The History and Anatomy of Auctorial Self-Criticism in the European Middle Ages

D1823381

32

Internationale Forschungen zur
Allgemeinen und
Vergleichenden Literaturwissenschaft

In Verbindung mit

Dietrich Briesemeister (Freie Universität Berlin) — Guillaume van Gemert (Universiteit Nijmegen) — Joachim Knape (Universität Tübingen) — Klaus Ley (Johannes Gutenberg-Universität Mainz) — John A. McCarthy (Vanderbilt University) — Manfred Pfister (Freie Universität Berlin) — Sven H. Rossel (University of Washington) — Azade Seyhan (Bryn Mawr College) — Horst Thomé (Universität Kiel)

herausgegeben von

Alberto Martino
(Universität Wien)

Redakteure:
Prof. Dr. Norbert Bachleitner. — Doz. Dr. Alfred Noe

Anschrift der Redaktion:
Institut für Vergleichende Literaturwissenschaft, Berggasse 11/5, A-1090 Wien

The History and Anatomy of Auctorial Self-Criticism in the European Middle Ages

Anita Obermeier

Amsterdam - Atlanta, GA 1999

∞ The paper on which this book is printed meets the requirements of "ISO 9706:1994, Information and documentation - Paper for documents - Requirements for permanence".

ISBN: 90-420-0405-3
©Editions Rodopi B.V., Amsterdam-Atlanta, GA 1999
Printed in The Netherlands

TABLE OF CONTENTS

Gewidmet meinem Vorbild,

meiner Mutter, Maria Obermeier

ACKNOWLEDGMENTS

I would like to thank the individuals and institutions whose aid, support, and advice have made this study possible. A Summer Research Award from the Women Studies Program at Arizona State University helped to underwrite my research on the specific role of medieval women authors in this study. In addition, I gratefully acknowledge permission from the Bodleian Library in Oxford and the Bayerische Staatsbibliothek in Munich for permission to publish the illustrations utilized in this book.

Both my readers and I have benefited from the willingness of my friends and colleagues to read and comment on the manuscript of this book at various stages. Any errors left in it are, of course, entirely my own. In particular I wish to thank: the late Daniel Brink, Alan Deyermond, the late John Doebler, William Hendrickson, Henry Ansgar Kelly, Rebecca Kennison, Dhira Mahoney, and Jean Monroe. I owe a special debt of gratitude to my mentor and friend Robert E. Bjork whose tireless support and excellent suggestions helped to mold me into a scholar.

My warmest thanks goes to my husband, David Buchholz, who has supported me patiently and lovingly in my quest for knowledge.

ABBREVIATIONS

A note on citations and translation: all numbers refer to page numbers, unless line numbers are indicated. Except for Arabic and Greek primary texts, which will be cited in translation only, quotations will be given in their original language in the text (if available), accompanied by an English translation in the footnotes. All translations will be properly identified; unidentified translations are my own. In order to reduce excessive citation clutter, the titles of some frequently-cited texts will be abbreviated and documented parenthetically in the text. These works do not appear in the footnotes but are listed below.

AP Lucian, *Apology for the "Salaried Posts in Great Houses,"* trans. K. Kilburn, Loeb Classics, 7 vols. (Cambridge: Harvard UP, 1959) 6: 191-213.

AS Geoffrey Chaucer, *A Treatise on the Astrolabe, The Riverside Chaucer*, ed. Larry D. Benson, 3rd ed. (Boston: Houghton Mifflin, 1987) 661-84.

BG Mary Inez Bogan, trans., *The Retractations*, by St. Augustine, The Fathers of the Church 60 (Washington, DC: Catholic U of America P, 1968).

DB Charles Dahlberg, trans., *The Romance of the Rose*, by Guillaume de Lorris and Jean de Meun (1971. Hanover: UP of New England, 1986).

Dec. Giovanni Boccaccio, *Decameron*, ed. Vittore Branca (Turin: Guilio Einaudi Editore, 1980).

DL Robert M. Durling, trans., *Petrarch's Lyric Poems: The* Rime Sparse *and Other Lyrics* (Cambridge: Harvard UP, 1976).

FM Lucian, *The Fisherman. Selected Satires of Lucian*, ed. and trans. Lionel Casson (Chicago: Aldine Publishing, 1962) 334-363.

GP Geoffrey Chaucer, General Prologue, *The Riverside Chaucer*, ed. Larry D. Benson, 3rd ed. (Boston: Houghton Mifflin, 1987) 23-36.

HR Adolf Harnack, "Die *Retractationen* Augustin's," *Sitzungsberichte der Königlichen preussischen Akademie der Wissenschaften* 53 (1905): 1096-1131.

JRN Guillaume de Machaut, *The Judgment of the King of Navarre*, ed. and trans. R. Barton Palmer (New York: Garland, 1988).

LGW Geoffrey Chaucer, *The Legend of Good Women, The Riverside Chaucer*, ed. Larry D. Benson, 3rd ed. (Boston: Houghton Mifflin, 1987) 587-630

MB Mark Musa and Peter Bondanella, trans., *The Decameron,* by Giovanni Boccaccio (New York: Norton, 1982).

MN Alistair J. Minnis, *Medieval Theory of Authorship: Scholastic Literary Attitudes in the Later Middle Ages*, 2nd ed. (Philadelphia: U of Pennsylvania P, 1988)

MP Apuleius, *Metamorphoseon oder Der Goldene Esel*, ed. and trans. Rudolf Helm, 6th ed. Schriften und Quellen der Alten Welt 1 (Berlin: Akademie-Verlag, 1970).

MilT Geoffrey Chaucer, Miller's Tale, *The Riverside Chaucer*, ed. Larry D. Benson, 3rd ed. (Boston: Houghton Mifflin, 1987) 66-77.

PM R. Barton Palmer, ed. and trans., *The Judgment of the King of Navarre*, Guillaume de Machaut (New York: Garland, 1988).

RR Jean de Meun and Guillaume de Lorris, *Le Roman de la Rose*, ed. Ernest Langlois, 5 vols. (Paris: Librairie Ancienne Edouard Champion, 1912).

Retr. Augustine, *Retractationum Libri II*, ed. Almut Mutzenbecher, Corpus Christianorum Series Latina 57 (Turnholti: Brepols, 1984).

RT Geoffrey Chaucer, Retraction, *The Riverside Chaucer*, ed. Larry D. Benson, 3rd ed. (Boston: Houghton Mifflin, 1987) 328.

RVF Francesco Petrarca, *Canzioniere*, ed. Gianfranco Contini (Turin: Giulio Einaudi, 1964).

TC Geoffrey Chaucer, *Troilus and Criseyde, The Riverside Chaucer*, ed. Larry D. Benson, 3rd ed. (Boston: Houghton Mifflin, 1987) 471-586.

CHAPTER 1

Introduction: Authorship and Authority

This book intends to delineate the history and anatomy of literary author apologies from Graeco-Roman times to the late Middle Ages. Critics might ask why I would wish to write a book that has as its partial topic the author, who, as a topic, should be so clearly passé after Roland Barthes' proclamation of the death of the author. My interest, however, is not limited to the author but resides in the realm of the interplay between the medieval author and the literary text, when the writer of the text becomes in turn his or her own published critic. In his provocatively-titled book, *The Death and Return of the Author,* Séan Burke concludes that "whilst authorial subjectivity is theoretically unassimilable, it cannot be practically circumvented."[1] Discussing Barthes', Foucault's, and Derrida's views on the boundaries between critic and author, Burke argues that the critic who pronounces the death of the author in his critical function becomes the author.[2] Although I am interested in the reverse process, how and why the medieval author becomes his own critic, two statements in Barthes' article "The Death of the Author" applied to the modern author elucidate the dilemma of the medieval author and touch upon issues that will surface in the Christian apology tradition. Barthes writes: "We know now that a text is not a line of words releasing a single 'theological' meaning (the 'message' of the Author-God) but a multidimensional space."[3] For Barthes, "Author-God" is a term to signal the glorification of the author; but for most medieval writers discussed here, their offense lies in imitating the creative function of God contrary to Christian doctrine, which is a different and reversed presumption. Because writing cannot mean on a singular level only, Barthes posits, it "liberates what may be called an antitheological activity, an activity that is truly revolutionary since to refuse to fix meaning is, in the end, to refuse God and his hypostases—reason, science, law."[4] Again, medieval authors chide themselves for having done what Barthes advocates modern texts should do.

Before I embark on illustrating how auctorial self-criticism[5] has developed over two thousand years, culminating in the medieval Christian tradition, I would like to proffer

---

1   Séan Burke, *The Death and Return of the Author: Criticism and Subjectivity in Barthes, Foucault and Derrida* (Edinburgh: Edinburgh UP, 1992) 173.

2   Burke, *The Death and Return of the Author* 162.

3   Roland Barthes, "The Death of the Author," *Falling into Theory: Conflicting Views on Reading Literature*, ed. David H. Richter (Boston: Bedford, 1994) 222-6; here 224.

4   Barthes, "The Death of the Author" 225.

5   J. F. Benton theorizes why there seems to be a proliferation of individual expression in the twelfth century ("Consciousness of Self and Perceptions of Individuality," *Culture, Power and Personality in Medieval France*, ed. Thomas N. Bisson [London: Hambledon, 1991] 327-56). He cites a renewed interest in Augustine's *Confessions*, the writing of biography, and the metamorphosis from a guilt to a shame culture. See also J. F. Benton, "Individualism and Conformity,"

a few recent modern examples and one medieval text situated outside the Graeco-Roman and Judeo-Christian realms that make up the bulk of this study. The recent cases of Salman Rushdie and Taslima Nasrin, as well as the medieval Arabic apology of Ibn Hazm, raise the same questions of authorship and censorship as the Graeco-Roman and medieval texts. These Arabic examples provide a topical modern point of departure for the medieval apology tradition and attest to the almost archetypal pervasiveness of auctorial apologies because of the hegemony of dominant cultural, political, and theological values. Let us first look at a metatextual theorizing statement by a Milan Kundera character on the "medieval" flavor of retractions, one form of medieval apologies.

In Kundera's 1984 novel, *The Unbearable Lightness of Being*, the chief surgeon asks his colleague, the protagonist Tomas, to recant his article on Oedipus, threatening that otherwise the communist regime in Czechoslovakia would make it impossible for Tomas to practice medicine; here, the chief surgeon ponders the concept of a retraction:

> "The pressure to make public retractions of past statements—there's something medieval about it. What does it mean, anyway, to 'retract' what you've said? How can anyone state categorically that a thought he once had is no longer valid? In modern times an idea can be *refuted*, yes, but not *retracted*. And since to retract an idea is impossible, merely verbal, formal sorcery, I see no reason why you shouldn't do as they wish. In a society run by terror, no statements whatsoever can be taken seriously. They are all forced, and it is the duty of every honest man to ignore them."[6]

This passage encapsulates the problem of creative license and censorship, pointing to the fact that self-criticism usually only is offered when an oppressive external force demands it and that such self-censure is inherently suspect. Totalitarian systems are more adept at providing that external force. But how medieval is the practice of retraction and how modern the practice of refutation? In February 1989, the entire literary world watched in horror as a political and religious quagmire developed around Rushdie's *The Satanic Verses*. Rushdie extended an apology to the members of the Islamic faith after the Ayatollah Khomeini issued the *fatwa*, the death sentence, against him, thus tying and subjecting literature to political and religious authority. In that context, the apology sounds precarious and functions both as a placating device for the insulted party—especially after Rushdie's 1988 comment, "'Frankly I wish I had written a more critical book'"[7]—and as a public relations boost for a rather mediocre book, which became known worldwide in a flash. On December 28, 1990, Rushdie took the initial apology a "logical" step further and embraced his Islamic faith anew, appending a disclaimer to his novel, agreeing:

Culture, Power and Personality in Medieval France, ed. Thomas N. Bisson [London: Hambledon, 1991] 313-26; Colin C. Morris, *The Discovery of the Individual, 1050-1200* (New York: Harper, 1973) and Walter Ullmann, *The Individual and Society in the Middle Ages* (Baltimore: Johns Hopkins UP, 1966).

6   Milan Kundera, *The Unbearable Lightness of Being*, trans. Michael Henry Heim (New York: Harper, 1984) 179-80.

7   Qtd. in John C. Swan, "The *Satanic Verses*, the *Fatwa*, and Its Aftermath: A Review Article," *Library Quarterly* 61:4 (1991): 429-43; here 431.

1) To witness that there is no God but Allah and Muhammad is His last Prophet.

2) To declare that I do not agree with any statement in my novel *The Satanic Verses* uttered by any of the characters who insult the prophet Mohammed or who cast aspersions upon Islam or upon the authenticity of the Holy Quran, or who reject the divinity of Allah.[8]

Applying the criteria of Kundera's chief surgeon to the Rushdie case, we can conclude that Rushdie—also pressured by a totalitarian force—neither refutes nor retracts, let alone regrets or repents anything, for he grants his text autonomy and disassociates himself from it. Since then, Rushdie has exposed his apology for what it was—a conciliatory move to stave off the *fatwa*—by denouncing his Islamic judges anew and by reaffirming his authorship.

Rushdie has a medieval Arabic predecessor, Ibn Hazm (994-1064), whose *The Ring of the Dove*, composed in Moslem Spain, exhibits auctorial concerns similar to the ones of the Graeco-Roman and medieval Christian writers at the heart of this study.[9] Like his Christian counterparts, Hazm addresses comments to both an earthly and a divine audience to place and justify his composition on love in the Moslem microcosm. His comment at the end of *The Ring* demonstrates that he is cognizant of his earthly critics: "I am aware that certain of my fanatical enemies will be shocked by my having composed a book of this kind. They will say, 'He has acted contrary to his professions, and deviated from his chosen path.'"[10] One cannot help but draw a comparison to Rushdie's case. Despite the fact that the Moslem establishment had not treated this medieval theologian and legal scholar kindly—Hazm spent some time in jail for political reasons and saw his books burned in Seville because his religious ideas and opinions clashed with the Moslem establishment[11]—he labels his critics "fanatics" and appears defiant toward them, rebuking them, as Augustine had his detractors, and proclaiming God as the only judge of sin.

In dealing with his Islamic divine audience, Hazm both parallels and differs from the Christian medieval writers. Like them, he places his only excursus into literature in a framework of metatextual and intratextual references, such as invocations to Allah, *The Ring*'s genesis, and quotations from Islamic scholars. Hazm furthermore claims to have undertaken this treatise on love only upon request from a friend. This is an *Exordialtopos* and a standard medieval stance in order to lessen his responsibility. Although distinctly influenced by Ovid, Hazm tries to de-emphasize carnal love and instead stress spiritual love in order to maintain an elevated moral level. Consequently, like other ancient and medieval works on human love that are intent on assuaging critics, his book progresses from the carnal to the spiritual (or condemning) side of

---

8   Salman Rushdie, "My Decision," *Index on Censorship* 2 (1991): 34. He furthermore agreed not to publish a paperback edition of the *Satanic Verses*.

9   For a treatment of the Arabic influence on medieval literature, see Maria Rosa Menocal, *The Arabic Role in Medieval Literary History: A Forgotten Heritage* (Philadelphia: U of Pennsylvania P, 1987).

10 Ibn Hazm, *The Ring of the Dove: A Treatise on the Art and Practice of Arab Love*, trans. A. J. Arberry (London: Luzac, 1953) 281.

11 Emilio Garcia Gomez, introduction, *El Collar de la Paloma*, by Ibn Hazm, 2nd ed. (Madrid: Sociedad de Estudios y Publicaciones, 1967) 31-83; here 38-39; A. J. Arberry, preface, *The Ring of the Dove*, by Ibn Hazm (London: Luzac, 1953) 7-14; here 9.

earthly love.[12] Intertextual quotations justify his composition: for instance, a "righteous and well-approved father of the faith declared, 'The man who has never known how to comport himself as a cavalier will never know how to be truly godfearing.'"[13] This way, earthly love is made respectable in association with religion. Despite these carefully arranged disclaimers, the poet expresses concern about how his composition might appear to Allah:

> I beg Allah's forgiveness for whatever the recording angels may note down, and the guardian angels enumerate against me, of this and the like; and I entreat His pardon as one who knows that his words shall be reckoned even as his deeds. If what I have said is not mere idle talk, for which no man shall be taken to task, yet my observations, God willing, shall prove to be pardonable peccadilloes; in any case they are hardly likely to rank as grave offences and abominations incurring Divine chastisement, nor do they count among those deadly sins specified in Holy Writ.[14]

Hazm's notion of accumulated sins is still similar to the Christian authors, as illustrated by the iconographic representation of Ingelard (see page 65), whose deeds are recorded by angels, as well as the popular account of Serlo of Wilton's conversion, whose vision of a tormented author in hell causes him to abandon secular writing. As in the Christian cosmos, the act of writing, like the committing of abominable deeds, may incur divine disfavor; thus given the background of the words-and-deeds theme, as some Christian authors have done, Hazm asks Allah's forgiveness, albeit in a conditional mode.

It is the perception of verbal sinning that separates the two religious philosophies. Christian medieval authors have to evaluate their own writing against the background of Matt. 12:36-37: "I assure you, on judgment day people will be held accountable for every unguarded word they speak. By your words you will be acquitted, and by your words you will be condemned." Whereas this meant that the medieval Christian authors were always in jeopardy of producing vanities and often criticized themselves for speaking in vain, in Hazm's religious establishment "idle talk" was not a sufficient enough reason for condemnation. Consequently, the bane of the Christian writer becomes the boon of the Islamic author. Hazm situates his possible offense at the bottom of the Islamic hierarchy of sins, which he delineates in order of increasing offense. His "idle talk" could not be any more damaging than "pardonable peccadilloes," never ranking as a grave violation or a deadly sin. The confidence with which Hazm gauges his own sinfulness might stem from the fact that Islam is less logocentric than Christianity, where a transgression with words is immediately an offense to Christ. When the New Testament was written there already existed in the Graeco-Roman empire a flourishing reading and writing tradition, whereas Arabic literature before Islam was mostly orally composed and performed. Since the Koran was the first book produced in Arabia,[15] it had no competition from other written sources, which might account for the absence of the notion of writing as a deadly sin. The history of

---

12   A. R. Nykl, introduction, *A Book Containing the Risala Known as the Dove's Neck-Ring: About Love and Lovers*, by Ibn Hazm (Paris: Librairie Orientaliste Paul Geuthner, 1931) xiii-cxxiv; here lxi. Arberry, preface 13.

13   Hazm, *The Ring of the Dove* 17.

14   Hazm, *The Ring of the Dove* 281.

15   Arberry, preface 11.

blasphemy shows that in a Christian context, blasphemy became identified as a verbal insult toward God.[16] Overall, Hazm's intratextual references perform the function of a preventative strategy in order to avert punishment, and the apology is extended for reasons of decorum rather than morals.

Several similarities appear between Hazm and Rushdie. Although injustices were levied upon Hazm, Rushdie seems subject to a religiously and politically oppressive establishment, a theocracy worse than that of Hazm's times. But both authors agree that writing does not constitute a serious enough offense; as Rushdie claims in 1993: "If there is a God, I don't think He's very bothered by *The Satanic Verses*, because he wouldn't be much of a God if He could be rocked on his throne by a book."[17] What bothered Rushdie's critics about the book, however, is an issue very close to Christian medieval authors' dilemma of imitating God's creative function: the divine inspiration of religious scriptures. This is how Leonard Levy chronicles it:

> The worst blasphemies in the book are those that seem to attribute the Koran, the revealed *ipsissima verba* of God, to Mohammed himself or, worse still, to Satan. A character in the novel who has Rushdie's first name serves as Mohammed's scribe, taking down the revelations. Salman gets a "diabolical idea." He begins changing words surreptitiously: "Little things at first. If Mahound recited a verse in which God was described as *all-hearing, all-knowing*, I would write, *all knowing, all wise*. Here's the point: Mahound did not notice the alterations. So there I was, actually writing the Book, or rewriting it, anyway, polluting the word of God with my own profane language." Salman could only conclude that, if his words could not be distinguished from the Revelation by God's own messenger, the book lacked divine quality. . . . Attributing the Koran to human composition indisputably constituted blasphemy as a matter of Islamic law. Yet Rushdie went further, if ambiguously, by allowing the inference that Satan was the real author of the Koran, at least of some verses. The very title of the novel, *The Satanic Verses*, as understood by literal-minded hostile Islamic critics, suggested diabolical authorship of the holy word of God.[18]

In a Manichean fashion, this passage questions the nature of the creative principles in the universe: is there an all-benevolent creator or does a dualistic principle of good and evil rule? Ultimately, the passage examines the relationship between signs and truths, language and reality.

Nowadays, of course, a literary apology is a rarity and by its sheer existence could be considered sincere, but Rushdie's disclaimer was prompted by the violent reactions of a "society run by terror," an Islamic fundamentalist nation; it is a political apology carefully tailored for the specific, extratextual intent of saving the author's life and does not have any aesthetic function in the novel. Hazm's apology is also a *post-facto* apology. Rushdie's apology was, nonetheless, immediately rejected by the Ayatollah Ali Khamenei,[19] who succeeded Khomeini, even though Khamenei had previously implied the *fatwa* would be rescinded with a Rushdie apology. The controversy con-

---

16 Leonard W. Levy, *Blasphemy: Verbal Offense against the Sacred from Moses to Salman Rushdie* (New York: Knopf, 1993) 552.

17 Salman Rushdie, "I Did Not Want to Gibber," *The Arizona Republic* 14 Feb. 1993: C2-3; here C2.

18 Levy, *Blasphemy* 560.

19 E. Salholz, "Rushdie Embraces the Faith," *Newsweek* 17 Jan. 1991, 52. Amir Taheri, however, writes that "the rulings of an ayatollah are automatically invalidated by his death" ("Reflections on an Invalid *Fatwa*," *Index on Censorship* 4 [1990]: 14-16; here 14).

tinued in September of 1998, as the more moderate president of Iran, Khatami, distanced himself from the Rushdie *fatwa*. This caused the western world and Rushdie to rejoice and celebrate his freedom, only to be repelled by the repeated warnings of Iranian clerics that the *fatwa* can never be rescinded. Iran's power struggle over this issue shows that even in a fundamentalist theocracy the clerical can overcome the secular power.

Furthermore, *The European* reported in September 1991 that Polish police were beefing up security for their team of translators working incognito on a Polish version of *The Satanic Verses*; these measures were deemed necessary after the killing of the Japanese translator and the stabbing of an Italian one by Middle Eastern terrorists.[20] This assault on the translators starkly parallels the medieval theory of *translatio*, in which translators are not responsible for the content of their sources. It does, however, fit with the *fatwa* hurled against Rushdie, as that called for the death of Rushdie and all involved in publishing the book. A German publisher had also been attacked for the same reason.

The 1993 case of Taslima Nasrin resembles Rushdie's dilemma. Nasrin, a Bangladeshi physician and poet, started to outrage the fundamentalist Moslems in Bangladesh as they tried to crack down on women's economic freedom gained from successful bank loan programs that allowed them to encroach on the turf of the patriarchal hierarchy. Nasrin, the author of sixteen books and a newspaper column, called for increased protection of women in an Islamic society, where just recently women were being killed through *fatwas*. Her own situation worsened with the publication of her 1993 novel, *Lajja* [Shame], as she became a target for several death threats issued by Islamic fundamentalist clerics. In an interview just before she went underground, she voiced strong opinions on the outdatedness of the Koran. Asked whether the Koran should be rewritten or modernized, Nasrin answered: "The Koran should no longer be the basis of law. . . . Religious books were written to serve one purpose: to assert men's superiority over women."[21] When she was subsequently quoted on the point of revising the Koran, fundamentalists were incensed, and Nasrin had to flee to Sweden. A proclaimed atheist, Nasrin actually had gone further and claimed that "'the Koran, the Vedas, the Bible and all such religious texts' were 'out of place and out of time.'"[22] She, however, issued a pseudo-apology, in which she claimed that she had been misquoted, that not the Koran but the "*Shariat* laws governing the marriage and divorce of women and men should be revised."[23] This apology was both a disavowal of text and a way for an author in jeopardy to assuage her critics and to buy time to leave the country. Even though Nasrin diverted attention from the Koran to the Shariat, she had been planning a feminist piece on women and the Koran.[24]

20 "Police in Rushdie Alert," *The European* 13-20 Sept. 1991, 7.

21 Birgit Schwarz, "Outspoken and in Hiding: Writer Decries Abuse of Women," *The Phoenix Gazette* 18 July 1994, B5.

22 Mary Anne Weaver, "A Fugitive from Injustice," *The New Yorker* Sept. 12, 1994: 48-60; here 56.

23 Bishnupriya Ghosh, "Feminist Critiques of Nationalism and Communalism from Bangladesh and India," *Interventions: Feminist Dialogues on Third World Literature and Film*, eds. Bishnupriya Ghosh and Brinda Bose (New York: Garland, 1997) 135-62; here 150.

24 Ghosh, "Feminist Critiques of Nationalism and Communalism from Bangladesh and India" 153.

Nevertheless, Nasrin does not see herself as a "female Salman Rushdie": "'We're very different: he has a huge *fatwa* on his head—more than two million dollars. Mine is very small compared to his. But the risk is the same. I respect Rushdie as a writer—he's very powerful. But he's repented, he's become a born-again Muslim, and that I don't respect. I will never be like him. I will never repent.'"[25] Four other writers in Bangladesh had *fatwas* issued against them.

While the Nasrin case received little attention—because Nasrin was relatively unknown in the West, some argue; because she is a woman, others claim[26]—the Rushdie case has elicited extraordinary publicity and has so far resulted in several books discussing, among other issues, the dynamics of literature and censorship.[27] The obvious major similarity between Rushdie and Nasrin—as well as Hazm—is that they are victims of Islamic fundamentalist theocracies because they criticized the Koran. Comparing their situation to that of medieval Christian writers may be illuminating. The question arises whether the literary apologies expressing varying degrees of auctorial self-criticism during the European Middle Ages are products of their prevalent philosophy, Christian logocentricity. Many medieval authors were indeed considered unsavory because of their violations of the logocentric Bible, but not all of them.

These self-critical expressions occur in the vernacular as well as the Latin compositions of English, French, German, Greek, Icelandic, Italian, Spanish, and Welsh authors. In this study, I examine examples by over seventy authors over a period of two thousand years. While this timeframe appears extensive and the number of authors modest, there are obvious periods of concentration during the two thousand years: the height of the Roman Empire, the end of late Antiquity and the start of the early Middle Ages, and 1100-1400, with specific national concentrations in specific centuries. The self-critical examples are not genre-bound and occur in tales, in lyrics, in epic, and in prose. In many cases the individual literary apology has been regarded as moral or personal rather than literary or aesthetic and has been associated with a religious, mainly Christian, conversion in old age. While Rushdie's well-documented modern apology is an isolated incident projecting a situation that could have been similar to the "Ur"-apology, the sheer number of medieval examples suggests a literary topos that has been largely unexamined up to now.

---

25   Qtd. in Weaver, "A Fugitive from Injustice" 58.

26   For a discussion of politics and gender concerning Taslima Nasrin, see Peter Priskil, *Taslima Nasrin: Der Mordaufruf und seine Hintergründe* (Ahriman Flugschrift 7, 1994).

27   See also M. M. Ahsan and A. R. Kidwai, eds., *Sacrilege versus Civility: Muslim Perspectives on the Satanic Verses Affair* (Markfield, UK: Islamic Foundation, 1991); Dab Cohn-Sherbok, ed., *The Salman Rushdie Controversy in Inter-Religious Perspective* (Lewiston: Mellon, 1990); Daniel Easterman, *New Jerusalems: Reflections on Islam: Fundamentalism and the Rushdie Affair* (London: Grafton, 1992); Daniel Pipes, *The Rushdie Affair: The Novel, the Ayatollah, and the West* (New York: Carol Pub. Group, 1990); Malise Ruthven, *A Satanic Affair: Salman Rushdie and the Rage of Islam* (London: Chatto & Windus, 1990); Ziauddin Sardar and Merryl Wyn Davies, *Distorted Imagination: Lessons from the Rushdie Affair* (London: Grey Seal, 1990); William J. Weatherby, *Salman Rushdie: Sentenced to Death* (New York: Carroll & Graf, 1990); and Michael Webster, *A Brief History of Blasphemy: Liberalism, Censorship and "The Satanic Verses"* (Southwold, UK: Orwell Press 1990).

Critical evaluation of apologies has been fragmentary and cursory; so far, only two articles have attempted to investigate one form of auctorial self-criticism, the retraction, as a European tradition, both in conjunction with Chaucer's Retraction at the end of *The Canterbury Tales*. In his 1913 article on Chaucer's Retraction, John Tatlock establishes "a well-marked though slim literary tradition" for Chaucer's Retraction.[28] Tatlock's study is limited to works featuring the term "retractatio" in their title, starting his tradition with Augustine's *Retractationes*. Half a century later, Olive Sayce expands on Tatlock's argument in her 1971 article, "Chaucer's 'Retractions': The Conclusion of *The Canterbury Tales* and Its Place in Literary Tradition," where she rightfully places Chaucer's Retraction in the prologue and epilogue tradition of medieval works and collects a valuable number of self-critical statements. Julius Schwietering lists still more in his book, *Die Demutsformel mittelhochdeutscher Dichter*. And Jill Mann concentrates on late medieval apologies to women in her 1990 inaugural lecture.[29] My study differs from these in scope as well as method; whereas Sayce recognizes a European tradition, I try to demonstrate both the geographical and temporal extent of that tradition from Iceland to Spain, from sixth-century BCE Greece to late fifteenth-century England. And whereas Sayce and Schwietering look for the tradition in prologues and epilogues only, I cover entire works, the whole canon of authors' works, and works that do not have prologues and epilogues.

Most self-critical authors provide references in their works to one or more of their previous works. This phenomenon can be linked to the concept of intertextuality—the relationship between texts—which takes us "beyond the traditional notion of the text as an autonomous, privileged, or originary object" and demonstrates how texts are related to each other in an "*imitatio veterum.*"[30] Laurie A. Finke and Martin B. Shichtman postulate that an intertextual approach would facilitate the examination of the "relationships among medieval literary works and other philosophical, historical, and religious texts."[31] Such an approach is ultimately a form of source study, although Manfred Pfister objects to considering intertextuality research a traditional "sources-and-analogues" study. Pfister's delineation of the five subcategories of intertextuality proposed in Gérard Genette's work *Palimpsestes: La littérature au second degré*, is useful: 1) intertextuality as the co-presence of two or more texts, the graspable presence of one text in another (quotation, allusion, plagiarism); 2) paratextuality in the references between a text and its title, preface, epilogue, motto; 3) metatextuality in the

---

28 John S. P. Tatlock, "Chaucer's *Retractions*," *Publications of the Modern Language Association* 21 (1913): 521-529; here 528.

29 Olive Sayce, "Chaucer's 'Retractions': The Conclusion of the *Canterbury Tales* and Its Place in Literary Tradition," *Medium Aevum* 40 (1971): 230-48; Julius Schwietering, *Die Demutsformel mittelhochdeutscher Dichter* (Berlin: 1921); Jill Mann, *Apologies to Women* (Cambridge: Cambridge UP, 1991).

30 Laurie A. Finke and Martin B. Shichtman, "Introduction: Critical Theory and the Study of the Middle Ages," *Medieval Texts & Contemporary Readers* (Ithaca: Cornell UP, 1987) 1-11; here 5. Manfred Pfister, "Konzepte der Intertextualität," *Intertextualität: Formen, Funktionen, anglistische Fallstudien*, eds. Ulrich Broich and Martin Pfister, Konzepte der Sprach- und Literaturwissenschaft 35 (Tübingen: Max Niemeyer, 1985) 1-30; here 1.

31 Finke and Shichtman, "Introduction" 5.

commenting and often critical reference of one text to a previous text; 4) hypertextual-ity, in which a text takes the other text as a foil (imitation, adaptation, continuation, parody); 5) architextuality as the genre references of a text.[32] Intertextuality, metatex-tuality, and hypertextuality are most closely related to the topic of auctorial self-criti-cism. Moreover, Pfister's concern that intertextuality would be utilized for the estab-lishment of the "'influence' theory"[33] is unfounded in this context because intertex-tuality in connection with self-criticism is an "announced" concept, an intentional backward reference by the author.

While intertextuality is usually concerned with the relationship between texts by different writers, auctorial self-criticism is mainly interested in autotextuality or autoreflexivity, where the author thematizes the intertextuality of the text.[34] There are examples in this study of authors referring to texts of other authors in a hypertextual manner by imitation or parody. Most of the self-critical statements, however, are either autotextual or intratextual. For the self-critical medieval author, we can examine how two or more texts of the same author autotextually relate to each other in their poetic genesis. In this analysis, independent texts of the same author as well as prefaces, epilogues, and letters are considered intertextual.[35] On the metatextual level, several classical and medieval authors lead us through almost their entire creative history, critiquing and criticizing their previous compositions. The notion of intratextuality manifests itself in texts that refer to themselves critically, posing the especially inter-esting conundrum of a literary creation that denies itself validity in a given political, social, literary, philosophical, or religious context.

Furthermore, it is not just the text or texts as aesthetic structures alone on which this study focuses, but also expressions of an individual auctorial consciousness. Various critical approaches have been diminishing not only the notion of the author but also the notion of the text. On one hand, for instance, structuralism and deconstructionism draw on a concept of intertextuality from which "the presence of a subject—a speaker, author, reader, someone who thinks and feels and communicates through the texts in question, someone who discovers the 'inter-' in intertextuality" has been omitted.[36] On the other hand, Jean Paul Sartre denies the existence of text: "'je m'oppose complète-ment à l'idée de texte'"[37] [I am completely against the notion of the text]. According to Sartre, disregarding the author commercializes literature, "'en le considérant comme

---

32 Pfister, "Konzepte der Intertextualität" 19, 16-17.

33 Thaïs E. Morgan, "Is There an Intertext in This Text?" *American Journal of Semiotics* 3 (1985): 1-40; here 10. Morgan postulates further that "Genette rejects the idea that all types of intertextu-ality must be implicit, hidden away in the deep matrix of the text and manifested only by ungrammaticalities on the surface of the text" (29).

34 Ulrich Broich, "Formen der Markierung von Intertextualität," *Intertextualität: Formen, Funktionen, anglistische Fallstudien*, eds. Ulrich Broich and Manfred Pfister, Konzepte der Sprach- und Literaturwissenschaft 35 (Tübingen: Max Niemeyer, 1985) 31-47; here 49. Pfister, "Konzepte der Intertextualität" 27.

35 Broich, "Formen der Markierung von Intertextualität" 50-51.

36 Morgan, "Is There an Intertext in This Text?" 18.

37 Qtd. in Ina Schabert, "Interauktorialität," *Deutsche Vierteljahresschrift für Literaturwissenschaft und Geistesgeschichte* 57 (1983): 679-701; here 681.

une chose qui parle et non comme la réalité d'un homme objectivée par son travail'"[38] [By considering it as a thing that talks rather than the objectified reality of a human being through his labor]. The fact that some modern critics have denied medieval writers auctorial consciousness is founded in the notion that an auctorial "I" did not surface until the Renaissance or possibly until the eighteenth century: "Firstly, the idea of literature as the expression of the individual and personal is one that has only been current since the mid-eighteenth century. . . . what is important is not the individual and personal, but the general and universally valid."[39] I, however, would like to center my analysis halfway between these extreme poles, working with the interplay between the authors and their texts.

Examining this interplay, I perceive great manipulative auctorial powers in the authors I discuss. Therefore, another modern critical concept that could help illuminate auctorial self-criticism is "interauctoriality," which means that a literary work depicts its author's contact with the "author personality" of a previously-read literary text, presenting two authors in the same work simultaneously.[40] While "interauctoriality" usually requires two different authors, it can be used to accommodate alternate selves of one author, clearly representing two authors in the intertextual self-critical work, the former and the current author. Thus "interauctoriality" could aid us in understanding the new concept of "intra-auctoriality" I am proposing. Coupled with self-criticism, intra-auctoriality creates a "negative" auctorial self-referentiality that challenges the notion of independent, autonomous works by weaving one continuous auctorial text, effectively writing the history of the author's creative development. In this light, medieval auctorial self-criticism evolves as an intricate interplay between intertextuality—a relationship between various texts, text patterns, and external influences on the literary text—and intra-auctoriality, reflexive and self-referential critiquing phases that help shape auctorial self-perception.

The roots of this intricate interplay can be found in classical and biblical literature. Although direct "influence" on medieval literature via external intertextuality between two authors cannot necessarily be proven, except maybe for Ovid, Augustine, and the Bible, the ancient tradition of writing literary apologies may serve as an archetypal pattern and theoretical framework for the auctorial self-criticism in the Middle Ages. When the forms and genres of texts in which an apology occurs do not illuminate the apology sufficiently, content and audience provide more decisive categories. Three different strands of the apology tradition can be proposed. The first and most pervasive strand features apologies to pagan deities and—later—to God, usually accompanied by the author expressing a sense of having jeopardized his spiritual well-being. The second most important strand contains literary apologies made to an earthly audience, usually of women. These examples generally come from authors repenting of earlier misogynistic attitudes. A third strand contains apologies for varying literary offenses that are directed to a more general audience. Against this framework, most medieval apologies are directed to God, for the composition of secular works, or to women.

---

38   Qtd. in Schabert, "Interauktorialität" 681.
39   Sayce, "Chaucer's 'Retractions'" 231.
40   Schabert, "Interauktorialität" 679. I derive the English term "interauctoriality" from this article.

Both of these strands are tied together by the specifically misogynistic treatment of women.

Chapter 2 traces the roots of the apology tradition from sixth-century BCE Greece to late Latin antiquity. During the Graeco-Roman period, self-critical authors apologize mainly to divinities and women, primarily in *post-culpam* attempts to alleviate or avert punishment. Most of the apologies to women are ironic and antifeminist. Other contributions to the tradition are the "youth vs. old-age" topos, the implication of the reader in the discourse, and the metatextual discussion of auctorial motives for apologies.

In Chapter 3, with the advent of Christianity, several new elements have been added to the recantation tradition. Apologies are now promoted by a theological concern about the place of one's literary works in the sight of God. The apologies are primarily addressed to God and secondarily to a general Christian audience, and combine Christian humility with Latin rhetorical devices. The tension between classical antiquity and Christianity lived on in the *trivium* education of medieval authors, causing a schizophrenic environment for writing and culminating in the medieval theory that language signifies only as an imitation of the Christian master narrative. This chapter also explores the biblical antifeminism that marginalized women in regard to writing and to the divine. Because of the abundance of nuances and variations in approach and tone in the tradition within even one particular author's canon, I have divided the medieval authors of this book into six chapters, grouped by language: Medieval Latin, German, French, Italian, British, and Spanish. Latin works of authors normally writing in the vernacular are also treated in the appropriate vernacular chapters. Within the individual chapters the medieval examples are examined diachronically to show a progression from the early to the later Middle Ages.

In Chapter 4, the self-critical medieval Latin writers from 700 to 1500 carry on the intellectual heritage of the late-antiquity Christian authors that grew out of the tension between the trivium of classical antiquity and the self-conscious fledgling Christian faith. The medieval Latin authors participate primarily in the first strand of apologies, those to God, but also in the third, apologies for unsavory literary practices. Both strands are influenced by Augustine.

In Chapter 5, *contemptus mundi* becomes the tradition's primary focus. This emphasis on *contemptus mundi* in German is the byproduct of a generic change in the tradition. Whereas so far the "enemy" was classical literature and to a degree amorous writings, German literature presents us with contemporary, vernacular "foes" in the form of the courtly epic, the *Minnelied*, and the *Spielmannslied*. Thus, we find in the German examples an intra-auctorial opposition to those genres, which explains why the German contingent divides into two generic groups: prologues to saints' legends and biblical epics as well as lyrical poetry.

In the medieval French literature of Chapter 6, we see for the first time a duality between the first and second strands of the apology tradition. Apologies to God for profane literature characterize some saints' legends and didactic poetry. A massive shift toward apologies to women occurred in the thirteenth century. This shift is rooted in the renewed interest in women in later medieval literature. Because both troubadour and Marian lyrics concentrate on the idolization of women, there is, coupled with classical and patristic influences, an increase in antifeminist literature to counterbalance this idolization.

In Chapter 7, the misogynistic and ironic nature of the French apologies to women stands in direct contrast to the three great poets of the Italian fourteenth century, who share in their writing a common passion for women. Dante Alighieri, Francesco Petrarch, and Giovanni Boccaccio utilize Beatrice, Laura, Fiammetta, and *le donne* as creative ancillas for their art. The *dolce stil nuovo* fuses aspects of the earthly troubadour lyric and the Marian lyric to create a sanctioned love of woman, in which *la donna* becomes a representation of the new poetry. All three poets, however, treat their creative ancillas differently and ultimately pay tribute to another female figure, the Virgin Mary.

Chapter 8 contains Old and Middle English as well as Welsh and Icelandic examples of auctorial self-criticism that are widely divergent in their genres and content. Although we can distinguish the two main apology strands, to God and to women, the more systematic uniformity achieved by the German, French, Italian and Spanish authors is lacking in the British self-critical passages; nevertheless the British authors invariably emulate the various continental models, such as the early Christian, the medieval translator, the scholastic compiler, and the writer accused of anti-feminism. In his canon, Chaucer dons all of these apologetic masks with great ease.

In Chapter 9, both main strands of the apology tradition (the third became mute) culminate in the Spanish apology tradition. What is most striking about both the Spanish troubadour's apology and the misogynist's excuse is their overt focus on women. For the latter that focal point is, of course, built into the design, but for the former, after classical times it has been more insinuated than openly expressed. Carnal love has always been included in the early Christian and early medieval authors' emphasis on their youthful errors in writing classically-influenced compositions that are vain, empty, and devoid of Christian truth. But it is not until the Spanish tradition that these implicit love compositions take the place of the untruthful pagan fables. Thus the immorality of illicit love becomes the center of the apologies to God, culminating in the establishment of the dichotomy of *cupiditas* and *caritas*. It is the Spanish apology tradition, however, in which that strange dichotomy culminates in the self-critical poets' dilemma of either composing love poetry, thus offending the contemporary Christian Zeitgeist, and then, repenting their literary sins, or writing antifeminist tracts, thus outraging women, and then apologizing to them.

In sum, while the apology tradition assumes a conventional character very early on, the tradition is by no means static but dynamic, allowing the individual authors to manipulate their self-critical strategies to various auctorial ends. These three strands coupled with variations in nuances of authorial sincerity, literary guiltiness, and expressions thereof, give rise to a number of varying apology structures. Auctorial nuances in expressions of guilt, such as the complete disavowal of the work, the partial disavowal of the work, the admission of guilt and a plea for correction by critics or a promise of making amends, the admission of guilt with remorse, the admission of guilt without remorse, or the admission of guilt with counterattack, are coupled with several other elements in the apology tradition: the pagan/Christian dichotomy expressed in the youth vs. old-age topos, the expected humility of the Christian author, and the integration of the reader into the writing process. The Graeco-Roman and early Christian apology scenarios follow the following pattern: offensive writing evokes a woman's or God's reaction, which in turn elicits an apology to ensure the writer's salvation. This pattern changes as the tradition transforms, becoming increasingly more literary and therefore more ambiguous and ironic as the Middle Ages progress and as the study moves through various linguistic traditions from Latin to Spanish. By the end of the Middle Ages, we can propose a new pattern: offensive writing evokes reaction of literary tradition, which in turn elicits an apology based on social, religious, and literary correctness. Thus the tradition has moved from behavior motivated by the reactions of God or a specific person to behavior lacking the impetus of a particular entity but dependent on societal conventions.

Finally, the conclusion in Chapter 10 explores linguistic signs and signifiers in the modern terminology applied to self-criticism, the establishment of literary tradition, intertextuality, and canon formation, all of which are significant both to this tradition and to medieval literature. It also examines the apologies of seven medieval women writers. Since women do not provide the same apologies as men, they initially were not part of the scope of this study. Despite the fact that women apologize for different purposes and reasons—mainly intertextually, mostly to men, and often for their gender—their examples illustrate, on yet another level, the antifeminist subtext inherent in the entire apology tradition.

CHAPTER 2

The Classical Tradition: The Stesichorean Paradigm

2.1. Stesichorus

Stesichorus of Himera (c. 630-553 BCE), a Western Greek writer of choral odes, fuses the earthly and divine strands in the earliest recorded literary apology, showing a conscious awareness of audience and authority.[1] Several ancient sources indicate that because Stesichorus had penned a poem called "Helen," in which he incorporated everything unflattering to Helen from the "myth cycle,"[2] and for which the gods punished him with blindness, he composed a fragmentary poem titled "Palinodia." The fragment of another poem illustrates that Stesichorus indeed did not deal kindly with Helen: in "Helen and Klytaimnestra," he refers to the sisters as "brides who deserted their husbands."[3] The poem "Helen" is lost and much speculation abounds as to its form; one of the questions significant to the issue of auctorial self-criticism is whether "Helen" and "Palinodia" are separate poems or parts of the same work,[4] whether inter-textuality or intratextuality is the underlying principle. Isocrate seems to favor the notion of intratextuality and provides evidence for the fusion of divinity and woman when he writes in the *Encomium of Helen*: "She revealed her power to Stesichorus the poet too, for when on beginning his song he uttered some blasphemy against her, he stood up deprived of sight; but when, recognizing the cause of his misfortune, he composed the so-called *Palinode*, she restored him to his normal condition."[5] Isocrate bestows the responsibility for blinding Stesichorus and subsequently restoring his sight

---

1   Jacqueline T. Miller writes that "[a]uthority and authorship are sometimes complementary, some-times conflicting concepts . . . [such as] individual authority or creative autonomy . . . [and] authoritative sanction that external sources provide. Authority,.both when it resides with the author and when it does not, implies restraint as well as freedom, limitation as well as power. A claim of personal authority may liberate and validate an author's activities; it may also restrict them, since it carries with it a constraining burden of responsibilities and is often acquired through an act of submission. . . . The author may accept authority that is conferred upon him; he may simply posit and assert his authority; he may deny or abdicate his authority. . . . Furthermore, a poet may disclaim his autonomy only to provide himself with a beneficial type of authorial anonymity: the formal acknowledgment of a higher authority may allow the imagination to roam freely under the guise of authoritative sanction" (*Poetic License: Authority and Authorship in Medieval and Renaissance Contexts* [Oxford: Oxford UP, 1986] 3-4).

2   C. A. Trypanis, *Greek Poetry: From Homer to Seferis* (Chicago: U of Chicago P, 1981) 104.

3   Stesichorus, "Helen and Klytaimnestra," trans. Richmond Lattimore, *Greek Lyrics*, 2nd ed. (Chicago: U of Chicago P, 1960) 37, line 6.

4   J. Vürtheim, *Stesichoros' Fragmente und Biographie* (Leiden: A. W. Sijthoff's Uitgevers-maatschappij N. V., 1919) 58-59.

5   Isocrate X 64, qtd. in J. A. Davison, "Stesichorus and Helen," *From Archilochus to Pindar* (New York: St Martin's, 1968) 196-225; here 202.

upon Helen alone, according her the powers usually reserved for the gods; he thus fuses earthly (female) with divine authority.[6] The account of Helen's divinity is not an aberration, for she was revered as a goddess in Sparta and other parts of Greece.[7] Furthermore, goddesses partake in Greek creation mythology.

The actual apology-poem, "Palinodia," deals with Helen's alleged presence at Troy but does not mention Stesichorus' imputed blindness.[8] The text and background to the "Palinodia" appear in Plato's *Phaedrus*, where, on the one hand, he weakens the thesis that Helen is the powerful party and, on the other hand, he fosters the notion of Stesichorus' application of intertextuality and of "Palinodia" and "Helen"'s being two separate poems. Plato (428-347 BCE) displays an intriguing example of both intertextuality and interauctoriality in this account, for he deals with Socrates, citing Stesichorus and mentioning Homer. Stesichorus' "Palinodia" is being utilized in the "playful" and partially ironic,[9] and thus hypertextual, context of Socrates' recognizing his literary error; Socrates, while preaching against love and therefore offending Eros, the son of Aphrodite, realizes his transgression. Since a superhuman voice reveals to him that he "had been guilty of impiety," Socrates comes to the same conclusion as later Christian poets: "'I feared that I might be buying honour from men at the price of sinning against the gods.' Now I recognize my error."[10] Because Socrates wants to atone for his sin of chasing after worldly poetic glory, he refers to another text and two other poets:

> And I bethink me of an ancient purgation of mythological error, which was devised, not by Homer, for he never had the wit to discover why he was blind, but by Stesichorus, who was a philosopher and knew the reason why; and therefore, when he lost his eyes, for that was the penalty which was inflicted upon him for reviling the lovely Helen, he at once purged himself. And the purgation was a recantation, which began thus,—"False is that word of mine—the truth is that thou didst not embark in ships, nor ever go to the walls of Troy;" and when he had completed his poem, which is called "the recantation," immediately his sight returned to him. Now I will be wiser than either Stesichorus or Homer, in that I am going to make my recantation for reviling love before I suffer.[11]

---

6   Pausanias claims that Helen sent a messenger to Stesichorus to inform him about the reason for his blindness; after that he composed the "Palinodia" (Vürtheim, *Stesichoros' Fragmente und Biographie* 67).

7   C. M. Bowra, *Greek Lyric Poetry: From Alcman to Simonides*, 2nd ed. (Oxford: Clarendon, 1961) 74-129; here 111.

8   For Helen's presence at Troy, the three theories are these: one, she went to Troy; two, she never left Greece, but Paris took an apparition with him; three, she was kidnapped and taken to Egypt, a thesis which Euripides employs in his tragedy *Helena* (Vürtheim: *Stesichoros' Fragmente und Biographie* 62, 65). C. M. Bowra finds the blindness story too much like "folk-lore" and cites other examples for divine punishment levied on human offenders in the form of blindness: Teiresias, Phineus, St. Paul, St. Zacharias (*Greek Lyric Poetry* 107). Bowra does not mention Homer's blindness, however.

9   W. H. Thompson, *Phaedrus of Plato with English Notes and Dissertations* (London: Whittaker, 1868) 38, fn. 243, 152.

10   Plato, *Phaedrus*, *Great Books of the Western World*, trans. Benjamin Jowett (Chicago: Encyclopedia Brittanica, Inc., 1952) 7: 115-41; here 122.

11   Plato, *Phaedrus* 122-23. For ancient references to Stesichorus' "Palinodia" aside from Plato and Isocrate, see Davison, "Stesichorus and Helen"; Vürtheim, *Stesichoros' Fragmente und Biographie* 58-72; and Bowra, *Greek Lyric Poetry* 106-13.

Plato differs from Isocrate in that he grants all power to the gods, of whom Socrates professes to be afraid, and illustrates three possible scenarios for poets who have offended deities and have been punished physically. The first one, Homer's inability to discover the reason for his blindness, has been considered Plato's preference of lyric poets over epic poets, since the former were supposed to have more insight into the causes of events.[12] The second one, Stesichorus' *post-facto* atonement, serves as a model for Socrates to repent his error. Socrates, however, regards his own choice as an improvement over Stesichorus' strategy, providing the third scenario: he is going to stave off any impending punishment before it might be inflicted upon him. Thus Stesichorus' "Palinodia" has started to assume conventional status as a tool to ward off punishment for literary errors as early as the fourth century BCE.

This extraordinary example of intertextuality and interauctoriality, where one author is dealing directly with the work and experience of two other authors, outlines many of the issues essential to the treatment of the apology tradition. One of the paradigmatic elements of Stesichorus' "Palinodia" is his admission of literary transgression— against the truth in this case. The Greeks viewed poetry as a didactic instrument, and the worst accusation a poet could suffer was to be called a liar, which would naturally thwart his highest aspirations of everlasting fame after his death.[13] Coupled with the elements of truth and fame, the legend that untruthful poets were punished by the gods through blinding asserts the dominant role truth plays in poetry.[14] Further significant elements are a withdrawal or modification of the erroneous statements and the punishment of the offender. One scholar adds another element to this list: an important power that "moves" the offender,[15] who in turn can atone for the literary offense with a new literary creation, as Socrates suggests by his account of Stesichorus' purification rite. Such a purification rite emphasizes the cathartic function and power of literature. Socrates, on the other hand, who had "told a lie," perceives recantation to be a preventative, not a reconstructive, measure and calls for the composition of a new speech on love, his "rhapsody on love."[16] Both Stesichorus and Socrates imply that the poet has recourse in case of literary misdemeanor, which, of course, actually enhances rather than diminishes the power of poetry.[17]

---

12 Vürtheim, *Stesichoros' Fragmente und Biographie*, 64. Homer is the poet who sees with his inner eye and is still famous now (G. J. de Vries, *A Commentary on the* Phaedrus *of Plato* [Amsterdam: Hakkert, 1969] 110); Stesichorus never gained such fame.

13 Rosemary Harriott, *Poetry and Criticism before Plato* (London: Methuen, 1969) 106, 110, 112.

14 Harriott, *Poetry and Criticism before Plato* 115.

15 Francis Cairns, "The Genre Palinode and Three Horatian Examples: *Epode*, 17; *Odes*, I, 16; *Odes*, I 34," *L'Antiquite Classique* 47 (1978): 546-52; here 547.

16 Plato, *Phaedrus* 244 and Thompson, *Phaedrus of Plato with English Notes and Dissertations* xv.

17 Plato utilizes Socrates again to express what may have been a change in attitude in his own works. For instance, current critical discussion argues over whether a change of view is evident in the later works of Plato, particularly about his theory of Forms. In his work *Parmenides*, Plato has young Socrates spell out the middle dialogues' conception of Forms, only to have the unhistorical but symbolic figures of Parmenides and Zeno rip them apart. In other late dialogues, many arguments do in fact undermine some of Plato's earlier uses of Forms. "This certainly looks like self-criticism," Julia Annas contends, "but Plato draws no explicit morals" ("Classical Greek Philosophy," *The Oxford History of the Classical World*, eds. John Broadman, Jasper Griffin, and

2.2. Euripides

A similar set of criteria applies to the analysis of Euripides' (480-407 BCE) auctorial self-criticism in conjunction with a purely earthly offended party: women. The playwright's external reason for the apology is the wrath of the offended women, who convince him to make amends for his offenses; Euripides never admits any guilt, however. Euripides' *Vita* contains two lines from his *Melanippe*, a lost play, in which he supposedly said, "'[i]n vain men shoot their criticism at women. The bow twangs and misses. Women—I say—are better than men!' (fr. 400 N)," thereby apologizing to the women of Athens, whom he had bitterly attacked in previous plays.[18] Euripides' *Vita* also mentions that "women lay in ambush for him at the Thesmophoria because of his criticisms of them in his poetry. They wanted to destroy him, but they spared him first because of the Muses and then because he promised never again to say anything bad about them."[19]

These fragments gain support from Aristophanes' *Thesmophoriazousae*. Before Plato, Aristophanes already exploits the same interauctorial situation in his comedy with the goal of ridiculing Euripides, as he treats the story of Euripides' quandary with the women. In the play, the figure of Euripides is accused of being a misogynist, for which the angry women are plotting his death: "Because, they say, I write lampoons upon them."[20] The character Euripides wisely offers to refrain from that activity from then on:

> Ladies, I offer terms. If well and truly
> Your honourable sex befriend me now,
> I won't abuse your honourable sex
> From this time forth forever. This I offer.[21]

The promise has been made in order to free Euripides' friend; no admission of guilt has been offered. According to Aristophanes, Euripides would have suffered death at the hands of his earthly accusers, while Stesichorus, Homer, and Socrates "only" feared and suffered blindness. Although the question arises whether the gods or women are more cruel, the women's blood-thirstiness is in itself an ironic characterization tool.

Oswyn Murray [Oxford: Oxford UP, 1986] 234-53; here 243). For a study utilizing Stesichorus' palinode examining Renaissance poetry through the Bakhtinian theory of dialogics, see Patricia Berrahou Phillippy, *Love's Remedies: Recantation and Renaissance Lyric Poetry* (Lewisburg: Bucknell UP, 1995).

18 Mary R. Lefkowitz, *The Lives of the Greek Poets* (Baltimore: Johns Hopkins UP, 1981) 168, 33.
19 Lefkowitz, *The Lives of the Greek Poets* 168.
20 Aristophanes, *The Thesmophoriazusae*, trans. Benjamin Bickley Rogers (Cambridge: Harvard UP, 1955) 130-241; here line 84.
21 Aristophanes, *The Thesmophoriazusae* lines 1160-63.

2.3. Callimachus

In addition to Stesichorus', Socrates', and Euripides' external concerns about blindness and death, the recantation tradition draws on the Hellenistic-influenced poetry that reaches from Alexandrian times to Christian late antiquity. The Alexandrian court poetry of the third century BCE developed a custom that allowed poets to attach autobiographical verses to an edition of their work with the intention of introducing themselves to their audience. From the Alexandrian poet Callimachus, who flourished in the third century BCE and greatly influenced later Roman poets, the practice assimilated the streak of self-justification more or less latent in most authors' self-criticism. Some authors utilize a fictional trial to bring a charge against themselves so that they can refute it. Callimachus follows this structure in the prologue to the *Aetia*, a fragmentary elegiac poem in four books telling a number of Greek aetiological legends in a frame structure.[22] The prologue contains two separate components: the poet's attack on the Telchines, his critics, and his explanation of his poetic gift. First, Callimachus repeats the charge of the Telchines, the malignant sorcerers of mythology,[23] that he does not produce long continuous epic poems but shorter ones. Consequently, to justify his choice of poetic style, Callimachus utilizes the concept of the *Dichterweihe*, anointing of the poet, to confirm that Apollo's divine intervention prescribed that particular poetic path for him: "Apollo said to me . . . 'tread a path which carriages do not trample; do not drive your chariot upon the common tracks of others, or along a wide road, but on unworn paths, though your course be more narrow.'"[24] With this concession, Callimachus obtains divine legitimation for his poetry and can finish his poem against the Telchines.[25] This strategy also removes responsibility from the poet's consciousness by making it look as if he has only conformed to the god's will, anticipating the Christian concept that all creativity stems from God; it further saves him from "explicit boasting"; Callimachus handed this "arresting play between modesty and pride" down to the Roman poets who took him as their model.[26] Because in genres other than the epic, Roman authors are garrulous about themselves and feature heavily in their own poetry, G. O. Hutchinson suggests something very much at the heart of this topic: attention has to be paid to how poets express information relevant to themselves and to the "division and the unity of the dramatic character and the author."[27] In one interpretative way, intertextuality and intra-auctoriality illustrate how authors measure their own poetic development.

---

22 Mario Puelma, "Kallimachos-Interpretationen II: Der Epilog zu den *Aitien*," *Kallimachos*, ed. Aristoxeneos D. Skiadas (Darmstadt: Wissenschaftliche Buchgesellschaft, 1975) 43-69; here 68.

23 G. O. Hutchinson, *Hellenistic Poetry* (Oxford: Clarendon, 1988) 78.

24 Callimachus, *Aetia*, trans. C. A. Trypanis (Cambridge: Harvard UP, 1975) 1-99; here lines 25-29.

25 Athanasios Kambylis, "Der Vollzug der Dichterweihe bei Kallimachos," *Kallimachos*, ed. Aristoxeneos D. Skiadas (Darmstadt: Wissenschaftliche Buchgesellschaft, 1975) 81-99; here 82.

26 Hutchinson, *Hellenistic Poetry* 80, 283.

27 Hutchinson, *Hellenistic Poetry* 283.

2.4. Catullus

The Roman poet Gaius Valerius Catullus (87-57 BCE) rewrites himself in his "Poem 42." Concerned with the practical task of regaining poems abducted by a certain woman, he resorts to the old Italian custom of forcing the offending party to comply by instigating a vocal public scolding, which would humiliate the other person immensely.[28] Therefore, the initially insulted author openly reviles his opponent with such strong epithets as "moecha turpis" ['filthy, naked whore'], "ore Gallicani" ['Gallic bitch'], and "'moecha putida'" ['dirty, little bitch'].[29] Like Helen (if credence is given to Isocrate's account), the woman, who seems untouched and quite amused by the spectacle, holds power over the author, who has just insulted her publicly. In a mock-Stesichorean manner, Catullus announces that he must change his strategy to regain what he lost: "mutanda est ratio modusque uobis" ['and we must change our tactics'] (line 22). Thus, after having previously announced her reputation as tarnished, he rewrites his own text, creating an intratextual case of self-criticism by calling her "pudica et proba, redde codicillos" ['O beautiful sweet untarnished virgin'] (line 24). The rewriting of the text, however, does not constitute erasure of the insults, especially since the text is completely devoid of any expression of auctorial guilt. Such an overt illustration of glaring insincerity and irony both points to Catullus' mock-conventional usage of the Stesichorean apology to a woman and anticipates the medieval antifeminist tradition with its ironic blanket insults and apologies which cannot be taken seriously by either the woman or the audience. Consequently, Catullus anchored the mocking of the convention in the secular apology tradition.

2.5. Horace

Catullus' successor Horace (65-8 BCE) contributes several interesting elements to the apology tradition. Not only is he responsible for the term "recantation," but he also illuminates and mocks Stesichorus' paradigm with his Canidia palinode, produces the first "erotic palinode," and introduces the topos of old age. Several critics maintain that Horace patterned his "Epode 17" after Stesichorus' "Palinodia."[30] The similarities are that both Stesichorus and Horace offend a woman—a woman with power, that is— both are punished for their offense, and both reverse their statements so that they may be delivered from their afflictions. Francis Cairns characterizes Horace's "Epode 17" as a "patently ironically insincere recantation" because of its blatant and repeated

---

28 Hans Peter Syndikus, *Catull: Eine Interpretation*, Impulse der Forschung 46 (Darmstadt: Wissenschaftliche Buchgesellschaft, 1984) 226. For the legal customs of Catullus' time, see Eduard Fraenkel, *Horace* (Oxford: Clarendon, 1957) 431-43.

29 Gaius Valerius Catullus, "Poem 42," *The Poems of Catullus*, trans. Horace Gregory (New York: Covici-Friede, 1931) 100-01; here lines 3, 9, 11 in facing page translation.

30 Bowra, *Greek Lyric Poetry* 109-10; Cairns, "The Genre Palinode" 546-52; Vürtheim, *Stesichoros' Fragmente und Biographie* 68-70.

stress on Canidia's power.[31] If it were not for her influence over the poet, who has spoken ill of her in "Epode 3," dedicated "Epode 5" entirely to a portrayal of her gruesome powers, and cursed her madly as well as derided her in *Sermones* I, 8, he would never have retracted. Horace's enumeration of the nasty effects Canidia had on him supports the coerced and insincere nature of his recantation, "ergo negatum vincor ut credam miser" ['And so I'm forced to believe what I denied'].[32] In the beginning of "Epode 17" then, Horace verbally prostrates himself before Canidia:

Iam iam efficaci do manus scientiae,
supplex et oro regna per Proserpinae

. . . .

Canidia, parce vocibus tandem sacris
citumque retro solve, solve turbinem.[33]

This little introduction sounds like a prayer to a goddess, a prayer much like the one Stesichorus could have made in the missing part of his "Palinodia." Bowra actually suggests that Horace might have had access to the entire "Palinodia" and thus would present a fuller picture than we can glean from Stesichorus' fragment.[34]

Although Horace acknowledges Canidia's magic power, he—unlike Stesichorus, who admits the falseness of his words—never concedes that he slandered Canidia in his writing, but he is willing to take punishment from her and "eagerly" wishes to atone:

. . . iussas cum fide poenas luam,
paratus expiare, seu poposceris
centum iuvencos, sive mendaci lyra
voles sonare 'tu pudica, tu proba
perambulabis astra sidus aureum.'
infamis Helenae Castor offensus vice
fraterque magni Castoris, victi prece
adempta vati reddidere lumina:
et tu (potes nam) solve me dementia.[35]

---

31 Cairns, "The Genre Palinode" 549.

32 Horace, "Epodon XVII," *Q. Horatius Flaccus: Oden und Epoden*, ed. A. Kiessling, 2 vols., 4th ed. (Berlin: Weidmann, 1901) 1: 458-64, line 27; translation by W. G. Shepherd, "Epode 17," *Horace: The Complete Odes and Epodes with the Centennial Hymn* (Harmondsworth: Penguin, 1983) 64-66; here 65.

33 Horace, "Epodon XVII" lines 1-2, 6-7.
    ['Now at last I salute your potent art,
    and kneeling I beg by Proserpina's realm,

    . . . .
    . . . . Canidia,
    leave off at length your supernatural spells
    and let the swift wheel reverse, reverse'] (Shepherd, "Epode 17" 64).

34 Bowra, *Greek Lyric Poetry* 100.

35 Horace, "Epodon XVII" lines 37-44.
    ['I will faithfully pay the punishment enjoined,
    prepared to expiate, should you demand
    a hundred bullocks, or wish to be sung
    to a disingenuous lyre—chaste and honest,

This passage has the greatest intertextual appeal, as it echoes both Stesichorus and Catullus. For one, just as Stesichorus did, Horace offers both a song to restore Canidia's virtue and a prayer to sway the gods. The reference to Castor and Pollux, Helen's stellar brothers, echoes Stesichorus' punishment and absolution for his slandering of Helen. This intertextual reference might, then, shed some light on the controversy about Helen's whereabouts that came to haunt Stesichorus. Horace promises to place Canidia among the stars, implying that Helen had also assumed a place in the sky next to her brothers; Bowra interprets Horace's utilization of that fact as a definite imitation of Stesichorus.[36] Horace's submissive and yet self-assertive trial structure prefigures later medieval poets, such as Machaut, Chaucer, and Hoccleve, who resort to similar constructs.

The second intertextual link connects Horace to Catullus and his use of the terms "pudica" and "proba," the same two adjectives Catullus employs in "Poem 42" when trying to change his adversary's mind. Some critics assume that Horace's word choice is purposefully modeled on Catullus. Lines 45 to 52 then give Horace the chance to deny what he said in *Sermones* I, 8, but also the satisfaction to repeat, in sordid detail, his charges of Canidia's grave robbery and childbirth. The poet is actually vindicated by Canidia's response and verdict that she is neither moved by his plea nor his eagerness to sing her praises. Her unforgiving stance is an ironic re-affirmation of the antifeminism for which he supposedly repented. Horace's adoption of both Stesichorus' and Catullus' texts illuminates his palinodes. Since it is evident that Catullus applied the virtuous terms in a similar highly ironic context, Horace could not possibly be serious himself. Furthermore, his offering to sing Canidia's praises and to place her among the stars emphasizes his literary power; how else would his poetic gift elevate her thus to the stature and immortality of both Helen and a star? On a metafictional level, however, Horace's offer insinuates that gods are made by poets and, therefore, affirms the power of poetry.

Horace's second—and the first ever erotic—palinode also follows a Stesichorean paradigm featuring another offended woman and the poet's concern over an external entity. Ancient commentators perceived intertextual ties of this poem to Stesichorus, especially the first line "O matre pulchra filia pulchrior" ['O lovelier daughter of a lovely mother']; Eduard Fraenkel denies the assertion that the apostrophe is reminiscent of Helen.[37] In "Ode I, 16," the poet employs self-criticism to achieve his amorous intent with a woman who is angry about some of his previous poetry. Stressing the woman's beauty, Horace surrenders his offending "iambs" to her for destruction by water, fire or whatever other form she wishes. This is the first case in which an author

---

a golden constellation, you'll walk among the stars.
Castor incensed at Helen's disrepute,
and Castor's great brother, were won by prayer:
so you (you have the power) deliver me from madness'] (Shepherd, "Epode 17" 65)

36 Vürtheim, *Stesichoros' Fragmente und Biographie* 68 and Bowra, *Greek Lyric Poetry* 110.

37 See R. G. M. Nisbet and Margaret Hubbard, *A Commentary on Horace: Odes Book 1* (Oxford: Clarendon, 1970) 202. Horace, "Carminum I.xvi," *Q. Horatius Flaccus: Oden und Epoden*, ed. A. Kiessling, 2 vols., 4th ed. (Berlin: Weidmannsche Buchhandlung, 1901) 1: 93-95; translation by W. G. Shepherd: "Ode I, 16," *Horace: The Complete Odes and Epodes* 84-85; here 84. Fraenkel, *Horace* 209.

offers the actual physical destruction of a literary piece, albeit only in an ironic context, and introduces the topos of literary sins in conjunction with youth: "temptavit in dulci iuventa / fervor et in celeres iambos / misit furentem" (lines 23-25) ['in sweet youth / heart's passion tried me too / and set me to raving / in rash lampoons . . .' (Fraenkel 209]. Horace's emphasis on his opponent's beauty and his own willingness to retract becomes clear as he reveals his real motives: "his recantation is conditional on her granting him her sexual favours."[38] Coining the new word "recantatis," modeled on Stesichorus' "Palinodia," Horace entices the female by promising recantation of his earlier verse:

> . . . nunc ego mitibus
> mutare quaero tristia, dum mihi
> fias recantatis amica
> opprobriis animumque reddas.[39]

The word "dum" harbors the author's intentions; only when she turns her favors once more toward him will he change his previous writing. This initial "sincerity" and offer to surrender his poems obviously enlist the ancient purification rite for a trivial purpose and thus mock it.

So far the auctorial apologies have mainly referred to one or several specific works. Horace, however, generalizes his newly-introduced "youth vs. old age" dichotomy by applying it to his entire canon. In "Epistulae II.2," Horace suggests a reason for his abandoning lyric poetry:

> nimirum sapere est abiectis utile nugis
> et tempestivum pueris concedere ludum
> ac non verba sequi fidibus modulanda Latinis,
> sed verae numerosque modosque ediscere vitae.[40]

This remark comments on Horace's progress as a poet, envisioning the poet in two different roles, the singer of love poetry and the disseminator of wisdom. Note,

---

38   Cairns, "The Genre Palinode" 549.

39   Horace, "Carminum I.xvi" lines 25-29.
['. . . Now I would change
those acid lines for sweet, if only (since I take
back all my taunts) you'll be my friend
and give me back my heart'] (Shepherd, "Ode I, 16" 85).
William Hardy Alexander postulates that this passage might actually refer to the verbal insults the lady heaped on Horace and subsequently be her recantation. As Linforth states, "[i]t is characteristically Horatian to work in a sly touch like this at the end, reminding the lady that she had been pretty abusive herself. Translate, therefore: 'provided you become my girl again, abjuring all the abusive epithets and taunts you heaped on me, and give me back your heart'" (qtd. in William Hardy Alexander, *Horace's Odes and Carmen Saeculare* [Berkeley: U of California P, 1947] 184). M. Dyson expands Alexander's theory in "Horace: Odes I 16," *Journal of the Australian Universities' Modern Language Association* 30 (1968): 169-79.

40   Horace, "Epistulae II.2," *Horaz: Satiren und Episteln*, ed. and trans. Otto Schönberger, Schriften und Quellen der Alten Welt 33 (Berlin: Akademie-Verlag, 1976) 223-35, lines 141-2. [It would of course be useful for me to stop the trifles, to be wise, to concede the game to the young people, to whose age it is more fitting, and not chase after words that should be sung to the Latin lyre but to learn the rhythm and harmony of a true way of life].

however, the use of the conditional mode, which makes the described intra-auctorial dichotomy a desirable state but does not confirm that Horace actually followed it. In both late antiquity and the Middle Ages, the old-age topos becomes a conventional structural element for many Christian writers who want to polarize their intra-auctorial careers as a movement from youth—the preferred but still misspent time for secular love poetry—to old age—the time for the true ("verae") things in life—as exemplified by a progression from literary and poetic explorations to austere and didactic prose, either truly autobiographical or purely fictional.[41]

2.6. Ovid

Autobiography and fiction also haunt Ovid (43 BCE-17 or 18 CE), who weaves an extensive apology text that functions diachronically on all four textual and auctorial levels—intertextually, intratextually, interauctorially and intra-auctorially—and involves half of his works: *Amores*, *Ars Amatoria*, *Remedia Amoris*, *Metamorphoses*, *Tristia*, and *Ex Ponto*. As half of his apologies are fictional devices and the others derive from external autobiographical concerns, such as his banishment, Ovid seems to have motives best assessed as mixed. Although he mostly apologizes to a general earthly audience, his nemesis, the Emperor Augustus, was also considered a deity—a parallel to Helen's divine status in the Stesichorus legend. In *Ars Amatoria*, Ovid demonstrates his knowledge of the Helen/Stesichorus incident: "probra Therapnaeae qui dixerat ante maritae / mox cecinit laudes prosperiore lyra."[42] In *Ex Ponto*, Ovid alludes to that divine power and makes further use of the Stesichorus legend in an interauctorial manner, as he theorizes about the gods and their way of punishing poets: "saepe levant poenas ereptaque lumina reddunt, / cum bene peccati paenituisse vident. / paenitet, o!" ['Often do they [the gods] mitigate penalties and restore the sight they have taken away when they behold sincere repentance for sin. I too repent!'].[43] The invocation of that ancient purification rite complements the magic formula of "sincere repentance." Through this allusion to sincerity Ovid implies that other apologies have lacked sincere repentance. Aside from unequivocally stating the sincerity issue, Ovid also establishes the audience as an active participant in the writing and reading process that takes place between the author, the text, and the reader. This becomes a major issue in the later Middle Ages.

Ovid's first opus on love, the *Amores*, a collection of erotic elegies, appeared in two editions, of which only the second is extant. We know this from the epigram with which Ovid prefaced the second edition of the *Amores*; this epigram, which derives

---

41 For a more extensive discussion of this topos, see footnote 4 in Chapter 4.

42 Ovid, *Ars Amatoria*, ed. E. J. Kenney (Oxford: Clarendon, 1961) 113-200; here lines 3.49-50. ['Who first reviled the bride from Therapnae / Soon sang her praises in a happier key'] (A. D. Melville, trans., *The Love Poems* [Oxford: Oxford UP, 1990] 129).

43 Ovid, *Tristia. Ex Ponto*, 2nd ed. Loeb Classics, 6 vols. (Cambridge: Harvard UP, 1988) vol. 6 with a facing page translation by Arthur Wheeler; here *Ex Ponto* lines I.i.57-59, 269.

from the Hellenistic introductory poem, is unprecedented in Ovid's time.[44] Here his personified books are speaking:

Qvi modo Nasonis fueramus quinque libelli,
   tres sumus: hoc illi praetulit auctor opus.
ut iam nulla tibi nos sit legisse uoluptas,
   at leuior demptis poena duobus erit.[45]

The hint at less pain implies that elegies have been removed. As Henry Riley suggests in the notes to his translation of the *Amores*, Ovid may have purged the more licentious pieces to avoid retribution.[46] If that is the case, this would be a true example of a retraction, in which an offending work was actually re-edited, perhaps rewritten, or pulled out entirely. The use of "leuior," not only in the sense of 'less burdensome' but rather with the meaning 'generically more modest,' hints at the eradication of some of the more licentious verses and at a "generic distinction."[47] This passage above also poses an interesting question. Should the second and revised edition be treated as the result of an intratextual self-criticism or as a separate text? Although two books have been removed, it cannot be safely determined whether certain poems have been cut or revised or simply been rearranged; additional new poems, however, seem to be out of the question.[48] Alan Cameron suggests that *Tristia* lines 4.x.59-62 might include some of those poems slashed from the first edition of the *Amores*, as Ovid writes:

moverat ingenium totam cantata per urbem
   nomine non vero dicta Corinna mihi.
multa quidem scripsi, sed, quae vitiosa putavi,
   emendaturis ignibus ipse dedi.[49]

At any rate, such ironic self-criticism is atypical for Ovid before his exile.[50]

In the "elaborate literary game"[51] of the *Ars Amatoria* and the *Remedia Amoris*, whose four books could be considered a literary unit, Ovid constructs an intertextual sequence of affirmation and negation. His *Remedia* has been characterized as a palin-

---

44 J. C. McKeown, *Ovid:* Amores *Text, Prolegomena and Commentary*, 2 vols., ARCA Classical and Medieval Texts, Papers and Monographs 22 (Leeds: Francis Cairns Ltd., 1989) 2: 1.

45 Ovid, *Amores*, ed. E. J. Kenney (Oxford: Clarendon, 1961) 1-107; here 5.
    ['We who before were Ovid's five slim volumes
       Are three: he thought it better to compress.
    Though reading us may still give you no pleasure,
       With two removed at least the pain is less'] (Melville, *The Love Poems* 1).

46 Henry T. Riley, trans., *The Heroides or Epistles of the Heroines, Amours, Art of Love, Remedy of Love, and Minor Works* (London: George Bell, 1879) 261.

47 McKeown, *Ovid* 6.

48 E. J. Kenney, introduction, *Ovid: The Love Poems*, trans. A. D. Melville (Oxford: Oxford UP, 1990) viii-xxix; here xiii. Alan Cameron, "The First Edition of Ovid's *Amores*," *Classical Quarterly* 18 (1968): 320-33; here 327.

49 Cameron, "The First Edition of Ovid's *Amores*" 328. Ovid, *Tristia* lines 4.x.59-62. ['My genius had been stirred by her who was sung throughout the city, whom I called, not by a real name, Corinna. Much did I write, but what I thought defective I gave in person to the flames for their revision'] (Wheeler 201).

50 McKeown, *Ovid:* Amores 3.

51 John A. Barsby, *Ovid* (Oxford: Clarendon, 1978) 20.

ode to the *Ars*, although certain critics claim that Book III of the *Ars* was penned after the *Remedia*.[52] Claiming to heal all the wounds that unhappy love can cause, the *Remedia* is "a neat reversal of what had been enjoined in the *Ars*,"[53] although Ovid tries to deny an implied self-criticism in his composing the *Remedia* with this intra-auctorial and metatextual comment that contradicts the question of erasure of the text: "nec te, blande puer, nec nostras prodimus artes, / nec nova praeteritum Musa retexit opus" ['Sweet boy [Amor], I've not betrayed you or my talent / And no new Muse unweaves work done before'].[54] He has to contradict himself on almost every count in the *Remedia*, nonetheless, and digresses in the middle of the work to refute the critics who found the Muse of his books to be wanton ("libellos / quorum censura Musa proterva mea est" [lines 361-62]). Keeping with the literary purpose of the *Remedia*, Ovid ends the work with fictional self-criticism; he has to advise his pupils of love to avoid poetic works about love, since they are trying to fall out of love, "eloquar invitus: teneros ne tange poetas / (summoveo dotes impius ipse meas!") ['I speak against the grain: don't touch love-poets; / For my gifts too—what sacrilege!—that goes'].[55] Once more, we witness the conflict of poetic pride and self-criticism.

Although there is some confusion as to why Ovid was banned by Augustus, he blames at least part of his banishment on his all-too-successful *Ars*, "duo crimina, carmen et error" (*Tristia* lines II.207) [two crimes, a poem and a blunder].[56] Writing a palinode to the *Ars*, however, did not give Ovid poetic license. He has to modify his statement in the *Ars*, "et mihi cedet Amor" ['So Love shall yield to me'] and accept the bitter reality that "cedunt Iouis omnia regno" ['all things yield to Jupiter's reign'].[57] He had angered the deity and had been punished for it. *Tristia* and *Ex Ponto* are laced with self-critical statements about his composition of the *Ars*, while allusions to the "error" stay purposefully hazy because Ovid did not want to incense Augustus any further. The *Ars* was said to have incited Roman wives to infidelity, but no action was taken against Ovid until seven years after its publication.[58] Arthur Leslie Wheeler cites a combination of reasons for Ovid's problems with the *Ars*. While Ovid was definitely not the first poet of erotic literature in Rome, he was the first who subordi-

---

52 See Charles E. Murgia, "Influence of Ovid's *Remedia Amoris* on *Ars Amatoria 3* and *Amores 3*," *Classical Philology* 8 (1986): 203-220.

53 Kenney, introduction xxiii.

54 Ovid, *Remedia Amoris*, ed. A. A. R. Henderson (Edinburgh: Scottish Academic Press, 1979) lines 11-12 with a translation by A. D. Melville, *The Love Poems* (Oxford: Oxford UP, 1990) 151.

55 Ovid, *Remedia Amoris* lines 757-59; Melville, *The Love Poems* 171.

56 For a comprehensive treatment of Ovid's exile, see John C. Thibault, *The Mystery of Ovid's Exile* (Berkeley: U of California P, 1964) and Alessandro Barchiesi's recent study on political power and literature in the Augustan age, *The Poet and the Prince: Ovid and Augustan Discourse* (Berkeley: U of California P, 1997). Sidonius seems to be the first medieval writer to point to Ovid's exile as a result of the *Ars* (Ralph J. Hexter, *Ovid and Medieval Schooling: Studies in Medieval School Commentaries on Ovid's* Ars Amatoria, Epistulae ex Ponto, *and* Epistulae Heroidum [Munich: Arbeo-Gesellschaft, 1986] 89).

57 Ovid, *Ars Amatoria* line 1.21 and Melville, *The Love Poems* 87; Ovid, *Metamorphoses* ed. and trans. Georges Lafaye, 3 vols. (Paris: Société d'Édition "Les Belles Lettres," 1985) 10.148.

58 Hermann Fränkel, *Ovid: A Poet Between Two Worlds*, Sather Classical Lectures 18 (Berkeley: U of California P, 1945) 111, 112.

nated the art of love to a "didactic system."[59] Not the content but the form and its influence on the public, coupled with the *Ars'* ever-increasing popularity, incurred the wrath of the emperor.[60]

Wavering between utter self-criticism and auctorial pride in the *Tristia* and *Ex Ponto*, Ovid consequently produces a rich textual tapestry. John Barsby attests that the "ego" in the letters from exile is "essentially Ovid, not an adopted persona."[61] Ovid conjures up an implied interauctorial setting in *Tristia* lines I.vii.15f. where he claims to atone for his literary sins by burning some of his verses, particularly all copies of the *Metamorphoses*, although several copies were saved by others. Harry B. Evans interprets this passage as a fictional imitation of Vergil's deathbed command to burn the *Aeneid* he could not finish to his satisfaction.[62] Additionally, the better part of Book II of Ovid's *Tristia* consists of references to the *Ars*, for which he reproaches and defends himself. He refers to the *Ars* as "iuvenalia carmina" (*Tristia* lines II.339) [the songs of youth], which seems either to exploit ironically Horace's sins-of-youth topos or to misinterpret it, for Ovid was in his early forties at the date of composition. In several passages, he condemns and hates his work ["damnat et odit opus"] (*Tristia* lines III.i.8), referring to his *Ars* as "foolish"; for instance, "est tamen his gravior noxa fatenda mihi. / neve roges, quae sit, stultam conscripsimus Artem" ['Yet I must confess a weightier sin. Ask not what it is. But I have composed a foolish "Art"'].[63] These passages are contrasted with certain defensive utterances. Although he admits that his book "non esse severae / scripta" ['has no serious mien'], he feels compelled to point out that courtesans, not married women, were the intended audience of his *Ars*.[64]

In another self-critical passage, he attacks his wanton Muse, demonstrating both literary repentance and a poet grappling with his creative power:

> at cur in nostra nimia est lascivia Musa,
>   curve meus cuiquam suadet amare liber?
> nil nisi peccatum manifestaque culpa fatenda est.
>   paenitet ingenii iudiciique mei.[65]

In yet another passage, Ovid shows all of his torn poetic self when he admits that he cannot help but write verses, which, on the other hand, end up burned:

> nec tamen, ut verum fatear tibi, nostra teneri
>   a componendo carmine Musa potest.
> scribimus et scriptos absumimus igne libellos:
>   exitus est studii parva favilla mei.
> nec possum et cupio non ullos ducere versus:

---

59 Arthur Leslie Wheeler, introduction, *Tristia. Ex Ponto* by Ovid, 2nd ed. Loeb Classics, 6 vols. (Cambridge: Harvard UP, 1988) 6: vii-xxxviii; here xx.

60 Wheeler, introduction, *Tristia* 6: xxiv.

61 Barsby, *Ovid* 42.

62 Harry B. Evans, *Publica Carmina: Ovid's Books from Exile* (Lincoln: U of Nebraska P, 1983) 43.

63 Ovid, *Ex Ponto* II.ix.72-73 and Wheeler 365. See also *Ex Ponto* lines III.iii.9-40.

64 Ovid, *Tristia* lines II.241-42 and Wheeler 73. Also *Tristia* lines II.251-54 and *Ex Ponto* lines III.iii.49-58.

65 Ovid, *Tristia* lines II.313-16. ['Yet why is my Muse so wanton? Why does my book advise anybody to love? There is naught for me but confession of my error and my obvious fault: I repent of my talent and my tastes'] (Wheeler 79).

. . . .
  . . . in cineres Ars mea versa foret![66]

This last quotation encapsulates the poet's state of mind. Although his poetic facility coerces him to write poetry, his inner censor forces him to destroy his creation, mostly because of the havoc the *Ars*, the work that unfortunately was not consumed by fire, has wreaked upon him.

Ovid adds two other strategies of defense to his repertoire, an interauctorial one and a reader-response one. First, he constantly points out the lasciviousness of contemporary authors who have nevertheless gone unscathed; this is especially true in passage II.421-572 of the *Tristia*. Second, Ovid is the first poet in the apology tradition who implicates the reader along with the author, a tactic imitated by several late-medieval writers:

> sic igitur carmen, recta si mente legatur,
>   constabit nulli posse nocere meum.
> atque ortum vitium quicumque hinc concipit, errat,
>   et nimium scriptis arrogat ille meis
>
> . . . .
> omnia perversas possunt corrumpere mentes;
>   stant tamen ipsa suis omnia tuta locis
>
> . . . .
> nec liber indicum est animi, sed honesta voluptas.[67]

Ovid suggests that the reading and writing process needs to be freed from the unilaterality of auctorial responsibility, in which the reader would merely be a victim and never an accomplice in the literary sinning process. Ovid affirms that the reader is as guilty in creating a literary text as the author. Ovid's textual and auctorial theory stands as an antithesis to what Roland Barthes calls the "'classical' bourgeois text" that "makes its reader into a passive 'consumer' because it is 'readable' ('lisible') only on the level of representation, where language is assumed to be transparently referential and ideologically innocent" but reinforces Barthes' theory that "the 'writable' ('scriptible') text liberates the reader to participate actively in the 'work' ('travail') or 'production' of literature itself. Each reader 'rewrites' the text by discovering a new arrangement of signification."[68] The theory of the reader's participation in the writing of the text is one feature of the apology tradition that becomes central to both Boccaccio and Chaucer in the Middle Ages. Although there is a definite difference between the *prae* and *post-culpam* Ovid, his last literary compositions, despite their

---

66   Ovid, *Tristia* lines V.xii.59-63, 68. ['And yet, to confess the truth to you, my Muse cannot be restrained from composing verses. I write poems which once written I consume in the fire; a few ashes are the result of my toil. I cannot and yet I long to refrain from writing verse; . . . I would that my "Art" . . . had been turned to ashes!'] (Wheeler 255, 257).

67   Ovid, *Tristia* lines II.275-78; 301-2; 357. ['So then with verse: if it be read with upright mind, it will be established that it can injure nobody—even though it be mine. Whoever believes that this has resulted in depravity is mistaken and attributes too much to my works . . . All things can corrupt perverted minds, yet all things stand harmless in their own proper places. . . . A book is not evidence of the writer's mind, but respectable entertainment'] (Wheeler 75, 77, 81).

68   Thaïs E. Morgan, "Is There an Intertext in This Text?" *American Journal of Semiotics* 3 (1985): 1-40; here 19.

sometimes ingratiating tone, demonstrate much grace under pressure and stand as a monument to a poet who was able to transform his punishment into an imperative to write poetry once more. They provide an intra-auctorial writing and rewriting of Ovid as a poet but prove that, while the sword might indeed be mightier than the pen, the former cannot necessarily completely vanquish the latter.

2.7. Apuleius

Another Latin work, Lucius Apuleius' second-century *Metamorphoseon*, which has puzzled most classical scholars as to its genre, autobiography or novel—that is, truth or fiction[69]—provides the first example of framed tales in the self-criticism tradition. Because of the inherent intratextual design of a framework structure in which all the information passes through one consciousness but originates from several sources, the narrator/auctor can be evasive about narrative responsibility. Ten of the eleven books narrate the story of Lucius, who, having been changed into an ass with the help of black magic, undergoes a journey of great humiliation and lewd adventures, in which "frivolous" and "serious" characteristics mingle.[70] The protagonist's adventures as an ass culminate in a graphic description of his sexual relationship with a woman; then in the eleventh book Lucius the ass becomes rehumanized and converts to the cult of Isis. Much has been written to explain this ten-to-one imbalance in the work.[71] For instance, portions of the work have been matched with Apuleius' biography, suggesting a strong autobiographical flavor, especially in the account of his conversion to Isis. I would like to add another theory to the existing ones. Apuleius previously had to defend himself against the charge of black magic, as recorded in his *Apologia*. It is generally presumed that the *Metamorphoseon* came after the *Apologia*, especially since that work could have helped him in his defense. Therefore, the particular structure of the *Metamorphoseon* might reflect the poet's wish to avoid another charge of black magic, since he puts forth a tale that transforms its hero into an ass through the help of witchcraft. By closing the story of the golden ass with a conversion, fusing the narrator and auctor, he can circumvent any criticism and avert any further legal action

69 John J. Winkler, *Auctor & Actor: A Narratological Reading of Apuleius's* Golden Ass (Berkeley: U of California P, 1985) 1. Not even Augustine was completely sure about its genre; see *De civitate Dei*, ed. Johann Divjak, 5th ed. (Stuttgart: Teubner, 1981) 18.18.

70 Winkler, *Auctor & Actor* 33.

71 See P. J. Enk, "A Propos d'Apulee," *Acta Classica* (1958): 85-91; Pierre Grimal, "L'originalité des Metamorphoses d'Apulée," *L'Information Littéraire* 9 (1957): 156-62; Léon Herrmann, "L'Ane d'or et le christianisme," *Latomus* 12 (1953): 188-91; M. Hicter, "L'Autobiographie dans l'âne d'or d'Apulée," *L'Antiquite Classique* 13 (1944-45): 61-68, 95-111; L. A. MacKay, "The Sin of the Golden Ass," *Arion* 4 (1965): 474-80; William Nethercut, "Apuleius' Metamorphoses: The Journey," *Agon* 3 (1969): 97-134; Francis Norwood, "The Magic Pilgrimage of Apuleius," *The Phoenix* 10 (1956): 1-12; Erwin Rohde, *Kleine Schriften* (Tübingen: J. C. B. Mohr, 1901) 2: 43-74; Carl Rubino, "Literary Intelligibility in Apuleius' *Metamorphoses*," *The Classical Bulletin* 5 (1966): 65-69; and Antonie Wlosok, "Zur Einheit der Metamorphosen des Apuleius," *Philologus* 113 (1969): 68-84.

contemplated against him. Apuleius could thus make use of both the cathartic and preventative function of the apology.

Because the framing-tales structure grants Apuleius the freedom the later medieval compiler also enjoyed, he can be evasive about the narrative center and rewrite both the *Metamorphoseon* and himself as an author. The work's structure can stand as a precursor to framed-story collections in the Middle Ages that move from the secular to the spiritual, in the sense Horace had already implied in his "Epistulae II.2." The *Metamorphoseon* demonstrates similarities to *The Canterbury Tales*: both works feature a frame-story and loosely connected tales narrated by individuals on a journey and relayed through one central character; they cope with a narrative center that cannot always be located very easily; and they move from the lewd and secular to the spiritual. Just as Chaucer cleverly shifts narrative centers, appearing polyphonous most of the time, Apuleius also plays hide-and-seek with the audience. The confusion of the narrative center starts in the prologue where the "I" asks the question "quis ille?" (*MP* I.5) [Who is talking?]. In a typical application of an *Exordialtopos*, the narrator excuses himself for his inferior command of Latin, posing as a mere translator (*MP* I.1), and, in an attempt to manipulate authorial intent, he proposes to entertain the audience with "fabulam Graecanicam" (*MP* I.1) [lewd Greek stories], adopting the role of a compiler or an anthologist. In Chapter 25 of Book I, the narrator is finally identified as Lucius. While the "I" from the prologue has promised the reader pleasurable stories, the narrator does not take any responsibility for them, for he becomes part of the audience as the other characters in the novel tell their stories; for instance, in Book VI, Chapter 25, the ass laments, "dolebam, mehercules, quod pugillares et stilum non habebam, qui tam bellam fabellam praenotarem" [and, by God, I was sorry that I did not have a pen and writing tablets to record this pretty story].

Book XI then places the work in a religious context with Stesichorean overtones. After paying homage to the deity Isis, Lucius, who is now identified as "Madaurensem" (*MP* XI.27) ['a man from Madaura'], participates in a Stesichorean purification rite in order to be delivered from an undesirable situation. The author equates his identity with the protagonist's, making the story autobiographical, since Apuleius was from that city.[72] While Book XI constitutes the intratextual negation of the entire work up to that point, the intra-auctorial rewriting of the narrator/auctor, who has avoided responsibility for the narrated stories, commences in Book X, Chapter 2, in which he returns to the metaphor of the written word and this time admits that the *Metamorphoseon* is his book: "Post dies plusculos ibidem dissignatum scelestum ac nefarium facinus memini, sed ut vos etiam legatis, ad librum profero" (*MP* 1-2) [I remember a wicked and abominable crime that had been instigated there, but so that you can read it, too, I will bring it forth in my book]. With this example the narrator/auctor distinction fades, and Lucius/Apuleius expresses some literary guilt, but by becoming a priest to Isis, he atones for all the objectionable aspects of the first ten books. In late antiquity, the entire *Metamorphoseon* was interpreted as a confession because of its religious ending.[73] Georg Misch also claims that Apuleius was serious

---

72 P. G. Walsh, "Lucius Madaurensis," *Phoenix* 22 (1968): 143-57; here 144.

73 Elizabeth Hazelton Haight, *Apuleius and His Influence* (New York: Longman, Green, 1927) 49.

about his surprising conclusion.[74] Some irony persists, however, since Apuleius, who could not tell his stories until he was a follower and priest of Isis, goes to great length and takes great pains to relate every detail of his vast sexual experience,[75] which expresses a great deal of authorial license.

2. 8. Lucian

Apuleius' contemporary Lucian (c. 120-190), whose biting satire left no human weakness unscathed,[76] is important to this study because he expands Callimachus' justification concept and provides an ironic model for the trial framework popular in the later Middle Ages. He blatantly converts "criticisms" to his own literary and satirical ends by employing the concept of intertextuality to create a new text as well as to assert the previous one, since his "apologies" are as offensive as the original offensive text. In a fictional trial scenario, he exploits the implied self-criticism as a means of justification. Similarly to Euripides in Aristophanes' *Thesmophoriazousae*, Lucian depicts himself in the prose satire *The Fisherman* as threatened by a hostile crowd of revived Greek philosophers. *The Fisherman* presents a constant intertextual reference to the *Philosophies for Sale*, in which Lucian has the gods sell off and ridicule "various types of the philosophic life."[77] Since during Lucian's times philosophers had gained great influence and were generally regarded as "authoritative role model[s],"[78] he exploits this self-critical structure to deride the bloodthirsty crowd of revenge-seekers even more. His portrayal of their vengefulness both underscores that tactic and echoes the dynamics of the antifeminist examples so far.

Lucian, the perfect example of the self-justifying aspects of the self-critical author who occasionally amuses himself by playing the role of the compiler, never explicitly admits any literary guilt. Although the fictional Plato enumerates Lucian's literary sins—"Or look into those charming dialogues you wrote in which you not only slandered Philosophy herself but humiliated us by hawking us like slaves on the block" (*FM* 336)—the accused affirms his innocence and counters: "How have I ever insulted you? When? All my life I've stood in awe of philosophy, sung your praises to the skies" (*FM* 337). The ensuing verbal trial illustrates several interesting intertextual and interauctorial points. Reminding us of the Stesichorean and post-Stesichorean apology, the philosophers call him a "blasphemer" and stress the "verbal craft" of that self-pronounced "Free-Speaker."[79] The act of granting Lucian "verbal license" encourages him to attack the philosophers anew in his defense. He contends that Diogenes had

---

74 Georg Misch, *Geschichte der Autobiographie*, 4 vols. (Bern: A. Francke, 1949-69) 1.1: 384.

75 Winkler, *Auctor & Actor* 141.

76 Misch, *Geschichte der Autobiographie* 1.1: 385.

77 Lucian, *Philosophies for Sale*, Loeb Classics, trans., A. M. Harmon, 7 vols. (New York: Macmillan, 1915) 2: 449-511; here 449.

78 Bracht R. Branham, *Unruly Eloquence: Lucian and the Comedy of Traditions* (Cambridge: Harvard UP, 1989) 122.

79 Branham, *Unruly Eloquence* 33.

"left out most of [his] criticisms and the more serious ones at that" (*FM* 349), which he generously repeats for the ears of the audience and of Philosophy, as did Horace in "Epode 17." The author furthermore disavows his own responsibility in creating those insults: "And, if what I'm going to say sounds slanderous or shocking, I think it would be fairer to put the blame on them for carrying on the way they do rather than on me— I'm simply submitting evidence" (*FM* 349). Although his defense and justification produce the desired dismissal of charges and prompt Diogenes to exclaim, "I retract the charges. He's a hero; he's my friend" (*FM* 354), Lucian cannot abstain from disparaging the philosophers: "Often the fakes are more convincing than the real philosophers" (*FM* 356). Overall, fishing for fake philosophers, Lucian emerges from the comedy vindicated, in an intertextual way re-affirming the initial premise in *Philosophies for Sale* but having turned seeming self-criticism and retribution into another triumph of his verbal craft.

Aside from the justification angle, Lucian is essential to the apology tradition because he is the first author who mocks the convention by elaborating on its potential motives. In his *Apology for the "Salaried Posts in Great Houses,"* he presents the dilemma of an author who has joined the ranks of those he sought to malign in a previous essay. Because he is now also writing under patronage, his *Salaried Posts in Great Houses*, which is not extant and is possibly a fictional reference, might now net him the charge of hypocrisy. He obscures his defense by taking into account the criticism of Sabrinus, although whatever Sabrinus says is expressed in the conditional mode and is therefore milder than the criticisms of the Philosophers. Sabrinus compares Lucian's apology to Stesichorus' recantation for Helen in a hypertextual way: "'recantation for the worse,' not for a Helen indeed, or what happened at Troy" (*AP* 195). This reference attests to the influential nature of Stesichorus' apology in the ancient world after so many centuries and implies that Lucian does not have the same lofty epic-related reason to apologize. Sabrinus furthermore advises Lucian to hide written copies of his first work, because the incongruity would obviously expose the poet to ridicule, and enumerates a long list of possible charges and unflattering criticism by would-be attackers (*AP* 197-201). Lucian naturally disarms all the hypothetical attacks upon him and actually lays open the thoughts and motives of an author who wishes to apologize, a tactic that has been unseen so far in the apology tradition:

> But now I am wondering to what defence I should turn. Is it best to play the coward, turn my back, and admit my wrong-doing, taking refuge in the universal defence, Fortune, Fate, Destiny? Shall I ask pardon from my critics, who know that we have no control and are driven by a mightier power, especially one of those I just mentioned? Shall I say we do not wish it, but have no responsibility at all for what we say or do? . . . Perhaps I have still one anchor left on board, to complain about old age and disease and poverty as well. (*AP* 203, 205)

His strategy emphasizes the satirical intent of the work, confirms the tradition of literary apologies, and identifies the concept of the literary apology as a defensive act. Lucian's list of potential motives and apologies is an invaluable document for the apology tradition because each of the outlined scenarios has been evoked by at least one author in the tradition. That enumeration can then actually be considered a metatextual document relating to auctorial apologies, for it discusses them more than it engages in them. The metatextual function of the list is accentuated by both the pervasive ridiculing tenor and the non-penitent closure of the work with a quotation from Herodotus, "Hippoclides doesn't care" (*AP* 213). Overall, Lucian employs intertextuality to create new texts but actually does not rewrite himself intra-auctorially, since the self-criticism is always reversed, the author vindicated, and his literary creatorship asserted.

Thus, during the Graeco-Roman period, self-critical authors apologize mainly to divinities and women, primarily in *post-culpam* attempts to alleviate or avert punishment. Stesichorus wishes to regain his sight; Euripides wants to stay alive; Horace yearns to be freed from the powers of a witch and wishes to gain a woman's sexual favors; Ovid suffers from the *Ars* and struggles with his banishment; Apuleius has his adventures as an ass and is finally changed back into a human being; both Callimachus and Lucian are under accusation and justify their actions. Other contributions to the tradition are the "youth vs. old age" topos, reader implication in discourse, and meta-textual discussion of auctorial motives for apologies. Additionally, most of the apologies refer back to Stesichorus in either a covertly intertextual or an overtly interauctorial fashion. This backward referentiality and indebtedness to the actual "Palinodia" as well as the to "pseudo-biographical"[80] recordings of Stesichorus' life strengthens Stesichorus' position as the father of the apology tradition. The majority of the authors heighten the irony inherent in the Stesichorean paradigm in their own literary frameworks, mainly because their apologies are addressed not to divinities but to women, who regain popularity as a target audience in the apology tradition of the high and later Middle Ages.

---

80 Francis Cairns, *Tibullus: A Hellenistic Poet at Rome* (Cambridge: Cambridge UP, 1979) 168.

CHAPTER 3

The Early Christian Tradition: Logocentricity and Patriarchy

As the apology tradition moves into the early Christian era, the Graeco-Roman antifeminist element of irony gives way to a theological concern about the place of one's literary works in the sight of God. These apologies are addressed primarily to God and secondarily to a general Christian audience, and combine Christian humility and Latin rhetorical devices. This new situation is implicitly antifeminist, but not iron-ically so, and can be traced to biblical precedents. Ironic apologies to women in the Graeco-Roman world were possible because women were part of the religious mythology of their cultures, whereas in the Judeo-Christian world, God is represented as male. In Greek mythology, a goddess created the world; and in the Babylonian cre-ation myth, male gods depose the great mother who had been ruling the universe and elect a male god who reigns supreme and creates with words.[1] By the time of the Judeo-Christian creation story, a male god who creates with words—the Logos—is already established, and a female creative principle is not even alluded to.[2] This male-privileging creation text, coupled with Jewish and early Christian patriarchal struc-tures, as well as Gnostic influences, branded the feminine as utterly undesirable in the production of text, even as a topic, and forms the beginning of an ingrained theory of creation that has ramifications for medieval authors. Although Christ by his actions effectively amended the solely male creation account concerning female authorship, the status quo remained. For instance, three of the four gospels describe the scene at the tomb of Christ in which He—the Word Incarnate—directly grants women author-ship rights. He privileges the women by appearing to them—especially to Mary Magdalen—before any other of his disciples, and empowers them to spread the good news. This call to creation (of the church) and authorship is later neutralized by the Pauline admonition that women should be silent in church, another removal from par-

---

1   Alexander Heidel, *The Babylonian Genesis: The Story of Creation*, 2nd ed. (Chicago: U of Chicago P, 1951) 82-3 as well as Charles Doria and Harris Lenowitz, eds. and trans., *Origins: Creation Texts from the Ancient Mediterranean* (Garden City, NY: Anchor Books, 1976) 136. Also, feminist critic Luce Irigaray claims that "'[a]ll of Western culture rests on the murder of the mother'" (*The Irigaray Reader,* ed. Margaret Whitford [Oxford: Blackwell, 1991] 7).

2   Even Gen. 1:27, "God created man in his image; in the divine image he created him; male and female he created them," does not allay the representational privileging of God as male. Irigaray points out the obvious by saying that "the gender of God, the guardian of every subject and discourse, is always *paternal and masculine* in the west" (*The Irigaray Reader* 166). For instance, second-century Christian apologist Justin considered the Greek belief that Aphrodite was the first conception—that the divine could have female form—as the "height of [pagan] folly" (Gerald Bray, "Explaining Christianity to Pagans: The Second-Century Apologists," *The Trinity in a Pluralistic Age: Theological Essays on Culture and Religion*, ed. Kevin J. Vanhoozer [Grand Rapids, MI: Eerdman, 1997] 9-25; here 16-17).

ticipation that served the medieval hierarchical and exclusionary view of authorship very well.

The Bible is also the source for the Christian humility topos that can be traced back to Moses' insistence on this inability to speak for God in Ex. 6:30: "'Since I am a poor speaker, how can it be that Pharaoh will listen to me?'" Christian writers of palinodes also employ penitential motives in their self-criticism. At first, confessions were public, but in the fourth century confessions that took place privately between the sinner and a priest were advocated, because too many immoral and scandalous things were being aired in public. Out of that penitential practice grew the literary confession of *confessio peccati*.[3] Writing one's literary sins down, however, returns the confession to the public realm. In the realm of auctorial self-criticism, the confessional spirit is coupled with a certain prescribed humility, whose sincerity has been doubted by Ernst Curtius.[4] The epideictic function of classical rhetoric, the praising or blaming of a person—in this context a blaming of the self stemming from a certain self-referential ambivalence—has also been assimilated into the apology context.

Early Christian authors are beset by a great ambivalence toward their own writing, an ambivalence that is tied to their understanding of and attitude toward pagan antiquity and the seven liberal arts, especially the *trivium*. Paulinus of Nola (c. 378-431) captures some of these attitudes in his "Poem 22" to Jovius:

Iam mihi polliceor sacris tua carmina libris
condere teque dei flammatum numine Christi
ora soluturum summo facunda parenti.
incipe diuinis tantum dare pectora rebus

. . . .
. . . abeat solitis inpensa facultas
carminibus, maior rerum tibi nascitur erdo.
non modo iudicium Paridis nec bella gigantum
falsa canis. fuerit puerili ludus in aeuo
iste tuus quondam; decuerunt ludicra paruum.
nunc animis grauior, quantum prouectior annis,
aspernare leues mature corde Camenas,
et qualem castis iam congrua moribus aetas
atque tui specimen uenerabile postulat oris,
suspice materiam, diuinos concipe sensus.
si decus e falsis aliquod nomenque tulisti
de nacuis magnum rebus, cum ficta uetustis
carminibus caneres . . . .

. . . .
quanto maior ab his cedet tibi gloria coeptis,
in quibus et linguam exercens mentem quoqua sanctam
erudies laudemque simul uitamque capesses?

. . . .
. . . hoc uerbum est, sine quo nihil, omnia per quod
facta uigent . . . .

---

3   Georg Misch, *Geschichte der Autobiographie*, 4 vols. (Bern: A. Francke, 1949-69) 1.2: 594-95.
4   Ernst Robert Curtius, *European Literature and the Latin Middle Ages*, trans. Willard R. Trask, Bollingen Series 36 (New York: Pantheon Books, 1953) 93-95, 410-15.

. . . .
his precor. his potius studiumque operamque legendis
scribendisque uoue . . . .

. . . .
tunc te diuinum uere memorabo poetam.[5]

Paulinus' mini-lecture summarizes the early Christian church's expectations of its
poets and touches upon several aspects of the two *trivium* arts important to this study:
grammar and rhetoric. Because of the absence of Christian schools during late antiquity, "the classical curriculum" became the means for education, and the study of Latin
grammar became the "central art" in which school boys were supposed to engage
between the age of seven and fourteen.[6] Most of the texts used in the grammar
schools, however, were of classical nature and dealt with pagan subjects, probably "the
works of Homer, Hesiod, the dramatists, and the lyric writers of Greece . . . the writings of the chief Latin poets, Virgil, Livius, Andronicus, Ennius, Plautus, Terence,
Horace, Lucan, and Statius."[7] After grammar had been mastered, the pupil was not to
concern himself anymore with the pagan culture but with the glorification of the
Christian God.[8] This division is expressed by Paulinus' poem, where he implores the
recently grown-up addressee to employ his learned eloquence now in the service of

5   Paulinus of Nola, "Carmen XII," *Corpus Scriptorum Ecclesiasticorum Latinorum* 29
     (Vindobonae: F. Tempsky, 1894) 186-93; here lines 1-4, 10-22, 26-8, 56-7, 148-9, 157. ['I
     promise myself that you are now basing your poems on the sacred books, and that inflamed with
     the power of Christ God you will loose your eloquent tongue to the highest Father. Start to devote
     your heart solely to God's affairs. . . let that fluency devoted to your customary songs give place,
     for a greater sequence of topics is now inaugurated for you. Your theme is now not the judgment
     of Paris or the fictitious war of giants. True, this was your sport of old in your childhood days, for
     games were appropriate to a young child. But now that you are more advanced in years, and
     accordingly more serious in purpose, you must spurn with adult mind the insubstantial Muses.
     You must take up subjects demanded by your age, for which chaste manners are now apposite,
     and by the venerable appearance of your countenance. You must conceive thoughts of God. If
     you have won any glory from fictitious themes or great fame from empty ones by singing of fan-
     ciful events in classical lays . . . How much greater fame will accrue to you from those themes
     which will not only exercise your tongue but will also inform your scrupulous mind, and from
     which you will obtain not only praise but also life! . . . This is *the Word without whom there is
     nothing*, by which all creation flourishes . . . I beg you, devote your studies and efforts rather to
     reading and writing about these events. . . Then I shall pronounce you truly a poet divinely
     inspired'] (P. G. Walsh, trans., "Poem 22," *The Poems of St. Paulinus of Nola* [New York:
     Newman Press, 1975] 202-08; here 202-207).
6   Joerg O. Fichte, *Chaucer's 'Art Poetical': A Study in Chaucerian Poetics* (Tübingen: Gunter
     Narr, 1983) 23; David L. Wagner, "The Seven Liberal Arts and Classical Scholarship," *The Seven
     Liberal Arts in the Middle Ages*, ed. David L. Wagner (Bloomington: Indiana UP, 1983) 1-31;
     here 21; Jeffrey F. Huntsman, "Grammar," *The Seven Liberal Arts in the Middle Ages*, ed. David
     L. Wagner (Bloomington: Indiana UP, 1983) 58-95; here 59.
7   Fichte, *Chaucer's 'Art Poetical'* 23.
8   Jean Leclercq confirms that notion: "In the secular schools the *auctores* studied, particularly the
     poets, are full of mythology, hence the danger which these studies, however necessary, present
     for Christians" (*The Love of Learning and the Desire for God: A Study of Monastic Culture*,
     trans. Catharine Misrahi [New York: Fordham UP, 1977] 23). For an account of versifying as part
     of the medieval curriculum, see also Peter Stotz "Dichten als Schulfach—Aspekte mittelalter-
     licher Schuldichtung," *Mittellateinisches Jahrbuch* 16 (1981): 1-16.

God, for talents given by God should be used in his service. Not to act in that way would deny a person the status of a divinely-inspired poet because he would only repeat the emptiness of the pagan culture, not the truths of Christianity.

The second part of the *trivium*, rhetoric, is equally important here. Rhetoric was partially the byproduct and partially the goal of the study of grammar. Owing to their ambivalence toward pagan antiquity, the church fathers rejected the arts as "empty" and especially condemned rhetoric and literature as "conduits of superstition, heresy, and pride."[9] Paul in his First Epistle to Timothy instructs his disciples to stay in Ephesus "in order to warn certain people there against teaching false doctrines and busying themselves with interminable myths and genealogies, which promote idle speculation rather than that training in faith which God requires" (1:3-4). In his *Etymologiae*, Isidore of Seville elaborates on this issue of truth, granting Latin pagan authors the status of "medieval authorities" but denying that they are disseminators of truth.[10] The main grievance Isidore has against pagan poetry is "its origin in the pagan religion"; he also clearly states the connection between poets and gods: "In quorum etiam laudibus accesserunt et poetae, et compositis carminibus in caelum eos substulerunt" ['And in their praises the poets, too, have helped, and by writing poems have raised them (the gods) up to the heavens'].[11] It is almost like a vicious cycle: the poets create the gods, and therefore the religion is a fable, which in turn invalidates the poetic effort in Isidore's eyes. The truths pagan writers held in such high esteem have now become questionable and partially invalidated in the search of the higher truth of Christianity. This search for truth posed specific problems for the early Christian writer, who would be painfully aware of Matt. 13:36-37: "I assure you, on judgment day people will be held accountable for every unguarded word they speak. By your words you will be acquitted and by your words you will be condemned." For the early Christian writer, not only content but also form became a dilemma.

Early Christian writing suffered from an inferiority complex because of the *sermo humilis* style of the Bible. Isidore's major criticism was therefore aimed at the artistic supremacy of the classical authors who produced fiction through stylistic embellishment, while medieval prose produced truth.[12] Christian poetry was not in the first place intended to be a vehicle for art but a medium for salvation.[13] Despite biblical exhortation and Isidore's damnation of pagan literature, the early Christian writers dip extensively into the pool of classical rhetoric, although they reject the content of classical literature as pagan and inferior to Christian logocentric teachings. The Venerable

---

9   Karl E. Morrison, "Incentives for Studying the Liberal Arts," *The Seven Liberal Arts in the Middle Ages*, ed. David L. Wagner (Bloomington: Indiana UP, 1983) 32-57; here 40, 53.

10 Jeanette M. A. Beer, *Narrative Conventions of Truth in the Middle Ages* (Geneva: Librairie Droz, 1981) 11.

11 Ernest Brehaut, *An Encyclopedist of the Dark Ages: Isidore of Seville* (New York: Burt Franklin, 1964) 75, 203 and Isidore of Seville, *Isidore of Seville on the Pagan Gods* (Origines *VIII.11*), ed. Katherine Nell MacFarlane (Philadelphia: The American Philosophical Society, 1980) VIII.11.2.

12 Beer, *Narrative Conventions of Truth in the Middle Ages* 13-14, 11.

13 Edward Kennard Rand, *Founders of the Middle Ages* (1928; New York: Dover Publications, 1957) 181.

Bede gives us a good example of this attitude in his *De Arte Metrica et De Schematibus et Tropis*:

> Et quidem gloriantur Graeci talium se figurarum siue troporum fuisse repertores. Sed ut cognoscas, dilectissime fili, cognoscant omnes qui haec legere uoluerint quia sancta Scriptura ceteris ommibus scripturis non solum auctoritate, quia diuina est, uel utilitate, quia ad uitam ducit aeternam, sed et antiquitate et ipsa praeeminet positione dicendi, placuit mihi collectis de ipsa exemplis ostendere quia nihil huiusmodi schematum siue troporum ualent praetendere saecularis eloquentiae magistri, quod non in illa praecesserit.[14]

Bede's urge to prove the rhetoricity and artistic value of the Bible would both justify and invalidate the use of classical rhetorical devices. For instance, in the apology tradition the usage of the following *Exordia/topoi* in prefaces demonstrates a rhetorical continuum between the late Latin and early Christian writers: use of diminutives, admissions of mediocrity, claims of deficiency in style, desire for correction, and appeals for divine assistance.[15] Deficiency in style was especially problematic for early Christian writers grappling with the *sermo humilis* style of the Bible, a style usually justified by a disavowal of "artistic language" as a hindrance to understanding God's Word.[16]

Although the third-century writer Juvencus does not express any self-criticism, only self-consciousness, he contrasts himself to the pagan poets to assert his own creation and demonstrate the pagan/Christian dichotomy:

> Quod si tam longam meruerunt carmina famam,
> quae veterum gestis hominum mendacia nectunt,
> nobis certa fides aeternae in saecula laudis
> immortale decus tribuet, meritumque rependet.
> Nam mihi carmen erit Christi vitalia gesta,
> divinum populis falsi sine crimine donum.
> Nec metus, ut mundi rapiant incendia secum
> hoc opus; hoc etenim forsan me subtrahet igni

---

14 Bede, *De Arte Metrica et De Schematibus et Tropis*, eds. C. B. Kendall and M. H. King, *Corpus Christianorum Series Latina* CXXIII A (Turnholti: Brepols, 1975) 60-171; here lines I.11-19. ['The Greeks pride themselves on having invented these figures or tropes. But, my beloved child, in order that you and all who wish to read this work may know that Holy Writ surpasses all other writings not merely in authority because it is divine, or in usefulness because it leads to eternal life, but also for its age and artistic composition, I have chosen to demonstrate by means of examples collected from Holy Writ that teachers of secular eloquence in any age have not been able to furnish us with any of these figures and tropes which did not appear first in Holy Writ'] (Gussie Hecht Tannenhaus, trans., "Concerning Figures and Tropes," by Bede, *Readings in Medieval Rhetoric*, eds. Joseph M. Miller, Michael H. Prosser, and Thomas W. Benson [Bloomington: Indiana UP, 1973] 96-122; here 97).

15 Tore Janson, *Latin Prose Prefaces: Studies in Literary Conventions* (Stockholm: Almqvist & Wiksell, 1964) 124-46 and Leonid Arbusow, *Colores Rhetorici: Eine Auswahl rhetorischer Figuren und Gemeinplätze als Hilfsmittel für akademische Übungen an mittelalterlichen Texten* (Göttingen: Vandenhoeck & Ruprecht, 1948) 104-6. Arbusow also asserts that *excusatio* is not so much biblical as influenced by the mannerisms of late antiquity (*Colores Rhetorici* 106).

16 Janson, *Latin Prose Prefaces* 129.

tunc, cum flammivoma descendet nube coruscans
Judex.[17]

Juvencus demonstrates the self-assertive side of the early Christian writer, for he emphasizes especially the salvific nature of his literary creation. It will be primarily his writing that will save him from the fires of Doomsday. Christian humility is being temporarily subsumed in the scheme of elevating Christian literature over pagan. See also Ingelard's picture on page 65.

Nonetheless, the church fathers used the very same style they condemned.[18] The discrepancy between utilizing the form of classical literature, but not the content, can be traced back to the grammatical and rhetorical training of most late-antiquity and medieval educated men. After the breakdown of the Roman Empire, the need for administrators trained in classical Latin was great; that need increased the teaching of classical rhetoric in school[19] but also laid the groundwork for creating rhetorically schizophrenic medieval minds. For instance, Peter Damian (1007-72), a former teacher of rhetoric, utterly rejects the liberal arts in his *On Holy Simplicity* and, like Paulinus of Nola to Jovius, exhorts his readers to "abandon secular learning for heavenly elo-quence."[20] Not surprisingly, however, Damian exhibits all the attributes of a master rhetorician, while "his text exemplifies the very arts that Damian's teaching urged his hearer to avoid: grammar, rhetoric (including poetry), and philosophy."[21] For the writers participating in the apology tradition, having to disavow the foundations of their sanctioned education in order to be accepted by the prevalent Christian Zeitgeist also facilitates an expected, conventional, and therefore inherently more questionable situation. According to Karl Morrison, literary ambivalence in early Christian times stems from an emphasis on conversion and manifests itself in the poets' intention to "integrate the segments of their lives before and after conversion, the early quest for erudition with the later quest for holiness."[22] This pre- and post-conversion dichotomy then becomes the focal point for the early Christian self-critical authors, who capitalize on this juxtaposition in their writing.

The *Kontrastierungstopos* (contrast topos) functions on both the literary and the biographical level: it contrasts the morally and religiously questionable, mendacious

---

17 Juvencus, "Praefatio," *Early Christian Latin Poets from the Fourth to the Sixth Century*, ed. and trans. Otto J. Kuhnmuench (Chicago: Loyola UP, 1929) 18-19, lines 15-24. ['And if poems, that weave lying fables into the deeds of the ancients, have merited so great praise, then our unshaken faith will win for us immortal glory and earn the reward of eternal praise through all the ages. For my song shall be the life and deeds of Christ, God's gift to mankind, without any falsehood. Nor need I fear that the earth's conflagration will destroy this work; perhaps even it will snatch me from that fire when in flaming clouds shall descend the Judge'] (Kuhnmuench 18).

18 Joerg Fichte also confirms this ambivalent attitude towards poetry by medieval clerics: "many of those who discounted the value of secular poetry and discouraged its reading make frequent use of it" (*Chaucer's 'Art Poetical'* 28).

19 R. R. Bolgar, "The Teaching of Rhetoric in the Middle Ages," *Rhetoric Revalued: Papers from the International Society for the History of Rhetoric*, ed. Brian Vickers (Binghamton, NY: Center for Medieval & Early Renaissance Studies, 1982) 79-86; here 80-81.

20 Morrison, "Incentives for Studying the Liberal Arts" 33-34.

21 Morrison, "Incentives for Studying the Liberal Arts" 34.

22 Morrison, "Incentives for Studying the Liberal Arts" 53.

pagan poetry with the Christian truth, underscoring that division by the author's abandonment of pagan poetry.[23] Thus the poet's withdrawal from pagan poetry and turn to Christian matter constitutes an intra-auctorial revision of the writing process that grows out of the conflict between classicism and Christianity. Strictly speaking, this self-epideictic rhetoric might have referred to realistic intra-auctorial quandaries in the early church, but its later medieval ramifications become formulaic and modular. This happened because the pagan/Christian ambivalence was kept alive "in the ascetic and theological core of the Church," whose "inner tension and potential for self-criticism kept it from stagnation."[24]

3.1. Proba

Faltonia Betitia Proba (322-70) is the first author and only woman to place her composition in the pagan/Christian dichotomy in a self-critical fashion. As a recent convert to Christianity, she needed to divest herself of pagan literature when she attempted her account of creation and Christ's life:[25]

> diuersasque neces, regum crudelia bella
> cognatasque acies, pollutos caede parentum
> insignis clipeos nulloque ex hoste tropaea,
> sanguine conspersos tulerat quos fama triumphos,
> innumeris totiens uiduatas ciuibus urbes,
> confiteor, scripsi: satis est meminisse malorum:
> nunc, deus omnipotens, sacrum, precor, accipe carmen
> . . . .
> non nunc ambrosium cura est mihi quaerere nectar,
> nec libet Aonio de uertice ducere Musas.[26]

Proba draws a very clear line between her former and her current intra-auctorial selves. We see again here the cathartic and salvific function of literature, since Proba offers her new song to God in atonement for the brutal pagan accounts she versified. Furthermore, Proba focuses on the destructive and belligerent aspects of pagan litera-

---

23 Paul Klopsch, *Einführung in die Dichtungslehren des lateinischen Mittelalters* (Darmstadt: Wissenschaftliche Buchgesellschaft, 1980) 15.

24 Morrison, "Incentives for Studying the Liberal Arts" 53.

25 Proba interjects her own account of salvation in lines 415-28.

26 Faltonia Betitia Proba, *Probae Cento*, trans. Elizabeth A. Clark and Diane F. Hatch, *The Golden Bough, The Oaken Cross: The Vergilian Cento of Faltonia Betitia Proba* (Chico, CA: Scholars Press, 1981) 12-95, lines 3-9, 13-14. ['And I have catalogued the different slayings, monarchs' cruel wars, and battle lines made up of hostile relatives. I sang of famous shields, their honor cheapened by a parent's blood, and trophies captured from no enemy; bloodstained parades of triumph "fame" had won, and cities orphaned of so many citizens, so many times. I do confess. It is enough to bring these errors back to mind. Now, God almighty, accept my sacred song . . . no longer do I care to seek the ambrosial drink, nor does it please to lead the Muses from Aonian peak'] (Clark and Hatch 15).

ture in order to highlight her conviction that Christianity advocates peace.[27] Although the poetess renounces the content of pagan literature, she is still very much indebted to its form, for her poem is fashioned out of lines from Vergil's *Aeneid*, with Christ showing a marked resemblance to Aeneas. It is also interesting to note that this early woman writer apologizes for the same reasons as her male colleagues—to demarcate her current position and beliefs from her previous pagan convictions. The later medieval women authors who wrote apologies, however, do so because they were women, pointing to a more entrenched antifeminism of the later Middle Ages when the common enemy of paganism had been vanquished and doctrinal Christianity no longer operated from an inferior position.[28]

3.2. Augustine

Disavowal of pagan rhetoric and such literary schizophrenia as Peter Damian's was pervasive, and also affected Augustine of Hippo (354-430), who participates in both the first and the third strand of the apology tradition. The first strand, an apology to God, can be found in his *Confessions*, the prototype of the Christian literary confession and conversion narrative, and concerns the disavowal of rhetoric. Augustine repudiates his previous literary practices, which is understandable in light of the ingrained Christian ambivalence about rhetoric and his initial rejection of the Bible's *sermo humilis* style (III.42). In Book I, 5 of his *Retractations*, Augustine mentions that before his baptism in Milan he had written six books about the liberal arts, of which only the introduction to the first volume survives. In Book IX of the *Confessions*, he then repudiates the study of rhetoric: "Et uenit dies, quo etiam etiam actu solueurer a professione rhetorica, unde iam cogitatu solutus eram. Et factum est, erusti linguam meam."[29] God converts Augustine to Christianity and, by rescuing his tongue, forgives him his literary sins as well. Consequently, Augustine intends to employ his verbal craft for the advancement of the heavenly kingdom, although he still admits to lingering literary pride.[30] Martin Camargo points out, however, that Augustine permits pagan rhetoric to the degree that it furthers the cause of the Church.[31]

---

27 Elizabeth A. Clark and Diane F. Hatch, *The Golden Bough, The Oaken Cross: The Vergilian Cento of Faltonia Betitia Proba* (Chico, CA: Scholars Press, 1981) 123.

28 For the letter Proba received from Augustine, see Anne-Marie la Bonnardière, "La lettre à Proba," *Saint Augustine et la Bible*, ed. Anne-Marie la Bonnardière (Paris: Beauchesne, 1986) 181-88.

29 Augustine, *Confessionum Libri XIII*, ed. Lucas Verheijen, *Corpus Christianorum Series Latina* 27 (Turnholti: Brepols, 1981) lines IV, 1-3. ['The day came on which I was actually to be released from the profession of rhetoric, from which I had already been released in my thinking. And the deed was done. Thou didst deliver my tongue'] (Vernon J. Bourke, trans., *Saint Augustine: Confessions*, by St. Augustine, The Fathers of the Church 21 [Washington, DC: Catholic U of America P, 1953] 233).

30 Bourke, *Saint Augustine: Confessions* 153.

31 Martin Camargo, "Rhetoric," *The Seven Liberal Arts in the Middle Ages*, ed. David L. Wagner (Bloomington: Indiana UP, 1983) 96-124; here 103. See also Jeffrey T. Schnapp, "Reading

Augustine's *Retractations*, which has been regarded as the cornerstone of the Christian apology tradition by Tatlock and Sayce, belongs to the third strand of auctorial self-criticism, which emphasizes textual revision. In the *Retractations*, Augustine practices intertextuality and intra-auctoriality on a grand scale, although he refers to the work with one of the Latin prefatory conventions as "opuscula mea" [my little work]. In this opus, which J. de Ghellinck calls "un genre nouveau," Augustine amends and corrects all of his former books, a practice which seems to hark back to the Hellenistic *de libris ac ratione studiorum* custom of authors cataloging their works and commenting on them, as exemplified by Isocrate and Galen.[32] Although the idea of commenting on one's work obviously had precursors, Augustine attempted to make it both a literary and religious endeavor. He first mentions the planned composition of the *Retractations* in a letter to Marcellinus in the year 412; in another letter in 427/28 to Bishop Quodvultdeus, Augustine asserts that he will censure anything in all of his accumulated writings that "'offends [him] or might offend others'" (BG 3, xiii). Augustine's main intent was to correct the erroneous things he had claimed in his writings so that no errors would mislead either his friends or enemies, and he insisted on correcting his works publicly before his audience (HN 1099) as well as on publishing this work to distribute his corrections to the people from whom he could not recall his previous works (Pro*Retr.* lines 43-45). In the prologue to his *Retractations*, Augustine employs the verb "recensare" to express his intention of "quod me offendit uelut censorio stilo denotem" (Pro*Retr.* lines 5-6) ['with the pen of a censor, I am indicating what dissatisfies me' (BG 3)]—which Augustine considers not to be the lengthy repetition of the Lord's word but false additions made to it (Pro*Retr.* lines 40-41). Augustine's intention to rewrite his texts and himself is furthermore recognized by the title *De recensione librorum*, which Augustine's biographer, Possodius, chose for the *Retractations*.[33] Adolf Harnack, who wrote the first and definitive article on the *Retractations*, likewise endorses the theory that this work should be viewed as corrections made to Augustine's previous works, and the title does not mean "Correcturen (im Sinne der Palinodie), sondern 'Durchsicht' (im Sinne von curae secundae)"; therefore, it is amply obvious that the Latin "retractationes" should not be equated with the English 'retractions' but rather with "'review,'" "'retreatment,'" or "'revision,'" as "[i]t is seldom that Augustine is compelled to "'retract' anything."[34]

Augustine's expressed wish to expose his errors mercilessly and to revise and rewrite his former works contrasts explicitly with his assertive justification of his literary craft, as he sends a warning to his earthly critics: "Neque enim quisquam nisi imprudens, ideo quia mea errata reprehendo, me reprehendere audebit" (Pro*Retr.* lines

---

Lessons: Augustine, Proba, and the Christian Detournement of Antiquity," *Stanford Literature Review* 9.2 (1992): 99-123.

32 J. de Ghellinck, "Les Rétractations de Saint Augustin examen de conscience de l'ecrivain," *Nouvelle Revue Theologique* 57 (1930): 481-500; here 481 and Georg Misch, *Geschichte der Autobiographie* 1.1: 173, 1.2: 341, 344.

33 Meredith F. Eller, "The *Retractationes* of Saint Augustine," *Church History* 18 (1949): 172-83; here 173.

34 HN 1097. [Corrections in the sense of a palinode but review in the sense of second attention]. Meredith F. Eller, "The *Retractationes* of Saint Augustine" 173.

6-7) ['For, truly, only an ignorant man will have the hardihood to criticize me for criticizing my own errors' (BG 3)]. This implies that Augustine wants both to correct his errors and to ward off any pending or future criticism, although he asserts that he would not undertake this endeavor if there had not been errors to correct (Pro*Retr.* lines 8-11). His earthly critics, however, are denied any jurisdiction in judgment matters, for God is the only qualified power to judge his auctorial achievement: "Restat igitur ut me ipse iudicem sub magistro uno, cuius de offensionibus meis iudicium euadere cupio" (Pro*Retr.* lines 35-37) ['Hence, it remains for me to judge myself before the sole Teacher whose judgment of my offenses I desire to avoid' (BG 4)]. Augustine's quotations from Scripture also echo Socrates' philosophy of doing preventative literary penance and support the theory that he is trying to stave off judgment by both humans and God; the apostolic saying that "If we judged ourselves, we should not be judged by the Lord" (qtd. in BG 3) invites unqualified self-criticism for security's sake. Another quotation from Prov. 10:19, "Where words are many, sin is not wanting," scares Augustine, but he immediately insists that his numerous compositions should not be considered superfluous or prone to sinning, for they were necessary (Pro*Retr.* lines 14-19). James 3:2, "[f]or in many things we all offend. If anyone does not offend in word, he is a perfect man," is also cited as justification (qtd. in BG 4). Last but not least, Augustine imitates Ovid and goes beyond the "writer and text" relationship to the "reader and text" relationship: "Sed ut uolet quisque accipiat hoc quod facio" (Pro*Retr.* line 12) ['But let each one, as he chooses, accept what I am doing' (BG 3)]. The responsibility has been unloaded onto the reader, and Augustine washes his hands of it. Further denial occurs when he claims that people have always forced him to speak and preach so that he was hardly accorded the privilege of silence and listening (Pro*Retr.* lines 32-35).

Although Augustine divided his writings into three categories, *libri*, *epistulae*, and *sermones*, he treats only the *libri* in his *Retractations*. In the scheme of the actual composition of the *Retractations*, Augustine uses the "youth and old-age" dichotomy as a structuring element, for the work is organized in chronological order so the reader can appreciate Augustine's progression as a writer. Augustine, who denies perfection in speech in his old age and much more so in his youth (Pro*Retr.* lines 30-32) and admits again to having been consumed by his indulgence in secular literature, wants to demonstrate how he rewrites himself. Therefore, he includes mention of his earliest works, which might, with modification, still be beneficial to the reader (Pro*Retr.* lines 45-50). Augustine employs self-criticism to demonstrate his intra-auctorial growth, growth which is reflected in the amount of criticism applied. In Book I, Augustine reviews his work as a layman and presbyter, and in Book II his compositions during his episcopate. In Book I, Augustine censures 167 passages in 26 works; in Book II, however, only 52 passages in 67 works are revised; and the last 30 works yield only 13 criticized passages,[35] a calculation which confirms the topos of errors committed in one's youth and the wisdom gained with age. The more recent the books are, the more background information about the genesis of the works Augustine provides; toward the end the *Retractations* seems merely a catalogue of books embellished with literary

---

35   HN 1102 and Eller, "The *Retractationes* of Saint Augustine" 173.

notes (HN 1103). Augustine's defining the final titles for his works and what should be included in them is quite reminiscent of an author's establishment of a definitive collected edition.

As for the actual organization of the two books, Augustine's intention was to provide a register for the content of his books and, therefore, he abstains from criticizing their literary forms (HN 1104). Several of his works are briefly criticized but not recalled for the sake of future generations. For example, Augustine says of his *De inmortalitate animae liber I* that it is too obscure in its reasoning and that not even he can grasp its meaning (*Retr.* lines I.v.6-9). *De Genesi ad litteram liber I imperfectus* is excluded from the revision because his other book about Genesis, *De Genesi ad litteram libri XII*, gives readers an opportunity to compare both works and to judge for themselves (HN 1104). Similarly, he preserves *De mendacio*, although he has written a second work on the subject and found the first one to be "obscurus et anfractuosus et omnino molestus" (*Retr.* lines I.xxvi.5-6) ['vague, complicated and entirely irksome' (BG 117)].[36] His additional critical strategy can be categorized as follows. First, he criticizes himself for using pagan terms in his early works (for instance, "fortuna"). Then he distances himself even more from the pagan philosophers and heterodox Christian theologians (in *De Academicis*). Finally, he deals with sections in which he feels to have obscured or not emphasized enough the specifically Christian. Numerous corrections deal with his earlier usage of biblical quotations and their interpretations, particularly terms that were unbiblical or against church usage in this area; thus he conscientiously tracks down every little imperfection.[37] Moving deeper into the realm of content, Augustine insists that he had asserted his current doctrine of free will, but that he preached wrongly about the creation of faith and predestination; the *Retractations* also shows that Augustine underwent quite a change of mind about free will and eschatology (HN 1115-16). Moreover, Augustine faults himself for overconfidence in his earlier writing (*De uera religione* I.12 section 3). Nonetheless, a large part of Augustine's compositions were polemical treatises against the Academics, Manicheans, Donatists, and Pelagians, who continued to suffer Augustine's critical pen in the *Retractations* (HN 1104).

Overall, Augustine serves as a twofold model for other Christian writers by his disavowal of his former rhetoric and his revision of his works. Nowhere, however, does he advise his audience not to read his works. Coupled with his air of personal modesty is a streak of vanity and auctorial self-assertion—"'A fine streak of vanity runs through [his] whole [life]'"—a combination that does not necessarily clash.[38] Augustine felt that he was a messenger of God and that his compositions were in their

---

36 There is discrepancy in numbering in Almut Mutzenbecher's edition. In the table of contents *De mendacio* is numbered as XXVI, but in the actual text it is numbered XXVII. I am choosing XXVI because *De mendacio* is referred to by that number in other references and also by Bogan.

37 For a list of examples, see HN 1108-15.

38 Comment made by Johann Gottfried Herder about both Augustine and Petrarch. Qtd. in Misch, *Geschichte der Autobiographie* 1.2: 638. On Petrarch's poetic ego, see P. Blanc, "Petrarca ou la poétique de l'ego: elements de psychopoétique Pétrarchienne," *Revue des Études Italiennes* 29 (1983): 122-69.

foundation sanctioned by God, and only God could pronounce a sentence over him.[39] Offenses committed by the word are atoned for by the word. Additionally, most early Christian apologies are directed to God or Christ (and later the Virgin), and demonstrate regret for former non-Christian, profane literary creations, drawing heavily on the youthful-error topos. By adopting this strategy, the early Christian writers emphasize their own conversion and participate in the ambivalence expressed toward the *trivium*. Some poets are more explicit about their errors than others. In many cases, their intertextual references merely exist to be discarded and to heighten the poet's religious sincerity. While such a formulaic practice still qualifies as intra-auctorial rewriting, the authors almost never follow in Augustine's footsteps by imitating the great detail of his *Retractations*.

3.3. Sedulius

The fifth-century poet Caelius Sedulius, of whom we know almost nothing personal, follows Augustine's Christian example of repudiating his former secular studies. Carl Springer confirms that the renunciation of pagan practices is "virtually a commonplace in early Christian literature," but ventures a guess that Sedulius' expression could be rooted in reality.[40] In a letter to his mentor Macedonius, Sedulius utilizes the pagan/Christian *Kontrastierungstopos* for self-criticism:

> Cum saecularibus igitur studiis occupatus vim inpatientis ingenii, quod divinitatis in me providentia generavit, non utilitati animae sed inani vitae dependerem, et litterariae sollertia disciplinae lusibus infructuosi operis, non auctori serviret: tandem misericors Deus, rerum conditor, clementius fabricam sui iuris aspexit et stultos in me mundanae sapientiae diutius haberi sensus indoluit ac fatuum prudentiae mortalis ingenium caelesti sale condivit.[41]

---

39 See lines 14-16 in the Prologue to the *Retractations*.

40 Carl P. E. Springer, *The Gospel as Epic in Late Antiquity: The* Paschale Carmen *of Sedulius*, Supplements to Vigiliae Christianae II (Leiden: Brill, 1988) 29. Reinhart Herzog also postulates: "Identifying sin with non-Christian poetry exemplifies a hermeneutic barrier modern interpretation faces when dealing with Christian literature: if one takes the authors at their (theological) word (misinterpreting the topos) specious biographical conclusions will result (schema: pagan or sinful youth and poetry, conversion, Christian poetic activity); if one does not take them seriously (categorizes them as topoi derived from antiquity) it will lead to the image of the genre faux (schema: the author forced into the Christian disguise seeks to keep cultivating the ancient form with some compromises and thus begins a tradition of [secular!] mistakes)" (*Die Bibelepik der lateinischen Spätantike: Formgeschichte einer erbaulichen Gattung* [Munich: Wilhelm Fink, 1975] 1: L n. 155).

41 Sedulius, *Paschale Carmen, Sedulii opera omni*, ed. Johannes Huemer, *Corpus Scriptorum Ecclesiasticorum Latinorum* 10, 1-146; here 2, lines 4-12. [When, therefore, as I was involved in worldly studies, I was spending the force of an impatient intelligence that divine providence had generated in me not on the good of my soul but on an empty life, and the adroitness of literary training was serving not the author but the games of an unfruitful work; finally the merciful God, creator of the world, looked more clemently on the fabric of his law and grieved to see the foolish

The one-time classical rhetorician and instructor of pagan literature regrets his former worldly poetry because now he is ready to fashion a different sort of discourse, one that would clash with his earlier writings. Sedulius does not completely disavow his pagan roots, for he wrote the *Paschale Carmen* in verse; thus he discards only the content but not the form of classical poetry and redirects his poetic energy toward God's praise, which is an acceptable activity in the eyes of the Church.

Sedulius' self-criticism is put into context and complemented by the introduction to Book I of the *Paschale Carmen*, which depicts the life story of Christ. There, he uses the *Kontrastierungstopos* in his favor and in a self-assertive, not a self-critical, way:

> Cum sua gentiles studeant figmenta poetae
> grandisonis pompare modis . . . .
> . . . .
> Cur ego, Davidicis adsuetus cantibus odas
> cordarum resonare decem sanctoque verentur
> stare choro et placidis caelestia psallere verbis,
> clara salutiferi taceam miracula Christi? . . .
> . . . .
> haec est via namque salutis.[42]

The begrudging admission that pagan authors are superior shapers of discourse surfaces repeatedly in contrast to the Christian authors' need for justification. The intent given is always the redemptive nature of writing biblical poetry, although Reinhart Herzog claims that the main impetus for Sedulius' poetic activity was his own moral improvement.[43]

3.4. Sidonius

Sidonius Apollonaris (431-489), on the other hand, is very expressive about his inten tions. Letters xii, xiii, and xvi in Book IX of his *Letters* map out the poetic philosophy of the poetry-composing bishop of France, who exemplifies the dilemma of an author of his era who was torn between donning priestly garb and poetic laurels. In "Letter IX.xii," Sidonius, who dedicated himself to epistolography, uses his friend Oresius' repeated entreaty for more of his poetry to practice what he had previously renounced: "primum ab exordio religiosae professionis huic principaliter exercitio renuntiavi."[44]

---

senses of worldly wisdom be held in me any longer, and seasoned the (my) fatuous genius of mortal prudence with heavenly salt].

42 Sedulius, *Paschale Carmen* lines 17-18, 23-26, 46. ['While pagan poets endeavor to parade their fictions in high-sounding phrases, why should I, who am accustomed to chant the psalms of David to the sound of the ten-stringed lyre and, at my place in the holy choir, to sing in quiet tones of heavenly things, why should I keep silent on the glorious miracles of Christ, our Savior? . . . for He is the way of salvation'] (Kuhnmuench, *Early Christian Latin Poets from the Fourth to the Sixth Century* 258).

43 Herzog, *Die Bibelepik der lateinischen Spätantike* LII n. 162.

44 Apollonaris Sidonius, "Letter IX.xii," *Poems and Letters*, trans W. B. Anderson, 2 vols. (Cambridge: Harvard UP, 1965) 2: 560-63, lines 8-9. ['But in the first place, I especially

The use of the term "exercitio" implies his classical education, while "primum" suggests that poetry was an occupation of the past. Whereas Sidonius professes that "tam pudeat novum poema conficere quam pigeat" ("Letter IX.xii" lines 22-23) ['I am as much ashamed as disinclined to compose a new poem' (Anderson 2: 563)], he does not seem to be able to renounce poetry completely. To that end, he performs a balancing act between keeping his promise and being able to deal with his own poetry, and oddly enough many of his letters contain both religious and secular poems.[45] This fence-sitting strategy illustrates that the writing of poetry per se was not the problem, but Sidonius could not reconcile it with his ecclesiastic role: "tenebimus igitur quippiam medium et sicut epigrammata recentia modo nulla dictabo, ita litteras, si quae iacebunt versu refertae, scilicet ante praesentis officii necessitatem, mittam tibi, petens."[46] This strategy serves him well as a pretense for writing more poetry, and it was later also utilized by Petrarch; Sidonius, for instance, uses it in "Letter IX.xiii": "Ecce, dum quaero quid cantes, ipse cantavi. tales enim nugas in imo scrinii fundo muribus perforatas post annos circiter viginti profero in lucem."[47] This possibly fictional ploy allows him to skirt around the charge of composing poetry when it is inappropriate to both his profession and his age.

Sidonius' self-criticism in "Letter IX.xvi" reveals those same concerns, especially the problem of writing poetry in one's youth and old age. On an intertextual level, Sidonius elaborates with pride on the various types of poetry he has written in his life but criticizes himself for having composed poetry, coupling that with the topos of youthful error:

> Nec recordari queo, quanta quondam
> scripserim primo iuvenis calore;
> unde pars maior utinam taceri
>   possit et abdi!
> Nam senectutis propriore meta
> quicquid extremis sociamur annis,
> plus pudet, si quid leve lusit aetas,
>   nunc reminisci.[48]

---

renounced this exercise of verse-writing from the very beginning of my religious profession']
(Anderson 2: 561).

45 Otto Bardenhewer, *Geschichte der altkirchlichen Literatur* (Darmstadt: Wissenschaftliche Buchgesellschaft, 1962) 4: 653.

46 Sidonius, "Letter IX.xii" lines 26-30. ['So I shall keep a sort of middle course; I shall not now write any new poems, but if there happen to be any letters lying about containing verses—written, of course, before the constraint imposed by my present profession—I will send them to you'] (Anderson 2: 563).

47 Sidonius, "Letter IX.xiii" lines 121-23. ['Lo and behold! In seeking something for you to sing, I have myself sung; for I now bring to light about twenty years after they were written some trifling verses which have been lying at the bottom of the book-case, nibbled full of holes by the mice'] (Anderson 2: 579).

48 Sidonius, "Letter IX.xvi" lines 41-48. ['Nor can I recall how many things I wrote in the first fervour of youth; I only wish that most of them might be buried in silence! For as the bourn of old age draws nearer, the closer I get to my last years, the more I am ashamed to remember now the flippant frolics of my youth'] (Anderson 2: 603). Sidonius, however, did not renounce his love for

Because he is guilty of wanton song, and in order not to implicate his office, Sidonius emphasizes his epistolographic career instead, which lacks the stigma attached to poetry. He openly admits that he does not want to jeopardize his position as a clergyman: "clerici ne quid maculet rigorem / fama poetae" ("Letter IX.xvi" lines 55-56) ['so that my fame as a poet might not cast a slur on my strictness as a cleric' (Anderson 2: 603)]. On an intratextual level, Sidonius is most evasive, since he asserts that he would be hard pressed to compose another poem ever again, while he is actually expressing that sentiment in a poem. He further qualifies that statement by proposing exceptions for poetry with a Christian content, while actually composing in that genre as he finishes his last poem, giving the reader a sample ("Letter IX.xvi" lines 57-64). Sidonius leaves the scene purposefully shrouded in ambiguity. He ends the letter in prose to avoid charges of having written poetry. Basically, Sidonius wants to have it both ways, the fame of the laurel wreath and the respectability of the bishop's mitre; therefore, he creates a contradictory self-critical and self-assertive tapestry of negating and affirming metafictional statements.

3.5. Dracontius

Aemilius Blossius Dracontius, a well-known lawyer and writer during the Vandal reign in North Africa, combined three texts and produced a double retraction, fusing both the earthly and the divine strands of the tradition and combining elements from both ancient writers and early Christian authors. Unlike Socrates, he did not realize his error fast enough to avert the punishment, as he was incarcerated by King Gunthamund sometime between 484 and 496:

> culpa mihi fuerat dominos reticere modestos
>   ignotumque mihi scribere vel dominum,
> qualis et ingratos sequitur qui mente profana,
>   cum dominum norunt, idola vana colunt.[49]

Because Dracontius had offended the Vandals' political establishment by composing a panegyric to a foreign ruler, whom some sources consider to be Zeno, Emperor of the East, he and his family suffered political persecution.[50] The offending poem is not extant, which is not surprising for a censured piece,[51] but we can infer its content from the elaborate counterstatement, *Satisfactio ad regnem Gunthamundum*, which Dracontius composed in prison to ask forgiveness for his literary sins. Dracontius'

---

ancient mythology (Karl Voretzsch, *Introduction to the Study of Old French Literature* [Geneva: Slatkine Reprints, 1976] 12).

49 Blossius Aemilius Dracontius, *Dracontii Satisfactio*, trans. M. Margaret (Diss. Philadelphia: U of Pennsylvania, 1936) lines 93-96. ['Mine was the blunder, being silent about forbearing lords, to celebrate one, though sovereign, unknown to me; such a fault as attends those ungrateful men who although they know their Lord, with unholy hearts worship vain idols'] (Margaret 33, 35).

50 M. Margaret, introduction, *Dracontii Satisfactio* (Diss. Philadelphia: U of Pennsylvania, 1936) 1-27; here 19.

51 David F. Bright, *The Miniature Epic in Vandal Africa* (Norman: U of Oklahoma P, 1987) 16.

situation is reminiscent of both Stesichorus and Ovid, in that they offended a higher power who was in a position to punish them.

The *Satisfactio* contains multiple confessions and pleas for pardon, as Dracontius repents and confesses to both Gunthamund and God, the latter as one who is omnipotent and can therefore influence rulers to pardon him. In lines 19 and 20, Dracontius first admits that he is a sinner, "sic mea corda deus, nostro peccante reatu / temporis immodici, pellit ad illicita" ['In this same way, because I am a culprit sinning times without number, God drives my thoughts to forbidden things' (Margaret 29)]. Not only does he accuse himself of being a sinner but blames God for pushing him in that direction. The poem culminates in a plea of temporary insanity (which Horace also claimed with Canidia), "quis nisi caelesti demens compulsus ab ira / aspera cuncta petat?" (*Satisfactio* lines 27-28) ['Who, but one driven to madness by God's anger, would strive for everything unpleasant'? (Margaret 29)]. Dracontius is aware of his offending organ, however, "heu mea quippe mihi vulnera lingua dedit" (*Satisfactio* line 44) ['while my own tongue has actually caused my wounds' (Margaret 31)]. He sustains his appeal for pardon to both the political and the divine power; here Dracontius yokes the two separate entities together:

te coram primum me carminis illius, ausu
quod male disposui, paenitet et fateor.
post te, summe deus, regi dominoque reus sum,
cuius ab imperio posco gemens veniam.[52]

While Dracontius has so far tried to use God to attain a pardon from Gunthamund, he now flatters Gunthamund by likening him to God in nature, "ignoscendo pius nobis imitare tonantem, / qui indulget culpas et veniam tribuit" (*Satisfactio* lines 149-50) ['In pardoning us you virtuously emulate the God of thunder Who has mercy on our faults and bestows pardon' (Margaret 37)]. In his defense, Dracontius resorts to the Ovidian and Augustinian strategy of implicating the reader (in this case Gunthamund) in the production of the text, pointing out the ambiguity of literature: "inde fit ut praestet littera vel noceat" (*Satisfactio* line 64) ['and from this it happens that the written word may benefit or it may harm' (Margaret 56)].

Because in contrast to Stesichorus, Dracontius' *Satisfactio* did not have the desired effect as a purification rite, the North African poet composed a second palinode, *De laudibus Dei*, all in praise of God. This new text counterbalanced the *Satisfactio*, in which he claims he was also not sufficiently reverent to God. The third book of the *De laudibus Dei* ends with another penitent confession of the author's sins in general terms, a plea to God for forgiveness, for release from imprisonment, and for temporal as well as eternal well-being.[53] Although all these prayers were intended for God, Otto Bardenhewer claims that Dracontius meant for *De laudibus Dei* to reach Gunthamund as well. Dracontius was finally released under the reign of Thrasamund and lived the

---

52 Dracontius, *Dracontii Satisfactio* lines 105-8. ['In Thy presence first of all, I repent of that poem which in my rashness I foolishly composed, and this do I confess. After Thee, God Supreme, I am answerable to my lord the king, whose sovereignty, sighing, I entreat mercy'] (Margaret 35).

53 Blossius Aemilius Dracontius, *De laudibus Dei*, ed. Friedrich Vollmer (Berlin: Weidmann, 1905) lines 565-755.

remainder of his life fairly peacefully, although it is not clear if his literary palinodes obtained the key to freedom for him.[54]

3.6. Boethius

The last of the representatives of late antiquity, Boethius (480-524), combines elements found in both classical writers and medieval authors.[55] Like Ovid and Dracontius, Boethius writes the work in question in jail, incarcerated by an offended ruler. Unlike Dracontius, however, Boethius does not try to appease the emperor but turns inward and finds consolation in philosophy. Boethius' self-criticism evident in Book I of the *De Consolatione Philosophiae* does not originate from the prior threat of having one's creativity stifled or thwarted but from the inability to create, which the poet laments:

> Carmina qui quondam studio florente peregi,
> flebilis, heu, maestos cogor inire modos.
> Ecce mihi lacerae dictant scribenda Camenae
> et ueris elegi fletibus ora rigant.
> Has saltem nullus potuit peruincere terror
> ne nostrum comites prosequerentur iter.

---

54 Bardenhewer, *Geschichte der altkirchlichen Literatur* 4: 659; Bright, *The Miniature Epic in Vandal Africa* 25; and Margaret, introduction, *Dracontii Satisfactio* 18.

55 The last important Italian poet of the sixth century, Arator includes some of the elements of the apology tradition but omits others. In his "Letter to Parthenius," Arator admits having composed youthful poetry:
Cura mihi dudum fuerat puerilibus annis,
Versibus assiduum concelebrare melos.
Scribere quas etiam simulavit fabula partes,
Et per inane fretum sub levitate rapi. (Arator, "Epistola ad Parthenium," ed. J. P. Migne, *Patrologiae Cursus Completus* 68 [Turnholti: Brepols, 1963] 245-52, lines 52-55). ['It had long been my concern in the youthful years to pursue continual song in my verses, to write of the roles which myth invented, and to be carried off in the power of shallowness through an empty channel'] (Richard J. Schrader et al, trans., "Epistle to Parthenius," *Arator's* On the Acts of the Apostles [De Actibus Apostolorum] [Atlanta: Scholars Press, 1987] 101-03; here 102). The passage bears witness to the admission of youthful poetic activity devoted to pagan subjects, which in themselves are shallow in a Christian context. That is the extent of his mild self-criticism, whose most accusatory element is his claim of shallowness, but the elements of contrition and atonement are largely missing. Arator brings this part of his career up in the context of Parthenius' admonishing him to redirect his love for pagan mythology to the more fruitful topic of Christian truth. In his "Letter to Vigilium," Arator also informs us that he had a conversion experience while under a Gothic siege and became a monk ("Epistola ad Vigilium," ed. J. P. Migne, *Patrologiae Cursus Completus* 68 [Turnholti: Brepols, 1963] 71-82). Furthermore, Arator has been familiar with Sedulius; see, Neil Wright, "Arator's Use of Caelius Sedulius: A Re-Examination," *Eranos* 87.1 (1989): 51-61.

Gloria felicis olim uiridisque iuuentae,
solantur maesti nunc mea fata senis.[56]

Poetry, he asserts, has been a friend in his youth and will remain so in old age, but all he does is take prompts from the Muses because they "dictate ('dictant') what Boethius writes."[57] Thus Lady Philosophy functions as a literary guide who wishes to teach him a new language by re-inventing him first as a reader and then as a writer.[58] In order to achieve that goal, Philosophy needs to eliminate the "poeticas Musas . . . scenicas meretriculas" (Prose I.23, 25-6) ['Muses of poetry . . . whores from the theater' (Green 4)], who personify all the "forensic, dramatic, and dialectical forms of expression" that stand between Boethius in his present state and Boethius the recreated author, who would then subscribe to a "purely philosophical mode of discourse."[59] Since Lady Philosophy is a projection of Boethius' mind, she is like an alter ego who is attempting to lead Boethius to a rational understanding of his situation. This Boethius does not yet accept gladly, since he sheds tears for the outcast Muses. By substituting her prose tracts for his poems, Philosophy is "acculturating old texts into new contexts."[60] She intends to teach Boethius how to create a language that surpasses the merely human and "literal" realm and aims higher, toward the eternal and permanent,[61] as the other early Christian writers had intended. Therefore, Boethius' self-criticism functions as an intratextual rewriting of the author and his creative craft. On an intertextual level, Boethius' rejection of poetry as transcendent influenced the

---

56 Anicius Manlius Severinus Boethius, *Philosophiae Consolatio*, ed. Ludwig Bieler (Turnholti: Brepols, 1984) Poem I.1-8. ['I who once wrote songs with keen delight am now by sorrow driven to take up melancholy measures. Wounded Muses tell me what I must write, and elegiac verses bathe my face with real tears. Not even terror could drive from me these faithful companions of my long journey. Poetry, which was once the glory of my happy and flourishing youth, is still my comfort in this misery of my old age'] (Richard Green, trans., *The Consolation of Philosophy*, by Anicius Manlius Severinus Boethius [New York: Macmillan, 1986] 3).

57 Anna Crabbe, "Literary Design in the *De Consolatione Philosophiae*," *Boethius: His Life, Thought and Influence*, ed. Margaret Gibson (Oxford: Blackwell, 1981) 237-74; here 248.

58 Seth Lerer, *Boethius and Dialogue: Literary Method in the* Consolation of Philosophy (Princeton: Princeton UP, 1985) 7.

59 Lerer, *Boethius and Dialogue* 7. Anna Crabbe adds the following to this discussion: Boethius "has chosen to fuse several traditional topoi, or characteristic elements, of programmatic poetry, namely (i) the claim to ascend the literary scale from an inferior to a superior genre and (ii) the reverse, generally called 'recusatio', that is a refusal to write, either at all or in some expected genre, usually epic. Both types of 'recusatio' function as an apology, often specious, for the work in hand, and either personal grief or the advent of an inspirational deity is used to account for the poet's inadequacy in other fields" (247). It should also be noted that Book I is still "more at home in poetry than in prose writing" (Crabbe, "Literary Design in the *De Consolatione Philosophiae*" 249).

60 Lerer, *Boethius and Dialogue* 23. Amy Blumenthal, however, argues that the "substitution of philosophical for elegiac muses grows out of Philosophy's realization that she needs poetry in order to accomplish her own work. . . . Lady Philosophy, then, implies that she recognizes some limitations in her traditional approach when she enlists the aid of poetry as a curative device" ("New Muses: Poetry in Boethius' *Consolatio*," *Pacific Coast Philology* 21 [1986]: 25-29; here 25).

61 Lerer, *Boethius and Dialogue* 102.

medieval conviction that prose was superior to poetry as a vehicle of truth. Furthermore, Boethius' concern for language points toward the Middle Ages when the emphasis on the role of language increases while external power factors diminish. Medieval authors were tightly enveloped by the Christian universe, which imprinted its notion of language and propriety onto them, but they rarely faced physical retribution as, for instance, Ovid and Dracontius did.

The threat to the medieval author was, rather, a spiritual one. These early examples of the apology tradition, both Graeco-Roman and early Christian, led to a surge of literary apologies in the Middle Ages. I contend that this surge—still rooted in the established tradition of the apology—has a clear connection to the medieval philosophies of language and notions of authorship as well as to antifeminism. Staunchly Christian, the Zeitgeist demanded that a literary piece must contain a Christian truth; without that, the work would be considered of no fundamental value, implying that an *auctor* ("someone who was at once a writer and an authority, someone not merely to be read but also to be respected and believed"—a person performing "the act of writing") had to adhere to the "right things" (MN 10) to say. The implication for this study is that authors then follow their ancient precursors by employing safety valves in the form of apologies in order to comply with an external standard; even monastic writers, who are already writing mainly about "safe subjects," participate in this practice, which smacks of conventionality and is still rooted in the pagan/Christian dichotomy. Only one medieval book treated in this study was banned by the Church in its time, suggesting that self-censure averts subsequent outside censure.

Self-censure would not be necessary if all medieval ideas of literature in general and the book in particular had been congruent with the Bible, the only book that held any significance. In contrast to the Bible, the "fabulas" of the poets were rejected as lies, ironically reminding us of the truth element regarded so highly in ancient Greek poetry. In the Middle Ages, spiritual truth was "based on written authority," and therefore information to be remembered "was in the process transformed into something bookish, or literary, a placed image preserved by the artificial memory."[62] Thus through the process of disseminating pagan literature in writing, a certain validity

---

62 Judson Boyce Allen, *The Ethical Poetic of the Later Middle Ages: A Decorum of Convenient Distinction* (Toronto: U of Toronto P, 1982) 269. Guibert de Nogent touches upon this aspect in his *Autobiography*: "Et qui in scripturis nunc jactantiam et verba quaero, immo ipsorum ethnicorum infamia dicta pro garrulitate contineo, tunc fletus dolorumque causas exinde exigebam, nec me legisse putabam, quotiens in ipsa lectione nihil contemplativum, nihil compunctioni habile attingebam. Scienter ego nescius sic agebam" (Guibert of Nogent, *Autobiographie*, ed. and trans. Edmond-René Labande [Paris: Société d'Édition Les Belles Lettres, 1981] XV, 114). ['Today I pore over the Scriptures for sheer display or to make speeches, going so far as to remember the disgraceful sayings of pagans to feed my chatter, whereas in those days I garnered from them reasons for tears and sorrow. I could never feel I had read unless I could gather from my reading something conducive to contemplation or compunction. Thus I was behaving wisely without realizing it'] (Paul J. Archambault, trans., *A Monk's Confession: The Memoirs of Guibert of Nogent* [University Park: Pennsylvania State UP, 1996] 50).

The Writer as Reporter. Oxford, Bodleian Library, MS Douce 213, fol 1[r]. Lawrence of Premierfait, French translation of Boccacio's *Decameron*.

Ingelard the Scribe at Judgment. From the Prüfening manuscript of Isidore of Seville's *Etymologiae*. Munich, Bayerische Staatsbibliothek MS Clm 13031 fol 1ʳ.

would be bestowed upon it that might at some level rival the truth inherent in the Incarnate Logos. Augustine was most keenly aware of the connections between Christ's redemption of language through his incarnation and the importance of human language in the dissemination of the divine Word. For Augustine, religious knowledge existed in verbal terms,[63] language to which everyone had access. By misdirecting one's literary efforts, the author would be guilty of offending the Logos. Whereas, according to Thomas Aquinas, God stands as the exclusive *auctor* of things that can signify, the human *auctor* creates words and can signify with words alone and is dependent on the imbuement of God's wisdom (MN 73, 97). The human writer imitates God in a creative act, and since creation with words resembles creation of the Word, an author stands responsible for any abuses of this godlike creative act. Therefore, the medieval author is caught in a quandary, since, as Albert the Great asserts, human poetry consists of the fallible fabrications of men, while sacred poetry embodies infallible truths (MN 139).

The medieval view of language leads inevitably to a hierarchical view of authorship. Following Bonaventure, Alistair Minnis, in his seminal study on medieval authorship, shows that the hierarchy of literary creation descends from God, possessing all *auctoritas*, through the *auctor*—imparting the most on a work and taking full responsibility; next the *commentator*—offering explanations of others' works; next the *compilator*—arranging the material of other people; to the *scriptor*—reporting and adding nothing of his own (MN 95) (see page 64 "The Writer as Reporter"). The closer a writer is to the top of that hierarchy, of course, the greater the risk—the further away, the lesser the responsibility. Naturally, several medieval authors classified themselves as *compilator* or *scriptor*, mere arrangers or reporters of the works and material of others, in an effort to circumvent certain literary taboos and to practice their authorial license; others, however, took full responsibility.[64] A twelfth-century

---

63 Marcia L. Colish, *The Mirror of Language: A Study in the Medieval Theory of Knowledge* (1968 rev. ed.; Lincoln: U of Nebraska P, 1983) 3, 34.

64 Vincent de Beauvais' *Apologia Actoris* to his four-part encyclopedia, the largest of medieval times (1256-59), is a good example of a real-life compiler's role and his self-justification. The Dominican Vincent attached the *Apologia Actoris* mainly to the *Speculum Historiale*, although it appears in varying forms in the beginning of the *Speculum Naturale*, *Speculum Doctrinale*, and *Speculum Morale* (Anna-Dorothee von den Brincken, "Geschichtsbetrachtung bei Vincenz von Beauvais: Die *Apologia Actoris* zum *Speculum Maius*," *Deutsches Archiv für Erforschung des Mittelalters* 34 [1978]: 410-99; here 411). There is some consensus that Vincent himself did only three *Specula* and that his disciples did the *Speculum Morale*. Its purpose is to explain the compiler's choice of sources. It is interesting that he uses the term *actor* to indicate the passages in which his meager contributions were most extensive. Minnis claims that Vincent uses the term *actor* in opposition to the term *auctor*, highlighting the distinction between the *auctoritates* and the modern scholars (MN 157). Anna-Dorothee von den Brincken, on the other hand, asserts that Vincent varies between both *actor* and *auctor* in several manuscripts. Another point pertinent to this study illustrates that Vincent enjoys putting certain guilt on the reader: if the reader or listener did not understand the Bible, the problem lies with the recipient of the word (Brincken, "Geschichtsbetrachtung bei Vincenz von Beauvais" 421-2). For more information on the *Apologia Actoris*, see the following authors: Ludwig Lieser, *Vinzenz von Beauvais, Kompilator und Philosoph: Untersuchung seiner Seelenlehre im* Speculum Maius (Leipzig: Felix Meiner,

manuscript illumination demonstrates the relationship language has to salvation and to Matt. 13:36-37 in this hierarchy proposed by Bonaventure. The Prüfening manuscript of Isidore of Seville's *Etymologiae* (Clm 13031) depicts on the first page the self-portrait of the scribe Ingelard (see page 65): the dead Ingelard lies on the ground while above him the archangel Michael holds the "soul scale" and another angel places Ingelard's book on the scale; at that point the devil that has been lurking around flees, and the soul of the deceased is transported to heaven.[65] The illumination takes Juvencus' hope and prediction a step further and affirms the positive power literary creation can have on the poet's salvation; on the other hand, literary activity that does not subscribe to, or further, the Christian Weltanschauung might easily have the opposite effect. Therefore, the picture stands both as an encouragement and a warning to the medieval author.

The direction of the history of the literary apology, then, seems fairly straightforward: it moves from Stesichorus and Ovid et al, with their practical concerns about external matters, through the early Christian authors' theological concerns about the place of their works in the sight of God, to a medieval philosophical concern about language and its role, and therefore the role of the author, in cosmic history. From its relatively simple beginning, the tradition becomes increasingly complex as the function of the apology develops broader ramifications—political, theological, philosophical, literary. It is against this background of increasing complexity that medieval literary apologies must be viewed. The classical apology examples create a paradigm for the foliating branches of auctorial self-criticism in the Middle Ages. The three different strands of apologies discernible in the Middle Ages are rooted in the three strands manifested in classical literature. In the first, apologies to pagan deities have been supplanted by homage to God. The second strand, apologies to women, has been established by Stesichorus, Euripides, and Horace in an ironic context and will be extended by the later medieval authors. The third strand contains examples that are

---

1928) 76-96, 194-200; Serge Lusignan, *Préface au* Speculum Maius *de Vincent de Beauvais: Réfraction et Diffraction* (Montreal: Bellarmin, 1979); M. Palmier, "Etude sur l'etat des connaissances au milieu du XIIIe siècle: Nouvelles recherches sur la genèse du *Speculum maius* de Vincent de Beauvais," *Spicae: cahiers de l'atelier Vincent de Beauvais* (Paris: Centre National de la Recherche Scientifique, 1978) 91-121; M. B. Parkes, "The Influence of the Concepts of *Ordinatio* and *Compilatio* on the Development of the Book," *Medieval Learning and Literature: Essays Presented to Richard William Hunt*, eds. J. J. G. Alexander and M. T. Gibson (Oxford: Clarendon Press, 1976) 115-38, esp. 128-33; J. Schneider, "Recherches sur une encyclopédie du XIIIe siècle: Le *Speculum Majus* de Vincent de Beauvais," *Comptes Rendus de L'Académie des Inscriptions* (Paris: Klincksieck, 1976) 174-89; J. B. Voorbij, "The *Speculum Historiale*: Some Aspects of Its Genesis and Manuscript Tradition," *Vincent of Beauvais and Alexander the Great: Studies on the* Speculum Maius *and Its Translations Into Medieval Vernaculars*, eds. W. J. Aerts, E. R. Smits, and J. B. Voorbij (Groningen: Egbert Forsten, 1986) 11-55.

65 For further examples of art as intended to stave off punishment, see Klopsch, *Einführung in die Dichtungslehren des lateinischen Mittelalters* 6-7. Also, there is discrepancy on the scribe's name. While Klopsch identifies him as Ingelard, Elisabeth Klemm proposes that, based on manuscript evidence, the codex was written by the scribe Swicher, who also wrote the *Glossarium Salomonis* (Clm 13002) ("Die Regensburger Buchmalerei des 12. Jahrhunderts," *Regensburger Buchmalerei: Von frühkarolingischer Zeit bis zum Ausgang des Mittelalters* [Munich: Prestel-Verlag, 1987] 39-58; here 49-50).

addressed to a general audience and are mainly textual criticism as modeled by Augustine in his *Retractations*.

There are very few apologies from the third strand in the Middle Ages. Most medieval apologies belong to the first and second strands, apologies for secular works and apologies to women, which are tied together by the specifically misogynistic treatment of women. Apologies to women appear in highly ironic contexts and are mainly insincere and often as misogynistic as the works for which they repent, because the antifeminist treatment is part of the game. These apologies for misogyny provide a highly overt outlet for misogynistic views; in contrast, apologies to God contain a more deeply-rooted and insidious antifeminism. Recantation of a youthful secular work initially implicitly and later explicitly denotes a rejection of love poetry, which has at its center—at least for the most part—women.[66] Therefore, a repudiation of love implies a rejection of woman; woman has become the literary "other," a "persona non grata" who has to be removed from the literary creation in order for the author to achieve spiritual union with divinity. Women were literally written out of the text. The only exception to this is Dante, but only because he spiritualizes Beatrice and removes all physical and earthly impurity from her image. Since the first apology strand does, by genre, contain nothing about women, one can conclude that, although almost the entire tradition centers on women, it assumes an antifeminist flavor. Nevertheless, the anti-feminism becomes its unifying quality, its underlying inter- and subtext.

Theories of the modern feminist critics Hélène Cixous and Luce Irigaray help highlight concerns relevant to the literary role of women in the apology tradition. Both Cixous and Irigaray attack the privileging of maleness in writing—a privileging that is similar to the logocentrically-inspired behavior of medieval authors.[67] For Cixous and Irigaray, women as subjects of male writing are reduced to their bodies and to roles as amorous seductresses. This sex-negative view, too, has analogues in the apology tradition in which youthful poetry dealing with women was disavowed because of its threat to the authors' salvation.[68] Ultimately then in the Middle Ages, women had to be rebuked for their connection to the non-rational. The prevailing medieval theological view was that Adam possessed a rational mind and Eve did not; Adam's and subsequently all men's ties to the Logos were greater and all claims to logocentric authorship were therefore more justifiable than those of women. As daughters of Eve, women, however, were suspect both as subjects of male writers, whom they undoubtedly enticed to write amorous verse, and as writers—claimants to logocentrality. In the context of the apology tradition, Irigaray reverses a biblical tenet by postulating "parousia, or 'second coming,' in which the flesh would be made word and women

---

66   There are some homosexual love lyrics attributed to Marbod de Rennes that could qualify as youthful examples later regretted.

67   Hélène Cixous claims that "logocentrism subjects thought—all of the concepts, the codes, the values—to a two-term system, related to 'the' couple man/woman" ("Sorties," *New French Feminisms: An Anthology*, eds. Elaine Marks and Isabelle de Courtivron [New York: Schocken Books, 1980] 90-98; here 91).

68   For a detailed history of sexuality and early Christianity, see Peter Brown, *The Body and Society: Men, Women and Sexual Renunciation in Early Christianity* (New York: Columbia UP, 1988).

would no longer be excluded from the divine."[69] Women in the Middle Ages were excluded from the divine because they were viewed as a sexual threat, as given to the passions of the flesh, without the saving grace of rational thought. By removing the feminine from male writing, medieval patriarchy in essence wanted to remove the female body, practicing a narrow form of *contemptus mundi* in *contemptus feminae*. Irigaray attacks the teleology of male discourse that relegates the feminine to the "traditional place of the repressed, the censured," while Cixous reads logocentricity as a form of phallocratism that subjugates the feminine to the masculine in writing.[70] One can conclude through application of these theories that all authors in the Middle Ages are subject to the confines of patriarchy; male authors, however, in Adam-like fashion pass that subjectivity, and therefore the blame, onto women, an act that liberates the male authors from at least one constraint. The seven medieval women authors that round out this study fully participate in this tripartite paradigm; in actuality, they add yet another level by themselves practicing auto-antifeminism.

---

69 Irigaray, *The Irigaray Reader* 7.
70 Irigaray, *The Irigaray Reader* 118 and Cixous, "Sorties" 92.

CHAPTER 4

The Medieval Latin Tradition: The Augustinian Legacy

The self-critical medieval Latin writers spanning 700 to 1500 carry on the intellectual heritage of the late-antiquity Christian authors that grew out of the tension between the *trivium* of classical antiquity and the self-conscious fledgling Christian faith. These medieval Latin authors participate primarily in the first strand of apologies, those made to (God commensurate with their sly antifeminism), and but also in the third, those made for unsavory literary practices. Both groups of apologies are influenced by Augustine.[1] The Venerable Bede and Gerald of Wales attempt to imitate Augustine's *Retractations,* and therefore their apologies lack the dimension of sinfulness. Wandalbert von Prüm, Marbod de Rennes, Guibert de Nogent, Peter of Blois, and Serlo of Wilton follow in the footsteps of the *Confessions,* and Aeneas Silvius Piccolomini incorporates both Augustinian models into his apologies. Most of the Latin authors cover the period between 800 to 1200, which R. R. Bolgar defines as the epoch in which "the rhetorical tradition of antiquity is explored from several points of view and its possibilities are developed."[2] The implications for the apology tradition are that theories of language and authorship were added and adapted to it. The *Kontrastierungstopos* between meaningful Christian compositions and empty pagan and amorous works is popular.[3] It appears in conjunction with the ubiquitous life-stage

---

1   Paul Lehmann postulates the following about Augustine's influence in the Middle Ages: "Already before the end of St. Augustine's life his *Confessions* had begun to exert profound influence on the public, and he increased their autobiographical character by publishing a series of *Retractationes*, and in doing so he gave the author-autobiographical tradition of antiquity a more spiritualized form. Both works were widely copied, read, and used in the Middle Ages, but were neither of them ever effectively imitated. The lists of his writings with which an author sometimes concludes his work, as for example that which Bede gives at the end of his *Historia ecclesiastica gentis Anglorum*, are simply book-lists in the style and after the model of St. Jerome; they are invaluable to the historian, but they do not form constructive pieces of self-criticism on the part of the author" ("Autobiographies of the Middle Ages," *Transactions of the Royal Historical Society*, 5th Series, 3 (1953): 41-52; here 42-43). I agree with Lehmann that Augustine has not been imitated in his entirety and that most of the book lists are not pieces of self-criticism but actually tools to establish a canon.

2   R. R. Bolgar, "The Teaching of Rhetoric in the Middle Ages," *Rhetoric Revalued: Papers from the International Society for the History of Rhetoric*, ed. Brian Vickers (Binghamton, NY: Center for Medieval & Early Renaissance Studies, 1982) 79-86; here 85.

3   Although not fully participating in the apology tradition, Otloh von Emmeram, an eleventh-century German monk, nevertheless depicts the continuing dichotomy between ancient learning and Christian truth. Emulating Augustine's *Confessions*, Otloh admits in his *Liber de tentatione* to his love for pagan writers and writing in verse; he is furthermore aware of the salvific nature of writing Christian doctrine. Otloh is, however, never really apologetic about these circumstances, rather exhibits academic pride in his learnedness and accomplishments as a scribe, enumerating all the works his has copied up to that point (Helga Schauwecker, *Otloh von St. Emmeram: Ein*

argument that assigns language an almost postmodern fluidity and vagueness: the same fixed text can "mean" differently in an author's youth than in his senectitude. The author has reached another intra-auctorial phase, in which the former text is no longer appropriate to its author. This philosophy reduces an author's creative choice to the Jungian *puer* or *senex*. The "youth vs. old age" topos has become a gesture of political correctness that is fueled by the requirements of Christian humility and repentance but manipulated by the authors to signal an intra-auctorial change.[4] The implications of this strategy are far reaching and highly susceptible to ironic treatment. This chapter traces the first strand of the apology tradition through the Middle Ages, from its relatively simple to its highly stylized applications—as, for instance, in Piccolomini.[5]

Beitrag zur Bildungs- und Frömmingkeitsgeschichte des 11. Jahrhundert [Munich: Verlag der Bayer. Benediktiner-Akademie, 1964] 22-24, 31). Like Ingelard, Otloh was primarily a scribe. If even the copying of a work can damn or save a soul in the Middle Ages, a primary author was in even greater peril. For a German translation of Otloh's *Book of Temptations*, see Wilhelm Blum, ed. and trans., *Das Buch von seinen Versuchungen* (Aschendorff Münster: Aschendorffsche Buchdruckerei, 1977).

4   Georges Minois' *History of Old Age* seems to contradict the value of old age, as he points out the poor treatment of old people in the Graeco-Roman world and the New Testament, a treatment which the Middle Ages carried on in the old man as an image of sin. The prevalence of the "youth vs. old age" topos in the Middle Ages might rest on the fact that an important part of the old population were clergy. For those clergy, who were also often writers, old age was a positive stage of life. This view must have solidified among the clergy when Bernard of Clairvaux connected wisdom and virtue with old age, no matter how old someone actually was (Georges Minois, *History of Old Age from Antiquity to the Renaissance*, trans. Sarah Hanbury Tenison [Oxford: Polity Press, 1989] 41-2, 48-9, 118-20, 149-52, 169, 182-8). This might explain why so many writers alluded to old age, regardless of their real chronological age, when they actually wanted to signal their improved wisdom.

5   After careful deliberation, I have decided not to treat Andreas Capellanus' *De amore* because it does not fit exactly into my taxonomy. Two elements in the prologue do need to be mentioned, however. The author employs the conventional topos of being urged to write and expresses slight reservations at the appropriateness of his endeavor: "Quamvis igitur non multum videatur expediens huiusmodi rebus insistere nec deceat, quemquam prudentem huiusmodi vacare venatibus, tamen propter affectum, quo tibi annector, tuae nullatenus valeo petitioni obstare" (Andreas Capellanus, *De amore*, ed. E. Trojel [Munich: Eidos Verlag, 1964] 2). ['Therefore, although it does not seem expedient to devote oneself to things of this kind or fitting for any prudent man to engage in this kind of hunting; nevertheless, because of the affection I have for you I can by no means refuse your request'] (John Jay Parry, trans., *The Art of Courtly Love*, by Andreas Capellanus [New York: Frederick Ungar, 1964] 27). This is the typical preventative exoneration strategy, but still too mild to qualify as full-blown self-criticism. Moreover, the self-criticism inherent in the calling himself not "prudentem" is immediately neutralized by the fact that Andreas is acting upon request. Also, the third part of the work, "The Rejection of Love," does not fit into the taxonomy either because it does not have an explicit auctorial statement. John Jay Parry claims that "Such a retraction was called for by the scheme of Ovid, which in a general way Andreas was following" (introduction, *The Art of Courtly Love*, by Andreas Capellanus [New York: Frederick Ungar, 1964] 3-24; here 18). *De amore*, then, boasts a palinodic structure, in which the last book presents a side of love, largely misogynistic, that seems to contradict the first two books.

4.1. Bede

The Venerable Bede's (c. 670-735) self-criticism focuses on his role as an exegete and follows Augustine's *Retractations*. Bede, who is best known in modern times for his *Ecclesiastical History of the English People*, although in the Middle Ages he was mainly regarded as an exegete, imitates the "hermeneutic procedures" of Augustine and Pope Gregory the Great in his exegetical strategies.[6] Bede practices the early medieval commentary system of cover-to-cover, phrase-by-phrase exegesis of a biblical work.[7] While his exegetical practice can be considered "eclectic and literary," the *Expositio Actuum Apostolorum et Retractatio* demonstrates an essentially historical approach.[8] Bede, who had composed his *Expositio Actus Apostolorum* as early as 709, returned to that work between 725 and 731 to find it wanting; instead of reworking it, he published *Retractatio*, in which four types of changes to the *Expositio* have been made: correction of "a small number of errors"; defense of choices; additions; and more in-depth usage of Greek.[9] Bede's self-criticism belongs in the third strand, as it features mainly textual alterations, and therefore the sinning dimension usually elemental to the other two strands is missing.

Well before his textual self-criticism in the *Retractatio*, Bede uses qualifying statements to define himself as an author in the *Expositio*. The preface to the *Expositio* contains auctorial remarks, elaborating on the genesis of the work, that prefigure the comments of later medieval authors. Bede, for instance, reminds us of Chaucer in his conditional approach to authorship in his preface:

> . . . quod interim potui feci. Misi enim opusculum in actus apostolorum, quoda ante non multos dies editum et velocissime quantum tempus dederat, ne tua sacrosancta voluntas impediretur, emendatum membranulis indieram, ubi ea quae vel mystice gesta vel obscurius dicta videbantur, ut potui, dilucidare temptavit. In quo me opusculo, cum alii plurimi fidei actholocae scriptores, tum maxime iuvavit Arator.[10]

Bede wants to apologize to Bishop Acca by qualifying his abilities and claiming the pressures of time. He employs the same strategies as the later medieval authors pre-

---

6   George Hardin Brown, *Bede the Venerable* (Boston: Twayne, 1987) 42, 44.

7   Brown, *Bede the Venerable* 44; Benedicta Ward, *The Venerable Bede* (London: Geoffrey Chapman, 1990) 58.

8   Brown, *Bede the Venerable* 46.

9   Lawrence T. Martin, trans., introduction, *Bede's Commentary on the Acts of the Apostles*, Cistercian Studies 117 (Kalamazoo, MI: Cistercian Publications, 1989) xv-xxxv; here xxiii. Eleanor Shipley Duckett still supports a post-731 composition date (*Anglo-Saxon Saints and Scholars* [New York: Macmillan, 1947] 320-21).

10 Bede, *Expositio Actuum Apostolorum*, ed. M. L. W. Laistner, The Medieval Academy of America Publication 35 (1939; New York: Kraus Reprint, 1970) Praefatio lines 3: 12-18. ['I have done what I could. I have sent [you] a little work on the Acts of the Apostles, which was produced not many days ago, and, so as not to impede your most holy will, I put it out as quickly as time permitted in corrected form on little parchments. Here I have attempted, insofar as I could, to shed light on those things which seemed to be treated mystically or stated somewhat obscurely. In this little work I have been aided by several other writers of the Catholic faith, especially Arator'] (Lawrence T. Martin, trans., *Bede's Commentary on the Acts of the Apostles*, Cistercian Studies 117 [Kalamazoo, MI: Cistercian Publications, 1989] 3).

tending to be compilers; he alludes to "little works," establishes the interauctorial link to the sources used, and even admits that, "Nonnulla vero in calce etiam proprio sudore subtextui" (Praefatio lines 5: 15-16) ['By my own labor I have added some things at the end' (Martin 6)]. The preface ends with another self-conscious remark catering to Christian humility: "in quo utroque opere, si quid utilitatis inveneris, dei donis adscribe; si quid superflui, meae fragilitati compatere" (lines 5: 16-17) ['If you should find anything useful in either of these works, attribute it to God's gifts; if you find anything useless, have compassion on my frailty' (Martin 6)].[11] This remark can be found almost verbatim in the beginning of Chaucer's Retraction, except that Bede only delineates "useful" and "superfluous," whereas Chaucer employs the Horatian distinction between *delectatio* and *utilitas*.

In the preface to *Retractatio,* Bede sets up a model intertextual and interauctorial relationship between the two texts and between Augustine and himself:

> Scimus eximium doctorem ac pontificem Augustinum, cum esset senior, libros retractationum in quaedam sua opuscula quae iuvenis condiderat fecisse, ut quae ex tempore melius crebro ex lectionis usu ac munere supernae largitatis didicerat; non ut de prisca confusus imperitia, sed ut de suo magis profectu gavisus monumentis inderet litterarum ac posteris legenda relinqueret. Cuius industriam nobis quoque pro modulo nostro placuit imitari, ut post expositionem actuum apostolorum, quam ante annos plures rogatu venerabilis episcopi Accae quanta valuimus sollertia conscripsimus, nunc in idem volumen brevem retractationis libellum condamus, studio maxime vel addendi quae minus dicta vel emendandi quae secus quam placuit dicta videbantur.[12]

Judging from Bede's intertextual and interauctorial announcement, it is doubtful whether Bede himself was perfectly sure what Augustine envisioned his *Retractations* to be. Bede characterizes Augustine's career as the reworking of his juvenilia in his later life, thereby assuming the topos of youthful error vs. old-age wisdom as the controlling stratagem of Augustine's *Retractations*. Augustine, however, had been revising his entire canon, not merely the earlier works, in order to establish a definitive edition. Granted, the earlier works were revised to a greater degree, but the more recent ones had not been exempted. The scope of Bede's intra-auctorial undertaking is simultaneously more limited and more extensive, since he only applies Augustine's method to one of his works but treats that work at much greater length (the project produced a work a little larger than half the size of the base text). At the same time, Bede is quick to assert that Augustine, while having the same intentions of correction and addition as Bede, had much less to correct but simply took pride in applying the

---

11 The Latin "superflui," however, means 'superfluous' rather than 'useless.'

12 Bede, *Retractatio in Actus Apostolorum* Praefatio lines 3: 1-11. ['I know that when he was older, the distinguished teacher and bishop Augustine wrote books of retractions on some of his works which he had written as a youth, as he learned things better in later time out of the practice of frequent reading and the gift of heavenly bounty; not as so erroneous in his early experience, but taking pleasure at his greater growth he should publish it in written monuments and leave it to be read by later ages. And it has pleased me to take his labor as a model for myself, so that after my exposition of the Acts of the Apostles, which I wrote as far as my skill enabled me, many years before, at the request of the venerable Bishop Acca, now I may make a small volume of retractions upon the same book, either by adding what seems to be missing or by correcting what seems to be wrong, with the greatest diligence'] (W. F. A. Bolton, *History of Anglo-Latin Literature 597-1066* [Princeton: Princeton UP, 1967] 1: 109).

added expertise and experience he had gained over the span of his life to improve his literary creations. Such a statement is equally self-reflexive and tempers the self-critical element by conveying that Bede might not have as much to correct as merely to improve. Some critics think that Bede's work is a conscious imitation of Augustine's reassessment of his works and contains corrections, reconsiderations, and revisions of the first version showing his surer hand as an exegete, whereas Tatlock declares that Bede revised to a smaller degree than Augustine and that his *Retractatio* "is really not much like the book it claims as a model."[13]

What exactly did Bede revise in his *Retractatio*? Most of the corrected errors comprise etymologies, poorly identified sources, and theological problems.[14] Here are several representative examples of his revision. With the *Retractatio* neatly organized, like Augustine's *Retractations* according to Bible verse, Bede did not want to neglect the linguistic and historical explanation of the Acts, and much of his revision focuses on the additional consultation of the original Greek text of Acts and its Latin translations.[15] He was able to reuse the bilingual Greek and Old Latin manuscript of the sixth century that he had utilized for his *Expositio*.[16] With at least three Latin and two Greek versions of the Acts as sources, Bede is mostly interested in textual variants and critical readings.[17] He unites all his grammatical, literary, and exegetical knowledge and applies it to Luke's text. One example of a corrected Greek term is: "Scripsi autem in

---

13   Franz Brunhölzl, *Geschichte der lateinischen Literatur des Mittelalters* (Munich: Wilhelm Fink Verlag, 1975) 1: 221 and John S. P. Tatlock, "Chaucer's *Retractions*," *Publications of the Modern Language Association* 21 (1913): 521-529; here 523. Although the catalogue of Bede's books in the *Ecclesiastical History* does not list the *Retractatio* (G. F. Browne, *The Venerable Bede* [New York: Pott, Young & Co., 1879] 17-20), it is considered authentic and probably composed after 731 (M. L. W. Laistner, *Thought and Letters in Western Europe* [London: Methuen, 1931] 157). The title *Retractatio* can be found in all manuscripts, except F, although *retractatus* is used in a few manuscripts (M. L. W. Laistner, introduction, *Expositio Actuum Apostolorum et Retractatio*, by the Venerable Bede, The Medieval Academy of America Publication 35, [1939, Reprint; New York: Kraus Reprint Co., 1970] xi-xlv; here xiv).

14   In the preface to the *Retractatio*, Bede elaborates on the reasons for errors and omissions: "quae, utrum neglegentia interpretis omissa vel aliter dicta an incuria librariorum sint depravata sive relicta nondum scire potuimus. Namque Graecum exemplar fuisse falsatum suspicari non audeo; unde lectorem admoneo ut haec ubicumque fecerimus gratia eruditionies legat, non in suo tamen volumine velut emendatturus interserat, nisi forte ea in Latino codice suae editionis antiquitus sic interpretata reppererit" (Bede, *Retractatio in Actus Apostolorum* Praefatio lines 93: 13-19). ['I have not yet been able to determine whether some changes and omissions are due to the negligence of the translator or to his use of different words or whether we are dealing with a case of scribes altering the text and omitting words. I hesitate to suppose that the Greek exemplar itself was a faulty one. Let my reader therefore accept whatever comments I make on these matters as scholarly comments and let him not on that account start to correct his own copy of Acts, unless perhaps he discovers a very old manuscript of the Latin version which confirms these comments'] (Ward, *The Venerable Bede* 59). As a writer dependent on sources, Bede naturally discusses translation and scribal problems, but his insistence on correcting his own text affirms both the autonomy he grants the text and the pride he takes in his literary and exegetical creation.

15   Karl Werner, *Beda der Ehrwührdige und seine Zeit* (Vienna: Wilhelm Braunmüller, 1881) 190 and Laistner, *Thought and Letters in Western Europe* 161.

16   Laistner, *Thought and Letters in Western Europe* 161.

17   Brown, *Bede the Venerable* 58.

praecedente libro Stephanum interpretari coronatum, nec longe est a vero quod scripsi; verum sollertius ediscens inveni non coronatum Graece, sed coronam significare Stephanum—est enic hoc nomen generis masculini apud eos ideoque viro conveniens."[18] Bede had, for instance, also found a better definition for the word "scapha," quoted from Isidore of Seville; M. L. W. Laistner considers Bede's textual criticism as sound and accords him competency in quoting from the original Greek, indicating a substantial increase in Bede's knowledge of Greek.[19] Bede furthermore rectifies Jerome's claim that the apostle Judas Thaddaus had been sent to King Abgar of Osroene, when it was actually not the apostle but a disciple.[20] In the same vein, he corrects an error in his chronological reasoning in the reign of kings, assigning twenty years to Samuel and twenty to Saul.[21]

Bede's eagerness to employ self-criticism[22] contrasts with his defense, in which he adumbrates the attitude of the twelfth-century scholastic compiler toward sources. Looking back to the *Expositio*, we can already note Bede's "apologetic tone."[23] Laistner concludes in his introduction to Bede's *Expositio Actuum Apostolorum et Retractatio* that Bede did not take the charges against his studies in Old Testament chronology lightly but was always keenly aware of criticism and prepared to reiterate his positions "with vigor."[24] For instance, Bede chides himself for bad scholarship but accuses Isidore of the same: "non ea quae scripsit scrupulosius discutientes, sed simpliciter eius dictis auscultantes, rati quod haec ipse de certis verterum historiis didicerit."[25] The interauctorial concept of the *auctoritates* is employed to avert

---

18 Bede, *Retractatio in Actus Apostolorum* lines VI, 8, 117: 1-5. ['I wrote in the previous book that Stephen means "crowned," nor is what I wrote far from what is true. But, learning more accurately, I have found that Stephen signifies in Greek not "crowned" but "a crown," for this name *corona* is, among the Greeks, of a masculine gender and therefore appropriate to a man'] (Ward, *The Venerable Bede* 59).

19 M. L. W. Laistner, "Bede as a Classical and Patristic Scholar," *Transactions of the Royal Historical Society* 16 (1933): 67-94; here 85-86.

20 Werner, *Beda der Ehrwührdige und seine Zeit* 190.

21 Bolton, *History of Anglo-Latin Literature 597-1066* 107.

22 Claude Jenkins, "Bede as Exegete and Theologian," *Bede: His Life, Times, and Writings*, ed. A. Hamilton Thompson (New York: Russell & Russell, 1966) 152-200; here 158.

23 Laistner, introduction xvi. It has been suggested that Bede had been accused of heresy in connection with the contents of the *De temporibus*, plus had been criticized for his explanation of the miracle of tongues at Pentecost in the *Expositio* (Laistner, introduction xvi). In the *De temporum ratione*, he confronts his critics with the words: "Quorum quisquis dicta perspexerit, credo mox nostro labori calumniam facere desistet si non hunc tamen liuidis, quod absit contemplatur obtutibus" (Bede, *De Temporum Ratione*, ed. Ch. W. Jones, *Corpus Christianorum Series Latina* CXXIII B [Turnholti: Brepols, 1977] Praefatio lines 35-37) [I believe that whoever looks at the sayings of these [persons] will soon desist calumniating our labor, if however he does not contemplate this book with envious (or spiteful) glances, which God forbid]. In later chronicles, the author demonstrates a similar sensitivity concerning questionable chronological issues that had to be discussed (Laistner, introduction xvii).

24 Laistner, introduction xvi.

25 Bede, *Retractatio in Actus Apostolorum* lines I, 13 96: 7-9. ['not examining what he wrote too scrupulously, but simply listening to his words, confident that he had learned them from proven histories of the ancients'] (Martin, *Bede's Commentary on the Acts of the Apostles* 23).

responsibility from Bede, who is very forthcoming about his errors but stresses his auctorial limitations: "Non autem mihi imputandum errorem reor, ubi auctoritatem magnorum sequens doctorum, quae in illorum opusculis inveni, absque scrupulo suscipienda credidi."[26] Bede touches upon the hierarchical view of language and authorship, in which the authority belongs to the previous, if not the original, author and gets diluted as it is handed down; therefore, Bede should not be held responsible for present errors. In another instance Bede turns the scenario around; instead of blaming the source he asserts that his interpretation has to be correct because his source could not possibly be wrong: "Scio me esse reprehensum a quibusdam, quod hanc sententiam duobus modis posse intelligi dixerim . . . sed ex verbis sancti et irreprehensibilis per omnia magistri, hoc est, Gregorii Nazianzeni assumpsi."[27] Overall, Laistner views the *Retractatio* as a solid and mature piece of exegetical research and interpretation.[28] Bede can correct and amend his former work, thus creating an intertextual and interauctorial connection and conscious imitation of Augustine, all on a plane devoid of moral repercussions, for the scope is mainly textual and linguistic; nevertheless, the author is a precursor to the scholastic compiler and engages in the same self-conscious, albeit less ironic, defense mechanisms.

4.2. Gerald of Wales

Gerald of Wales (1147-1223) also produced a work reminiscent in title of Augustine's *Retractations*. Gerald's "Retractationes," which belongs in the third category of apologies and basically deals with unsavory literary practices, has been quite neglected by scholarship. Even in Robert Bartlett's recent literary biography of Gerald of Wales, the "Retractationes" is conspicuously absent.[29] Although its element of self-criticism is slight, it should not be neglected, says Michael Richter.[30] Gerald's self-criticism completely lacks the dimension of guilt often associated with apologies to deities and sounds combative and begrudging. In the introductory statement to "Retractationes," Gerald juxtaposes the general fallibility of man, of the writer, and even more of the reader: "ea quae in opusculis nostris retractanda decrevimus, quatinus et lector caveat

---

26 Bede, *Expositio Actuum Apostolorum et Retractatio* lines I, 13, 96: 23-25. ['I do not think that that error should be imputed to me when, following the authority of the great doctors [Jerome in this case], I believed that I should adopt without scruple what I found in their writings'] (Martin, *Bede's Commentary on the Acts of the Apostles* 24).

27 Bede, *Retractatio in Actus Apostolorum* lines II, 6, 99: 1-2, 6-7. ['I know that I have been blamed by some because I said that this sentence [Ac 2:6] can be understood in two ways . . . I have taken the words of a holy and completely irreprehensible master, Gregory of Nazianzus'] (Martin, *Bede's Commentary on the Acts of the Apostles* 39).

28 Laistner, "Bede as a Classical and Patristic Scholar" 87.

29 Robert Bartlett, *Gerald of Wales 1146-1223* (Oxford: Clarendon, 1982).

30 Michael Richter, "Gerald of Wales: A Reassessment on the 750th Anniversary of His Death," *Traditio* 29 (1973): 379-90; here 389.

et pro certis incerta non habeat, hic proponere dignum duximus."[31] Like Ovid, Gerald disassociates himself from his former text and puts the weight on the reader and the statements as if they were self-standing units without a tie to their creator. The implication of the reader as not discerning and skeptical enough toward the written text questions the truth and graspability of the text. He furthermore applies the errors-of-youth topos in conjunction with interauctoriality in order to exonerate himself for what he has to admit to: "Quoniam, ut ait Jeronimus, 'Errores adolescentiae aetas matura condemnat'" ("Ret." 425) [Since Jerome says, "One condemns the errors of youth at a maturer age"]. Gerald's evocation of Jerome and the old-age topos demonstrate both how generally acknowledged this practice was and how elemental and prescribed it was in an author's development. The formulaic nature of the old-age topos goes hand in hand with the absence of guilt for Gerald.

Gerald basically apologizes for three literary misdemeanors that characterize him as a negligent author. He counts among the errors of his youth certain "inaccuracies and hasty assertions in his published works,"[32] acknowledging first that not all his sources for the *Topographia Hibernica* were valid. The first self-criticism has to do with intertextuality in the abusing of sources. Secondly, he admits to having claimed several poems in the *Symbolum Electorum* as his own ("Ret." 426), an offense that deals with undisclosed interauctoriality. Third, he confesses that some of the more scandalous passages about Hubert Walter in the *De Invectionibus* and the *De Gestis Giraldi* were not true: "De his inquam omnibus et similibus, magis absque dubio credendum, quod ea famae malignae confictio quam ulla rei gestae perpetratio publicare praesumpserit. Similiter etsi in libro *Gestis Giraldi* haec forte aut his similia reperiantur, eadem habenda est consideratio."[33] This third admission lies outside the realm of literature, in the area of personal slander. Gerald raised the old question of the quarrel of the metropolitan rights of St. David and now admits that rumors had played a bigger part in the quarrel than historical certainty and that most of the charges brought against the Archbishop Hubert stemmed from the heat of the bitter battle; therefore, he tempers those remarks and portrays the bishop less negatively: half of "Retractationes" describes the prelate's character.[34] This ratio suggests that the "revision" is more polit-

---

31 Gerald of Wales, "Retractationes," *Opera*, ed. J. S. Brewer, 6 vols. (London: Longman, 1861) 1: 425-27; here 425. [We will set forth what needs to be reconsidered in earlier writing, and will tell the readers how far they have to be on their guard against taking uncertain statements for certainties].

32 E. A. Williams, "A Bibliography of Giraldus Cambrensis," *Cylchgrawn Llyfrgell Genedlaethol Cymru: The National Library of Wales Journal* 12 (1961): 97-140; here 113.

33 Gerald of Wales, "Retractationes" 426. [Concerning all these and similar things, I say, it is without doubt preferable to presume that the fabrication of a bad story rather than the perpetration of a deed incites to publish. Similarly, when that or something like that can accidentally be found in the book of Gerald's deeds, the same consideration should be applied to it].

34 Henry Owen, *Gerald the Welshman* (London: David Nutt, 1904) 31 and W. S. Davies, "Giraldus Cambrensis: *De Invectionibus*," *Y Commrodor: The Magazine of the Honorable Society of Cymmrodorion* 30 (1920): 16. On the controversy between Gerald of Wales and Hubert Walter, see C. R. Cheney, *Hubert Walter,* Leaders of Religion (London: Nelson, 1967); I. P. Shaw, "Giraldus Cambrensis and the Primacy of Canterbury," *The Church Quarterly Review* 148

ical than literary and therefore less deserving of a comparison with Augustine's works, although Augustine also used political polemic against the Pelagians, even in the *Retractations*. In keeping with the example of Augustine, however, Gerald writes two lists of his works, the *Epistle to the Chapter of Hereford* (a catalogue of books) and the *Lesser Catalogue of His Books* (a similar list). Whereas Augustine systematically revised his books and combined the revision with a catalogue to provide a definitive edition, Gerald separates the two issues, producing only a faintly Augustinian imitation, in which he mostly tries to exonerate himself from accusations of unsavory literary practices and possibly attempts to preserve his canon as well.

4.3. Wandalbert von Prüm

The remaining medieval Latin authors in this chapter practice to self-criticism of the first strand, apologies to God, which are rooted in medieval theories of language. Because these writers follow Augustine's *Confessions*, the added dimension of sinfulness in the Christian universe elicits professions of guilt, often coupled with the youth-vs.-age topos. In order to prove himself acceptable in a cosmos that rejects literary works that are amorous in content and pagan in origin, the ninth-century West-Frankish monk Wandalbert von Prüm contrasts his former writing practices with his current project, the metric *Martyrologium*, which had been commissioned in 847:[35]

> Carmine qui vacuas captavi saepius auras
> Rumores vulgi quaerendo stultus inanes,
> Adgrediar tandem veram de carmine laudem
> Quaerere et aeternum mihi conciliare favorem.
> Spectandos breviter signans actusque virosque
> Atque dies anni reditu volvente per orbem,
> Ordine quae lustrent scribens sollemnia quaeque.[36]

(1949): 82-101; and Charles R. Young, *Hubert Walter: Lord of Canterbury and Lord of England* (Durham: Duke UP, 1968).

35 F. J. E. Raby, *A History of Christian-Latin Poetry from the Beginning to the Close of the Middle Ages*, 2nd ed. (Oxford: Clarendon, 1966) 178 and Max Manitius, *Geschichte der Lateinischen Literatur des Mittelalters*, 3 vols. (1911, 1931, Reprint; Munich: C. H. Beck, 1974) 1: 557. For background information relating to the Abbey of Prüm and Wandalbert, see Wolfgang Haubrichs, *Die Kultur der Abtei Prüm zur Karolingerzeit: Studien zur Heimat des althochdeutschen Georgsliedes* (Bonn: Ludwig Röhrscheid, 1979) 54-65. For a critical article on the merits of his *Martyrologium*, see Jacques Dubois, "Le martyrologe métrique de Wandelbert: ses sources, son originalité, son influence sur le martyrologe d'Usard," *Analecta Bollandiana* 79 (1961): 257-93.

36 Wandalbert von Prüm, *Martyrologium*, ed. J. P. Migne, *Patrologiae Cursus Completus* 121 (Turnholti: Brepols, 1963) 567-622; here Propositio 576, lines 1-7. [I who often held the empty breezes with song, seeking stupid, inane rumors of the common crowd, let me come at last to seek true praise concerning song and win for myself eternal favor, briefly pointing out the noteworthy acts and men and days of the year as it returns in its orbit, writing in order each solemnity that occurs].

Not only does the author accuse himself of desire for fame but he also re-enacts the patristic criticism of classical literature by contrasting the "empty" with the "true" composition. The creation of a metrical saints' and holy day almanac, then, could lend his auctorial abilities the necessary salvific content and provide a good opportunity to wipe the slate clean in God's eyes (see Ingelard, page 65). Wandalbert overtly expresses this sentiment. The "empty" and "true" contrast highlights the two different stages of his intra-auctorial development.

Additionally, Wandalbert apologizes both for technical difficulties and for the poem itself. He points out that certain stubborn names refuse to comply with pure meter:[37] "Hic mihi nonnumquam sanctorum nomina leges / Carminis excedent, sed non mutilanda vocandi / Est censura bonos; veniam pietate merebor."[38] Wandalbert sounds tongue in cheek when evoking piety in conjunction with faulty scansion. His confidence and lightheartedness here, however, are diametrically opposed to his exaggerated humility in the conclusion. Besides the usual self-flagellation for worldly vanities and the coveting of auctorial fame, Wandalbert criticizes himself excessively by bemoaning the fact that during the thirty-five years of his life he has not achieved anything good. This exaggerated display of humility does not match his earlier aspiration to piety and it demonstrates the conventionality of his self-criticism, as composing the *Martyrologium* should signal that he has now rewritten himself and that the past should therefore no longer be a point of concern for him.

4.4. Marbod de Rennes

Marbod de Rennes (1035-1123) is equally torn on matters of humility. At the alleged age of sixty-seven, the bishop of Rennes furnishes one of the most extensive discussions of the literary old-age topos in the self-critical introduction to his *Liber decem capitulorum* (1107). Like Lucian, Marbod goes beyond the self-epideictic structure of the apology and enters the metatextual realm, not merely admitting to his literary errors but elaborating on the rationale behind the self-critical process. The first chapter, the "Apto de genere scribendi," contains Marbod's recantation of his juvenilia.[39] This hinges on the dichotomy of youth and old age as well as the works' creative repercussions:

Quae iuvenis scripsi, senior dum plura retracto,
Paenitet et quaedam vel scripta vel edita nollem,
Tum quia materies inhonesta levisque videtur,

---

37 Wolfgang Stammler, *Die Deutsche Literatur des Mittelalters: Verfasserlexikon* (Berlin: Walter de Gruyter, 1933-55) 832.

38 Wandalbert von Prüm, *Martyrologium*, Propositio 576, lines 8-10. [Here for me the names of saints will sometimes exceed the laws of verse [i.e., they cannot be scanned metrically], but they should not be mutilated. Because of my piety I merit forgiveness].

39 F. A. Wright and T. A. Sinclair, *A History of Later Latin Literature: From the Middle of the Fourth to the End of the Seventeenth Century* (New York: Macmillan, 1931) 294.

Tum quia dicendi potuit modus aptior esse:
Unde nec inventu pretiosa nec arte loquendi
Vel delenda cito vel non edenda fuissent.
Sed quia missa semel vox irrevocabilis exit
Erroremque nefas est emendare priorem,
Restat ut in reliquum iam cautior esse laborem,
Ne quid inornate vel ne quid inutile promam,
Praecipue quia iam veniae locus esse nequibit,
Qui quondam fuerat, dum stulta rudisque iuventus
Et levis in culpam poterat toleranda videri.[40]

Marbod, who has been neglected by Tatlock, also uses the verb "retractare" in the sense of 'reconsidering.' Marbod's unusually explicit and detailed self-criticism sets up the intra-auctorial dichotomy of the young poet and the old poet, with the latter commenting on the performance of the former. His self-criticism concentrates on both form and content, while other authors mainly adhere either to one or to the other. Walther Bulst, in fact, considers it amazing that in the twelfth century an admired poet on the threshold of senectitude obliges himself to undertake writing poetry with a new form and content.[41] Marbod's assertion that published words cannot be recalled nor corrected seconds Socrates', Piccolomini's, and Kundera's opinion, but opposes both Augustine's and Bede's attempts to correct past literary works. Since Marbod considers earlier literary efforts part of the unalterable auctorial past, he joins rank with those authors that, rather than improve an existing work, set out to ameliorate their track record with a new work.

Marbod expounds on the errors-of-youth topos in several more passages. He very specifically stresses the fallibility of both youth and old age, although the maturation process eradicates the "grace period" for the older poet:

Nunc vitae studiique simul diuturnior usus
Acrius exspectat rigidi censoris acumen.
Ergo propositum mihi sit neque ludicra quaedam
Scribere nec verbis aures mulcere canoris.[42]

The poet equates more mature age and knowledge with conditions that would make the reader increasingly critical of his poetic work, which in turn incites the poet to

---

40 Marbod de Rennes, *Liber decem capitulorum*, ed. Rosario Leotta (Rome: Herder, 1984) lines I. 1-13. [As I am, an old man reconsidering the many things I wrote as a young man, I regret them, wish not to have written and published this or that: some because the contents seem too facile and appear without dignity; some because the presentation could have been more suitable. Hence, what was lacking both in form and invention should have been immediately stricken or never published. Once the word is released, it is gone and cannot be recalled. It is also not possible to correct the former error; what is left for me is to be more careful in the future in order not to present anything without finesse or profit, especially since now there is no more room for forgiveness, as was available earlier when youth, stupid, inexperienced and careless in guilt, could be tolerated].

41 Walther Bulst, "Studien zu Marbods *Carmina varia* und *Liber decem capitulorum*," *Nachrichten von der Gesellschaft der Wissenschaften zu Göttingen* (1939): 173-241; here 214.

42 Marbod, *Liber decem capitulorum* lines I. 14-17. [Advanced age and knowledge now have to expect the harsh criticism of the severe censor much more; therefore, I pledge not to write anything else ludicrous nor to flatter the ear with well-sounding words].

stave off criticism with self-criticism. He spells out the boundaries of his future literary activity, but the criteria of not being ludicrous and mellifluous are still subjective and fluid, giving his critics great leeway of interpretation and himself increased auctorial license. Marbod, furthermore, polarizes the youth-and-age issue by assigning a certain code of decorum, not Christian morality, to them:[43] "Sed mihi nunc melius suadet maturior aetas, / Quam decet ut facili contenta sit utilitate / Utque supervacuum studeat vitare laborem."[44] Older age is characterized as less likely to lead the poet astray. Horatian "profit" has become the desirable goal, rather than self-defeating poetic exercises, although Marbod accords the latter literary activity its place as a part of the creative development process:

> Nec tamen omnino me paenitet illa secutum,
> In quibus exercens animum sudare solebam;
> . . . .
> Praeterea iuvenem cantare iocosa decebat,
> Quod manifesta seni ratio docet esse negatum,
> Cuius morali condiri verba sapore
> Convenit et vitiis obsistere fronte severa.[45]

Marbod's clear distinction between what is appropriate to each of the two ages and his slight defensiveness about it are rooted in the *trivium* training experienced by grammar-school students dealing with non-Christian literature. It is obvious from Marbod's comments and literary production that he draws on both the classical and the Christian world in his literary endeavors. F. J. E. Raby and Joachim Suchomski hypothesize that Marbod's recanted poems might have been "school-exercises in which a certain license was allowed," a thesis supported by Marbod's own insistence on his youthful creation of classically influenced amorous poems or epigrams.[46] On the other hand, we actually do not have to look beyond his extant lyrical production to find material that might have been suspect in his times.[47]

The second apology strand, addressed to women, makes one of its first appearances in Marbod and should be briefly mentioned here. In chapter four of the *Liber*, Marbod posits a possible self-criticism about his previous treatment of women in his poems. In

---

43   Bulst, "Studien zu Marbods *Carmina varia* und *Liber decem capitulorum*" 215.

44   Marbod, *Liber decem capitulorum* lines I. 26-28. [More mature age now gives me better advice; it behooves this age that it takes pleasure in mild profit and tries to avoid superfluous labors].

45   Marbod, *Liber decem capitulorum* lines I. 43-44, 47-50. [I do not entirely regret that I indulged in what my mind had been trained and was used to labor in . . . Besides, it was suitable for the young man to make poems about the jocular, which, clear reason dictates as forbidden to the old man, for whom it is suitable to season the word with an ethical tone and resist vices with a stern brow].

46   F. J. E. Raby, *A History of the Secular Latin Poetry in the Middle Ages*, 2 vols., 2nd ed. (Oxford: Clarendon, 1957) 2: 333 and Joachim Suchomski, *Delectatio und Utilitas: Ein Beitrag zum Verständnis mittelalterlicher komischer Literatur*, Bibliotheca Germanica 18 (Bern: A. Francke, 1975) 69-70.

47   For a sampling of Marbod's love lyrics, addressed to women as well as men, see Karl Langosch, *Lyrische Anthologie des lateinischen Mittelalters* (Darmstadt: Wissenschaftliche Buchgesellschaft, 1968) 260-69; Thomas Stehling, trans., *Medieval Latin Poems of Male Love and Friendship* (New York: Garland, 1984) 30-39; and Bulst, "Studien zu Marbods *Carmina varia* und *Liber decem capitulorum*."

one of the first medieval apologies for antifeminist writing, he says: "Quod neque culpari mulier, quia femina tantum, / Nec quia vir tantum, debet quis laude beari" (*Liber* IV, lines 122-23) [One can never accuse a woman merely for being a woman or praise a man for merely being a man]. Although this statement is very general, it suggests belated self-criticism of his vicious attacks on women, even as late as chapter three in the *Liber*, where he assails woman as the worst tool of the devil. His stipulation that women should not be maligned because of their gender leaves plenty of room for denunciation of women for other reasons, however.

Despite this extensive explanation and apology, the poet demonstrates a healthy dose of self-assertion, as he claims, "Nec mihi sit summos fas attemptare poetas / Nec nimis abiecte me deterioribus addam" (*Liber* IV, lines 57-58) [Neither do I dare count myself among the greatest poets nor humiliate myself to count among the lowly ones].[48] Marbod's admonition to infuse old-age compositions with a certain seriousness implies a very rigid and premeditated approach to literature, one in which an author does not follow his creative development but instead performs in accordance with a prescribed intra-auctorial formula dictating appropriate content, and to some degree form, at the various stages of his life, without doubt a rationalization of the constraints the Christian Zeitgeist placed on him. With this interauctorial statement the self-criticism has been put into perspective; a realistic assessment and a value judgment have been made contrasting starkly to Wandalbert von Prüm's expressed poetic self-presentation. Marbod's approach to literature is modified, but literature itself never abandoned; the newly announced change of literary practice and intra-auctoriality is supposed to start in chapter two of the *Liber*. Despite the poet's age of sixty-seven, this passage is far from a deathbed confession, for he indeed projects his continued and improved poetic activity into the future, a strategy which would preclude any implication that he was laying down the proverbial pen.

4.5. Guibert de Nogent

The Benedictine monk Guibert de Nogent (1053-1124)[49] demonstrates the same love for writing in his *Autobiography*, which imitates Augustine's *Confessions*.[50] The most remarkable aspect of Guibert's discussion of his development is that he takes some of the established topoi and reverses them. Since the work emulates Augustine's confessional work, it is fraught with penitential expressions and a gamut of confessions of

---

48 For an example of a poem praising Marbod's poetic prowess, see Baudri of Bourgueil in Langosch, *Lyrische Anthologie des lateinischen Mittelalters* 228-31.

49 For an alternate date of birth and explanation, see J. F. Benton, "The Personality of Guibert of Nogent," *Culture, Power and Personality in Medieval France* (London: Hambledon, 1991) 293-312.

50 For a detailed comparison, see S. Hallenstein, *Nachbildung und Umformung der Bekenntnisse Augustins in der Lebensgeschichte Guiberts* (Diss. Hamburg, 1935) and Frederic Amory, "The Confessional Superstructure of Guibert of Nogent's *Vita*," *Classica et Medieavalia* 25 (1964): 224-40.

sins. In Book XV of his *Autobiography*, Guibert informs the reader that "divina volumina"[51] [holy books] supplied the material for his "prosulas versiculosque" [short pieces of prose and verse]. Guibert's word choice is neutral, not pejorative as in later cases, and clearly shows that he has been producing compositions with a religious bent until he discovered classical literature:

> Interea cum versificandi studio ultra omnem modum meum animum immersissem, ita ut universa divinae paginae seria pro tam ridicula vanitate seponerem, ad hoc ipsum, duce mea levitate, jam veneram, ut ovidiana et bucolicorum dicta praesumerem, et lepores amatorios in specierum distributionibus epistolisque nexilibus affectarem.[52]

Four aspects of this quotation are noteworthy. First, it shows that Guibert's auctorial progression moves from religious to secular, reversing the usual order of secular to spiritual. Second, the passage is crucial because the author delineates specifically what the folly of his youth entails, whereas many medieval authors, like Marbod, for instance, only supply cryptic statements. Third, the passage represents the kind of literature closed-mouthed authors allude to and the alleged pernicious influence of that kind of literary work. Fourth, it openly introduces the aspect of amorous writing into the medieval apology tradition.

The writing of erotic verse, instigated by the reading of such classical love poetry, might be compounded by the advent of hormonal changes, which explains why many authors allot a person's youth to amorous activity. Guibert confirms this fact by openly spelling it out: "Nimirum utrobique raptabar, dum non solum verborum dulcium, quae a poetis acceperam, sed et quae ego profuderam lasciviis irretirer, verum etiam per horum et his similium revolutiones immodica aliquotiens carnis meae titillatione tenerer."[53] Despite his candid admission of these offenses, Guibert portrays himself as a victim, as expressed by his word choice and use of passive construction of "raptabar," "irretirer," "tenerer." The implied passivity on his part and the outright perpetration on literature's part removes most of his responsibility for this abominable violation of monastic rules. The following passage also capitalizes on his role as a victim: "Inde accidit, ut, effervescente interiori rabie, ad obscaenula quaedam verba devolverer, et aliquas literulas minus pensi ac moderati habentes, immo totius

---

51 Guibert de Nogent, *Autobiographie*, ed. and trans. Edmond-René Labande (Paris: Société d'Édition Les Belles Lettres, 1981) lines 110, 112.

52 Guibert, *Autobiographie* XVII, 134. ['Meanwhile, I had fully immersed my soul in the study of verse-making. Consequently I left aside all the seriousness of sacred Scripture for this vain and ludicrous activity. Sustained by my folly I had reached a point where I was competing with Ovid and the pastoral poets, and striving to achieve an amorous charm in my way of arranging images in well-crafted letters'] (Paul J. Archambault, trans., *A Monk's Confession: The Memoirs of Guibert of Nogent* [University Park: Pennsylvania State UP, 1996] 58).

53 Guibert, *Autobiographie* XVII, 134. ['In point of fact, I was doubly chained for I was enmeshed not only by the sweet words I had taken from the poets but also by the lascivious ones I poured forth myself. Moreover, by repeating these poetic expressions, I was sometimes prone to immod-est stirrings of my flesh'] (Archambault, *A Monk's Confession* 59). For a discussion of Guibert's sexuality and writing, see Seth Lerer, "Transgressio studii: Writing and Sexuality in Guibert of Nogent," *Stanford French Review* 14:1-2 (1990): 243-66.

honestatis nescias dictitarem."[54] Once more, Guibert is not to blame, since the "rabies," the combination of lust and love poetry, drove him to write.

He is further exonerated in a Christian sense through a dream in which God Himself appears and reprimands Guibert, exerting His divine power and mirroring the medieval auctorial pyramid—God at the top, and the author a shadowy image of Him—because Guibert has offended the divinity by imitating the divine creative act: "'Volo . . . ut de literis quae factae sunt mihi rationem reddas; verum manus quae literas ipsas scripsit non est sua ipsius quae scripsit.'"[55] This metonymic statement makes a clear intra-auctorial case for the existence of two different authors within the same person. Guibert interprets the dream in that way too: "plane non permansura in illa ignominiosa sua actione indubie denotatur . . . quasi ex necessitate rejectis imaginationibus, spiritualitate recepta, ad exercitia commodiora perveni."[56] The impersonal construction used in the first phrase attests again to the victim-role of the author, who has been gripped by frenzy but who is now completing the cycle of his career. He has moved from religious to secular and back to spiritual. His poetic development differs from Augustine's in that Augustine's progression is linear, moving from pagan to Christian literature, Guibert's is circular and he presents his "trifles" as hurdles in the path to greater spirituality.

4.6. Peter of Blois

Peter of Blois (1135-1212), the secretary and chaplain to Henry II and Eleanor of Aquitaine, was also one of the four important twelfth-century Latin poets of the English court.[57] The poet is vexed by the "lasciviousness of his youthful songs," rejecting them;[58] he cannot, however, refrain from returning to them. The author provides several statements about his alleged youthful compositions in his letters. He writes: "'ego quidem nugis et cantibus venereis quandoque operam dedi, sed per gratiam Eius qui me segregavit ab utero matris meae, reieci haec omnia a primo limine iuventutis . . . omitte penitus cantus inutiles et aniles fabulas.'"[59] The poet's attitude

---

54 Guibert, *Autobiographie* XVII, 136. ['My inner turmoil reached such a point that I began to use a few slightly obscene words and to compose little poems entirely bereft of any sense of weight and measure, indeed shorn of all decency'] (Archambault, *A Monk's Confession* 59).

55 Guibert, *Autobiographie* XVII, 136. ['"I want you to render an account of these poems that were composed; the hand that wrote them is not that of the man who drew these letters'"] (Archambault, *A Monk's Confession* 59).

56 Guibert, *Autobiographie* XVII, 136, 138. ['clearly this meant that this hand would not persevere in these shameful activities . . . it was almost inevitable that I should reject vain fantasies, and, paying heed to spiritual things once again, I took up more appropriate exercises'] (Archambault, *A Monk's Confession* 59, 60).

57 Peter Dronke, "Peter of Blois and the Poetry at the Court of Henry II," *Mediaeval Studies* 38 (1976): 184-235; here 191.

58 Dronke, "Peter of Blois and the Poetry at the Court of Henry II" 193.

59 Peter of Blois, "Letter 76" qtd. in Raby, *A History of the Secular Latin Poetry in the Middle Ages* 2: 323. ['I too at one time occupied myself in writing frivolities and amorous poems, but by the

toward repentance seems lukewarm, and as Richard Southern points out, these statements were made rather late in Blois' life.[60] He gave up his trifles, but only because of an external impetus, and regrets them less than he discourages the addressee from paying attention to them. Yet in another letter he asks that they be returned to him: "mitte mihi versus et ludicra, quae feci Turonis"[61] [Send me the verses and trifles that I wrote in Tours].

Additional correspondence sheds light on his ambivalent attitude towards court life and his own literary creation. In a letter written at the time of a serious illness, Peter of Blois condemns the life of courtiers as vain and empty, but in another letter he comments hypertextually on the first letter: "For at that time, stricken by grievous illness, and thus impelled by grievous repentance, I deemed not only the court but the world and all worldly things unclean and damnable. . . . yet I do not condemn the life of courtiers."[62] On the one hand, Peter admits that a serious physical illness caused him to practice *contemptus mundi* toward a world epitomized by court life. On the other hand, he is aware of his contradictory intertextuality, when he writes "'I shall be convicted of having written diverse and perhaps contrary things in this letter and in the one I previously sent you.'"[63]

Peter of Blois has puzzled scholars with a number of letters addressed by one Peter of Blois to another. Raby interprets the latter as a namesake of the famous Peter, whereas Peter Dronke reports that historians have not been able to identify him.[64] Reto Bezzola has suggested that Peter set the letters up in the trial framework of the ancient poets, such as Callimachus and Lucian adumbrating Petrarch's *Secretum*.[65] If this is the case, Peter of Blois, like Guibert de Nogent, presents a very distinct example of intra-auctoriality by fabricating two author personae representing contradictory literary views. For instance, the proper persona representative of the spirit of the age approaches the poet thus:

> quid tibi ad vanitates et insanias falsas? quid tibi ad deorum gentilium fabulosos amores, qui debueras esse organum veritatis? . . . et quae insania est de Hercule et Jove canere fabulosa: et a

---

Grace of Him who set me apart from my mother's womb, I put away such things when I became a man . . . *omit entirely the idle songs and old-wives' tales*'] (Richard W. Southern, *Medieval Humanism and Other Studies* [Oxford: Blackwell, 1970] 120); italics indicate my translation. Marc Wolterbeek presents a chapter on "*Nugae*: The Trifles of Learned Latin Poets." He classifies *nugae* as "school exercises, amatory verses, comic narratives" belonging to erudite clergymen. None of the Latin poets examined in this study are included, but Wolterbeek draws an interesting conclusion for the phenomenon: "The *nugae*, then, are documents of a most peculiar sense of humor at the dawn of the High Middle Ages. They are the pioneering efforts of somewhat isolated scholars struggling to find a medium for a secular impulse" (*Comic Tales of the Middle Ages: An Anthology and Commentary*, Contributions to the Study of World Literature 39 [New York: Greenwood, 1991] 43, 97).

60 Southern, *Medieval Humanism and Other Studies* 120.
61 Qtd. in Raby, *A History of the Secular Latin Poetry in the Middle Ages* 2: 323.
62 Dronke, "Peter of Blois and the Poetry at the Court of Henry II" 195.
63 Qtd. in Dronke, "Peter of Blois and the Poetry at the Court of Henry II" 196.
64 Raby, *A History of the Secular Latin Poetry in the Middle Ages* 2: 324.
65 Qtd. in Dronke, "Peter of Blois and the Poetry at the Court of Henry II" 196.

Deo, qui est via, veritas et vita, recedere? . . . insani capitis est, amores illicitos canere et se corruptorem virginum iactitare . . . quid tibi ad Iovem, et ad Herculem?[66]

This reprimand by the politically-correct Peter of Blois is rooted in the dichotomy between the pagan lies and Christian truth, and capitalizes on the old-age topos. Raby, who did not have access to the newly-attributed poems of Peter of Blois, ascribes the criticism to the "usual school exercises,"[67] but the poem "Flora" fits the description in the passage perfectly. The reply letter by the accused Peter of Blois features a persona who is proud of his poetic creation, desires fame, and does not blame himself or his alter-ego accuser.[68]

Peter of Blois capitalizes heavily on the life-stage argument that is so prevalent in the "youth vs. old age" topos for *literati*. Presenting both sides of the issue in another dialogue, "Dialogus inter dehortantem a curia et curialem," the author simultaneously attacks and defends the court. As expected, the courtier asserts his right to wait for penitence until old age because youth is meant for joy and pleasure.[69] The "Dialogus" ties in with another of Peter's poems that delineates the age dynamic in life in general and bears implication on the literary process:

Dum iuventus floruit,
licuit et libuit
facere, quod placuit,
   iuxta voluntatem
currere, peragere
carnis voluptatem.

Amondo sic agere,
vivere tam libere,
talem vitam ducere
   viri vetat etas,
perimit et eximit
leges assuetas.

Etas illa monuit,
docuit, consuluit,
sic et etas annuit:
   'Nichil est exclusum!'
Omnia cum venia
   contulit ad usum.

Volo resipiscere,
linquere, corrigere,

---

66   Qtd. in Raby, *A History of the Secular Latin Poetry in the Middle Ages* 2: 324. ['What are they to you, these vanities and false insanities? What are they to you, the fabled loves of pagan gods, you who should have been an organ of truth? What madness to sing fabled songs of Hercules and Jupiter, and to recede from the God who is "way, truth, and life" . . . Already you have a sprinkling of white hairs, and still you spend your time on puerilities . . . It's a madcap thing to sing of illicit loves, and vaunt yourself a seducer of young girls . . . What's Jove to you, what's Hercules to you?'] (qtd. in Dronke, "Peter of Blois and the Poetry at the Court of Henry II" 197).

67   Raby, *A History of the Secular Latin Poetry in the Middle Ages* 2: 324.

68   Dronke, "Peter of Blois and the Poetry at the Court of Henry II" 195.

69   Dronke, "Peter of Blois and the Poetry at the Court of Henry II" 206-9.

quod commisi temere;
    deinceps intendam
seriis, pro vitiis
    virtutes rependam.[70]

Peter of Blois is an author enamored with writing but keenly aware of its implications. Like Marbod, he pays homage to the correct literary requirement of forced retirement for a love poet at a certain age. By claiming that his poems are the work of his youth, he can keep working on them without reprimand, which he likely did, for Dronke regards the poetic work of Peter of Blois as too polished to be merely juvenilia.[71] Like Petrarch, Blois acknowledges the concept society expects him to follow, but he cannot come to terms with it and indulges in dichotomies and contradiction that ensure that he can keep writing about the subjects he likes. His example demonstrates again that self-criticism is not a mode that prohibits but actually promote writing.

---

70   Peter of Blois, "Letter XVII ['A new leaf']," *The Virgin and the Nightingale: Medieval Latin Poems*, trans. Fleur Adcock (Newcastle: Bloodaxe Books, 1983) 70-71:
['While my youth was fresh and green
my routine was quite serene:
all was pleasure: I was keen
  on the scent of action,
quick to chase and then embrace
carnal satisfaction.

Now my age begins to tell:
raising hell's all very well,
but the middle years compel
  sober introspection;
then a man will try to plan
changes of direction.

Youth advised me to be free—
actively encouraged me;
when I ventured on a spree
  there was no restriction:
'Go ahead,' my conscience said,
  with its benediction.

Now it's time for penitence,
continence and abstinence;
now I want to learn some sense;
  henceforth I'll be graver:
I'll go straight, and cultivate
  ways to Heaven's favour.']

71   Dronke, "Peter of Blois and the Poetry at the Court of Henry II" 203.

4.7. Serlo of Wilton

I am indebted to Raby and A. G. Rigg[72] for the sparse account of Serlo of Wilton's life and literary self-criticism. Serlo (1105-81), a twelfth-century learned Englishman who lived the worldly life of a Parisian scholastic and wrote Goliardic poetry, underwent a conversion and became a monk, and later an abbot. Popular medieval accounts embellish Serlo's conversion with the following story:

> While still a master at Paris he found a colleague or a pupil at death's door, and begged him, when he died, to return to him and tell him how he fared in purgatory. Shortly afterwards the dead man appeared to him, clad in a gown of parchment covered with the sophisms of the schools. He explained that he was clad in the vain arguments in which he had once delighted, and that the gown weighed him down more heavily than a church tower. Further he had to endure the fires of purgatory. Serlo nervously made light of the torment, until the dead man stretched out his hand and touched him. The torture of that touch decided him; he deserted the world, and, enter[ed] the cloister.[73]

This popular account provides an interesting complement to Ingelard's iconographic rendition of the salvific function of literature. Vain literature and erudition would not lead to salvation but to the opposite, because the dead man's erudite endeavors are directly responsible for the inflicted pain and punishment. Serlo punctuates his *contemptus mundi* with these lines, "linquo *coax* ranis, *cra* corvis vanaque vanis, / ad logicam pergo quae mortis non timet ergo."[74] Based on the eighteen Serlonian poems reprinted in Dronke's and Jan Öberg's edition of his poems, Serlo had participated fully in the writing of amorous verse in the Ovidian vein.[75] Therefore, his supposed personal conversion elicits an intra-auctorial change, an abandonment of Goliardic poetry and an embracing of *contemptus mundi* literature, as evidenced by his composition "Farewell to the World."[76] For Raby, Serlo represents the fledgling secular literature that cannot quite stand up to the Church and the threat of damnation it holds over its sheep.

4.8. Aeneas Silvius Piccolomini: Pope Pius II

The apology tradition's pervasiveness, much like the plague, seemed to affect all levels of society, even popes. Aeneas Silvius Piccolomini (1405-64), later Pope Pius II, emulates both Augustinian self-critical models and thus participates in the first and third strands of the apology tradition. The threat of damnation, however, is not the rea-

---

72   A. G. Rigg, "Serlo of Wilton: Biographical Notes," *Medium Aevum* 65:1 (1996) 96-99.

73   Raby, *A History of Christian-Latin Poetry* 340.

74   Qtd. in Raby, *A History of Christian-Latin Poetry* 341. [I leave the *coax* to the frog, the *cra* to the raven and the worthless vanities to the vain; I proceed with logic because it does not fear death].

75   Peter Dronke, *Medieval Latin and the Rise of European Love-Lyric*, 2nd ed., 2 vols. (Oxford: Clarendon, 1968) 1: 493-509 and Jan Öberg, ed., *Serlon de Wilton: Poèmes latins* (Stockholm: Almqvist and Wiskell, 1965).

76   Raby, *A History of Christian-Latin Poetry* 341.

son for Piccolomini's two public apologies. The first was issued to clarify some theological and political issues surrounding his role at the Council of Basle, and the other was made because of "the gap between the pagan sensual libertine and the austere Christian moralist."[77] Textual evidence for these issues is spread over two documents. The first apology is contained in his 1447 address as bishop to the Rector of the University of Frankfurt—*Commentaries on the Council of Basle*:

> I am but a man and therefore born to sin; I have gone astray, and am fully aware of it. And I give thanks to God who rescued me from further error. No one who reads my writings will deem that I was so perfectly convinced, so entirely rooted in my opinions, as to be incapable of change. It were unfortunate for men if they could not alter their judgements! Augustine denounced the books he had written. We are free agents while life lasts, and are judged by our final state of mind; the evildoer may find salvation by remorseful repentance. In the spirit of Saul going to Damascus, an enemy of Christianity, I went to Frankfort.[78]

With this passage Piccolomini wishes to exonerate himself as much as possible for the issues at the Council of Basle. He summons the Christian concepts of human sinfulness, contrition, and repentance to his side, thus characterizing his compositions as youthful errors in judgment. To aid his case the author extends the interauctorial bridge to the most famous sinner-turned-convert models of Christianity, Paul and Augustine, each of whom serves a different purpose. Paul exemplifies the personal side of the converted human being, Piccolomini's changed attitudes about the Church, whereas Augustine portrays the public and literary side. At the same time, Piccolomini seems unsure about Augustine's exact use of self-criticism, for Augustine denounced works of rhetoric that he used in his pre-conversion stage in his *Confessions*, but the *Retractations* is a revision, not a retraction. Retraction is not what Piccolomini has in mind, for he still invites people to read his works and find redeeming qualities in them. The reader is being drawn into the creative process again because the bishop has granted the text fluidity, openness to interpretation, a vagueness of expression that could exonerate him. Piccolomini's opinion of the life-stage argument furthermore corroborates the views expressed by Marbod and Peter of Blois. Ferdinand Gregorovius claims that, based on the universality of human error, Piccolomini displays neither hypocrisy nor repentance.[79]

While the latter is true, the former rests on shaky ground. Piccolomini, like Petrarch, was a passionate poet who had to come to terms with the role of his creative activity in his vocation as a bishop and later pope. In the preface to the *Commentaries* he professes his passion:

---

77 Keith Whinnom, "The *Historia de Duobus Amantibus* of Aeneas Sylvius Piccolomini (Pope Pius II) and the Development of Spanish Golden-Age Fiction," *Essays on Narrative Fiction in the Iberian Peninsula in Honour of Frank Pierce*, ed. R. B. Tate (Valencia: Dolphin Book, 1982) 243-55; here 246.

78 Qtd. in William Boulting, *Aeneas Silvius (Enea Silvio de' Piccolomini-Pius II) Orator, Man of Letters, Statesman, and Pope* (London: Archibald Constable, 1908) 179. The original Latin was unavailable.

79 Ferdinand Gregorovius, *History of the City of Rome in the Middle Ages*, trans. Annie Hamilton, 4th ed., 8 vols. (New York: AMS, 1967) 7.1: 172.

Quid agis tandem Aenea? Tene quamdiu uiuis poetica possidebit? . . . abieci oratorios codices, abieci historias, omneisque huiusmodi literas ut meae salutis inimicas pepuli. At sicut auiculae quaedam ignem candelae nequeunt dimittere, in eoque, priusquam fugiant, aduruntur, sic ego ad meum malum et ubi mihi pereundum est redeo; nec aliud mihi (ut uideo) hoc studium quam mors adimet. . . . Deus donet . . . nec turpem senectam degere nec cithara carentem.[80]

It is abundantly evident that Aeneas Piccolomini was an ardent writer,[81] who, like Petrarch, recognized both the destructive and the redemptive nature of literature, but the vagueness of his statement leaves ample auctorial license. In 1442, the Emperor Frederick crowned him poet laureate, an honor that Cardinal Piccolomini displayed very proudly by signing all his correspondence "Aeneas Silvius poeta."[82] Piccolomini's generous admission that he threw away much of his writing also gives him the chance to flaunt his literary prolificacy. The one work conveniently omitted here or subsumed under the vague category of detrimental writing is the amorous *De duobus amantibus* [Two Lovers].[83] Although most of his youthful poetry is lost, this— then immensely popular—story of illicit love, which he did not consider suitable for his new position, is extant despite Piccolomini's best efforts to suppress it.[84]

And Piccolomini kept his promise to literature. In the five-year span after his first apology he busied himself literarily by writing "a novel, a comedy, many poems, and treatises on such different subjects as the Authority of General Councils, the Nature and Care of Horses, Fortune, Education, and the Miseries of the Courtiers."[85] This continued literary activity, coupled with his election as pope, prompted him to compose a second apology, the *Bulla Retractationum*, because he felt his former literary activity might compromise the authority of his new office. More than half of that

---

80 Aeneas Sylvius Piccolomini (Pius II), *De Gestis Consilii Basiliensis Commentariorum Libri II*, eds. and trans. Denys Hay and W. K. Smith (Oxford: Clarendon, 1967) 2, 4. ['What in the world are you after, Aeneas? Is poetry going to claim you all your days? . . . I threw away my oratorical writings, my histories too, and I banished all literary efforts of that kind as hostile to my welfare. But just as some small birds cannot leave the flame of a candle and are burnt in it before they can escape, even so do I come back to my own hurt and the place where I must perish, and nothing, I see, save death will take this interest from me. . . . May God . . . grant me . . . to pass an old age that is neither without honour nor lacking a lyre'] (Hay and Smith 3, 5).

81 For Piccolomini's defense of literature, see Albert R. Baca, "Enea Silvio Piccolominis Verteidigung der Literatur," *Antike und Abendland* 17 (1971): 162-72.

82 R. J. Mitchell, *The Laurels and the Tiara: Pope Pius II 1458-1464* (Garden City, NY: Doubleday, 1962) 76 and Albert A. Baca, trans., introduction, *Selected Letters of Aeneas Silvius Piccolomini* (Northridge, CA: San Fernando Valley State College, 1969) xi-xiv; here xii.

83 See the new edition of an English version of *De duobus amantibus*: *The Goodli History of the Ladye Lucres of Scene and of her Lover Eurialus*, ed. E. J. Morrall, Early English Text Society 308 (Oxford: Oxford UP, 1996).

84 Cecilia M. Ady, *Pius II (Aeneas Silvius Piccolomini the Humanist Pope)* (London: Methuen, 1913) 281. For an account of its influence on Spanish golden-age literature, see Keith Whinnom's "*Historia*"': "Pius II did all in his power to suppress it, and, albeit posthumously, achieved some measure of success in this, for most of the copies of the various editions of the *Opera omnia* held by the Biblioteca Nacional lack *De duobus amantibus*, dutifully excised by friars who countersign the mutilation and quote the Papal authority for their censorship" ("The *Historia de Duobus Amantibus* of Aeneas Sylvius Piccolomini (Pope Pius II) and the Development of Spanish Golden-Age Fiction" 248).

85 Ady, *Pius II (Aeneas Silvius Piccolomini the Humanist Pope)* 281.

document deals with his errors at Basle, which he would have strongly wished to have erased from memory, whereas the other half attempts to contextualize his literary creativity:

> Delicta iuuentutis meae, & ignorantias ne memineris, & c. Pudet erroris, poenitet male fecisse, & male dictorum scriptorumque, uehementer poenitet: plus scripto, quam facto nocuimus. Sed quid agamus? Scriptum et semel emissum uolat irreuocabile uerbum. Non sunt in potestate nostra scripta, quae in multas inciderunt manus, & uulgo leguntur. utinam latuissent quae sunt edita. nam si futuro in seculo manserint, & aut malignas mentes inciderint, aut incautas fortasse scandalum patientur. . . . Cogimur igitur, dilecti filii, beatum Augustinum imitari, qui, cum aliqua in suis uoluminibus erronea inseruisset, retractationes edidit. Humilis, & probatissimi uir ingenii, qui suas ineptias uerecunde confiteri, ac corrigere, quam impudenter defendere maluit. Idem & nos faciemus: confitebimur ingenue ignorantias nostras, ne per ea, quae scripsimus, iuuenes error irrepat, qui possit in futurum Apostolicam sanctam sedem oppugnare.[86]

The Pope varies several of the apology topoi examined so far. He contextualizes his self-criticism as errors of his youth, although his literary output has been high up to that point. He is trying to manipulate his audience into thinking that his intra-auctorial skin-shedding had started earlier than it did. The author joins ranks with Ovid and Marbod in granting the text autonomy after it has been released; that process implicates the reader, who has the power to interpret the text according to his or her disposition. Pius II uses this strategy to establish a certain distance between himself and the text. The third manipulation connects interauctorially to Augustine; although Pius mentions Paul in the *Bulla Retractationum* in the same vein as in the *Commentary*, in this case the Pope wants to impress upon his readers that he is indeed emulating Augustine's *Retractations* by confessing in shame and correcting, but not defending. Augustine, however, approached his subject with much more detachment, devoid of shame, correcting but also heavily defending what he had written. Also, Augustine's remedy was not silence but continued literary activity in the service of God, which would make Pius' offer the wrong strategy.

Piccolomini places even greater emphasis on the reader in the creative triangle between the author, the text, and the reader when he pleads that the audience should favor his later person over his former, thus explicitly exemplifying the concept of intra-auctoriality in the "youth vs. old-age" topos. Pius pleads thus:

---

86 Aeneas Sylvius Piccolomini (Pius II), "Bulla Retractationum," *Opera Omnia* (Reprint; Frankfurt: Minerva, 1967) 1-8; here 1. [O Lord, do not think about the misdemeanors of my youth and my ignorance. I am ashamed of my error, I regret my bad words and writings, I regret them immensely; I have sinned more through my writings than my actions. But what should We do? One cannot recall the written and sent-out word. That writings that have fallen into many hand and are widely ready are not under my control. I wish that what has appeared had remained hidden, for if it should remain in the future and incise the minds of either the wicked or the uncautious, it may meet with scandal. . . . We are compelled, dear sons, to imitate St. Augustine, who, since he had inserted some erroneous material in his volumes, produced retractations. Being a humble man and of upright mind, he preferred to confess with shame his ineptitudes and to correct them than to defend them imprudently. And we will do likewise: We will ingenuously confess our ignorances lest through what we wrote as a youth an error will creep in that could harm the holy apostolic see in the future].

> Si quid aduersus hanc doctrinam inueneritis aut in dialogis, aut in epistolis nostris, quae plures a nobis sunt editae, aut in aliis opusculis nostris (multa enim scripsimus adhuc iuuenes) respuite atque contemnite. Sequimini quae nunc dicimus & seni magis, quam iuueni credite, nec priuatum hominem pluris facite, quam Pontificem. Aeneam rejicite, Pium recipite. . . . Dicent fortasse aliqui cum Pontificatu hanc nobis opinionem aduenisse, & cum dignitate mutatam esse sententiam.[87]

This plea, which Keith Whinnom denies the validity of a "Pauline or Augustine palinode, a change of heart marked by his ordination,"[88] mirrors the most-marked intra-auctorial dichotomy. The author wants to convey the change in his creativity with the assumption of a new name, much like Paul who used to be Saul. It should be noted that Pius uses the conditional mode to express rejection of his works, a mode that is not inclusive and affirms that he did make worthwhile compositions. The gap in credibility between the youthful private person, who should be given less credit than the mature public pope, contains an interesting fallacy that ties in with Piccolomini's remark from the *Commentaries,* in which he postulates that a person's final disposition in the eyes of God counts more than previous ones. Credibility should naturally be higher in an author's youth when he is most likely still a private person, although the act of writing to an audience makes literary creation invariably public and therefore inhibited. The Pope's apology is an expression of religious/political correctness, made by a public person who had a purpose to achieve. By its very nature it is more highly suspect. The Pope even tries to counteract his critics by revealing his possible motive. He needs to do so because they might remember his profession in the *Commentaries* of undying love and dedication to poetry, which only death could take from him. The papacy is then forcing him to renounce it himself, although he is still able to show off his proficiency in the process.

In order to elude his critics and to prove his sincerity, Pius gives an account of his life, especially the incident at Basle. He describes his literary activity at Basle thus:

> scripsimus epistolas, & opuscula. hoc omnibus passim datur: docti et indocti scribunt: & quae scripsit ipse, nemo contemnit, nisi editionis feruorem tempus extinxerit. nobis placebant scripta nostra more poetarum, qui poemata sua tanquam filios amant. Nec in Basilea quenqua jouens ebamus qui ea damnaret: probant enim similia similes: applaudebamus nobis ipsis, & in editionibus nostris gloriabamur.[89]

Pius is the only self-critical author who admits that the rejection of one's creation is unnatural and has to be brought on by the lapse of time. His analogy between poetic

---

87 Piccolomini (Pius II), "Bulla Retractationum" 2-3. [If you should find anything against this teaching either in my dialogues or in my many published letters, or in other works of ours—for we wrote a lot as a youth—reject and despise it; heed what we say now and give more credit to the old man than the young man; do not esteem the private person higher than the pope. Reject Aeneas and accept Pius. . . . Some will maybe say that we assimilated this opinion with the papacy and changed our opinion with the office].

88 Whinnom, "The *Historia de Duobus Amantibus*" 246.

89 Piccolomini (Pius II), "Bulla Retractationum" 4. [We wrote letters and small compositions, as anyone can do. Scholars and uneducated people alike write and no one despises what he himself has written, unless time dampens his fervor to publish. We delighted in our works, like the poets who love their poems like children. Aside from that there was no one at Basle who would have rejected them because birds of a feather flock together. Therefore, we applauded ourselves and triumphed at the appearance of our works].

works and children underscores the creative engendering power of the author, but also functions as an apologetic device to reduce auctorial responsibility. He qualifies his accountability even further by accusing his fellow clergymen of not having criticized him at that time and ends the *Bulla Retractationum* with the same conditional sentence he employed earlier: "Si qua uel uobis, uel aliis conscripsimus aliquando, quae huic doctrinae repugnent, illa, tanquam erronea, & iuuenilis animi parum pensata iudica, reuocamus, arque omnino respuimus."[90] Once more, the self-criticism is conditional, thus partial, hypocritical, and political in purpose. It is evident that Piccolomini had been writing all his life, and, judging from his own statements, he would not have produced the various apologies had the tiara not forced the lyre out of his hand.

Understandably, all of these Latin authors granting us a glimpse into the makings of their literary minds are clergymen. After the twelfth century, Latin examples of apologies become more scarce because vernacular literature emerged as universities proliferated[91] and ancient texts were newly appreciated in the twelfth-century Renaissance. The late Latin example of Piccolomini can be explained by his clerical office. It also has to be noted that both Petrarch and Ramon Llull produced Latin apologies in the thirteenth and fourteenth century that will be treated in the appropriate vernacular chapters.

Overall, the medieval Latin poets in their interauctorial references to Augustine parallel the Graeco-Roman poets in their allusions to Stesichorus as their father of the literary apology. But because the ramifications of Augustine's self-criticism in the Christian realm are more complex, its cornerstone function is more important than Stesichorus' in antiquity. Augustine's models, like Stesichorus', however, are manipulated by the emulating poets, who fit them to their own purposes. The first strand of the apology tradition has furthermore undergone a subtle change from antiquity to the high and then late Middle Ages. For the Christian writer of late antiquity the goal was to triumph over the pagan writers and their works. The contrast evoked by many of those authors culminates in the issue of glory and praise; if the vacuous pagan poets could gain fame, the Christian writer, who spreads the truth, should be able to gain fame and possibly salvation more easily. Despite self-criticism, the overall tone is positive and hopeful. For the medieval Latin authors the contrast is still alive and well, but its dynamic has been altered. Although salvation is the ultimate goal, it is often expressed in negative terms. Salvation is desired covertly, but overtly the fear of damnation becomes the *modus operandi*, a fear that influences the denigration of women-specific youthful literature. As seen in Piccolomini, that fear later vanishes completely. In the next chapter the apology tradition moves toward *contemptus mundi*.

---

90 Piccolomini (Pius II), "Bulla Retractationum" 8. [If we have ever written anything to you [the faculty at the University of Cologne] or to others that goes against this teaching, we revoke it as entirely erroneous and the fruit of a lack of contemplation in our younger years].

91 Bolgar, "The Teaching of Rhetoric in the Middle Ages" 84.

CHAPTER 5

The German Tradition:
The World behind, the Cross before Me

Julius Schwietering, compiler of medieval expressions of humility, posits that German authors apologize for a sinful literary youth because of Christianity's ongoing battle with the educational *trivium* and the ensuing ambivalent situation in which the grammar and rhetoric learned from classical literature could only be applied to the glorification of Christianity and not used in the context in which they were studied.[1] Although this tension still underlies German self-critical literature, the German tradition's primary focus has become *contemptus mundi*. For the German medieval poet, the important dichotomy is the "Poet and God," not the poet and a worldly patron.[2] But most authors utilizing apologies in their works appeal equally to an earthly audience, especially when their work is intended to fulfill a dual purpose and effect a spiritual uplift in their listeners or readers. The emphasis on *contemptus mundi* in German is the byproduct of a generic focus in the tradition. Whereas so far in this study the "enemy" has been classical literature and to a degree amorous writings, German literature presents us with contemporary, vernacular "foes" in the form of the courtly epic, the *Minnelied*, and the *Spielmannslied*, all of which flourished in the twelfth century.[3] Thus we find in the German examples an intra-auctorial opposition to those genres, which explains why the German manifestation of the tradition divides into two generic groups: prologues to saints' legends and biblical poetry as well as lyrical poetry.[4] For

---

1   Julius Schwietering, *Die Demutsformel mittelhochdeutscher Dichter* (Berlin: 1921) 76-77. Nikolaus Henkel provides a list of the texts which had been used between the ninth and fifteenth/sixteenth centuries in German schools. Among those were the pagan writers Terence, Horace, Vergil, Cicero, Sallust, Ovid, Persius, Juvenal, Lucan, Statius, Seneca, Cato, and Avian (*Deutsche Übersetzungen lateinischer Schultexte: Ihre Verbreitung und Funktion im Mittelalter und in der frühen Neuzeit* [Munich: Artemis Verlag 1988] 57-58). For the entire curriculum list see Henkel 56-64. Also see Peter Stotz for an account of versifying as part of the medieval curriculum ("Dichten als Schulfach—Aspekte mittelalterlicher Schuldichtung," *Mittellateinisches Jahrbuch* 16 [1981]: 1-16) and specifically for Ovid, Ralph J. Hexter, *Ovid and Medieval Schooling: Studies in Medieval School Commentaries on Ovid's* Ars Amatoria, Epistulae ex Ponto, *and* Epistulae Heroidum (Munich: Arbeo-Gesellschaft, 1986).

2   Julius Schwietering, "The Origins of the Medieval Humility Formula," *Publications of the Modern Language Association* 69 (1954): 1279-91; here 1280.

3   W. Scherer, *A History of German Literature*, trans. F. C. Conybeare, ed. F. Max Müller (New York: Haskell House, 1971) 1: 73, 94, 135.

4   In his dissertation, *Einleitungen der altdeutschen Epen* (Bonn: Carl Georgi, 1908), Richard Ritter extensively analyzes introductory statements of medieval German epic poets. Some of his findings are as follows: most Old High German poets go *in medias res* or waste only a few words (5). Poets ask God to open their mouths, to give them the correct frame of mind, to enable them to speak the truth, to help them so that the work would honor God and the saints and to make people

the German epic poets Hartmann von Aue, Konrad von Fußesbrunnen, Ulrich von Türheim, and Rudolf von Ems, intertextual statements pursue an intratextual purpose by rejecting courtly literature and the courtly world in order to heighten the effect of the Christian tales. The lyric poets Walther von der Vogelweide and Neidhart von Reuental grapple with their role as *Minnesänger* und *Spielmann*. All of the German authors fit into the first strand of apologies, the ones made to divinity, and thus carry on Augustine's legacy of the *Confessions*. They enlist *contemptus mundi*, the "youth vs. old-age" dichotomy, and statements about the instability and sinfulness of both the world and themselves in order to propose an atonement with words that would facilitate their salvation.[5]

5.1. Hartmann von Aue

The *contemptus mundi* and confession of literary sins in Hartmann von Aue's (c. 1165-1220) *Gregorius* can be both placed in and illuminated by his intra-auctorial development. Although Volker Schupp maintains that Hartmann's intertextual references do not permit an integration of his *Gregorius* into his oeuvre without question marks, Karl Lachmann's chronology of his major works—"Das Büchlein," *Erec*, *Gregorius*, *Armer Heinrich*, and *Iwein*—demonstrates a circular intra-auctorial progression.[6] Hartmann

---

better and instruct them (9). The poets often admit that, because of their sinfulness, they are not good enough to fulfill the task, and because of their ineptitude they are not up to it (15). God is more often mentioned than Christ (33). The poets revere Mary as the Virgin and the Lady (34). Often the poets request that the audience pray for their salvation with the emphasis that God would also save the merciful petitioner (36). Aside from admissions of ineptitude, poets often confess to their audience that they do not have a good enough command of the language, especially courtly speech, that their versification is not up to par, or that the present work is their first endeavor (49-50). Even if the authors display a certain modesty and subjugate themselves to their audience, they are very conscious of their value and dignity as didactic instruments (55). Some poets, like the ones in this chapter, regard their compositions as an act of penance (74). Similarly, Käthe Iwand examines how medieval German poets close their epics. According to her, most epics conclude with a reference to God (*Die Schlüsse der mittelhochdeutschen Epen* [Berlin: Emil Ebering, 1922] 16). More references to Mary begin to appear with the rise of the Marian cult (50). Expressions of auctorial pride, such as names, are often contrasted with admission of poetic failure (104). And Volker Mertens links the self-criticism to the genre of the legend (*Gregorius Eremita: Eine Lebensform des Adels bei Hartmann von Aue in ihrer Problematik und ihrer Wandlung in der Rezeption* [Munich: Artemis Verlag, 1978] 77).

5   As evident so far, the topos of youthful auctorial sins dates back further than the Latin legends, in which authors started to name themselves mostly in epilogues, as Eckart Conrad Lutz speculates (*Rhetorica Divina: Mittelhochdeutsche Prologgebete und die rhetorische Kultur des Mittelalters* [Berlin: Walter de Gruyter, 1984] 96).

6   Volker Schupp, "Gregorius-*der guote sündaere* unter Rittern, Mönchen und Devoten," *Bild und Gedanke: Festschrift für Gerhart Baumann zum 60. Geburtstag*, eds. Günter Schnitzler et al. (Munich: Wilhelm Fink, 1980) 165-86; here 170 and J. C. de Jong, *Hartmann von Aue als Moralist in seinen Artusepen* (Amsterdam: Wed. G. van Soest N. V., 1964) 9. For further discussion of Hartmann's chronology also, see Eduard Sievers, "Zur inneren und äußeren Chronology

commences with a treatise on love and an Arthurian romance; he then turns to the diametrically-opposed story of the world-negating penitent Gregorius; balances out his otherworldly vision in the *Armer Heinrich*;[7] and finally returns to the Arthurian epic, despite his rejection of it and his self-chastisement in the *Gregorius*. This circularity should mute all assumptions of a possible deathbed confession.[8] Actually, in the prologue to the *Gregorius*, his most elaborate one, Hartmann attacks the concept of near-death repentance and professes his youthful literary sins and enslavement to the world:

Mîn herze hât betwungen
dicke mîne zungen
daz si des vil gesprochen hât
daz nâch der werlde lône stât:
daz rieten im diu tumben jâr.
nû weiz ich daz wol vür wâr:
swer durch des helleschergen rât
den trôst ze sîner jugent hât
daz er dar ûf sündet,
als in diu jugent schündet,
und er gedenket dar an:
'dû bist noch ein junger man,
aller dîner missetât
der wirt noch vil guot rât:
du gebüezest si in dem alter wol',
der gedenket anders danne er sol.[9]

---

der Werke Hartmanns von Aue," *Festgabe Philipp Strauch*, eds. Georg Baesecke and Ferdinand Joseph Schneider (Halle: Max Niemeyer, 1932) 53-66. See also, Will Hasty, *Adventures in Interpretation: The Works of Hartmann von Aue and Their Critical Reception* (Columbia, SC: Camden House, 1996).

7   Helmut de Boor, *Die höfische Literatur: Vorbereitung,Blüte, Ausklang, 1170-1250,* 9th ed. (Munich: C. H. Beck, 1974) 80.

8   Walter Haug, *Literaturtheorie im Deutschen Mittelalter von den Anfängen bis zum Ende des 13. Jahrhunderts: Eine Einführung* (Darmstadt: Wissenschaftliche Buchgesellschaft, 1985) 134. Helmut de Boor postulates that Hartmann's shift to penitential material was influenced by biographical circumstances, such as the death of his lord and the poet's decision to join the crusades, which resulted in a spiritual crisis out of which the *Gregorius* was born (*Die höfische Literatur* 73-74).

9   Hartmann von Aue, *Gregorius*, ed. Hermann Paul, 13th ed. (Tübingen: Max Niemeyer, 1984) lines 1-16. [My heart has often overcome my tongue, so that it has often spoken of that which inclines toward the reward of the world: that is what the naive years advised it to do. Now I know this truly: anyone who has sinned, through the advice of the devil, the consolation in his youth, when youth pressed hard on him, and thinks: "You are still a young man, all your misdeeds will still be taken care of eventually; you can still do penance for them in your old age" is not thinking as he should]. In his article about Hartmann's prologues and epilogues, Siegfried Grosse reaches the conclusion that there the poet, much like his Hellenistic predecessors, can express himself personally and address his audience directly ("Beginn und Ende der erzählenden Dichtungen Hartmanns von Aue," *Hartmann von Aue*, eds. Hugo Kuhn and Christoph Cormeau, Wege der Forschung 359 [Darmstadt: Wissenschaftliche Buchgesellschaft, 1973] 172-94; here 173). In contrast, Olive Sayce raises the question of the narrator in Middle High German works and how much of the "I" in the *Gregorius* prologue could actually be attributed to the poet. The fact that the prologue is spoken by an "I" until line 170 and then Hartmann von Aue is named as the author

The phrase "diu tumben jâr" has traditionally been interpreted as Hartmann's sinful youth, but Sayce asserts that age references are less biographical than appropriate for the topic; in the prologue to his "Klage," Hartmann calls himself a "jungelinc" [a youth], since that age is suitable for the young lover he portrays in the work.[10] In his self-critical stance on worldly fame and glory, Hartmann insinuates that the probably courtly audience is equally guilty, since they obviously wanted to hear the sinful creations.[11] *Minnelieder* and courtly romances (the Arthurian *Erec*) were exercises in futility,[12] but the author's redirection of his material is reflected in his change of focus from a worldly audience to a heavenly one. Furthermore, Hartmann exposes the fallacy inherent in the life-stage argument and its ensuing emphasis on repentance when the author gets older, as well as in the subsequent and predictable intra-auctorial redirection. Because Hartmann appears concerned with his salvation and the salvation of his fellow Christians, he inadvertently criticizes this lackadaisical approach in the works of Marbod de Rennes, Peter of Blois, and Guto'r Glyn, who all discuss the issue of a calculatedly late repentance.

Since no one knows the hour of one's death, Hartmann unmasks the speciousness of the dichotomy between youth as the time for sinning and old age as the time for repentance, and intends to atone while he is still young. The purpose of his self-criticism is

---

in third person has been interpreted by Sayce as the dichotomy between the narrator and the poet ("Prolog, Epilog und das Problem des Erzählens," *Probleme mittelhochdeutscher Erzählformen*, eds. Peter F. Ganz and Werner Schröder [Berlin: Erich Schmidt Verlag, 1972] 63-72; here 71). On the other hand, Grosse claims that the use of the first person during the majority of the prologue expresses personal thoughts in contrast to "official" messages—in all of his other prologues Hartmann only uses the third person for himself—strengthening his theory by pointing out that Hartmann never uses the first-person form in any other prologue or epilogue of his entire opus ("Beginn und Ende der erzählenden Dichtungen Hartmanns von Aue" 177). Sayce seems to argue that Hartmann utilizes a prominent narrator in one work, something that could be regarded as an advance in narratological technique, and then completely drops that concept again in any subsequent work. Neither Sayce's view of medieval poets being completely formulaic without showing any subjectivity and personality ("Prolog, Epilog und das Problem des Erzählens" 63), nor the purely personal interpretation should be endorsed entirely. The confession, while showing personal traits and being surely meant in the Christian spirit, is nonetheless made in the context of a work dealing with penance and contrition, dictated by certain conventional events and attitudes. Furthermore, H. Sparnaay draws a parallel between Sedulius' *Paschale Carmen* and denies the *Gregorius* prologue any independent value (*Hartmann von Aue: Studien zu einer Biographie*, 2 vols. [Darmstadt: Wissenschaftliche Buchgesellschaft, 1975] 2: 73).

10 Sayce, "Prolog, Epilog und das Problem des Erzählens" 63, 70. The apology is specific to Hartmann's auctorial stance because both the French source—which is only a third in length (M. O'C. Walshe, "The Prologue to Hartmann's *Gregorius*," *London Mediaeval Studies* 2 [1951]: 87-100; here 89)—and Arnold's subsequent Latin translation of Hartmann's *Gregorius*, *Gregorius Peccator*, lacks the apology.

11 Frank J. Tobin, Gregorius *and* Der Arme Heinrich: *Hartmann's Dualistic and Gradualistic Views of Reality*, Stanford German Studies 3 (Bern: Herbert Lang, 1973) 39.

12 Mertens, *Gregorius Eremita* 78. William C. McDonald posits that Hartmann wrote the *Erec* for his patron, Duke Berthold IV of Zähringen (*German Medieval Literary Patronage from Charlemagne to Maximilian I: A Critical Commentary with Special Emphasis on Imperial Promotion of Literature* [Amsterdam: Rodopi, 1973] 112).

literary atonement and ultimately proclamation of the truth prescribed by Christian linguistic theories:

> Durch daz waere ich gerne bereit
> ze sprechenne die wârheit
> daz gotes wille waere
> und daz diu grôze swaere
> der süntlîchen bürde
> ein teil ringer würde
> die ich durch mîne müezikeit
> ûf mich mit worten hân geleit.[13]

Hartmann also stresses the redeeming quality of language, of one kind of discourse over another, as he contrasts his "idle words" with the truth to follow. In contrast to Ibn Hazm, who argues that idle words should not condemn him, Hartmann needs to fear that his "idle talk" would be considered inappropriate and thought detrimental to his salvation, although he never really admits guilt for his works. Moreover, the apology also functions in the *Gregorius* on an intratextual level. To that end, the author utilizes his confession as an exhortation and as an example for his audience, moving from his personal situation to the story of the good sinner, Gregorius, who undergoes penance for his "schulde . . . groz unde vil" (line 53) [great sin] and through God's grace becomes pope in the end. By associating his own sins with sins of his main character, Hartmann obviously draws a parallel between the two situations, implying that, if Gregorius' heinous crimes were pardoned, his own literary sins must also be forgiven.[14] Hartmann's willingness to atone with words for the sins committed with words conforms readily to the logocentric Christian worldview and shows his intention to escape the traditional pattern of belated penance in old age. Hartmann's insistence on man's obligation to render confession and atonement to God (lines 76-78) gives Hartmann's own literary confession and atonement the flavor of a religiously correct action.

In the *Gregorius'* quite extensive epilogue, Hartmann reiterates his exhortations to the reader. He warns the reader not to fall prey to the fallacy of expecting grace without "riuwe" and "buoze" (lines 3987-88) [repentance and penance] but to follow the example set forth in his work, although he hopes to attain expiation himself first of all by writing the *Gregorius* and secondly by having people pray for him as a reward for his endeavor,[15] the traditional pattern first found in clerical Christian writers. By facilitating his own salvation through the writing of the *Gregorius* and its presumed subsequent reward, and by utilizing his personal confession as an example of how penance and grace can work closer to home than in a remote saint's legend, Hartmann demonstrates the expiatory function of his narrative on two more levels.[16] The intertextual

---

13 Hartmann, *Gregorius* lines 35-42. [Therefore, I am gladly willing to speak the truth of God's will so that the great heaviness of the sinful burden, which I have heaped upon myself with my idle words, would be somewhat relieved].

14 Haug, *Literaturtheorie im Deutschen Mittelalter* 132.

15 Iwand, *Die Schlüsse der mittelhochdeutschen Epen* 157.

16 Haug contends that the *Gregorius* prologue lacks the characteristics of the legend prologue: the general invocation, the plea for assistance, the invocation of the saints, and the humility formula (*Literaturtheorie im Deutschen Mittelalter* 132). Christoph Cormeau warns against taking the

structure and intratextual purpose of the apology—and the fact that Hartmann resumes in the *Iwein* the composition of Arthurian material for which he apologized so profusely in the *Gregorius*—tend to support M. O'C. Walshe's assessment of Hartmann's intentions: "the mood which Hartmann displays in his religious writings of this period is serious, but there is no need to postulate a severe conversion-crisis in his life."[17] Rather than retracting previous writings, Hartmann lends a "deeper sense of seriousness" to the present work[18] and charts his circular auctorial itinerary appropriately to the works he was writing.

5.2. Konrad von Fußesbrunnen

Konrad von Fußesbrunnen (late twelfth/early thirteenth century), possibly a learned layman, wanted to alleviate the sins of his worldly life by writing the *Kindheit Jesu* [Christ's Childhood].[19] Like the other legend writers, Konrad has supposedly been influenced by Hartmann. Konrad adds to his only extant work a profession of his literary sin and atonement. In the apocryphal story of Christ's childhood, or Pseudo-Matthew,[20] he depicts the story of Christ from before his conception until the Holy Family's return after Herod's death, emphasizing the struggle between good and evil. Although Konrad imitates Hartmann's intertextual structure by alluding to his own literary sins and seeking worldly praise, he fails to connect the prologue with the story so that they form an intratextual whole. Konrad also focuses on the issue of truth in writing, implying that even sinners can express truth with God's help: "daz manec sundiger munt / die wârheit fur brâhte" [that some sinful mouth can speak the truth].[21] Having sinned with words, like Hartmann, Konrad is now ready to atone with words:

> Der *nacketen* ich einer bin,
> wand ich ie want mînen sin
> ze der werlde lôn unt niht nâch got.
> luge, schimph unde spot,
> dar ûf stuont aller mîn gedanc.
> diu wîle dûhte mich vil lanc,

---

narrative merely as an explanation of the prologue (*Hartmanns von Aue* Armer Heinrich *und* Gregorius: *Studien zur Interpretation mit dem Blick auf die Theologie zur Zeit Hartmanns* [Munich: C. H. Beck, 1966] 42).

17 Walshe, "The Prologue to Hartmann's *Gregorius*" 99-100; see also Mertens *Gregorius Eremita* 82.

18 Tobin, Gregorius *and* Der Arme Heinrich 38.

19 Robert Reinsch, *Die Pseudo-Evangelien von Jesu und Maria's Kindheit in der romanischen und germanischen Literatur* (Halle: Max Niemeyer, 1879) 111.

20 Hans Fromm and Klaus Grubmüller, introduction, *Die Kindheit Jesu*, by Konrad von Fußesbrunnen (Berlin: Walter de Gruyter, 1973) 1-70; here 5.

21 Konrad von Fußesbrunnen, *Die Kindheit Jesu*, eds. Hans Fromm and Klaus Grubmüller (Berlin: Walter de Gruyter, 1973) lines 32-3. For an evaluation of this edition, see Kurt Gärtner, "Zur neuen Ausgabe und zu neuen Handschriften der 'Kindheit Jesu' Konrads zu Fußesbrunnen," *Zeitschrift für deutsches Altertum und deutsche Literatur* 105 (1976): 11-53.

swâ man die wârheit las
od iht von got ze reden was.
swie gerne ich nû wider chêrte
unt im sîn lop gemêrte.

. . . .

swâ mich der werlde süeze
ûf ander rede geschundet hât
daz der mit dirre werde rât.[22]

In this passage, Konrad encapsulates his transitional state by charting the wickedness of the former author, who was captivated by worldliness and embroiled in lies, and the proposed new author, who will further Christian goals. Konrad wishes to atone for his "sweet" worldly poetry, none of which has survived[23] or else never existed, by praising God in his new sacrally-tinted poetry. Achim Masser, however, rejects the usual age topos as an explanation for that,[24] especially since Konrad does not mention his age. Masser asserts that the pious attitude that drove Konrad to assume the writing of the *Kindheit Jesu* is exhausted in the choice of topic and that no trace of an inner conflict with the religious theme is evident.[25] This contrasts with Hartmann von Aue's ability to exploit intertextuality for an intratextual purpose, a strategy Konrad's poetic skill, or lack thereof, failed to accomplish. While Hartmann transforms himself into an example demonstrating that forgiveness could be obtained by any sinner, Konrad hopes to be forgiven himself because of Christ's salvation of humankind.[26]

5.3. Ulrich von Türheim

Ulrich von Türheim (1195-c. 1250) follows Hartmann's and Konrad's pattern of intertextual and intratextual references in his legend framework. In his *Rennewart*, his literary sins, the idea of truth in poetry, and his indebtedness to the world play a role in his wish to atone with another literary creation. The *Rennewart* poses a specific interauctorial problem, since it is Ulrich's continuation of Wolfram von Eschenbach's *Willehalm*, albeit established from the French source, the *Bataille d'Aliscans*,[27] and not directly from Wolfram's work. Taking interauctorial and intertextual liberty, Ulrich starts his *Rennewart* at a much earlier point than Wolfram ends his *Willehalm*,

---

22   Konrad von Fußesbrunnen, *Die Kindheit Jesu* lines 65-74, 88-90. [I am one of the naked ones, for previously I turned my mind to the reward of the world and not towards God. Lying, cursing, and ridiculing were on my mind. The time when the truth was read or God was talked about seemed long to me. How I would like to turn around now and further His praise. . . . Wherever the sweetness of the world has pressed me to other speech, that will be made right with this one].

23   Wolfgang Stammler, *Die Deutsche Literatur des Mittelalters: Verfasserlexikon* (Berlin: Walter de Gruyter, 1933-55) 547.

24   Achim Masser, *Bibel- und Legendenepik des deutschen Mittelalters*, Grundlagen der Germanistik 19 (Berlin: Erich Schmidt, 1976) 96-7.

25   Masser, *Bibel- und Legendenepik des Deutschen Mittelalters* 96.

26   Lutz, *Rhetorica Divina* 94.

27   Eberhard Kurt Busse, *Ulrich von Türheim*, Palaestra 121 (Berlin: Mayer & Müller, 1913) 115.

and since Wolfram intended Willehalm as the hero of his work, Ulrich exercises poetic license by differing from the source and diminishing Rennewart's part.[28] Scholars, therefore, believe that Ulrich did not simply want to be an epigone but planned to embark on a new work with his *Rennewart*, in which the two knights turn into monks and move onto a more elevated plane of being, although still fighting non-believers with the same worldly weapons.[29] Christa Westphal-Schmidt suggests that rigorous *contemptus mundi* indicates the dissolution of a courtly ideal: the balanced relationship between the world and God, the fragile equilibrium between *Diesseitsbejahung* [affirmation of the world] and *Gottbezogenheit* [reference to God], is destroyed by the one-sided moralistic attitude of the late Middle Ages.[30] The contradiction between the ideal of the knight and the monk, between the *contemptus mundi* and the continuing tie to the world, cannot be eliminated. That Westphal-Schmidt rightly perceives the *Rennewart* to be a mixture of contradictory value systems and Weltanschauungen only confirms how entrenched the two opposing poles were, and Wolfram's Christian knight, having turned into Ulrich's world-denying monk, emphasizes the heightened religiosity of the text.

In the *Rennewart* prologue, Ulrich's sinful and untrue creations are contrasted with God's, the owner of the "rehten warheit" (line 11) [the right truth]:

Des beginnes ich hie beginne,
daz ich den hie so gespreche
daz ez die sünde breche.
sprach ich ie daz gelogen was,
daz man doch leider gerne las,
wan ez gezoch sich gein der welte,
herre, mit disem gelte
wil ich die lüge büzen
und wilz mit worten süzen,
daz nie tütshe bezzer wart.
sit daz dir nihsnit ist verspart,
so erkenne, herre Adonay,
daz ditz getihte din dienst si;[31]

Embedded in eschatological concerns, the apology—which is touted as stopping the sinning cycle—is directed solely to God, who would also be the recipient of the atonement for his literary *faux-pas*, either the *Cliges* or the *Tristan*. The *Tristan* is the more likely choice, since it deals with adulterous love and would be grounds enough to

28 Busse, *Ulrich von Türheim* 148-9.
29 Busse, *Ulrich von Türheim* 149; Gustav Ehrismann, *Studien über Rudolf von Ems: Beiträge zur Geschichte der Rhetorik und Ethik im Mittelalter*, Sitzungsberichte der Heidelberger Akademie der Wissenschaften 8 (Heidelberg: Carl Winter, 1919) 67.
30 Christa Westphal-Schmidt, *Studien zum "Rennewart" Ulrichs von Türheim* (Frankfurt: Haag & Herchen, 1979) 262.
31 Ulrich von Türheim, *Rennewart*, ed. Alfred Hübner, Deutsche Texte des Mittelalters (Berlin: Weidmann, 1964) lines 114-26. [I start here with the beginning, that I speak in a way that breaks the sin. If I spoke lies, which alas people liked to read, and which inclined toward the world, Lord, with this currency I will atone for the lie and want to sweeten it with words, better German words there never were. Lord Adonai, since everything is revealed to you, recognize that this poem is made in your service].

induce guilt feelings, especially since Thomas Kerth maintains that Ulrich's continuation of the *Tristan* sank from the elevated plane of Gottfried's work to an undemanding level of exaggerated, almost obscene, *Spielmanns*-like sexuality.[32] Ulrich furthermore emphasizes the concept of atonement with words by explicitly referring to "worten süzen" [sweet words], which are used in a context quite different from the "sweet joys" of the world to be rejected by Guto'r Glyn and Konrad von Fußesbrunnen. On the other hand, a healthy portion of auctorial pride is intermingled with this self-criticism; he boasts that his atoning words will be the best German words ever. Additionally, Eberhard Kurt Busse attests to Ulrich's well-developed sense of self—a sense that is based on his literary achievement.[33] Ulrich, like Hartmann, practices audience-chastisement by insinuating that his worldly works were popular. It appears that, even if we acknowledge the sincerity of his attempt, Ulrich could not fully divorce himself from the earthly realm.

5. 4. Rudolf von Ems

How well did Rudolf von Ems (1200-c. 1254) fare with this approach? Like Hartmann's, Rudolf's self-criticism fits into an intra-auctorial pattern. He moves from the *Gute Gerhard*, a story with a balanced view of the world, to *Barlaam und Josaphat*, the legend of the hermit Barlaam and his converted follower Josaphat, to the pseudo-histories *Willehalm*, *Alexander*, and *Weltchronik*, which all demonstrate a turn back to the world and a circular intra-auctorial design.[34] Rudolf uses self-criticism to underscore the ascetic tenor of the *Barlaam*. The confession of youthful literary sins, the contrast to Christian truth, the *contemptus mundi*, as well as the desired atonement are all strategies to conform to the sacramental theory of language and its requirement of Christian truth that can oppose the amorous and carnal content of both *Minnelied* and courtly romance:

> ich hân dâ her in mînen tagen
> leider dicke vil gelogen
> und die liute betrogen
> mit trügelîchen maeren:
> ze trôste uns sündaeren
> wil ich diz maere tihten,
> durch got in tiusche berihten.
>
> . . . .
>
> diz maere ist niht von ritterschaft,

---

32 Thomas Kerth, ed., introduction, *Tristan*, by Ulrich von Türheim, Altdeutsche Textbibliothek 89 (Tübingen: Max Niemayer, 1979) vii-xvi; here vii.

33 Busse, *Ulrich von Türheim*.

34 For a comparison of Rudolf's *Barlaam und Josaphat* with other renditions of the Barlaam and Josaphat legend, see Salvatore Calomino, *From Verse to Prose: The Barlaam and Josaphat Legend in Fifteenth-Century Germany*, Scripta Humanistica 63 (Potomac, MD: Scripta Humanistica, 1990). Furthermore, de Boor claims that Rudolf composed additional saints' legends, none of which is extant (*Die höfische Literatur* 180).

noch von minnen, diu mit kraft
an zwein gelieben geschiht;
es ist von âventiure niht,
noch von der liehten sumerzît:
ez ist der welte widerstrît
mit ganzer wârheit, âne lüge;
sunder spot und âne trüge
ist ez an tiuscher lêre
der kristenheit ein êre.[35]

Rudolf's metatextual remarks are controlled by the contrast between lies and truth. His characterization of what the *Barlaam* is not defines the lies of the author's youth. Rudolf's deceitful fables are aligned with courtly literature, which deals with the adventures of knights and carnal love and is rejected in favor of the doctrinal truth in the *Barlaam*, a truth that should shine in contrast to the depravity of the world.[36]

Heinz Rupp, however, finds the pure *contemptus mundi* approach too simplistic for the *Barlaam*,[37] especially since Rudolf's intertextual comments depict varying levels of self-criticism. Despite the pronounced *contemptus mundi* element, Rupp cautions against the postulation of a religious crisis, which had also been suggested of Hartmann.[38] Although Rudolf von Ems gives the impression of being a devout Christian in his works, he does not seem to identify himself with the ideal hermit Josaphat; this is evident in several passages in which the author intrudes on the narration to comment on or counterbalance the story. Rudolf, for instance, contrasts the happily retreating Josaphat with the wailing people of his kingdom (*Barlaam* lines 14691-14720). The poet's philosophy can be summed up in the term "maze" [restraint], for anything done in an exaggerated fashion disturbs Rudolf's sense of propriety.[39] Josaphat's complete withdrawal clashes with Rudolf's philosophy that God put man in this world to prove himself here and to be saved. Furthermore, by defending virtuous women against the accusation of being devils, Rudolf stands up for the life philosophy of his class and the right to a more liberated worldly morality, compared to the ascetic monkish morality of his source.[40] The middle ground for Rudolf, therefore, lies in an equilibrium between effecting good in this world and keeping an eye on the afterlife.

---

35 Rudolf von Ems, *Barlaam und Josaphat*, ed. Franz Pfeiffer (Berlin: Walter de Gruyter, 1965) lines 150-56, 16105-14. [I have, therefore, lied a lot in my days and cheated people with deceitful fables; as a consolation to us sinners, I will compose this story in German with the help of God. . . . This tale deals neither with knights nor love, which happens with force to two lovers; it is neither about adventure nor about the light summertime: it is about the fight against the world, in all truth, without a lie, without mocking and without illusion; it is a German teaching, an honor for Christendom].

36 For similar values, see Thomasin of Zirclaere's *Der Wälsche Gast*, ed. Heinrich Rückert (Quendlinburg and Leipzig 1852).

37 Heinz Rupp, "Rudolfs von Ems *Baarlam und Josaphat*," *Dienendes Wort: Eine Festschrift für Ernst Bender zum 70. Geburtstag*, ed. Walter Franke (Karlsruhe: Braun, 1959) 11-37; here 15.

38 Rupp, "Rudolfs von Ems *Baarlam und Josaphat*" 26.

39 Rüdiger Schnell, *Rudolf von Ems: Studien zur inneren Einheit seines Gesamtwerkes*, Basler Studien zur deutschen Sprache und Literatur 41 (Bern: A. Francke, 1969) 85.

40 Ehrismann, *Studien über Rudolf von Ems* 199.

In the epilogue to the *Barlaam*, Rudolf's metatextual comments illuminate the prologue. A sense of deflation pervades this passage:

> Nû lât mich vürbaz sprechen mê.
> ich hâte mich vermezzen ê,
> dô ich daz maere enbarte
> von dem guoten Gêrharte,
> haet ich mich dran versûmet iht
> daz lîhte tumbem man geschiht,
> daz ich ze buoze wolde stân,
> ob mir würde kunt getân
> ein ander maere: dêst geschehen.
> nû kann ich des niht verjehen,
> ob ich hân iht gebezzert mich:
> dez weiz ich niht. noch wil ich
> mit dirre buoze mich bewarn,
> mîn sprechen an ein anderz sparn,
> swes ich mich hie versûmet hân.[41]

Rudolf's contextualization of the *Gerhard* as unacceptable to the contemporary sacramental theory of language brings up the question of its intratextual connection to the youthful sins mentioned in the prologue. If there were compositions before the *Gerhard*, they are not extant.[42] If there were not, the disavowing of courtly literature concentrates on the *Gerhard*, as Rudolf insists. Applying Rudolf's anti-courtly criteria from the prologue to the *Gerhard* raises contradictions because the protagonist belongs to the merchant class and not the court.[43] Maybe Rudolf rejects the presence of courtly elements and the absence of *contemptus mundi* as a valid outlook on life in the *Gerhard*. Rudolf also places himself in the medieval auctorial hierarchy by subordinating his creative power to God's, from whom he derives it. Rudolf's further metatextual and intra-auctorial remarks give a deflated impression that clashes with his ardent rejection of courtly literature in the prologue. Rudolf's questioning himself about his intra-auctorial rewriting might be connected to the fact that he wrote the work for his

---

41 Rudolf, *Barlaam und Josaphat* lines 16130-43. [Let me still speak. I erred previously in putting forth the story of the good Gerhard; I wasted my time with that, which easily happens to a naive man; I wanted to bear my atonement if another story were revealed to me: this has happened. I cannot say now whether I improved: I do not know that. But I still want to protect myself with this penance and save my speaking for something else, something I have missed so far]. Rüdiger Schnell associates this quotation with the poet's confession in the prologue and concludes that Rudolf neutralizes his former statement in that he puts both works on the same level, assigning the same language to them: "versumet" (lines 16133, 16143), "buoze" (lines 16135, 16141), and "ein ander maere" (line 16137) as well as "an ein anderz sparn" (line 16142) are applied to both texts (*Rudolf von Ems* 114).

42 Schnell assumes that the touted youthful compositions of Rudolf are an illusion and that no religious crisis of the poet took place (*Rudolf von Ems* 115).

43 For a recent study on the merchant-class aspects of the *Gute Gerhard*, see Sonja Zöller, *Kaiser, Kaufmann und die Macht des Geldes: Gerhard Unmaze von Köln als Finanzier der Reichspolitik und der "Gute Gerhard" des Rudolf von Ems* (Munich: Wilhelm Fink, 1993).

patron, Abbot Wido von Kappel, as a didactic exemplar for the audience and himself.[44]

We can draw interauctorial parallels between Rudolf and Guto'r Glyn. Both poets wrote their respective works upon request, both openly discuss their endeavor's hoped-for preventative and redemptive function, and both seem to regard their writing as an expected literary exercise. Because the *Barlaam* is earmarked as a saint's legend with the explicit purpose of fighting Dame World, the author feels that he needs to contrast his and courtly literature in general negatively with the genre devoted to the afterlife. (The figure of Dame World in Middle-High German verse is used by the clergy to sum up all the worldly courtly ideals that would lead to damnation.)[45] In his intra-auctorial progression, however, he returns to courtly literature and *Minne* in the form of the *Willehalm*, which became one of the most popular *Minneromane* of the thirteenth and fourteenth centuries.[46] He has completed a cyclic auctorial design, demonstrating that his apology is aesthetically appropriate to the *Barlaam*.

5.5. Walther von der Vogelweide

As fashioners of *Minnesang* and *Spielmannslied*, both Walther von der Vogelweide (c. 1170-1230) and Neidhart von Reuental (c. 1180-1236) created poetry opposed to the medieval sacramental theory of language. Instead of focusing on meaningful *Gottesminne*, they busy themselves with transitory *Frauenminne*. Woman becomes the epitome of the authors' "this-worldliness"; therefore, in their self-critical lyrical poetry, *contemptus mundi* is personified as "Frowe Werlt" [Dame World]. Walther and Neidhart provide an evaluative metastructure that aids the poets in understanding their role in cosmic history as they oscillate between their own creative impulses and the rigidity of the enveloping medieval linguistic system. As Walther expresses it in his poem "Vil wol gelopter got" [Much praised God]:

> Vil wol gelobter got, wie selten ich dich prîse,
> sît ich von dir beide wort hân unde wîse,
> wie getar ich sô gevreveln under dîme rîse?
> ich entuon diu rehten werk, ich enhân die wâren minne
>
> . . . .
>
> vergip mir anders mîne schulde, ich wil noch haben den muot.[47]

---

44 Gustav Ehrismann considers Rudolf's expression to be another instance of auctorial modesty (qtd. in Schnell, *Rudolf von Ems* 114), whereas, instead of modesty, Schnell advocates Rudolf's self-assertive distance toward his respective theme (115).

45 Scherer, *A History of German Literature* 1: 71-2.

46 Rupp, "Rudolfs von Ems *Baarlam und Josaphat*" 31.

47 Walther von der Vogelweide, "Vil wol gelopter got," *Walther von der Vogelweide: Leich, Lieder, Sangsprüche*, eds. Karl Lachmann and Christoph Cormeau, 14th ed. (Berlin: Walter de Gruyter, 1996) 49, lines 1-4, 10. [Much-praised God, how seldom I praise you! How do I dare to sin under your auspices, since I owe you both word and melody. I am still not doing the right deeds; I lack true love. . . . Forgive me otherwise my sins: I still have that frame of mind]. Walther's canon

Walther's self-criticism expresses the poet's obligation to give praise to God but equally affirms that the poet has not reached that stage in his intra-auctorial development yet.[48] It is against this background that Walther's other apologies must be viewed.

Walther's affirmation of the world is juxtaposed with his self-critical usage of *contemptus mundi* in three other poems. Although these poems are generally thought to be compositions of his old age, his "Ir reiniu wîp, ir werden man" and "Mîn sêle müeze wol gevarn" would fit that category better. The first of Walther's examples, titled "Owê war sint verswunden alliu mîniu jâr!" ['Return'] by Karl Simrock or "Palinodie" by Gustav Ehrismann, contrasts the author's desire for the (courtly) world with his expected negation thereof:[49]

Owê war sint verswunden alliu mîniu jâr?
. . . .
waz wunders ist, ob ich dâ von verzage?
waz spriche ich tumber man durch mînen boesen zorn?
swer dirre wunne volget, der hât jene dort verlorn,
iemer mêr ouwê.[50]

Walther's self-castigation stems from the central medieval dualism between serving the world and serving the Lord. Both this and the next world are modified by the term "sweet," but a Christian can only obtain the latter if he or she renounces the former, which makes the term "sweet" mutually exclusive and forces the poet to make a choice.[51] Konrad Burdach sees the "Palinodie" less as a public statement than as an

---

boasts around 70 poems dedicated to women, around 90 to worldly patrons, about 20 to God, and about 30 miscellanies.

48   For an analysis of Walther's poetic consciousness, see Helen Adolf, "Walther von der Vogelweide and the Awakening of Personality," *Germanic Studies in Honor of Edward Henry Sehrt*. Eds. Frithjof Andersen Raven et al. (Coral Gables, FL: U of Miami P, 1968) 1-13.

49   The poem has been interpreted as societal criticism, the lamenting of ephemerality, or crusading propaganda (Max Wehrli, "Die Elegie Walthers von der Vogelweide," *Walther von der Vogelweide*, ed. Siegfried Beyschlag, Wege der Forschung 112 [Darmstadt: Wissenschaftliche Buchgesellschaft, 1971] 190-209; here 194). For other poems in that penitential mood, see F. W. Wentzlaff-Eggebert, *Kreuzzugsdichtung des Mittelalters: Studien zu ihrer geschichtlichen und dichterischen Wirklichkeit* (Berlin: Walter de Gruyter, 1960).

50   Walther von der Vogelweide, "Owê war sint verswunden alliu mîniu jâr?," *Walther von der Vogelweide: Leich, Lieder, Sangsprüche*, eds. Karl Lachmann and Christoph Cormeau, 14th ed. (Berlin: Walter de Gruyter, 1996) 264, lines I.1, II.14-17. [Alas, where have all my years gone? . . . Is it any wonder if I am totally desperate? What am I, naive man, saying in my anger? Whoever follows this joy will have lost the other one. Always more, alas].

51   For the supporters of the poem as a crusading slogan, the penitential tone appears appropriate (W. T. H. Jackson, "The Ambivalent Image in the Poetry of Walther von der Vogelweide," *Spectrum Medii Aevi: Essays in Early German Literature in Honor of George Fenwick Jones*, ed. William C. McDonald [Göppingen: Kümmerle, 1983] 157-76; here 172). For Max Wehrli, on the other hand, Walther possesses the ability to assign importance to both the earthly and the heavenly realm, providing a poetic progression from lamentation, to accusation, to retraction and to solicitation for the crusade ("Die Elegie Walthers von der Vogelweide" 195); according to that view the self-criticism serves as ploy to draw the attention of the would-be crusaders to the important eschatological realities.

intra-auctorial comment, the poet's swan song and tragic palinode to an essential part of his life, his vain endeavors towards unimportant worldly affairs. One can clearly hear the sound of his worldly harp, shattering as it is thrust away by the poet himself; W. T. H. Jackson agrees with Burdach and labels the poem a "recantation."[52] Walther is comparing the real world around him to the "timeless world of poetry," his long-time stomping ground. Sobered by the reality of the physical world, he now seeks another realm of permanent values: Christianity. The imagery in the third stanza supports this interpretation. Walther has "awakened from the dream of the Minnesang, represented by images of spring, of flowers, of woods, trees, and rivers and . . . now embraces the images of Christian redemption."[53]

The mainstay of Walther's poetic career, *Minnesang*, and its antithesis, *contemptus mundi*, are also at the heart of his second self-critical poem, "Mîn sêle müeze wol gevarn!" [I wish my soul found salvation]. The poet places himself in the middle of several sets of medieval dichotomies that demonstrate the difficulty of serving both God and the world:

> Mîn sêle müeze wol gevarn!
> ich hân zer welte manegen lîp
> gemachet frô, man unde wîp:
> künd ich dar under mich bewarn!
> Lobe ich des lîbes minne, daz der sêle leit,
> und giht, ez sî ein lüge, ich tobe.
> der wâren minne giht si ganzer staetekeit,
> wie guot si sî, wie sie iemer wer.
> Lîp, lâ die minne, diu dich lât,
> und habe die staeten minne wert.[54]

The poet enlists the dichotomies of body and soul, lies and truth, transitory love and eternal love to chart his own intra-auctorial dichotomy: he brings into focus the potentially detrimental influence of his creative ability on his salvation. His creation with words brought joy to the world and could rival the Logos' function of redeeming the world. Since Walther's joy-giving is transitory and questionable in the Christian universe, he has to subordinate it to the eternal one and reject it as worthless, as belonging to the world. Because of the worldliness of his poetry, he cannot claim that he has fulfilled the Horatian requirement of *utilitas*. Walther, however, expresses a certain calculatedness by the word "bewarn," which is also used by Rudolf von Ems in

---

52 Konrad Burdach, "Walthers Aufruf zum Kreuzzug Kaiser Friedrichs II," *Walther von der Vogelweide*, ed. Siegfried Beyschlag, Wege der Forschung 112 (Darmstadt: Wissenschaftliche Buchgesellschaft, 1971) 117-39; here 136-37 and Jackson, "The Ambivalent Image in the Poetry of Walther von der Vogelweide" 173.

53 Jackson, "The Ambivalent Image in the Poetry of Walther von der Vogelweide" 173.

54 Walther von der Vogelweide, "Mîn sêle müeze wol gevarn!," *Walther von der Vogelweide: Leich, Lieder, Sangsprüche*, eds. Karl Lachmann and Christoph Cormeau, 14th ed. (Berlin: Walter de Gruyter, 1996) 149, lines 1-10. [I wish my soul would find joyous salvation! I have brought joy with my song to many in the world, man and woman. If only I could have saved myself from it! If I praise the love of the body, my soul suffers. The soul says it is a lie; I am mad. It speaks of the complete reliability of true love, of how good it is, of how it always was. Body, leave the love that leaves you and appreciate eternal love].

the context of averting punishment for not conforming to the Christian worldview. Furthermore, Walther's commanding the body to take the religiously correct action—to give up earthly love and reject *Frauenminne*—implies an impotence on the author's part to change things and confirms the unrepentant state of his "Confession." Opposing H. Böhm, who claims that this poem would be more deserving of the title "Palinodie" than the poem so titled above, Günther Jungbluth thinks that Walther does not have a reason to be ashamed of his worldly compositions, since his continual striving for true inner nobility now simply culminates in a turn towards true love.[55] But for Walther that dichotomy exists and characterizes his auctorial path.

Another of Walther's poems illustrates the dichotomy between auctorial negation and affirmation. In his poem "Ir reiniu wîp, ir werden man" [You pure women and honorable men], Walther describes how many years he spent as a love poet:

wol vierzec jâr hân ich gesungen unde mê
von minnen und als iemen sol
Dô was ich sin mit den andern geil:
nu *enwirt mirs niht*, ez wirt iu gar,
mîn minnesanc, der diene iu dar
und iuwer hulde sî mîn teil.[56]

The passage reflects several aspects of the apology tradition. Walther seems to say that love poetry was a matter of his youth only and thus contextualizes it as time-specific. The length of his poetic career, however, seems to argue against this. His aspiration for salvation is supported by the audience and patronage argument. He composed love songs for this extended period of time for the profit and delight of the audience who appreciated them. Now the audience can intercede for the poet, while Walther demonstrates that he is still upholding his earlier ideal of *Minnesang* and takes pride in it. The benevolence of his courtly audience should also extend to the actual poems, as Walther entrusts them to his audience in his farewell to courtly literature.[57]

5.6. Neidhart von Reuental

Neidhart has either imitated or parodied Walther's *contemptus mundi* theme in respect to Dame World in his "Werltsüezelieder" [Songs of the Sweet World] "which appear

55 H. Böhm, *Walther von der Vogelweide* (Stuttgart: Köhler, 1949) 144 and Günther Jungbluth, "Walthers Abschied," *Walther von der Vogelweide*, ed. Siegfried Beyschlag, Wege der Forschung 112 (Darmstadt: Wissenschaftliche Buchgesellschaft, 1971) 514-38; here 529-30.

56 Walther von der Vogelweide, "Ir reiniu wîp, ir werden man," *Walther von der Vogelweide: Leich, Lieder, Sangsprüche*, eds. Karl Lachmann and Christoph Cormeau, 14th ed. (Berlin: Walter de Gruyter, 1996) 147, lines 7-12. [Forty years or more I have sung of love, and, as behooves one, I was then as ardent as the rest. Now that is all nothing to me, but you alone. My song should serve you, and your benevolence be my reward in it].

57 Jungbluth, "Walthers Abschied" 524, 529. L. Kerstiens claims that "min minnesanc" refers to true love and not to his worldly songs, but Jungbluth denies that such an interpretation can be maintained (515-17).

to be serious statements of an older poet who advocates abnegation and renunciation of the world"[58] but are, in fact, highly ironic. These belong to the category of his "Winter Songs," in which love, seduction, and sexual encounters are predominant. They utilize courtly language and roles in paradoxically peasant settings. The three "Werltsüezelieder" show an escalation in their ironic self-criticism and form an inter-textual and intratextual web of comment on the poet's auctorial ability, tied together by the personification of Dame World, the old-age topos, and a repudiation of his own poetic style. The poet has experienced a sense of remorse before writing the "Werltsüezelieder":

Zwîvel mînes lônes und der werltfreude krenke
    diu zwei diu machent, daz ich mînes sanges wil verpflegen.

dar zuo fürhte ich sêre, daz er mich ze helle senke.
    ich wil die swaeren bürde schiere ab mînem rucke legen.

daz wir vil gesünden, deist von hove niht erloubet.
    jâ zimt ez niht uns beiden, mir und mînem grîsen houbet.[59]

The poet's metatextual remarks concern three aspects of the apology tradition. First, Neidhart theorizes that the questionable reward and the transitory nature of life might bring him to abandon his poetic calling. Outside factors, not the poet's own conviction, are to blame for this attitude. Second, Neidhart bluntly verbalizes what many poets couch euphemistically, evoking with words the opposite of the salvific quality of liter-ature as exemplified by Ingelard's manuscript portrait. Third, the old-age topos is employed in conjunction with decorum, which does not look kindly on either the aging poet or lover. Because the poet-lover has been wooing his lady unsuccessfully, he wonders about his reward. The implication is that the only function of his poetry is seduction, a goal that would both scandalize the court and jeopardize the poet's salva-tion. The ironic and superficial nature of this metatextual statement is corroborated in the conclusion to "Poem L 84": "wizzet, daz ich noch ein niuwez liedel von in tihte!" (line VIII, 6) [You know that I will still write a new song about them]. Neidhart is not ready to rewrite himself, for *Dörperspott* [mocking of the boors], coupled with a paro-dying of *Minnesang*, still characterizes his poetry.[60]

In this triptych of world-negating songs, Neidhart augments the theme from "Poem L 84." In the first poem, "Poem L 54," entitled "Frau Welt" [Dame World], Neidhart complains bitterly about his lady, Dame World, whose service bears ill reward:

Swaz ich nû gesinge, daz sint klageliet.
    dâ envreut sich lützel leider iemen von.
    ê dô sang ich, daz den guoten liuten wol gezam.

58   Eckehard Simon, *Neidhart von Reuental* (Boston: Twayne, 1975) 63-4.

59   Neidhart von Reuental, "Poem L 84," *Die Lieder Neidharts*, ed. Siegfried Beyschlag (Darmstadt: Wissenschaftliche Buchgesellschaft, 1975) 462-67; here lines VI, 1-6. [Both doubt at the reward and the ephemerality of worldly joys cause me to renounce my singing. Furthermore, I am much afraid that it will send me to hell. I want to get rid of the heavy burden from my back quickly. The court does not allow us to live in sin; it behooves neither me nor my grey head].

60   Walter Weidmann, *Studien zur Entwicklung von Neidharts Lyrik*, Basler Studien zur deutschen Literatur 5 (Basel: Benno Schwabe, 1947) 119.

sît daz mich daz alter von der jugende schiet,
    muoz ich dulden, des ich ê was ungewon.[61]

This passage parallels Boethius' lament over the loss of his former poetic ability. It, too, echoes several other poets' admissions that they composed under patronage, although Neidhart implies a repudiation by the court for age reasons. He is artificially separated from the love poetry he used to compose and is forced to do what is unnatural to him because of standards of seemliness. Arriving at a new assessment of his poetic craft[62] in the second "Frau Welt," "Poem L 55," he renounces worldly poetry:

Ahzic niuwer wîse
    loufent mir nu ledic bî,
            diech ze hôhem prîse
        mîner vrouwen lange her ze dienste gesungen hân.

    ditze ist nû diu leste,
        die ich mêre singen wil.[63]

The "new" songs show poetic activity up to that point and a rejection of the old-age topos. In this passage, Neidhart, who has been rebuffed by the court, in turn rejects the court in the form of his "Lady" and in the process renounces love lyrics.

The third and last sweet-life poem, "Poem L 56," reflects ironically on the first two and illustrates that Neidhart, unlike Boethius, does not undergo the metamorphosis from a worldly poet to an eternal one. First of all, the poet has made another song, thus contradicting his previous promise. Second, canceling out his *contemptus mundi* self-criticism and new poetic paradigm, he regresses to his old-style *Dörper* theme:[64]

    sô muoz ich mich ir gewaltes mit verzîhen wern.

    sî endarf mich nimmer mê an sich geladen.
    von ir dienest umbe ein scheiden sô stêt aller mîn gedanc.
        ich bin in dem willen, daz ich wil die sêle nern,

    diech von gote geverret hân
            mit üppiclîchem sange.
        der engel müeze ir bî gestân
            und hüete ir vor getwange![65]

---

61 Neidhart, "Poem L 54," *Die Lieder Neidharts*, ed. Siegfried Beyschlag (Darmstadt: Wissenschaftliche Buchgesellschaft, 1975) 324-32, lines IV, 1-5. [Whatever I sing now will be songs of lament. No one can enjoy them. I used to sing what the court liked. Since age separates me from youth, I have to endure what I have not previously been used to].

62 Günther Schweikle, *Neidhart*, Realien zur Literatur 253 (Stuttgart: Metzler, 1990) 87.

63 Neidhart, "Poem L 55," *Die Lieder Neidharts*, ed. Siegfried Beyschlag (Darmstadt: Wissenschaftliche Buchgesellschaft, 1975) 332-41, lines VI, 1-6. [Eighty new single songs, which I sang as praise in my Lady's service long ago, accompany me. This will be the last one that I will still sing].

64 Simon, *Neidhart von Reuental* 75.

65 Neidhart, "Poem L 56," *Die Lieder Neidharts*, ed. Siegfried Beyschlag (Darmstadt: Wissenschaftliche Buchgesellschaft, 1975) 342-51, lines III, 3-10. [Thus I have to defend myself against Dame World's power by leaving. She can never again summon me to her. All my thoughts con-

Like the other German authors, the poet recognizes worldly poetry as an obstacle to salvation. The way to remove that obstacle is to abandon his poetic calling, to parallel a change of heart with a change in poetry. Neidhart, however, only talks about his intentions and implies a certain powerlessness in the transformation process, for he asks an angel for help. His well-intentioned but passive author persona immediately retracts his own ambitions and complies with the request from the audience for a song, engaging in his typical verbal attacks on the peasants, a regression into the poetry that he made all his life and that he could not quite renounce or imbue with fresh motives. Neidhart tries to recover from this obvious *faux-pas* and weakness with the conclusion: "unde enwil niht mêre singen von ihr gogelheit / jâ wil ich mich rihten in ein ander leben" ("Poem L 56," lines X, 3-4) [I won't sing about their stupidity again; I am now turning to a different life]. Despite Eckehard Simon's conclusion that Neidhart's personal expressions are "confessional" and not diminished by being intermixed with less-serious themes,[66] it is obvious that Neidhart is a die-hard poet who parodies the medieval poet's dilemma in being caught between the assertion and the negation of the world.

Although the homogeneity of the German examples, both epic and lyric, and their emphasis on *contemptus mundi* are characteristic of the poetry of the eleventh and twelfth centuries in which God and the World are once again portrayed in conflict, their self-critical authors persistently utilize the characteristic topoi of the apology tradition. Christian poetry oscillates between hymn-like praise and desperate admonition, between *Weltverklärung* [praise of the world] and *Weltabsage* [turning away from the world].[67] All these German authors participate in this oscillation, marking their respective creations appropriately in an intertextual and intratextual web, uncovering their auctorial itineraries and paying tribute to the medieval sacramental theory of language. The epic poets Hartmann von Aue, Konrad von Fußesbrunnen, Ulrich von Türheim, and Rudolf von Ems, as well as the lyric poets Walther von der Vogelweide and Neidhart, intra-auctorially oppose courtly literature and *Minnesang* in the *contemptus mundi* framework. The old conflict between negation and affirmation of the world lives on in the centuries to come; secularized, it resurfaces as a fundamental aesthetic conflict between the provocative and affirmative function of art.[68] The self-critical authors fit into this dichotomy because they provoke the artistic, literary, religious, and political establishments with their art and then through their self-criticism seem to reaffirm the established aesthetics. This dichotomy becomes more apparent in the following chapters. With the increased presence of women in the French apology tradition, its explicit antifeminism is only equaled by some Spanish examples.

---

centrate on leaving her service. I still intend to save my soul, which I removed so far from God with this vain singing. May the angel stand by my soul and protect it from hell].

66 Simon, *Neidhart von Reuental* 76.
67 Haug, *Literaturtheorie im Deutschen Mittelalter* 24.
68 Haug, *Literaturtheorie im Deutschen Mittelalter* 24.

CHAPTER 6

The French Tradition: Breeding Ground for Misogyny

In medieval French literature, we see for the first time a distinction between the implicit antifeminism of the first strand and the explicit antifeminism of the second strand of the apology tradition. Apologies to God for profane literature characterize some saints' legends and didactic poetry. Like the *Spielmann* in German literature, the medieval French *jongleur* was equally condemned and prosecuted by the Church for his amorous tales and stories of *aventure*, especially *fabliaux, dits*, etc.[1] A massive shift toward apologies to women occurred in the thirteenth century, rooted in later medieval literature's renewed interest in women. At the end of the twelfth and the beginning of the thirteenth century, *Minnesang* and troubadour lyric were at their peak in Germany and France. Even women troubadours, trobaritz, composed and sang love songs, much to the chagrin of the Church,[2] which launched counterattacks, especially on the troubadour lyric, with that literary exemplification of the Marian cult, the Marian lyric.[3] Because both troubadour and Marian lyric concentrate on the idolization of women, antifeminist literature, assisted by classical and patristic influences, increased to counterbalance this idolization. Apologies to women are powered by a dynamic quite different from the *contemptus mundi* apologies we have encountered so far. Dormant from classical times to the thirteenth century, these apologies derive their theme of the mock-elevation of women to a status of power from Stesichorus, Euripides, Catullus, Horace, and Ovid. In the Middle Ages, this ironic treatment of women branches out. The particular readiness of the poets to apologize is ironically modified by Bonaventure's hierarchical concept of compiler, translator, and scribe. Poets claim these roles, which are low in the hierarchy and thus removed from the concept of the *auctor*, to avert blame and responsibility from themselves and to facilitate the actual justification and re-affirmation of the offensive misogynist stance. Both Denis Piramus and Guillaume le Clerc de Normandie oppose courtly literature and employ tactics similar to the German epic poets with their confessions of worldly works and wishes to atone.[4] Rutebeuf links the eschatologically-based apology for

---

1   Paul John Jones, *Prologue and Epilogue in Old French Lives of Saints Before 1400* (Philadelphia: Pennsylvania University Publications, 1933) 43. See also, John W. Baldwin, "The Image of the *Jongleur* in Northern France around 1200," *Speculum* 72.3 (1997): 635-63.

2   Michel Zink, *Medieval French Literature: An Introduction*, trans. Jeff Rider (Binghamton, NY: Medieval & Renaissance Texts & Studies, 1995) 34.

3   Eduard Wechssler, *Das Kulturproblem des Minnesangs: Studien zur Vorgeschichte der Renaissance*, 2 vols. (Halle: Max Niemeyer, 1909) 1: 434-35. For a discussion of theories on the genesis of the Marian lyric, see Karl-Hubert Fischer, *Zwischen Minne und Gott: Die geistesgeschichtlichen Voraussetzungen des deutschen Minnesangs mit besonderer Berücksichtigung der Frömmigkeitsgeschichte* (Frankfurt: Peter Lang, 1985) 156-59.

profane works with the apology to a general earthly audience. The post-1200 contingent of French medieval authors—Jean de Meun, Nicole Bozon, Guillaume de Machaut, Jean le Fèvre, and Alain Chartier—apologize primarily to women.

6.1. Denis Piramus

In Denis Piramus' saint's life, *La Vie Seint Edmunt*, self-criticism augments the truth claim of the saint's-life genre. He parallels the German epic poets and contrasts the truth of the saint's life with his former courtly writing activity and that of other secular authors:[5]

> Mult ai usé cume pechere
> Ma vie en trop fole manere,
> E trop ai usée ma vie
> E en peché e en folie.
> Kant court hanteie of [sic] les curteis,
> Si feseie les serventeis,
> Chanceunettes, rimes, saluz
> Entre les drues e les druz
>
> . . . .
> Ceo me fist fere l'enemi,
> Si me tinc ore a malbaili;
> Jamés ne me burdera plus.
> Jeo ai noun Denis Piramus;
> Les jurs jolifs de ma jeofnesce
> S'en vunt, si trei jeo a veilesce,
> Si est bien dreit ke me repente.
> En autre ovre mettrai m'entente,
> Ke mult mieldre est e plus nutable.[6]

---

4   Other scholars have suggested that Thibaut d'Amiens, Watriquet de Couvin, le Clerc de Voudai, and the anonymous author of *La Vie de Saint André* partake in the penitential convention. They do indeed participate in a confessional tradition, but in more general terms. Thibaut d'Amiens implores the saints for intercession for his sins (qtd. in Charles V. Langlois, *La Vie en France au Moyen Age* [Paris: Librairie Hachette, 1925] 25-26). The anonymous author of *La Vie de Saint André*, le Clerc de Voudai, and Watriquet de Couvin regret the follies of their youth (see Edward Faral, *Jongleurs en France au Moyen Age*, 2nd ed. [Paris: Librairie Honoré Champion, 1964] 155, 174, 209, 218; Achille Jubinal, *Nouveau Recueil de contes, dits, fabliaux et autres pièces inédites des XIII, XIV, et XV siècles I-II* [Geneva: Slatkine Reprints, 1975] 132-49; and August Scheler, ed., *Dits de Watriquet de Couvin* [Brussels: Victor Devaux, 1868] 113-15.

5   Denis Piramus does not only parallel German epic poets but also other French hagiographical writers who attack worldly literature by contrasting it with accounts of a saint's life (Jones, *Prologue and Epilogue in Old French Lives of Saints* 43-44). Among those, Denis Piramus is the only author who makes intertextual and intra-auctorial statements (Josef Merk, *Die literarische Gestaltung der altfranzösischen Heiligenleben bis Ende des 12. Jahrhunderts* [Diss. Zurich: Zurich University, 1946] 191).

6   Denis Piramus, *La Vie Seint Edmund le rei: Poème anglo-normand du XIIe siècle*, ed. Hilding Kjellman (Geneva: Slatkine Reprints, 1974) lines 1-8, 13-21. ['I have spent much of my life like a

The author emphasizes the veracity of the saint's life with the by-then fixed topoi of the apology tradition. His sinful past is characterized by his empty, "this-worldly," courtly writing activity, which even culminated in the poet's function as a messenger between lovers, thereby implicating him as an aide to adultery.[7] His claims about the detrimental nature of his former poetry, coupled with the well-established old-age topos, signal an expected appropriateness for repentance—a convention that Hartmann criticizes in the prologue to his *Gregorius*. All protestations of repentance and sincerity are nullified because Piramus evades his responsibility by claiming that the "devil made him do it." Furthermore, intratextual evidence allows us to compare Piramus' self-criticism to the intra-auctorial experiments Guto'r Glyn and Rudolf von Ems underwent. Piramus' admissions in line 3279 that he is the translator of the work and that he wrote it for "del eglise li segnur" (line 3285) [a church prelate] function as further distancing elements. The translator's remark represents the rudimentary application of this later highly developed and stylized topos: writing under patronage implies restricted auctorial freedom, for patrons would want the author to conform to their literary taste. Therefore, the poet can divert responsibility for questionable writings to the patron by mentioning him. It is noteworthy that so far when self-critical medieval poets have referred to their patrons they have always been members of the clergy.

Piramus does not stop at accusing himself of writing sinful and foolish works but emulates the attacks of early Christian writers on the lies and fables of pagan poets. Piramus attacks two poets specifically, the author of the *Partonope* and Marie de France, although "it is with a bit of spite mingled with regret that he looks upon the success of *Dame Marie*":[8] "Ki en rime fist e basti / E compassa les vers de lais, / Ke ne sunt pas del tut verais" (lines 35-37) ['Who made and constructed and thought out in rhyme the verses of lays, which are not at all true' (Legge 82)]. Thus the author contrasts the entertainment value of treacherous lais with the Horatian *utilitas* and *delectatio* produced by his saint's life, which he hails as a paragon of truth: "Un dedut par vers vus dirrai, / Ke sunt de sen e si verrai / K'unkes rien ne pout plus veir estre" (lines 69-71) ['I will tell you a pastime in verses which are full of wisdom and so true that nothing can be truer' (Legge 82)]. The progression from the author's literary foolishness to other authors' literary sins and from falsehood to truth provides an apt introduction to the story of the childhood and miracle-working of St. Edmund of East

---

sinner, in a very foolish manner, and I have spent my life much in sin and folly. When I frequented the court of the courtly, I made sirventes, songs, rhymes, and messages between lovers and their beloveds. . . . The enemy made me do this, and I now consider myself in an evil plight. Never will I jest again. My name is Denis Pyramus, the happy days of my youth are passing and I approach old age. So it is fitting that I should repent; I shall turn my mind to other things *which are much better and more notable*' (Dominica M. Legge, *Anglo-Norman Literature and Its Background* [Oxford: Clarendon, 1963] 81) (italics indicate my own translation).

7 None of his former compositions is extant.

8 Henry Haxo, "Denis Piramus: La Vie Seint Edmunt," *Modern Philology* 12 (1914): 345-66; here 359. See also footnote 7 in Chapter 10.

Anglia, who ends up a king after a journey to Jerusalem and several miracles[9] and who should be considered an ideal for other courtly people.

6.2. Guillaume le Clerc de Normandie

Guillaume le Clerc de Normandie (c. 1170-1230) also patterns himself after Denis Piramus and the German poets. His intertextual confession achieves the intratextual purpose of optimizing the didactic content of *Le Besant de Dieu* (1227). In accordance with the *contemptus mundi* flavor of *Le Besant*—the author actually quotes from Innocent III's *Contemptus mundi*[10]—the poet evokes the typical Christian fears of doomsday. Guillaume bemoans the depravity, folly, and sin of humanity as well as attacks avarice, rich people, pride, and the miserable state of the Church in its failure as humanity's guide through the waves of life. His penitential tenor and auctorial repentance are intended to incite his readers to repent as well:

> Guillame, uns clers qui fu normanz,
> Qui versefia en romanz
> Fablels e contes soleit dire.
> En fole e en vaine matire
> Peccha sovent: Deus li pardont!
> Mult ama les desliz del mond
> E mult servi ses enemis
> Qui le guerreeint tut dis.[11]

Guillaume le Clerc's overarching world-negating strategy requires that he renounce the joys of the world, especially his former works, whose genres he carefully mentions. Interestingly enough, we can match the author's extant works with the given genres. His proposed intra-auctorial progression from profane to literarily correct material can be seen in his *fabliau*, "Le prest et Alison," and the courtly romance, *Le roman des aventures de Fregus*.[12] The general and conventional character of his apology, however, is evidenced by the existence of the already politically-correct *Bestiaire Divin* (1211). Although the *Bestiaire* does not offend, Guillaume le Clerc seems to lump it with his offending fables. By rejecting the genre of the *fabliau* and the courtly *aventure*, he wishes to emphasize the redemptive character of his current work. That

---

9   Phyllis Johnson and Brigitte Cazelles, *Le Vain Siecle Guerir: A Literary Approach to Sainthood through Old French Hagiography of the Twelfth Century*, North Carolina Studies in the Romance Languages and Literatures 205 (Chapel Hill: U of North Carolina P, 1979) 229-33.

10 Jean-Charles Payen, *Le Motif du repentir dans la littérature française médiévale (dès origines à 1230)* (Geneva: Librairie Droz, 1967) 512.

11 Guillaume le Clerc de Normandie, *Le Besant de Dieu*, ed. Pierre Ruelle, Université Libre de Bruxelles 54 (Brussels: Editions de l'Université de Bruxelles, 1973) lines 79-86. [Guillaume, a clerk from Normandy, used to versify romance and narrate fabliaux and tales. In foolish and futile matters he often committed sins: God forgive him! He loved the delights of the world greatly and served his enemies, who fought him constantly].

12 Ernst Martin, introduction, *Le Besant de Dieu*, by Guillaume le Clerc de Normandie (Geneva: Slatkine Reprints, 1975) i-xlviii; here xlvi.

move, nevertheless, accentuates the poet's assertion that he does not wish to bury his talents in oratory and rhetoric, especially in a work focusing on such God-given talents. Ernst Martin asserts that Guillaume le Clerc was as enthusiastic about the knightly ideal in his youth as he was eager to admonish people to repent in old age, to relinquish pride, and to cultivate piety.[13]

6.3. Rutebeuf

Rutebeuf "le jongleur" (c. 1250-85), a prolific poet experimenting with a great number of different non-courtly genres, exploits the "'subgenre' of the *jongleur's* repentance for having sung worldly songs" to express intra-auctorial self-criticism concerning both his salvation and his polemic writing.[14] "La Repentance de Rutebeuf" combines two apologetic strands usually kept separate: the first, the eschatological one, and the third, the earthly one made for offenses that do not concern women. Rutebeuf's application of the apology tradition echoes those of many other poets:[15]

> Laissier m'estuet le rimoier,
> Car je me doi moult esmaier
> Quant tenu l'ai si longuement.
> Bien me doit li cuers larmoier,
> C'onques ne me soi amoier
> A Deu servir parfaitement,
> Ainz ai mis mon entendement
> En geu et en esbatement
> . . . .
> Tart serai mais au repentir,
> Las moi, c'onques ne sot sentir
> Mes soz cuers que c'est repentance
> N'a bien faire lui assentir
> . . . .
> J'ai fait rimes et s'ai chantei
> Sus les uns por aux autres plaire,
> Dont Anemis m'a enchantei.[16]

---

13 Martin, introduction xlvi.

14 Nancy Freeman Regalado, *Poetic Patterns in Rutebeuf: A Study in Noncourtly Poetic Modes of the Thirteenth Century* (New Haven: Yale UP, 1970) 6, 275. Although Nancy Freeman Regalado postulates a subgenre, she does not define the overarching genre.

15 Michel Zink likens him to Guillaume le Clerc de Normandie in his approach. In penance terms, writing worldly vanities is objectionable; quitting writing altogether and joining a convent would be preferable; thus both Guillaume and Rutebeuf strike a compromise by writing things pleasing to God (introduction, *Rutebeuf: Oeuvres complètes* [Paris: Bordas, 1989] 1: 1-40; here 24).

16 Rutebeuf, "La Repentance de Rutebeuf," *Rutebeuf: Oeuvres complètes*, ed. Michel Zink (Paris: Bordas, 1989) 1: 298-303; here lines 1-8, 13-16, 38-40. [I have to quit making verse, because I have reason to trouble myself about having cultivated it that long! My heart has great reason to weep: never have I applied myself to serve God completely. I have not occupied my spirit except for jest and amusements . . . It is pretty late for me to repent now, poor me: I will never remedy

The poet weighs his extended worldly poetic activity against projects the medieval spirit of the age would approve of, and he falls short in the comparison because he has misused his God-given talents on vacuous jests and amusement. By this comparison, Rutebeuf is rudely reminded that his gift flows from God and that He will want to find these talents multiplied on Judgment Day. The poet's sense of urgency in the first line is explained by the allegedly belated hour for penance, a concept he greatly elaborates on throughout. For instance, Rutebeuf echoes Guto'r Glyn and Rudolf von Ems in doubting that repentance can reform a heart and mind so completely steeped in creating earthly, meaningless poetry.

Moreover, the author combines his general literary apology with a particular topical instance, his polemic works against the universities,[17] making this poem one of the few examples of the third strand of the apology tradition, apologies for unsavory literary practices. At that point, however, Rutebeuf invalidates forty lines of apology with another exculpating element, the devil's ensnaring influence, which was also responsible for Piramus' plight. Rutebeuf's outcry, "je le las" (line 84) [I quit the jesting] as his conclusion is highly ironic and signals merely his intention to abstain from writing deceitful and profane works. It does not mean the end of his entire career because it is generally assumed that he composed his religious works after "La Repentance." This would mean that Rutebeuf's apology marks a definite caesura in his poetic career but that, instead of stopping him, it allows his redirection and abjuration of vain and culpable literature in favor of more God-pleasing and correct works that correspond to the sacramental nature of Augustine's theory of language.

6.4. Jean de Meun

Jean de Meun's part of the Le Roman de la Rose (1275) restarts the tradition of apologies to women. These apologies are charged with a more explicit antifeminism than the contemptus mundi apologies we have encountered.[18] The ironic treatment of women in the apology tradition in the Middle Ages appears in three generic scenarios: the lyrical poet's "auctorial" apology, the debate or trial construct—in which the poet is the defendant—and the poet's assumption of a translator or compiler role, located at the low end of the auctorial hierarchy and further removed from the concept of the auctor. Because of the shifting of responsibility, ironic possibilities abound. While most of the self-critical authors have shouldered their blame and faced the world and God as auctores, Jean de Meun, as well as other authors to come, create a more elusive

---

that stupid heart, which is what repentance is, nor resolve to make it well. . . . I have made poetry and I have sung at the expense of some in order to please others: thus the devil has seduced me].

17 Zink, *Rutebeuf: Oeuvres complètes* 489.

18 Robert Gregg Pucci's dissertation examines the unity of the two parts of the *Roman* and concludes that there "are elements within the carefully established 'courtly' structure of Guillaume's poem that suggest a parody, if not a palinode, of the literary convention of *fin'amors*" ("The Metaphorical Rose: Mythology, Language and Poetics in the *Roman de la Rose*" DA 34 [1974]: 7323A. Brown U).

auctorial concept that surpasses the triangular relationship between author, audience, and text, and meshes intertextuality, intratextuality, and interauctoriality in order to obfuscate intra-auctoriality in an almost postmodern effort to dislocate the narrative center of the text. Intra-auctorially mitigating circumstances, such as the follies of one's youth, are replaced by interauctorial references to the *auctores* the author relies on and uses faithfully, shifting any value judgment to the previous *auctor* and enabling the author to avoid responsibility himself. As a result of this strategy, the self-criticism of the second strand becomes increasingly ironic and heavily intertwined with self-defense. Jean de Meun writes to this effect when promising lovers an adequate art of love:

Ailleurs vueil un petit entendre,
Pour mei de males genz defendre;
Non pas pour vous faire muser,
Mais pour mei contre aus escuser.[19]

Jean de Meun's case demonstrates the author's indebtedness to both the compiler and the *auctor* concept.[20] The intratextual apology/defense in the *Le Roman de la Rose* occurs more than two thirds of the way through the poem, indicating that Jean is answering specific criticisms leveled against him because of the *Roman* and, drawing on the compiler function, addresses three distinct audiences: the lovers, women, and the clergy. The gap in intention between "defendre" and "escuser" adumbrates the irony in his treatment. Later in the *Testament*, Jean abandons the compiler notion and assumes the status of an *auctor*, apologizing to God.

---

19 *RR* lines 15155-58. ['I want to move aside a little to defend myself against wicked people, not so much to delay you as to excuse myself to them'] (DB 258). I am using the Ernest Langlois edition of the *Roman* instead of the more recent Felix Lecoy edition (*Le Roman de la Rose*, ed. Félix Lecoy, 3 vols. [Paris: Librairie Honoré Champion, 1968]) because Charles Dahlberg's translation still relies on Langlois.

20 Sylvia Huot contributes an interesting point to this discussion concerning the manuscript rubrications: "The association of the *Rose* rubrication with that of encyclopedias raises an interesting question with regard to the word *aucteur*. Old French orthography was, of course, highly variable; in many manuscripts, the rubric is not *aucteur* but *acteur*. The distinction between narrator and protagonist is clear enough; what is not entirely clear is whether the narrator is meant to be understood as an *aucteur*—vernacular equivalent of the Latin poets, philosophers, and theologians—or an *acteur*, vernacular equivalent of the Latin compilers. The latter interpretation is more consistent with the view of the *Rose* as a compendium; and in this case, Jean de Meun's address to the reader toward the end, normally introduced with a rubric stating 'Ci s'excuse Maistre Jehan de Meun' or 'Comment l'aucteur/l'acteur s'excuse' (Here Master Jean de Meun excuses himself; How the author excuses himself), would correspond to Vincent of Beauvais' *Apologia actoris*. Like Vincent, Jean assures the reader that he is merely the faithful transmitter of the words of others: a compiler. It is probable, however, that the ambiguous *aucteur-acteur* was at least sometimes understood in the former sense as well, especially since Jean de Meun was also known as the author of learned translations; participants in the literary debate, or *querelle*, of 1401-02 refer to him by such terms as *poëte, docteur, philosophe*. Perhaps the very instability of the term *a(u)cteur* is itself indicative of a certain ambiguity in the changing status of the vernacular poetry during the later Middle Ages" (*From Song to Book: The Poetics of Writing in Old French Lyric and Lyrical Narrative Poetry* [Ithaca: Cornell UP, 1987] 101-2).

In a *captatio benevolentiae* move in the *Roman*, Jean enlists his most obvious followers, the "seigneur amoureus" (*RR* line 15159) ['amorous lords' (DB 258)] to oppose his slanderous critics. Philosophy of language, not content, has now come under attack; the signifier, not the signified, is being questioned: "Que, se vous i trouvez paroles / Semblanz trop baudes ou trop foles" (*RR* lines 15161-62) ['if you find here any speeches that are too bawdy or silly' (DB 258)]. Although Jean de Meun asks pardon for his offense, he justifies his signifiers with his subject matter, insisting that in order to give his audience "D'Amours . . . art soufisant" (*RR* line 15144) ['an adequate art of love' (DB 258)], he has to employ a certain set of signifiers for the signified:

ce requerait la matire,
Qui vers teus paroles me tire
Par les proprietez de sei;
E pour ce teus paroles ai;[21]

The linguistic criticisms aimed at Jean de Meun by the slanderous critics focus on his use of more "realistic" bourgeois love terms contrary to the courtly language of *fin'amors*.[22] Jean couples his claim of verisimilitude with the claim of truth.

Because of its relation to the author's compiler or translator roles, the concept of truth in the medieval apology tradition has undergone a drastic change. Whereas in the first apology strand many authors utilize a lack of transcendent truth to apologize, making their usual contrast between the lies of the pagan poets and the truth of God, classical authors have now been turned into fountains of truth. Jean de Meun exemplifies this attitude when he cites Cato interauctorially: "Qu'il fait bon creire les paiens / Con de leur diz grand biens aiens" (*RR* lines 7061-62) ['It is good to believe the pagans, for we may gain great benefit from their sayings' (DB 134-35)]. He has Reason elaborate on that concept:

La verité dedenz reposte
Serait clere s'ele iert eposte;
Bien l'entendras se bien repetes
Les integumenz aus poetes:

---

21 *RR* lines 15173-76. ['my subject matter demanded these things; it draws me toward such things by its own properties, and therefore I have such speeches'] (DB 258).

22 See also *RR* lines 6928-7229, Reason's and the Dreamer's discussion about the explicit or euphemistic naming of male sexual organs. During that debate the Dreamer makes an interesting point about God's creation of words:
Car, tout ait Deus les choses faites
Que ci devant m'avez retraites,
Les moz au meins ne fist il mie
Qui sont tuit plein de vilenie. (*RR* lines 6983-86)
['even if God made the things that you have mentioned before here, at least he did not make the words, which are filled with villainy'] (DB 133). The Dreamer's semiotic argument fits with the dichotomy between content and form in the apology tradition as well as the theory of the creation of language. For instance, while God creates the earth and its inhabitants, Adam has the privilege of naming the animals. Therefore, man is responsible for language, which relates to the notion that God is the only perfect author who creates truth and perfection, whereas the human author creates imperfections.

La verras une grant partie
Des secrez de philosophie,
Ou mout te voudras deliter,
E si pourras mout profiter;
En delitant profiteras,
En profitant deliteras,
Car en leur jeus e en leur fables
Gisent deliz mout profitables,
Souz cui leur pensees couvrirent
Quant le veir des fables vestirent;
Si te couvendrait a ce tendre,
Se bien veauz la parole entendre.[23]

When they serve an auctorial purpose the fables are acceptable, especially given the background of Horatian *delectatio* and *utilitas*. Despite these accolades for truth, Jean de Meun lectures the audience on the pitfalls of written representations of reality, obfuscating the issue of whether truth can be attained through writing at all.

In the second segment of his three-pronged apology/defense, the dynamics change. In regard to women, the signified, not the signifier—content, not language—is criticized in connection with the requirement of truth. This passage is especially important for the rest of this study, since it was seminal in the pro- and antifeminist debate that ensued over it, the *Querelle de Roman de la Rose*, and harbors most of the defensive arguments cited by misogynist authors both in their offensive and their apologetic compositions. The poet, who addresses all the "vaillanz fames, / Seiez dameiseles ou dames" (*RR* lines 15195-96) ['worthy women, whether girls or ladies' (DB 258)], ironically claims he has never harmed any woman alive in his writing (*RR* line 15208). His subsequent denial of any blame rests on several defensive and evasive strategies. The poet, like Chaucer in his Retraction, enlists Pauline wisdom (Rom. 15:4) to justify antifeminism biblically:

Que, se moz i trouvez ja mis
Qui semblent mordanz e chenins
Encontre les meurs femenins,
Que ne m'en voilliez pas blasmer,
Ne m'escriture diffamer,
Qui toute est pour enseignement.[24]

The author sanctions his own creation as doctrinal and instrumental for erudition, because "il fait bon de tout saveir" (*RR* line 15214) ['it is good to know everything' (DB 259)]. Thus the critical women are labeled enemies of learning.

---

23 *RR* lines 7165-80. ['The truth hidden within would be clear if it were explained. You will understand it well if you review the integuments on the poets. There you will see a large part of the secrets of philosophy. There you will want to take your great delight, and you will thus be able to profit a great deal. You will profit in delight and delight in profit, for in the playful fables of the poets lie very profitable delights beneath which they cover their thoughts when they clothe the truth in fables'] (DB 136). The original actually reads "in their games and in their fables."

24 *RR* lines 15198-204. ['that if you ever find set down here any words that seem critical and abusive of feminine ways, then please do not blame me for them nor abuse my writing, which is all for our instruction'] (DB 258). The original French does not use "our."

The second excuse in this segment focuses on the translator or compiler role of Jean de Meun, the reteller of somebody else's stories, based on the concept of interauctoriality. The author tries to escape the accusation of being a liar by hiding behind the *auctoritates*:

S'il vous semble que je di fables,
Pour menteeur ne me'en tenez,
Mais aus aucteurs vous en prenez
Qui en leur livres ont escrites
Les paroles que j'en ai dites,
E ceus avec que j'en dirai;
Ne ja de riens n'en mentirai,
Se li preudome n'en mentirent
Qui les anciens livres firent.[25]

By equating fables with lies, Jean de Meun participates in the medieval conception of literature that is still rooted in ambivalence toward classical literature. Minnis considers the *Roman* "the greatest medieval compilation of *auctoritates* on love" (MN 197). Jean de Meun's deferment tactic to shift the blame from himself to the old *auctoritates*, who, on the one hand, were considered "authorities" and, on the other hand, were powerless to defend themselves, can be recognized as the "compiler's typical defence" (MN 197).[26] This tactic alleviates Jean's guilt in composing the work, since he is simply repeating what the masters have said and, in the worst-case scenario, is merely echoing a lie, not fabricating one himself.

In the third part of his defense against women, Jean de Meun adds insult to injury, rejecting the insinuation that the *auctoritates* could be lying. In so doing he drops the carefully raised smoke screen of the compiler and admits some original authorship:

Cil les meurs femenins savaient,
. . . .
Par quei meauz m'en devez quiter:
Je n'i faz riens fors reciter,
Se par mon jeu, qui po vous couste,
Quelque parole n'i ajouste,
Si con font entr'aus li poete,
Quant chascuns la matire traite
Don il li plaist a entremetre;
Car, si con tesmoigne la letre,
Profiz e delectacion,
C'est toute leur entencion.[27]

---

25 *RR* lines 15216-24. ['if it seems to you that I tell fables, don't consider me a liar, but apply to the authors who in their works have written the things that I have said and will say. I shall never lie in anything as long as the worthy men who wrote the old books did not lie'] (DB 259).

26 Jean Leclercq lists as the *auctores* considered by the Middle Ages "the writers of the Latin Golden Age" as well as "Lucan, Statius, Persius, and others; Christian poets like Juvencus and Sedulius; and finally grammarians, Quintillian, Donatus and the others" (*The Love of Learning and the Desire for God: A Study of Monastic Culture*, trans. Catharine Misrahi [New York: Fordham UP, 1977] 142).

27 *RR* lines 15229, 15233-42. ['They knew about the ways of women . . . For this reason you should the sooner absolve me; I do nothing but retell just what the poets have written between them,

The apology to women confirms that the "authorities" are correct. Although Jean de Meun swears that he followed his sources faithfully, he ironically admits that he is not entirely indebted to the *auctoritates*, thus breaking out of his assumed role of compiler and taking responsibility for his creation, raising himself a few notches on the auctorial ladder. The poet has furthermore amended his compositional intention, which has moved from the biblical "everything is written for our doctrine" to the classical Horatian *utilitas* and *delectatio*, as expounded earlier by Reason. The author seems to concede that, in order to fulfill his intent of profit and delight, he will adjust his material to fit that plan, which in turn would put him above the role of the compiler. Alan Gunn asserts, "[n]o mere transmitter of oldtime wisdom speaks here, but a bold and skillful ironist, a poet with a profound understanding of the truths of life and of the purpose of poetry, an artist who is the master and not the servant of the materials with which he is working."[28]

Toward the third group of critics, the clergy, Jean de Meun is the most unapologetic. The author takes the Lover's "false-seeming" and transforms it into an embodiment of religious hypocrisy by attacking the friars over the dispute between the mendicants and the arts faculty of the University of Paris in the 1250s and 60s.[29] Jean, employing the same tactic as he does with the women, denies ever having wanted to harm any religious person *alive* (*RR* lines 15253-56), while at the same time admitting his intent of hitting those religious individuals whom "Jesus apele ypocrites" (*RR* line 15264) ['Jesus calls hypocrites' (DB 259)]. The author further excuses himself from any guilt on his part should people have been injured when associating themselves with one of his targets, again providing the evidence for his innocence by implicating the previously-written word:

Onc riens n'en dis, mien escient,
Comment qu'il m'aut contrariant,
Qui ne seit en escrit trouvé
E par esperiment prouvé
Ou par raison au meins prouvable.[30]

Jean de Meun's proffered submission to the Church—his announcement that he will make changes to his work as required by the Holy Church—is ironically qualified with a conditional clause about his ability to do so.[31] Overall, one can deduce that he avoids admission of any wrongdoing by using his sources as the scapegoats, albeit without

---

when each of them treats the subject matter that he is pleased to undertake, except that my treatment, which costs you little, may add a few speeches. For, as the text witnesses, the whole intent of the poets is profit and delight'] (DB 259).

28 Alan Gunn, *The Mirror of Love: A Reinterpretation of* The Romance of the Rose (Lubbock: Texas Tech P, 1952) 57.

29 Charles Muscatine, *Chaucer and the French Tradition* (Berkeley: U of California P, 1969) 91.

30 *RR* lines 15293-7. ['I have never said anything that may not be found in writing, either proved by experience or at least capable of being proved by reason, no matter whom it may displease'] (DB 260).

31 "As I said, one should not take seriously the plea that he should be forgiven for the rudeness of his insult" (August Wulff, *Die Frauenfeindlichen Dichtungen in den Romanischen Literaturen des Mittelalters bis zum Ende des XIII Jahrhunderts*, Romanische Arbeiten 4 [Halle: Max Niemeyer, 1914] 100-101).

accusing them directly. Generally, the apology functions as a repeated endorsement of his earlier antifeminist and anticlerical satires in that the author adjusts every self-criticism so that the blame ends up in the readers' or critics' lap.

In his other self-critical legacy, the didactic poem *Le Testament* (1291-1295), Jean de Meun finally drops the compiler role and assumes responsibility for his literary creation:[32]

> J'ay fait en ma jeunesce maint dit par vanité,
> Ou maintes genz se sont pluseurs foiz delité.
> Or m'en doint Dieux un faire par vraye charité
> Pour amender les autres, qui pou m'ont proffité.[33]

This apology contains the typical elements seen in apologies to God: the youthful literary error, the "guilty" audience, who nonetheless delighted in his works, and the wish to atone with this *Testament*. The author furthermore agrees with Hartmann von Aue, Marbod de Rennes, and Peter of Blois when he claims that youth is for sinning, but the sinner has to repent before it is too late, since death could always be imminent. This penitent feeling, however, contrasts with his great auctorial pride in his literary achievement, which he says the reader should not criticize but laud. The *Testament* ends with another apology to God. Its tone is adumbrating Chaucer's Retraction because it, too, asks God to disregard anything offensive. It parallels Chaucer's suggestion that the reader turn to another tale in *The Canterbury Tales* if he finds certain tales unsuitable. Consequently, the reader/God, not just the author himself, becomes the judge of literary impropriety.

Jean de Meun is a strong author who mostly justifies himself, his self-criticism hinging on only one aspect for his work. When comparing the *Roman* and the *Testament* for their intra-auctorial content it becomes obvious that the latter repeats many of the theological tenets of the former[34] and simply reiterates most of the examples of sinful clergy and women. That comparison demonstrates that Jean's position on women and the clergy has not changed and that he keeps earthly and heavenly apologies distinctly separate. John V. Fleming does not subscribe to the speculation that the *Roman* could be among the vain "dits" of Jean's youth.[35] Since Jean keeps with the apology convention and does not identify the offending works, we cannot completely exclude the *Roman* but must agree with Gunn that Jean's recantation of his youthful literary follies implies that his own conception of the *Roman* has changed from that of a "collection of dissertations on matters philosophical, theological, and scientific, or as a rendering into French verse of 'the useful teachings of ancient sages'" to that of a

---

32 For questions concerning Jean de Meun's authorship of the *Testament*, see Gunn, *The Mirror of Love* 30, footnote 43.

33 Jean de Meun, *Le Testament*, ed. Aimee Celest Bourneuf (Diss. New York: Fordham University, 1956) lines 5-8. [I have in my youth made many dits because of vanity, in which many people have been delighted several times. Now may God give me one through true charity so that I can make amends for the ones which have profited me little].

34 John V. Fleming, *The* Roman de la Rose: *A Study in Allegory and Iconography* (Princeton: Princeton UP, 1969) 49.

35 Fleming, *The* Roman de la Rose 49.

"'carnal'" creation.[36] This does not mean that Jean would have to reject the entire *Roman*, only its carnal aspects, which would be the politically correct action; at some level the recantation in the *Testament* also annuls his mock-apology in the *Roman*.

6.5. Nicole Bozon

The Anglo-Norman Franciscan friar Nicole Bozon, living in northern England in the late thirteenth or early fourteenth century, engages in antifeminist clerical writings, although his apology lacks the notion of the compiler and is more implicit than explicit. The poet produces works in which completely opposite views of women are offered, obviously raising some intra-auctorial questions. The offending work, the *Char d'Orgueil* (1304), a vehicle for stock misogynist attacks, contains a violent diatribe against women. It lambastes their coquetry, their greediness for pleasure, and their vanity in the persona of Orgueil, the daughter of the devil, in her sinful reign, and her wagon, whose parts represent the vices. During the diatribe, women are identified with the vices—the wagon and the horses—in a sustained misogynistic attitude. His *Les femmes a la pie* is cut from the same cloth and presents a "raucous antifeminist satire."[37]

Two other works by Bozon seem to contradict the *Char d'Orgueil*: *De la Bonté des femmes* (1330) and *Plainte d'Amour*.[38] Bozon's exuberant praise of women in the *Bonté* devaluates itself by its exaggeration, which becomes at some level as offensive as the diatribe because there is no middle ground:

> Ja n'est trovee en tere ou en mer
> Piere preciouse nule si chere
>   Que vayle a femme,
> Ne charbuche q'est si cler
> Ne diamand qe dure entier
>   Ne autre gemme.[39]

The author's echoing the cart of the *Char d'Orgueil*, however, strengthens the ironic self-critical intention of the poem:

---

36 Gunn, *The Mirror of Love* 30.

37 David L. Jeffrey and Brian J. Levy, introduction, *The Anglo-Norman Lyric: An Anthology* (Toronto: Pontifical Institute of Mediaeval Studies, 1990) 1-30; here 15.

38 Three critics accept the praise poem *De la Bonté des femmes* as a palinode to the *Char d'Orgueil*: F. N. Robinson in his preface to *The Legend of Good Women* (*The Works of Geoffrey Chaucer*, 2nd ed. [Oxford: Oxford UP, 1957]) as well as Lucy Toulmin Smith and Paul Meyer in their introduction to *Les Contes moralisés de Nicole Bozon* [Reprint. Paris: Librairie de Firmin Didot, 1968] i-lxxiv).

39 Nicole Bozon, *De la Bonté des femmes*, *Les Contes moralisés de Nicole Bozon*, eds. Lucy Toulmin Smith and Paul Meyer (Reprint. Paris: Librairie de Firmin Didot, 1968) xxxiii-xli; here lines 229-34. [I have not found on land nor at sea a more precious stone so dear as the value of a woman; no carbuncle so clear, no diamond, which lasts forever, no other gem].

Pur un char q'ay charpenté
Ou tut le mounde i est entré,
    Haut e bas,
Une feme fu coroucée.[40]

Therefore, Vising rejects the *Bonté* as a palinode; Bozon's claim that a particular woman had felt insulted by the misogynistic character of the *Char d'Orgueil*[41] would put the apology in line with the Graeco-Roman examples, in which apologies were extended to specific women.

Although Vising does not consider the *Bonté* a palinode, he perceives a statement in Bozon's *Plainte d'Amour* that is completely contradictory to the vicious satire aimed at women in the *Char d'Orgueil*:

Jeo ne voyl
Si bien nun de femme dire;
Tute ey jeo grant matire
En ceo toyl.
Mes benet seient totes gens
Ke funt as femmes reverens
Pur m'amye.[42]

Vising attributes Bozon's apology in the *Plainte* to his reverence for the Virgin Mary,[43] whose womanhood would be compromised by such antifeminist slogans. Since Bozon's canon is still being developed, it is difficult to ascertain whether his then-conventional antifeminist slogans in his didactic preaching incensed a real contemporary woman, a situation which subsequently prompted these mitigating words as retribution, or whether both the antifeminism and the apologies belong to the purely fictional literary world, representing two exaggerated positions in the battle of the sexes.[44]

6.6. Guillaume de Machaut

Guillaume de Machaut, a low-born cleric, "professional writer,"[45] and one of the most influential French poets of the fourteenth century, joins in the ironic treatment of

---

40   Bozon, *De la Bonté des femme* lines 7-10. [Because I made a cart aboard which the whole world climbed, both high and low, a woman was filled with wrath].

41   Johan Vising, introduction, *Deux Poemes de Nicholas Bozon* (Göteborg: Elanders, 1919) iii-xxii; here x and Legge, *Anglo-Norman Literature and Its Background* 230.

42   Bozon, *Plainte d'Amour* lines 525-31; qtd. in Vising, introduction x. [I don't want to say anything but good about woman in that I have a great subject on which I toil. But blessed be all people who regard women with reverence for the sake of my female friend].

43   Vising, introduction x.

44   Legge points out that "anti-feminism in preachers is nothing new, but amends are rare" (*Anglo-Norman Literature and Its Background* 230).

45   Kevin Brownlee, *Poetic Identity in Guillaume de Machaut* (Madison, WI: U of Wisconsin P, 1984) 19.

antifeminism and *fin'amors* with the intertextual structure connecting three of his works. The self-criticism is inherent in the structure of his *Le Jugement dou Roy de Navarre contre le Jugement dou Roy de Behaigne* (1350), in which the author resorts to the Graeco-Roman trial framework, allowing himself ample defense.[46] The author's self-criticism and treatment of love and women are ironic because he provides "a retraction of the earlier judgment that cunningly does not refute it."[47] As with Bozon, the same question of topicality arises. Was there still an external reaction that prompted the self-criticism or had it become a matter of literary fiction and decorum? William Calin speculates that the external reason for Machaut's composing the *Navarre* was that the release of the *Behaigne* in the late 1330's might have given rise to a "minor literary furor" and Machaut might have been accused of crimes against *fin'amors* and therefore against women.[48] Machaut was not the first French poet to attack the concept of *fin'amors*, for Jean de Meun had already undermined that literary cliché[49] with a more realistic picture of love in the Middle Ages in his *Roman*, a strategy that also brought him the charge of being too unseemly in his language.

The antifeminist action Machaut is being accused of in the *Behaigne* hardly compares to the vitriolic tirades of the *Roman*, the *Char*, or *Lamentations*. In the *Behaigne*, Machaut has the King of Bohemia arbitrate a debate concerning who suffers more deeply: a lady grieving for her dead lover or a knight whom his lover has left for another man; he decides in favor of the knight. In the appeals court set up in the *Navarre*, the Lady Bonneürté confronts the poet with intertextual evidence that he has sinned against women ("Vers les dames estes forfais") (*JRN* line 811) in his writing: "Car le fait devers vous avez / En l'un de vos livres escript" (*JRN* lines 866-67) ['Because the case against you is something / You've written in one of your books' (PM 39)]. Machaut responds to the accusation without an admission of guilt: "Mais seürs fui qu'enforfaiture / N'avoie fait en ma vie onques / Envers nulles dames quelsquonques" (*JRN* lines 836-38).[50] His declaration of innocence reinforces the slightness of the offense in the poet's eyes but also ironically highlights the conventions of *fin'amors* under whose rule a fourteen-century courtly woman could easily take offense at the depiction of the women in the *Behaigne* as well as the insinuation, to quote Calin's observation, that in the *Behaigne* "the men love 'better' than the women."[51]

---

46 "Hoepffner has satisfactorily explained why *Navarre* is found out of place chronologically in the manuscripts: being a palinode for *Jugement*, the maker of the manuscript moved it up to follow that poem directly" (James I. Wimsatt and William W. Kibler, introduction, *Le Jugement du Roy de Behaigne and Remede de Fortune*, by Guillaume de Machaut [Athens: U of Georgia P, 1988] 3-57; here 33).

47 R. Barton Palmer, ed. and trans., introduction, *The Judgment of the King of Navarre*, by Guillaume de Machaut (New York: Garland, 1988) xi-l; here xxviii.

48 William Calin, *A Poet at the Fountain: Essays on the Narrative Verse of Guillaume de Machaut* (Lexington: UP of Kentucky, 1974) 41.

49 Calin, *A Poet at the Fountain* 42.

50 ['But I was certain that I had done / No harm in my entire life / To any lady whomsoever'] (PM 39). The original French actually uses the plural "no ladies."

51 Calin, *A Poet at the Fountain* 45.

In the ensuing debate, now chaired by the King of Navarre, about Machaut's unfavorable auctorial decision, several of the self-critical elements other authors level against themselves surface as accusations the debaters bring against Guillaume. Lady Bonneürté requests atonement through a reversal of opinion: "Mais de vostre descouvenue, / Qui est contre dames si grande, / Afferroit bien crueuse amende" (*JRN* lines 918-20).[52] Self-imposed atonement has played a crucial role so far in the apology tradition, and that atonement has been mostly linked with untruthfulness, which keeps coming up in this debate also. The irony of Machaut's strategy, however, is that his self-imposed atonement reinforces the justification angle of his work and retaliates against most of the anti-truth accusations.[53] The judge, for instance, announces, "Tout pour Guillaume qui se tort / De verité dont il ha tort" (*JRN* lines 1632-33) ['And this is for the sake of Guillaume, who has turned / Away from the truth, and therefore erred' (PM 75)]. Since the poet's sin was to award to the knight the title of main sufferer, the lady asserts now that "On ne porroit trouver en homme / Si grant loyauté comme en femme" (*JRN* lines 2810-11) ['No man ever is as loyal / As women are' (PM 127)]. The author, however, is stubborn on that particular point and reiterates his charge of feminine fickleness by claiming that maybe one in five hundred thousand might not be (*JRN* lines 3105-8), after which Sufficiency also confronts Machaut with the issue of truth in literature: "Car nuls homs qui vueille voir dire / Ne porroit des dames mesdire" (*JRN* lines 3133-34) ['For no man who wishes to speak truth / Can defame women' (PM 141)]. Moderation finds him guilty because of things that he did, which were "[s]imples, foles, vuides, et veinnes" (*JRN* line 3630) ['stupid, foolish, empty, and vain' (PM 163)], epithets echoing the first strand of the apology tradition. Reason finishes off Machaut with a discourse on the function of love poetry:

Se vous heüssiez compassé
En vous aucune congnoissance
Qui fust signes de repentence
De ce que vous aviez mespris
Contre les dames de haut pris,
Vous heüssiez fait moult que sages.
Car d'Amours est tels li usages
Que s'aucuns des dames mesdit,
S'il ne s'en refreint et desdit,
Amender le doit hautement
Ou comparer moult chierement.[54]

---

52 ['But concerning your false opinion, / Which is so seriously biased against women, / A severe penance is called for'] (PM 43).

53 This is especially interesting in contrast to Machaut's *Prologue* (although written later), in which he had to promise the God of Love not to slander women. The God of Love asserts that continued antifeminism could harm his standing as a poet (Palmer, introduction xx-xxiv).

54 *JRN* lines 3795-3804:
"If you had shown
Any sign in your manner
Which would have indicated repentance
For the wrong you did
To ladies of great worth,

Unlike the humble poet-narrator of his *Prologue*, Machaut does not retract anything but rather justifies the attitudes he is accused of with the blanket claim that his antifeminist statements reflect public opinion. But, like the Graeco-Roman antifeminist authors, he readily accepts his punishment because this offers him another chance at poetic creation as well as a potential affirmation of his previous stance.

It comes as no surprise that Machaut's sentence is the command to write three more poems, a lay, a song, and a ballad, mirroring the triple offense: the composition of the *Behaigne*, his persistent argument with the ladies, and his attacks upon women's loyalty. The poet pronounces his only real admission of error after the judgment, but it is not a literary one: his mistake was to take on a lady of such high standing (*JRN* lines 4195-8). Guillaume points out another intra-auctorial and psychological notion: "Pour miex congnoistre mon meffait, / Ay ce livret rimé et fait" (*JRN* lines 4201-2) ['In order the better to understand my fault, / Have [I] composed and rhymed this little book' (PM 189)]. The poet assigns art the function of imposing order on chaos, self-criticism being a vehicle for structuring his personal ineptitude with his poetic aptness. Without admission of guilt, but eager to succumb to his punishment, Machaut asks for forgiveness: "Li priant que tout me pardoint" (*JRN* line 4205) ['And begging her to pardon me for everything' (PM 189)]. Douglas Kelly claims that Machaut was willing to adjust his previous "conception of love": "love by desire replaces love by hope"; for Calin, however, Machaut does not reject courtly love altogether but seeks a compromise between the courtly and anticourtly.[55]

We have evidence of Machaut's partial penance in the "Le Lay de Plour"; the existence of the *chanson* and *balade* cannot be proven.[56] "Le Lay de Plour" very

---

You would have been acting wisely.
For the custom of love is such
That if anyone defames women,
And does not retract doing so, afterwards refraining,
He must make severe amends
Or pay quite dearly." (PM 171)

55   Douglas Kelly, *Medieval Imagination: Rhetoric and the Poetry of Courtly Love* (Madison: U of Wisconsin P, 1978) 138-9; Calin, *A Poet at the Fountain* 46. In his work on Machaut, Calin has touched upon the major division in the apology tradition between religious and antifeminist: "The *JRN* as a whole is a palinode, a recantation in the medieval tradition. But unlike Andreas Capellanus, Petrarch, Juan Ruiz, and the author of the *Canterbury Tales*, Machaut does not renounce love poetry in favor of a higher truth, the only Truth and Love for a canon at Reims. Instead following Nicole Bozon and anticipating Jean le Fèvre and the Chaucer of the *Legend of Good Women*, he recants misogyny for *fin'amor*, the inspiration of poets, and he continues to write" (*A Poet at the Fountain* 128). Calin's perceptive view needs some adjustment, however, since the element of irony contained in most of the cited authors makes it doubtful that we can assert whether they stopped or continued writing. Petrarch, for instance, never quit writing. Bozon's and le Fèvre's apologies are rather panegyrics and exercises in virtue catalogs incited by an external reason—to gain the favor of a woman—than true abjurations of misogyny. Taking these statements with an ironic grain of salt might be prudent.

56   James Wimsatt, *Chaucer and the French Love Poets: The Literary Background of the* Book *of the Duchess* (Chapel Hill: U of North Carolina P, 1968) 95. R. Barton Palmer also discusses Machaut's metapoetical dialogue with himself in the three poems examined here

obviously conforms to the task given the poet. He forges a female version of the suffering lover, asserting that "Qui bien aimme a tart oublie" (line 1) ['Whoever loves well forgets slowly' (PM 191)], which echoes intertextually both the initial conflict in the *Behaigne* and Frankness' statement in the *JRN* that women love more loyally than men (*JRN* lines 2810-22).[57] The author further suggests that "Ne que jamais, par nul art, / Soit sa pointure garie" ("Lay" lines 15-16) ['Nor ever, by any art, / Will that wound be healed' (PM 191)]; however, after moving through numerous examples of suffering and not forgetting one's dead lover, the poet concludes with an unmistakable allusion to poetic art, beyond the obvious Christian symbolism:

> Humblement mes cuers supplie
> Au vray Dieu qu'il nous regart
> De si amoureus regart
> Qu'en livre soiens de vie.[58]

The poet fulfills his sentence of pleasing his audience, but simultaneously asserts the life-giving quality of poetry by prescribing it as the way of dealing with the loss of a lover, although he had claimed earlier that nothing could heal those wounds caused by love. Furthermore, Machaut's confidence in the written word equals that of the picture of Ingelard (see page 65), in which the salvific function of writing has been captured.

6.7. Jean le Fèvre

Unlike Nicole Bozon and Guillaume de Machaut, who did not enlist the compiler or translator role to excuse themselves, Jean le Fèvre (1320-1376) seems to imitate Jean de Meun's *apologia* in the *Roman*. As the French translator of the Latin *Lamentationes de Matholeus* (1375), a violently antifeminist satire written by Mahieu, a bigamist cleric from Boulogne-sur-Mer a century prior, le Fèvre feels compelled to temper the contents of this—along with the *Quinze Joyes de mariage*—most extensively misogynist work of the Middle Ages[59] with an apology to a particular set of women.[60] The

---

   ("Transtextuality and the Producing-I in Guillaume de Machaut's Judgement Series," *Exemplaria: A Journal of Theory in Medieval and Renaissance Studies* 5:2 (1993): 282-304).
57   Guillaume de Machaut, "Le Lay de Plour," *The Judgment of the King of Navarre*, ed. and trans. R. Barton Palmer (New York: Garland, 1988) 190-213.
58   Machaut, "Le Lay de Plour" lines 207-10:
      My heart humbly begs
      The true God to look upon us
      With such loving countenance
      That in a book we'll find life. (PM 213)
59   Alfred Schmitt, *Matheus von Boulogne: "Lamentationes Matheoluli" (Kommentierte und kritische Edition der beiden ersten Bücher)* (Diss. Bonn: Rheinisch Friedrich-Wilhelm-University, 1974) 7.
60   For opinions on le Fèvre's work in the context of the French pro- and antifeminist debate, see Renate Blumenfeld-Kosinski, "Jean le Fèvre's *Livre de Leesce*: Praise or Blame of Women?" *Speculum* 69.3 (1994): 705-25; Karen Pratt, "Analogy or Logic; Authority or Experience? Rhetorical Strategies for and against Women," *Literary Aspects of Courtly Culture*, eds. Donald

author finds himself in the peculiar situation of making an intratextual comment that is actually backgrounded by intertextuality and interauctoriality, for he is apologizing for somebody else's work. Jean de Meun and his augmentation of his sources spring to mind, although A. G. van Hamel confirms that le Fèvre has, for the most part, translated Mahieu faithfully. Nevertheless, le Fèvre wishes to counteract the blanket and cliché-like condemnations of women as quarrelsome, devious and treacherous, disobedient by nature, envious, cold, etc., by rendering homage to all virtuous, loyal, and worthy women. The equation is already uneven and ironic, since the accusations still remain for most women and have not been retracted as generally as they have been brought forth. The following passage in le Fèvre's *Lamentations de Matheolus* could also be an imitation of Mahieu's own admission that a few choice women have to be exempted from his charges:

> Excuser me vueil en mes dis
> Que des bonnes point ne mesdis
> Ne n'ay voulenté de mesdire.
> J'ameroye mieulx moy desdire
> Que'estre haï pour fol langage.
> Dieux le scet et j'en tens mon gage,
> Qu'envers femmes je n'ay haïne
> Ne rien n'en di par attaïne,
> Fors pour mon propos coulourer.
> On ne pourroit trop honnourer
> Les bonnes et les vertueuses
>
> . . . .
>
> Se je ment, je vueil qu'en me bate.
> Il convient, puis que je translate,
> Que je die ou que je me taise.
> Pour ce suppli qu'il ne desplaise,
> S'en c'est dittié suy recordans
> Aucuns mos qui soient mordans.
> Car de moy ne procede mie.
> N'y a denrée ne demie
> Qui ne soit trouvée es histoires
> Et es anciennes memoires.[61]

Le Fèvre utilizes several elements of the apology tradition. First, he emphasizes his wish to atone in writing. Second, the ironies in his apology, which features the usual

Maddox and Sara Sturm-Maddox (Cambridge: Brewer, 1994) 57-66; and Alcuin Blamires, *The Case for Women in the Medieval Culture* (Oxford: Clarendon, 1997), esp. 36-44.

61 Jean le Fèvre, *Les Lamentations des Matheolus et le Livre de Leesce*, ed. A. G. van Hamel, 2 vols. (Paris: Librairie Émile Bouillon, 1905) 2: lines 1541-51, 1559-68. [I wish to excuse myself in my writing, since I do not slander the good women nor do I desire to slander. I would rather retract than be hated for foolish language. God knows it, and I keep my wager for it, for I have no ill will toward women. Nor do I say anything in anger, except to color my statements. Good and virtuous women can never be honored too much. If I lie, I want to be beaten. It is fitting, since I translate, for me to speak or be silent. For this I beg that it be not displeasing if in this moral treatise I record words which may be biting. For nothing proceeds from me, not the smallest bit, which is not found in histories and in ancient memories]. See also *Les Lamentations des Matheolus et le Livre de Leesce* 2: lines 1658-74.

topoi for this strand—assurance of no ill will against women, especially virtuous ones, emphasis on the translator role, emphasis on faithfulness to sources—are evident. For instance, le Fèvre's claim to faithfulness cannot be entirely maintained because, like Jean de Meun, he molds his material to expand the historical elements.[62] Additionally, his excuses notwithstanding, the insults keep accumulating for several thousand more lines.[63] Furthermore, he makes an interesting announcement about modifying his statements that parallels Jean de Meun's approach to his own authorship.

Subsequently, le Fèvre utilizes this interauctorial scenario and the compiler role to atone for his sins with another work, *Livre de Leësce* [The Book of Joy], designed to refute the tenets of *Lamentations*. The author prefaces this point-by-point palinode[64] with a forty-line apology for the rudeness expressed in the *Lamentations*, thus either questioning the apology already extended in that work or reiterating it for the audience that has not read it:

> Mes dames, je requier mercy.
> A vous me vueil excuser cy
> De ce que sans vostre licence
> J'ai parlé de la grant dissence
> Et des tourmens de mariage.
> Se j'ay mesdit par mon oultrage,
> Je puis bien dire sans flater
> Que je n'ay fait que translater
> Ce que j'ay en latin trouvé;
> Assés pourra estre prouvé
> Ou livre de Matheolule.[65]

The author apologizes to women with arguments similar to those in the *Lamentations* and uses Jean de Meun's excuse that the insults were present in the source material. Therefore, his protestations of remorse only apply to the fact of his translation, not for its contents, and he does not sound too sorry for the translation either.

Le Fèvre establishes an intertextual tie between the two works in order to explain and justify why he is now writing a work completely contrary to his previous translation. Like the ancient poets offending women, as well as the medieval authors insulting God, he wishes to atone with another literary creation. Furthermore, he reveals an ulterior motive for his move, an external reason reminiscent of the reasoning of the Graeco-Roman poets:

---

62 A. G. van Hamel, ed., introduction, *Les Lamentations des Matheolus et le Livre de Leesce*, 2 vols. (Paris: Librairie Émile Bouillon, 1905) 2: xxvii-ccxxvi; here lxii, lxiii.

63 The antifeminist arguments expounded in the *Lamentations* coincide with the generally held views of women and their role in sacred and profane history (for example, Eve as the temptress) as evident in the biblical, patristic as well as pagan "authorities" (Pierre-Yves Badel, *Le Roman de la Rose au XIV siècle: Étude de la réception de l'oeuvre* [Geneva: Librairie Droz, 1980] 186).

64 Aside from the palinodic part, le Fèvre enlarged his topic by discussing world order, the history of salvation, the human faculties and nature (Badel, *Le Roman de la Rose au XIV siècle* 187).

65 Le Fèvre, *Les Lamentations des Matheolus et le Livre de Leesce* 2: lines 1-11. [My ladies, I request mercy. I would like to apologize to you that I have spoken about the great strife and the torment of marriage without permission. If I have spoken amiss through my flagrant insult, I can say without flattering that I only translate what I found in Latin; I could well prove that from the book of Matheolule].

Car je suy tout prest que je face
Un livre pour moy excuser;
Ne le me vueilliés refuser. . . .
Sans vostre grace ne vueil vivre.
Et s'aucun requiert de cest livre
Comment entitulé sera,
Je dy que l'en l'appellera
Par droit nom "Livre de Leesce";
Car pour l'amour de celle est ce
Qu'ay fait cest livre, pour complaire
Par argument de sens contraire,
Pour vous excuser loyaument
Et monstrer especiaument
Que nul ne doit femmes blasmer;
On les doit loer et amer,
Cherir, honnourer et servir,
Qui leur grace veult desservir.[66]

Fueled by his desire, le Fèvre's wish for literary atonement has moved from a general to a specific plane, shifting from addressing all women in his audience, to addressing a very specific person. But van Hamel, the modern editor of the poem, believes that the reader should not be surprised to find this refutation of the former satire, for the author's previous interpolated apology, along with the subject matter of a complete list of negative feminine attributes, would already have laid the groundwork for a sequel, aside from the external topical reason for the composition of the poem.[67] Le Fèvre, being merely the translator, did not have to shoulder the blame for Mahieu's misogyny, unless he did not now wish to explore that subject from the other extreme, a panegyric on women. The entire situation, however, is infused with the usual irony surrounding antifeminist recantation. First, although in the *Leesce* le Fèvre refers to the *Lamentations* as a "libelle diffamatoire" (line 3522) [slanderous satire], his supposed repentance is marred by his statement in *Lamentations* I, 55 that calls the *Lamentations* "l'ouevre du sage" [the work of a wise man]. Second, because the author mirrors the structure of the *Lamentations*—he relies on biblical and classical examples to back up his theses, employs opposites, and puts in an occasional theological or philosophical digression or a list of good women or bad men to liven up the monotonous point-by-point countering of the tirades of the *Lamentations*—he generously repeats its antifeminist accusations. The work concludes with the never-ending quarrel over male versus female superiority, for le Fèvre wants to compromise so that he would not ultimately have to take sides.

---

66 Le Fèvre, *Les Lamentations des Matheolus et le Livre de Leesce* lines 18-20, 27-40. [Because I am ready to make a book to excuse myself; don't refuse me that. Without your mercy I don't want to live. And if anyone requests how this book is going to be titled, I say that I will give it a right name, "The Book of Joy"; because I have made this book for her love, to please by argument of opposite meaning in order to apologize to you loyally and demonstrate particularly that no one should blame women; one should praise, love, cherish, honor, and serve them, for their mercy deserves this].

67 van Hamel, ed., introduction cxcv.

6.8. Alain Chartier

Fifteenth-century author Alain Chartier (1380/90-1430) also becomes embroiled in the antifeminist controversy, less by textual design than by extratextual circumstances. His story should be related because it shows how ridiculous and stylized the second apology strand has become by this time. His *La Belle dame sans mercy* is a typical love-debate poem in the courtly tradition between a pursuing man and a resisting woman. In the beginning of the poem, imitating the Boethian consolation strategy, the poet reasserts his conviction, expressed in his *Complainte*, that he will no longer create happy verse because his lady has died. *La Belle* ends with the lady successfully resisting the lover, who subsequently dies of a broken heart. The author warns the women in the audience, "Ne soyés mie si crüelles . . . Qu'on appellera, ce me semble, / La belle dame sans mercy!"[68] Chartier, like Jean de Meun before him, endows his heroine with the qualities of a "self-sufficient bourgeois"[69] who did not swallow the courtly lines fed to her. Such behavior could imply criticism of courtly literature, and for some people it did.

The author's work spawned extratextual action—professional court suitors who felt their endeavors jeopardized wrote a letter, *Requeste baillée aux Dames*, to the ladies of the royal court, complaining that Chartier had to be punished in order to deter other writers from following in his footsteps.[70] They were heard by sympathetic ears because three ladies by the names of "Katherine, Marie, Jehanne" wrote a letter to Chartier requesting his appearance at the court of Issoudun to "make a general retraction."[71] Such consequences of a literary work might puzzle the modern reader but become more understandable when regarded in the context of the Court of Love that had been established about two decades before *La Belle* was written; the suing courtiers considered Chartier's poem to be contrary to the Court's charter forbidding the slandering of women.[72]

Faced with this extratextual situation, the author returns the discussion to a literary level by penning an intertextual reply in a second poem, titled *Excusacion aux dames*.[73] Following the example of Guillaume de Machaut and, to a lesser extent, Jean de Meun, Chartier uses the structural design of the dream-vision to stage an encounter with the God of Love, who accuses the author, as Chaucer had been accused, of having served him badly. Like Machaut, Chartier denies any wrongdoing and attests himself the God of Love's most humble servant. He exactly reverses Machaut's situation by claiming that he, the author, should not be confused with the lover in the poem and should not be held accountable for the latter's words, since, after all, he was only the

68 Alain Chartier, *La Belle dame sans mercy, The Poetical Works of Alain Chartier*, ed. J. C. Laidlaw (London: Cambridge UP, 1974) 328-60; lines 795, 799-800. [Don't be so cruel . . . so that you won't be called, as it seems to me, the beautiful lady without mercy].

69 Edward Joseph Hoffman, *Alain Chartier: His Work and Reputation* (Geneva: Slatkine Reprints, 1975) 58.

70 Hoffman, *Alain Chartier* 59.

71 Hoffman, *Alain Chartier* 59.

72 Hoffman, *Alain Chartier* 59-60.

73 Alain Chartier, *Excusacion aux dames, The Poetical Works of Alain Chartier*, ed. J. C. Laidlaw (London: Cambridge UP, 1974) 362-70.

transcriber of what went on, a defense that smacks of the compiler's and translator's defense used by Jean de Meun and Jean le Fèvre. (Machaut, on the other hand, having been a mere observer in the *Behaigne*, explicitly equates the narrator with the author in *Navarre*.) But here, without any admission of guilt, Alain Chartier could intratextually convince the God of Love—the highest authority and one picked by the author on purpose—that he was innocent. Extratextually, unfortunately, the controversy continued, as the three court women could not be placated by his "apology" and in their *Response de Dames* renewed their attacks and summons to court for the purpose of a retraction. The final outcome is not quite clear. Interestingly enough, in the ensuing mania of imitating, repudiating, defending, and condemning *La Belle*, Chartier "was often considered the defender of the feminine sex," in contrast to such offenders as Juvenal, Jean de Meun, and Mahieu.[74] Like Rushdie and Nasrin, Chartier would not have altered his auctorial path—and, actually, he did not—if it had not been for extratextual reasons.

Both main strands of the apology tradition, the heavenly and the antifeminist one, are powered by different dynamics. Whereas Denis Piramus', Guillaume le Clerc de Normandie's, Rutebeuf's, and Jean de Meun's apologies to God feature the fixed topoi of youth vs. old-age, confessions of literary faux-pas in the form of mendacious worldly poetry, and a generally self-imposed atonement with another literary work, the antifeminist authors' apologies use the highly ironic strategy of shifting blame and averting responsibility, which usually does not effect any intra-auctorial rewriting, since it reaffirms the misogynist position. Among these, Nicole Bozon gives a lyrical example; Guillaume de Machaut and Alain Chartier utilize a debate or trial; while Jean de Meun and Jean le Fèvre employ the compiler's defense and hide behind their *auctoritates*. Overall, there seems to be a more pronounced antifeminist streak in medieval French literature than in German literature. In the Italian tradition, this explicit antifeminism of the French apologies to women is almost entirely submerged in the *dolce stil nuovo*'s fusion of earthly women with heavenly attributes, reappears more implicitly in the English tradition, and strikes back with a vengeance in the Spanish tradition.

---

74 Hoffman, *Alain Chartier* 62-3, 68-9.

CHAPTER 7

The Italian Tradition:
"Always Drawn to the Eternally Feminine"

The misogynistic and ironic nature of the French apologies to women contrasts directly to the three great poets of the Italian fourteenth century, who share in their writing a common passion for women. According to Peter Hainsworth, "Dante, Petrarch and Boccaccio all create autobiographical love-stories";[1] while such a statement is still being disputed because the historical authenticity of the respective women cannot always be proven, the point is not whether Beatrice, Laura, Fiammetta, and *le donne* were real women and lovers but to what degree these poetic myths function as creative ancillas for the poets' art.[2] The *dolce stil nuovo* fuses aspects of the troubadour lyric and the Marian lyric to create a sanctioned love of woman, in which *la donna* becomes a representation of the new poetry. All three poets, however, treat their creative ancillas differently and ultimately pay tribute to another female figure, the Virgin Mary. Dante Alighieri sublimates earthly sexual love into heavenly Christian love in the *Vita Nuova* without repudiating Beatrice as a woman; he actually creates her as a *donna angelicata*.[3] Francesco Petrarch occupies the middle ground between Dante and Giovanni Boccaccio in his attitude toward a woman's inspirational guidance; he alternates between affirmation and rejection of Laura as a positive guiding force. Boccaccio, the poet who most blatantly caters to earthly women, becomes the most fervently opposed to women, moving from his literary inspiration— Fiammetta and *le donne* of the *Decameron*—to an antifeminist stance, a rejection of earthly love, and finally to the Virgin Mary. The three authors employ self-criticism of

---

1   Peter Hainsworth, *Petrarch the Poet: An Introduction to the* Rerum vulgarium fragmenta (London: Routledge, 1988) 114.

2   Aldo Scaglione stresses that point also and adds that the women "were nothing but objectified, symbolic extensions of the poet's self" ("Classical Heritage and Petrarchan Self-Consciousness in the Literary Emergence of the Interior 'I'," *Petrarch: Modern Critical Views* ed. Harold Bloom [New York: Chelsea House, 1989] 125-37; here 130). Sara Sturm maintains that in the "*Canzoniere* Petrarch is concerned, as Bosco notes, with the creation of a 'poetic myth' rather than with an autobiographical account of his love for Laura, and the emphasis on poetic activity is an essential part of that myth-making" ("The Poet-Persona in the *Canzoniere*," *Francis Petrarch Six Centuries Later: A Symposium*, ed. Aldo Scaglione [Chapel Hill: U of North Carolina, 1975] 192-212; here 192).

3   "Beatrice, for instance, is often described in the *Vita Nuova* as 'mirabile,' and in the poetry of other *stilnovisti*, women are desexualized as seemingly 'angelic' or they become 'intelligences'" (Jerome Mazzaro, *The Figure of Dante: An Essay on the* Vita Nuova, Princeton Essays in Literature [Princeton: Princeton UP, 1981] 11). In the *dolce stil nuovo*, the *donna angelicata* "was the path to the knowledge and enjoyment of God through one of His creatures" (Aldo Scaglione, *Nature and Love in the Late Middle Ages* [Berkeley: U of California P, 1963] 57).

the first and second strands in varying degrees in order to cope with a Weltanschauung opposed to their writing of love poetry and their indebtedness to female inspiration in their creative acts. All three poets, but especially Petrarch and Boccaccio, weave conflicting tapestries depicting their auctorial itineraries. Dante uses a new kind of forward-projecting apology; Petrarch capitalizes on the traditional "youth vs. old age" dichotomy; and Boccaccio exploits, among other topoi, the compiler's defense.

7.1. Dante Alighieri

Dante (1265-1321) capitalizes on an adumbrating intertextuality with an unconventional form of self-criticism that enables him to keep writing about his beloved Beatrice under the umbrella of Christian truth and salvation. Mark Musa considers the *Vita Nuova* "the most original form of recantation in medieval literature—a recantation that takes the form of a re-enactment, from a new perspective, of the sin recanted."[4] Dante has tried to come to terms with his youthful experiences and, therefore, has to relive them as he is writing them down. This writing experience is punctuated by intra-auctorial statements demonstrating the author's finding and changing his style and material. For instance, in *Vita Nuova* XVII, the poet revises his creative approach: "Poi che dissi questi tre sonetti . . . credendomi tacere e non dire più . . . avvegna che sempre poi tacesse di dire a lei, a me covenne ripigliare matera nuova e più nobile che la passata."[5] The poet seems to work with a trial-and-error method that delineates exactly his intra-auctorial approach and ultimately leads to the last statement of the *Vita Nuova*, a "literary impasse":[6]

> Appresso questo sonetto apparve a me una mirabile visione, ne la quale io vidi cose che mi fecero proporre di non dire più di questa benedetta infino a tanto che io potesse più degnamente trattare di lei. . . . io spero di dicer di lei quello che mai non fue detto d'alcuna. E poi piaccia a colui che è sire de la cortesia, che la mia anima se ne possa gire a vedere la gloria de la sua donna, cioè di quella benedetta Beatrice.[7]

---

4   Mark Musa, *Dante's Vita Nuova: A Translation and an Essay* (Bloomington: Indiana UP, 1973) 174.

5   Dante Alighieri, *Vita Nuova*, ed. Vittorio Cozzoli (Milan: EDIS Edizione Culturali, 1995) 65. ['After I had written these three sonnets . . . believing I should be silent and say no more . . . even at the cost of never again writing to her . . . I felt forced to find a new theme, one nobler than the last'] (Musa, *Dante's Vita Nuova* 30).

6   Robert Pogue Harrison, *The Body of Beatrice* (Baltimore: Johns Hopkins UP, 1988) 133.

7   Dante Alighieri, *Vita Nuova* XLII, 136 ['After I wrote this sonnet there came to me a miraculous vision in which I saw things that made me resolve to say no more about this blessèd one until I would be capable of writing about her in a nobler way. . . . I hope to write of her that which has never been written of any other woman. And then may it please the One who is the Lord of graciousness that my soul ascend to the glory of its lady, that is of that blessèd Beatrice'] (Musa, *Dante's Vita Nuova* 86). Some critics believe that "Dante revised the original ending of the work much later in his career" (Harrison, *The Body of Beatrice* 130), which would eliminate the imme-

In this passage, Dante combines several elements of the recantation tradition, as seen in other authors so far: God, woman, writing, and writing as an improvement or atonement, with which Dante achieves his forward-pointing intertextuality. The standard trappings of the "youth-and-age" dichotomy and the protestations of sinfulness are conspicuously absent because the poet is constantly redefining himself and does not feel guilty in a religious sense. His vision provides him with the realization that he has treated Beatrice, in the light of the troubadour tradition, as the earthly beloved; now he sees her as a spiritual guide, expressing "that love of the *donna*, or at least of Beatrice, led upwards."[8] The implication is that his writing about love so far has been lacking and that a person like Beatrice surpasses the earthly conventions of love poetry; therefore, he recreates her as a *donna angelicata* in the *Divina Commedia*. Dante, however, uses Beatrice's death ironically to keep their relationship absolutely devoid of the corporeal, demonstrating the virtue of their love by the absence of her demands for fulfillment and satisfaction.[9] When the author moves his temptation to a heavenly sphere, she becomes a "religiously correct" subject and can serve him further as his creative handmaiden, whereas keeping her on earth would have meant that the poet would have been caught in the dichotomy between the corporeal and the heavenly.

Several other aspects demonstrate that Dante's self-criticism is not altogether selfless and purposeless. First, the poet expresses an unmitigated wish to keep writing, but to move onto another plane, implying that writing itself is a worthwhile pursuit and only his approach has to be altered. Second, he involves God as the blessing force, which, so he hopes, will allow him finally to behold his beloved in heaven. Third, the poet's ultimate goal derives from both his writing and the grace of the Lord, culminating in his beholding Beatrice in heaven. The poet exhibits both a very assured attitude about himself and his poetic ability and an almost blasphemous sentiment about his motivations for going to heaven. He claims he wishes to see Beatrice, "la quale gloriosamente mira ne la faccia di colui *qui est per omnia secula benedictus*" (*Vita Nuova* XLII, 136) ['who in glory contemplates the countenance of the One who is through all ages blessed' (Musa 86)], assigning a salvific mediator role to Beatrice: Dante beholds Beatrice, who in turn beholds God. The poet ventures even closer to religious blasphemy when he proclaims that Beatrice, not the Virgin Mary, is both the "lady of his soul" and the recipient of writing never written for another woman before, and that he wants to go to heaven to look upon her, not upon the ultimate woman, the Virgin. The Virgin eventually receives top billing. Dante's move toward a more spiritual view of love of woman is suggested in the ending of the *Vita Nuova* and the *Commedia*, the former ending with praise of Beatrice and the latter with a poem to Mary.

It is an accepted idea that the Italian poets were influenced by the troubadours of Southern France, of whom a third took up a religious life in their later years. "In one

---

diacy of the intra-auctorial refashioning. See also Diane Hichwa Senior, "The Politics of Self and Dante's *Vita Nuova*," *NEMLA Italian Studies* 18 (1994): 5-12.

8   Hainsworth, *Petrarch the Poet* 153.

9   Scaglione, "Classical Heritage and Petrarchan Self-Consciousness" 130.

form or another repentance did come to be a part of the tradition of courtly love," Charles Singleton postulates.[10] In the *Vita Nuova*, Dante begins in the spirit of the troubadour lyrics, but by sublimating his sexual love into a Christian love, he proves his indebtedness to a worldview that would expect such a turn. Dante removes the God of Love from the *Vita Nuova*, which equals a retraction of the troubadour love.[11] Dante, however, differs from both Petrarch and Boccaccio, as well as other medieval

---

10 Charles S. Singleton, *An Essay on the* Vita Nuova (Cambridge: Harvard UP, 1958) 66. For the conversion of Bernart de Ventadorn, see J. Boutière and A. H. Schutz, *Biographies des Troubadours: Textes Provençaux des XIII et XIV Siècles* (Paris: A. G. Nizet, 1964) 26-28, 98-102) and Thomas G. Bergin, *Petrarch* (New York: Twayne, 1970) 171-74. Eduard Wechssler postulates that the phenomenon of aged French troubadours flocking to monasteries did not result from conversion experiences but represents the conclusions of the lives of men who had become superfluous in the world (*Das Kulturproblem des Minnesangs: Studien zur Vorgeschichte der Renaissance*, 2 vols. [Halle: Max Niemeyer, 1909] 1: 434-35). Also compare William of Aquitaine's (1071-1127) "Pos de chantar m'es pres talentz" ['Religious Song']:
Pos de chantar m'es pres talentz
Farai un vers don sui dolenz

. . . .
Qu'era m'en irai en eisil:

. . . .
De proeza e de joi fui,
Mas ara partem ambedui,
Et eu irai m'en a sellui
On tuit peccador troban fi.
Mout ai estat cuendes e gais,
Mas Nostre Seigner no'l vol mais;
Ar non puesc plus soffrir lo fais,
Tan soi aprochatz de la fi.

. . . .
Aissi guerpisc joi e deport
E vair e gris sembeli.
['Since I feel a need to sing
I will make a song about my sorrow;

. . . .
For now I shall go into exile:

. . . .
I have belonged to prowess and joy,
But now we part company,
And I go away to the One
With whom all sinners find rest.
I have been most charming and gay,
But our Lord wants that no more;
Now I can no longer carry the burden
So close have I come to the end.

. . . .
Thus I leave joy and pleasure
And rich fur and sable.'] (*The Medieval Lyric: Anthology 1* [Mount Holyoke College: 1988] 42-43; lines 1-2, 5, 25-32, 41-42)
11 Singleton, *An Essay on the* Vita Nuova 74.

writers, in that he does not reject woman per se, a practice abundantly illustrated in this study, in which an author's rejection of earthly love often equals implied antifeminism. Beatrice is removed from the realm of earthly love with its amorous passions and exalted to the heavenly sphere where she can act as a mediator between God and Dante, and truly facilitate the latter's salvation. After the *Vita Nuova*, she has actually become a static figure[12] and in her desexualized form is less dangerous to Dante. To resolve the tension between love of woman and love of God, Dante writes the spirit of Beatrice, while Petrarch, who thrives on that tension throughout his career, writes the body of Laura.

7.2. Francesco Petrarch

Petrarch (1304-74), the most ambivalent of the medieval Italian writers, weaves a perplexingly complex intra-auctorial web; unlike Dante, he cannot fuse love of God and love of woman, although he tries; unlike Boccaccio, he would not even consider abandoning his writing career. While he attempts to portray Laura as a divine representative on earth, he does not fuse but instead polarize the issue, wavering excessively between self-criticism and self-justification. On the one hand, with his poems to Laura, he heeds Irigaray by trying to write the flesh and make it word; on the other hand, he is aware of the implications of writing love poetry in the medieval Christian cosmos. Because he never quite achieves the *donna angelicata*, he has to use the conventional apology trappings of old-age repentance. Given the contemporary philosophy of language, Petrarch theorizes about the feasibility of an old poet's writing love songs, the appropriate language for love poetry, and Laura's role in the composition of that love poetry, which is illustrated by a pattern of affirmation and negation.[13] These auctorial concerns and "flashes of lucid self-criticism"[14] manifest themselves metatextually in several of his letters, intratextually in the *Canzoniere* (*Rerum vulgarium fragmenta*), and intertextually in the *Trionfi* as well as the *Secretum*.

In the best tradition of the topos of youthful error vs. wisdom in old age, Petrarch confesses to the very same in his "Epistle to Posterity": "Adolescentia me fefellit, iuventa corripuit, senecta autem correxit, experimentoque perdocuit verum illud quod diu ante perlegeram: quoniam adolescentia et voluptas vana sunt."[15] In that letter

---

12 Adriano Seroni, *Apologia di Laura e Altri Saggi* (Milan: Bompiani, 1948) 14.

13 Marguerite R. Waller interprets the recurring retractions in the *Canzoniere* as "thematic focusing device[s]," which very pointedly fail to "reassure us of a change of heart on the part of the poet" (*Petrarch's Poetics and Literary History* [Amherst: U of Massachusetts P, 1980] 57).

14 Kenelm Foster, "Beatrice or Medusa," *Italian Studies Presented to E. R. Vincent*, eds. C. P. Brand, K. Foster, and U. Limentani (Cambridge: W. Heffer, 1962) 41-56; here 45.

15 Francesco Petrarch, "*Sen.* XVIII, 1," *Epistole*, ed. Ugo Dotti (Turin: Unione Tipografico, 1978) 870-89; here 870. ['Adolescence misled me, youth swept me away, but old age set me right, and taught me by experience that truth I had read long before: that adolescence and pleasure are vain'] (Aldo S. Bernardo, Saul Levin, and Reta A. Bernardo, trans., *Francis Petrarch: Letters of Old Age:* Rerum senilium libri I-XVIII, 2 vols. [Baltimore: Johns Hopkins UP, 1992] 2: 672).

Petrarch also delineates his poetic path as it supposedly turns from poetry to sacred literature. He admits to the same prejudice toward the Bible's *sermo humilis* style as Augustine does in the *Confessions*: "Ingenio fui equo potius quam acuto, ad omne bonum et salubre studium apto, sed ad moralem precipue philosophiam et ad poeticam prono; quam ipse processu temporis neglexi, sacris literis delectatus, in quibus sensi dulcedinem abditam, quam aliquando contempseram, poeticis literis non nisi ornatum reservatis."[16] His claim that poetry has now been pushed to the fringes of his literary creation reveals an inversion in creative thinking; while form—poetry—has so far had precedence over content, content now surpasses form. In more concrete terms, the author prefers the truths of the lower biblical style to the stylistically more perfect classical literature.

Nevertheless, Petrarch is quite indebted to and enamored with classical authors and has to contextualize them in his intra-auctorial development because of the ambivalence toward classical literature that still lingered despite the *trivium* education of medieval students. He writes, "[n]eque ideo tamen quia hos pretulerim, illos abicio, quod se fecisse. . . . ego utrosque simul amare posse videor, modo quos in verborum, quos in rerum consilio preferam non ignorem."[17] This passage furthermore illustrates the inherent medieval mode of thinking inculcated by the *trivium* education that forced its pupils to use the style of classical literature but to reject its content. Petrarch's phrasing of this statement identifies the shortcoming of each group along with its forte. While classical literature lacks substance, Christian literature lacks style. Petrarch adds several other elements to the discussion of ancient versus Christian writers: "presertim cum veteres illi nil aliud me requirant, nisi ne oblivione deleantur et primitiis studiorum contenti, omne iam melioribus tempus cedant?"[18] As part of the life-stage argument and the *trivium* education, pagan, sinful, "insignificant" literature has been

---

16 Petrarch, *"Sen. XVIII, 1"* 874. ['I had a well-balanced rather than a keen intellect, fit for all kinds of good and wholesome study, but especially inclined to moral philosophy and poetry. Yet in the course of time I abandoned the latter, when I found delight in sacred letters, in which I felt the hidden sweetness I once despised; for I limit poetry to embellishment only'] (Bernardo, Levin, and Bernardo, *Francis Petrarch: Letters of Old Age* 2: 673). Here follows a partial genesis of the "Epistle to Posterity" according to Ernest Hatch Wilkins: "(6) The self-portrait that now opens the Letter was written after 1368: it probably contains some elements of the self-portrait that Petrarch had drafted, at least in part, in 1350. (7) Insertions were made in the autobiographical portion in 1371 or the first half of 1372. (8) The Letter was not revised after August 1372." Petrarch's work on what ultimately became the "Letter to Posterity" began in or shortly before 1355, and came to an end in 1371 or the first half of 1372 (*Studies on Petrarch and Boccaccio*, ed. Aldo S. Bernardo [Padua: Editrice Antenore, 1978] 292).

17 Francesco Petrarch, *"Fam. XXII, 10,"* *Epistole*, ed. Ugo Dotti (Turin: Unione Tipografico, 1978) 480-86; here 484. ['But if I do prefer these [Christian works], I do not reject the others [classical works]. . . . I seem capable of loving both at the same time, provided I distinguish between the ones preferred for their style and the others preferred for their substance'] (Aldo S. Bernardo, trans., *Francesco Petrarca: Letters on Familiar Matters: Rerum familiarium libri XVII-XXIV*, [Baltimore: Johns Hopkins UP, 1985] 233).

18 Petrarch, *"Fam. XXII, 10"* 484. ['especially since the ancients demand nothing of me save that I not let them fall into oblivion; and happy about my devoting my youth to them, they now allow me to dedicate all my time to more important matters'] (Bernardo, *Francesco Petrarca: Letters on Familiar Matters* 233).

assigned to Petrarch's youth, whereas his old age is supposed to concentrate on "significant" Christian compositions. Petrarch ironically portrays the dilemma of the poet in the Christian cosmos but also alludes to the fact that the lingering ambivalence toward classical authors is unfounded, for they are powerless and only require remembrance from him as a writer and a human being. Supposedly, the Christian universe is less gentle with its authors, for the requirements for him as a Christian writer and person are more severe and threatening. Noncompliance with the contemporary logocentric philosophy of language would imperil his soul; therefore, deference to the Christian worldview has to be paid.

In letter *"Fam. XXII, 10,"* Petrarch also expands and qualifies his ideas about language and poetry. He gives us another insight into the his psyche as a reader. Since Petrarch draws on the authors he reads, his attitude towards reading mirrors his approach to writing. Like Lucian, he very openly discusses his motives: "Sed iam michi maius agitur negotium, maiorque salutis quam eloquentie cura est; legi que delectabant, lego que prosint; is michi nunc animus est, imo vero iampridem fuit, neque enim nunc incipio, neque vero me id ante tempus agere coma probat albescens."[19] In the medieval spirit of polarization between the earthly and the heavenly, Petrarch touches upon important issues. First, he very bluntly admits that he does not want to jeopardize his salvation. Second, he implies that his usage of language plays a paramount role in his soul's deliverance. Third, he ties language to pleasure and profit, which is actually the Horatian litmus test of good literature. Fourth, he hastily adds a timeframe to his change of mind.[20] In the conflict between pleasure and profit, Petrarch encapsulates the central medieval philosophy of language with its logocentric emphasis on language as the vehicle of truth. According to that philosophy, on the one hand, literature intended to please alone does not signify, since only biblical truths can signify; on the other hand, the backhanded insinuation is that profitable literature could not delight.

Petrarch's repeated emphasis on the life-stage argument, as in "ut qui iuvenilibus iuventam studiis dedi, maturiorem etatem melioribus curis dem" (*"Fam. XXII, 10,"* 480) ['I can devote my riper years to more important matters after devoting my early years to youthful studies' (Bernardo 232)], functions as one of Petrarch's smoke screens for his continued efforts on the *Canzoniere*. Singleton considers Petrarch the "last troubadour," who recants in the last poem of the *Canzoniere* as well as the first poem,[21] but in between abounds a vast array of love poetry, along with evidence of the poet's grappling with it. In order to do justice to Petrarch's self-expression, we have to

---

19 Petrarch, *"Fam. XXII, 10"* 482. ['But now I must think of more serious matters, for I am more concerned with salvation than eloquence; I used to read works that gave me pleasure, now I am reading works that are good for me. This is my present state of mind, and it has been so for some time. Nor am I just beginning, from and my graying hair I can see that I began none too soon'] (Bernardo, *Francesco Petrarca: Letters on Familiar Matters* 233).

20 Walter Savage Landor writes, "Petrarca, like Boccaccio, regretted at the close of life, not only the pleasure he had enjoyed, but also the pleasure he had imparted to the world" ("Francesco Petrarca," ed. Beatrice Corrigan, *Italian Poets and English Critics, 1755-1859: A Collection of Critical Essays*, Patterns of Literary Criticisms [Chicago: U of Chicago P, 1969] 168).

21 Singleton, *An Essay on the* Vita Nuova 66.

look at almost the entirety of his literary production and most of his intra-auctorial statements. In his own time, Petrarch was famous for his Latin rather than his Italian works, which only totaled seventy-eight pages in contrast to fourteen hundred Latin pages in his 1554 edition. The Italian poems are love poems influenced by the Provençal and Tuscan tradition; the Latin works derive from antiquity, and love is not found in them, although Petrarch's self-criticisms apply to both language strands. Petrarch's claim to have turned to more serious matters contradicts the known fact that he worked on the *RVF* between 1330 and the year before his death, when he gave the collection its final form.[22]

Petrarch presents the first recorded and documented case of the way an important literary figure produced his works on a detailed, almost day-to-day basis; making a final and fully authorized version of his *Canzoniere* represents Petrarch's attempt to stem an "absorption of his poetry into an oral culture."[23] By 1350 he has admitted to having given up poetry entirely, which was true for his Latin poetry; for Italian poetry he has better excuses:

> Italian poetry, as he conceived and wrote it, was not to be reconciled with humanism in any intellectually coherent fashion . . . There could be no justification for indulgence in sexual love, however refined, nor for love-poetry. It was available to the vulgar at large, and . . . to women. It had to be judged frivolous, immoral, and, as literature, inferior in every way to what might be written in Latin.[24]

With his continued efforts on the *RVF*, Petrarch opens himself to criticism as an aging poet still writing love lyrics, like, for instance, Neidhart von Reuental. As we have seen in the apology tradition, youth and love are aligned, whereas old age teams with wisdom and a traditional disavowal of love. Petrarch caters to that tradition by bracketing his Italian collection with two intratextual palinodic poems, "*RVF* 1" and "*RVF* 366," in order to preserve his *RVF* in written form. With the last poems, Petrarch fosters and confirms the attitude that they are poems of an era long past and that the end of his *RVF* is a reflection of a long-past phase in his *vita*. As a septuagenarian, he can no longer write love lyrics or even deal with old poems without claiming that they are ancient ones.

Therefore, Petrarch employs two strategies to disguise his real intentions. First, he has to make newer poems look older; second, he utilizes extratextual or metatextual self-criticism by writing letters and notes to friends expressing his hesitation to shoulder such a project but his resolve to do it because there is a demand and because the

---

22 Hainsworth, *Petrarch the Poet* 7.

23 Also Scaglione, "The Structure of the *Canzoniere* and Petrarch's Method of Composition," *Francesco Petrarca, Citizen of the World: Proceedings of the World Petrarch Congress, Washington, DC, April 6-13, 1974*, ed. Aldo S. Bernardo (Albany: State U of New York P, 1980) 301-13; here 301. Hainsworth, *Petrarch the Poet* 18. Petrarch writes in "*Sen.* V, 2": "although those brief and scattered vernacular works of my youth are no longer mine, as I have said, but have become the multitude's, I shall see to it that they do not butcher my major ones'] (Bernardo, Levin, and Bernardo, *Francis Petrarch: Letters of Old Age* 1: 163). The Latin original was not available to me.

24 Hainsworth, *Petrarch the Poet* 7-8.

poems are already known.[25] That way he can allay possible criticisms leveled against a mature poet who is still writing love songs. In the notes to several poems, he refers in derogatory terms to the vernacular poems that make demands on his time: "post multos annos, 1350 Aprilis 3 mane quodiam triduo exacto institi ad supremam manum vulgarium, ne diutius inter curas distrahar."[26] Another passage reflects the same sentiment: "1356, novembris 4, sero. dum cognito de fine harum nugarum."[27] Toward the end of his literary career, he employs the opposite tactic. Instead of being harsh on his vernacular creations, he sketches a favorable picture of the mature poet reorganizing youthful poems when time permits. In "*Sen.* XIII, 9," a letter to Pandolfo Malatesta, to whom Petrarch sent a copy of the *RVF* in 1373 with the words: "nugellas meas vulgares . . . in quibus multa sunt excusationis egentia"[28] [my vulgar trifles . . . in which there is much in need of excuse], he describes the aging love-poet positively; while he may be speaking truthfully, the "dubious status of vernacular love-poetry,[29] especially for an aging writer who claims to have renounced poetry altogether," seems to provide ample necessity to devise such a smoke screen in the first place. In any event, Petrarch's maneuvers illustrate how difficult it is for him to maintain the equilibrium between subscribing to the sacramental theory of language and being true to his poetic inclinations.

7.2.1. *Canzoniere*

The first poem of the *Canzoniere* bears intratextual witness to that difficulty. Baring his "public self," Petrarch delivers the standard medieval apology for the errors of his

---

25   Bernhard König, "Das letzte Sonett des *Canzoniere*. Zur 'architektonischen' Funktion und Gestaltung der *Ultime Rime* Petrarcas," *Interpretation: Das Paradigma der europäischen Renaissance-Literatur. Festschrift für Alfred Noyer-Weidner zum 60. Geburtstag*, eds. Klaus Hempfer and Gerhard Regn (Wiesbaden: Franz Steiner, 1983) 239-57; here 246.

26   ['after many years, 1350, April 3, morning. Since at the end of three days I pressed on to give the last touch to the vernacular pieces, in order not to be further distracted in the midst of my cares'] (qtd. in Hainsworth, *Petrarch the Poet* 35).

27   ['in the evening, whilst thinking of (making) an end of these trifles'] (qtd. in Hainsworth, *Petrarch the Poet* 36). "In more than six hundred letters now extant he mentions them [*RVF*] only eight times—usually with some disparaging remark: In the Preface (to Socrates); *Ep. Metr.* I.i; *F.* VII, 18, VIII, 3, X, 3, XXI, 15; *Sen.* V, 3, and XIII, 10" (Edward H. R. Tatham, *Francesco Petrarca, the First Modern Man of Letters, His Life and Correspondence: A Study of the Early Fourteenth Century (1304-1347)*, 2 vols. [London: Seldon Press, 1925] 1: 277). In 1349, at the age of 45, he called his Italian poems: "illa vulgaria iuvenilium laborum meorum cantica, quorum hodie pudet ac penitet" ("*Fam.* VIII, 3," *Epistole*, ed. Ugo Dotti [Turin: Unione Tipografico, 1978] 196-204; here 202) [those ordinary songs of the labor of my youth, of which I am ashamed today and which I regret].

28   Petrarch, "*Sen.* XIII, 9," *Epistole*, ed. Ugo Dotti (Turin: Unione Tipografico, 1978) 754-59; here 756.

29   Hainsworth, *Petrarch the Poet* 32-33.

youth "with a voice of moral authority."[30] Such moral authority, however, bestows a certain superiority on the poet. One difference between Petrarch's first sonnet and other authors' work in the apology tradition is that Petrarch's confession heads the presentation of his "giovenile errore" ("*RVF* 1" line 3), basically warning the reader that what is to come will not measure up to the prevalent Christian Zeitgeist. This is unlike most other self-critical authors, who would mention their literary sins in an intertextual context. The term "errore" is ambiguous, since it can refer to his admission of an earthly love, "[a]more acerrimo sed unico et honesto in adolescentia laboravi"[31] or to the fruits of that love, the ensuing love songs. As we know from the extensive research conducted by scholars like Ruth Shepard Phelps and Ernest Hatch Wilkins,[32] Petrarch devoted almost fifty years to writing this collection of his poems, culminating in a final version ordered and partially transcribed by himself. Therefore, the order in which the poet arranges his largest vernacular work cannot be taken as the original order of composition. Wilkins attributes "*RVF* 1" to the second form of the *Canzoniere* between the period of 1345-47,[33] which is almost twenty years after the proposed beginning of the collection.

In the best apology tradition, the first poem of the *Canzoniere* is riddled with ambiguity, alluding to both his love for Laura and his "early" writings, expressing repentance as well as a certain underlying pride:

Voi ch' ascoltate in rime sparse il suono
di quei sospiri ond'io nudriva 'l core
in sul mio primo giovenile errore,

---

30 Giuseppe Mazzotta, "The *Canzoniere* and the Language of Self," *Petrarch: Modern Critical Views* ed. Harold Bloom (New York: Chelsea House, 1989) 57-78; here 57. This article is also reprinted in Guiseppe Mazzotta, *The Worlds of Petrarch* (Durham: Duke UP, 1993). Sturm notes, the "apparent apology of this opening sonnet has been related to well-known medieval patterns. Montanari notes in it 'la figura tipica dell'introduzione medievale,' including the author's apology for the limitations of his talent, his inability to do justice to the important theme which he is about to attempt; . . . however, in the first sonnet his apparent apology is not for the inadequacy of his talent, but rather for offering a work made up of *rime sparse*, the final result of a poetic effort which the poet himself questions even while offering it to the reader" ("The Poet-Persona in the *Canzoniere*" 194). Ugo Foscolo considers the first sonnet an "apology to the world . . . which he resolved to prepare in his old age, rejecting those pieces which were apocryphal, and those which he considered unworthy of him" ("An Essay on the Poetry of Petrarch," *Italian Poets and English Critics, 1755-1859: A Collection of Critical Essays*, ed. Beatrice Corrigan [Chicago: U of Chicago P, 1969] 78-97; here 79).

31 Petrarch, "*Sen.* XVIII, 1" 872. ['I struggled in my adolescence with the most intense but constant and honorable love'] (Bernardo, Levin, and Bernardo, *Francis Petrarch: Letters of Old Age* 2: 673).

32 Ruth Shepard Phelps, *The Earlier and Later Forms of Petrarch's* Canzoniere (Chicago: U of Chicago P, 1925) and Ernest Hatch Wilkins, *The Making of the* "Canzoniere" *and other Petrarchan Studies*, Storia E Letteratura Raccolta di Studi e Testi 38 (1955. Rome: Folcroft, 1977). On the chronology of Petrarch's *Canzoniere*, see also König, "Das letzte Sonett des *Canzoniere*" 239-57 and "Die Anordnung der Gedichte des *Canzoniere* als Problem der Literaturkritik und der Petrarca-Editionen des 15. bis 19. Jahrhunderts," *Romanistisches Jahrbuch* 44 (1993): 124-38.

33 Wilkins, *The Making of the* "Canzoniere" 352.

quand'era in parte altr'uom da quel ch'i' sono:

. . . .

spero trovar pietà, nonché perdono.[34]

"Rime sparse," the first ambiguity, insinuates, on the one hand, that his work is scattered, unfinished, partial, incomplete, and possibly incidental—all of which have a negative connotation. On the other hand, in "*Sen*. V, 2," he admits that he wanted to make a definitive version of his lyrics because they had become so scattered and commonly available. He wanted to protect his creation and, despite his protestations about the inferiority of the vernacular, he wishes to preserve his poetry in a form he deems final. It is overwhelmingly clear that "an artist of his calibre" would not have bothered for most of his life with works of "minor or marginal importance."[35] "Scattered rhymes" equally connect to lines 9-10, "Ma ben veggio or sì como al popol tutto / favola fui gran tempo . . ." ['But now I see well how for a long time I was the talk of the crowd . . .' (DL 36)] and illustrate that he was publicly humiliated because of his love aspirations and because he was known for his poetic creation. The second ambiguity, the "primo giovenile errore," can refer both to his love for Laura, which he now criticizes, and his writing of love lyrics, especially when he is still polishing this collection as an old man, who—according to himself in his letters—should no longer write love poetry. He opens himself up to criticism and mockery and therefore asks for "pietà" and "perdono." The third ambiguity lies in the phrase "in parte," signaling that the poet has partly changed but is still partly the same man as before, which in turn affirms that he "remains committed to the errancy of his 'vaneggiar.'"[36] The poem even ends on an ambiguous note: while it professes repentance and resignation that life and experience on earth are fleeting, "che quanto piace al mondo è breve sogno" ("*RVF* 1" line 14) ['whatever pleases in the world is a brief dream' (DL 36)], Petrarch, like Chaucer, also invokes pleasure, telling his readers or listeners that what they are about to read or hear caters to pleasure and was once pleasurable to him. In summary, while the first poem openly seems to warn the readers of what lies ahead, and what they might not want to read in the first place, one is inevitably attracted to the promise of love poetry, albeit "defective in literary, moral, social and ontological terms."[37]

Indeed, the majority of the *Canzoniere* is love poetry about Laura, his one and only love and poetic inspiration. Among these three hundred sixty-six poems, Kenelm Foster classifies a handful as "decidedly penitential" (*RVF*s 1, 62, 81, 142, 264, 355, 364-366), containing three recurring charges against Petrarch's love for Laura: "a loss of moral liberty," "a loss of spiritual dignity," and "the waste of natural gift."[38] While these particular poems reveal the poet's concern for these issues, only some of them deal explicitly with his intra-auctoriality. They depict a blaming, self-reproaching, defensive, repentant, and proud poet-persona, who tries to grapple with the experience

---

34 "*RVF* 1" lines 1-4, 8. ['You who hear in scattered rhymes the sounds of those sighs with which I nourished my heart during my first youthful error, when I was in part another man from what I am now: . . . I hope to find pity, not only pardon'] (DL 36).

35 Kenelm Foster, *Petrarch: Poet and Humanist* (Edinburgh: Edinburgh UP, 1984) 47.

36 Harrison, *The Body of Beatrice* 107.

37 Hainsworth, *Petrarch the Poet* 103, 104.

38 Foster, *Petrarch* 46.

of love and its subsequent birthing of literary creation. The God of Love and Laura directly and indirectly incite him to love and, therefore, to write. Protestations of modesty, self-doubt, avoidance of responsibility, claims of old age, and contradictory attitudes toward Laura are all mixed together.

One manifestation of Petrarch's view of his own poetic craft, which actually underscores his abilities, is his use of modesty formulas. For instance, in "*RVF* 20," he criticizes himself for not being able to write about Laura: "Piú volte incominciai di scriver versi: / ma la penna et la mano et l'intellecto / rimaser vinti nel primier assalto."[39] In "*RVF* 125," he still complains, "a voler poi ritrarla / per me non basto . . ." (lines 36-37) ['I am not sufficient to describe her by myself' (DL 240)]. He further faults himself for his inability to praise Laura in verse: "So io ben ch'a voler chiuder in versi / suo laudi fôra stancho / chi piú degna la mano a scriver porse."[40] The poet voices a similar sentiment in "*RVF* 221," lines 12-14, and bemoans his too humble words ("dir troppo humile") which must definitely offend her ("*RVF* 247," lines 5-6). All of these formulas actually illustrate a vain streak in Petrarch, for their appearance in a collection of three hundred sixty-six lyrics and statements from other poems in the collection both contradict this modesty.

The poet that could not help but proclaim his ability to pen poems about his lady contrasts with the poet who laments having written about her at all. In a general sense, he exhibits the understandably human tendency of trying to obliterate the offending action: "Mai non vo' piú cantar com'io soleva, / ch'altri no m'intendeva, ond'ebbi scorno; / et puossi in bel soggiorno esser molesto."[41] Rejected love and Laura's death—which is detrimental to a poet dependent on female inspiration—seemingly make him want to abandon his writing love songs, but he does not do so, as we know, until shortly before his death, "Or sia qui fine al mio amoroso canto: / secca è la vena de l'usato ingegno, / et la cetera mia rivolta in pianto."[42] Although this passage seems to signal the end of his poetic creativity, there are over seventy poems to go before the end.

Yet another Petrarchan persona is that of a defensive poet who does not want to take personal responsibility for his craft and who expresses satisfaction with his poetic capability. He takes refuge in the fact that other factors drove him to certain actions, "fame amorosa e 'l non poter mi scuse" ("*RVF* 207" line 26) ['let my amorous hunger and my powerlessness excuse me' (DL 356)]. Striking an even more self-confident note, the beginning of "*RVF* 293" both reminds the reader of "*RVF* 1" and contradicts it. Petrarch writes:

S'io avesse pensato che sí care
fossin le voci de' sospir' miei in rima,

---

39 "*RVF* 20" lines 12-14. ['Many times have I begun to write verses, but my pen and my hand and my intellect have been vanquished in the first assault'] (DL 54).

40 "*RVF* 29" lines 50-2. ['I know well that to enclose her praises in verse would vanquish whoever put the worthiest hand to writing'] (DL 85).

41 "*RVF* 105" lines 1-3. ['I never wish to sing again as I used to, for I was not understood, wherefore I was scorned, and one can be miserable in a pleasant place'] (DL 208).

42 "*RVF* 105" lines 12-14. ['Now here let there be an end to my song of love; dry is the vein of my accustomed wit, and my lyre is turned to weeping'] (DL 470).

fatte l'avrei, dal sospirar mio prima
in numero piú spesse, in stil piú rare.[43]

Both "sospir" and "sospirar" echo "sospiri" from the first poem, especially since "*RVF* 293" specifically refers to the first sigh. There, "sospiri" was used in a negative context; here it assumes a positive meaning, since the poet proposes an even larger number of such sighs, albeit with fewer forms. (Again, Petrarch mentions content and form.) Nonetheless, the entire passage annuls the first poem, in which the poet regrets ever having written these poems. Another contradiction illustrating the same point exists in "*RVF* 296": "I' mi soglio accusare, et or mi scuso, / anzi mi pregio et tengo assai piú caro, / de l'onesta pregion . . . ."[44] A very defiant Petrarch defends his decision to keep writing for Laura and not to abandon his devotion to her or lavish his skills upon another focal point—implying that Laura is his only Muse. Laura is a contrast to Dante's Beatrice, who is a way to God; Laura is an antagonist to God and could mean spiritual death to the poet. Not until she dies, and Petrarch reconciles that notion with a heavenly one, does she become a mediatrix figure. Not until Laura has been neutralized as a physical, sexual woman and, therefore, a threat to the poet's salvation, does he become more comfortable with her in the Christian cosmos.

Although Laura is his only Muse, Petrarch likes to deny the voluntariness of his decision to write love poetry, making the external force, Love, assume both a motivational and scapegoat role. For instance:

Poi che per mio destino
a dir me sforza quell'accesa voglia
che m'à sforzato a sospirar mai sempre,
Amor, ch'a ciò m'invoglia,
sia la mia scorta e 'nsignimi 'l camino
et col desio le mie rime contempre.[45]

Petrarch actually begs Love, albeit out of necessity, to take on an active role and to assist him in his compositions; such a move is conventional, but in the scheme of Petrarch's palinodic poems, it relieves the poet of some of the responsibility. In "*RVF* 93," Love becomes even more active, for it now commands the poet: "Piú volte Amor m'avea già detto: 'Scrivi, / scrivi quel che vedesti in lettre d'oro'" (lines 1-2) ['Many times had Love already said to me: "Write, write in letters of gold what you have seen"' (DL 196)]. In "*RVF* 309," then, the poet fuses both self-criticism and absolution of responsibility:

vuol ch'i' depinga a chi nol vide, e 'l mostri
Amor, che 'n prima la mia lingua sciolse;

---

43   "*RVF* 293" lines 1-4. ['If I had thought that the sound of my sighs in rhyme would be so pleasing, from the time of my first sighs I would have made them in number more frequent, in style more rare'] (DL 472).

44   "*RVF* 296" lines 1-3. ['I used to accuse myself and now I excuse, rather I praise myself and hold myself much more dear for the worthy prison . . . '] (DL 474).

45   "*RVF* 73" lines 1-6. ['Since through my destiny that flaming desire forces me to speak which has forced me to sigh always, you, O Love, who arouse me to it, be my guide, and show me the way, and tune my rhymes to my desire'] (DL 168).

poi mille volte indarno a l'opra volse
ingegno, tempo, penne, carte, e 'nchiostri.[46]

The incentive to write was provided by Love, who asked the poet to recreate Laura's reality in poetry, releasing the poet from responsibility; the fact that Love has employed the paraphernalia of writing in vain self-critically states that the poet has not been successful in his task and the poet loves understatement. Ultimately, in "*RVF* 74," the poet utilizes the persona of Love he has set up in the previous passages to exempt his art from criticism: "et onde vien l'enchiostro, onde le carte / chi'i' vo empiendo di voi: se 'n ciò fallassi, / colpa d'Amor, non già defecto d'arte."[47] This statement is the culmination of Petrarch's commentary on his poetic inspiration. He falls in love with Laura; therefore, Love causes him to compose. It is not bad art, but bad love, and his art does not have be implicated. Thus Petrarch has achieved an interesting reversal of the tradition, which would postulate that art ignited by human love is always questionable.

It is love—synonymous with Laura—the poet implies he should have abandoned earlier. The conflict between love and old age is also addressed by Petrarch in the *RVF*, in which he tends to paint a more negative and self-critical picture, in contrast to his metatextual letters and notes to the poems. The first passage most closely relates to the letters in presenting an older man still dabbling in love:

Se bianche non son prima ambe le tempie
ch' a poco a poco par che 'l tempo mischi,
securo non sarò ben ch' io m'arrischi
talor ov' Amor l'arco tira et empie.[48]

Petrarch shows his awareness of the dangers of love in old age, but either apologizes for his weakness in dealing with love or excuses himself with the inevitability of such a situation when the God of Love chooses to target him.[49] In "*RVF* 168," the author

---

46 "*RVF* 309" lines 5-8. ['Love, who first set free my tongue, wishes me to depict and show her to whoever did not see her, and therefore a thousand times he has vainly put to work wit, time, pens, papers, inks'] (DL 488).

47 "*RVF* 74" lines 12-14. ['and whence comes the ink, whence the pages that I fill with words of you (if in that I err, it is the fault of Love, not at all a lack of art)'] (DL 174).

48 "*RVF* 83" lines 1-4. ['As long as both my temples are not white, which now time variegates little by little, I shall not be fully secure in risking myself where Love draws and loads his bow'] (DL 186).

49 In the *Secretum*, Petrarch is bombarded by a fictional Augustine with advice about old age and its place in a person's life; there Petrarch also denies feeling a change: "Secundum est, quia inter iocos et falsa gaudia senescitis . . . Nonne enim pudet hoc scienti canos nil mutationis attulisse? Pudet, piget et penitet, sed ultra non valeo. Scis autem quid hic michi solatii est? Quod illa mecum senescit" (*Secretum*, *Opere latine*, ed. Antonietta Bufano et al, 2 vols. [Turin: Unione Tipografico, 1975] 1: 44-259; here 1: 222-24, 226). ['The second reason for your stupidity is that old age comes on you still living a frivolous life of empty pleasures . . . Knowing what you know, are you not ashamed that your gray hairs have brought with them no change in you? Yes, and I am filled with regret and repentance, but there is nothing more I can do. Do you know what truly consoles me? She grows old along with me'] (Davy A. Carozza and H. James Shey, trans., *Petrarch's* Secretum *with Introduction, Notes, and Critical Anthology* [New York: Peter Lang, 1989] 127, 129).

intensifies the "love in old age" issue by moving from a passive to an active pattern of participation. He says, "[o]r sia che pò: già sol io non invecchio: / già per etate il mio desir non varia, / ben temo il viver breve che n'avanza."⁵⁰ Petrarch actually compromises his smoke screen of the indignant, aging poet just trying to get rid of those trifles; at the same time he does not cite an outside force that should take the blame for them. This is a step away from the blaming pattern.

In "*RVF* 32," Petrarch takes another step in the direction of sentiment uninfluenced by other forces. Musing on the ephemerality and the end of his life, the poet considers it the natural end of his creating love songs, "I' dico a' miei pensier': Non molto andremo / d'amor parlando omai . . ." ("*RVF* 32," lines 4-5) ['I say to my thoughts: Not much further now will we go speaking of love . . .' (DL 90)]. He alludes to the length of his creative life in lines 9 and 10, "'perché co·llui cadrà quella speranza / che ne fe' vaneggiar sí lungamente" ['for with it will fall the hope that made us rave so long' (DL 90)]. This self-criticism culminates in a statement that is purposefully kept general but is inevitably pertinent to the poet himself: "'sí vedrem chiaro poi come sovente / per le cose dubbiose altri s'avanza, / et come spesso indarno si sospira.'"⁵¹ The use of "sospira," 'sighs' made in vain, alone provides the intratextual reference to the collection itself, as it picks up the red thread of sighs woven through the *Canzoniere*. The poet's resigned tone of voice points to a low point in his creative life, when he doubts the usefulness of his poems.

Three other poems, 264, 311, and 332, his last metatextual *ubi sunt* poem about writing, illustrate Petrarch's real or feigned *contemptus mundi*. He criticizes himself for wanting to hang on to a place, earth, where nothing pleases or endures. "*RVF* 70" and "*RVF* 334" contradict these sentiments and affirm the poet as a righteous creator. In the former poem, the poet implores God to sanction his creative act. He begs, ". . . io il ripreghi / di dir libero un dí tra l'erba e i fiori: / *Drez et rayson es qu' ieu ciant e· m demori.*"⁵² This passage harbors a rebellious attitude toward the contemporary medieval philosophy which regards language as sacramental and restricts the poet to Christian-oriented literary creation. Petrarch demands songs, implicit love poetry, in an unabashed "this-worldliness" accentuated by the nature topos. Like Callimachus, Petrarch seeks divine justification, but in the process questions the medieval theory of signs. If only texts containing a Christian truth can signify, then asking God to acknowledge love poetry, deemed devoid of any spiritual value by many medieval philosophical minds, is revolutionary. Furthermore, in "*RVF* 334," Petrarch exhibits great indebtedness to the world he decries in previous poems:

S' onesto amor pò meritar mercede
et se Pietà anchor po quant'ella suole,

---

50 "*RVF* 168" lines 12-14. ['Now come what will: I am not the only one who is growing old, and my desire does not vary at all with age; but I do fear that what remains of life may be short'] (DL 314).

51 "*RVF* 32" lines 12-14. ['we shall see clearly then how often people put themselves forward for uncertain things and how often they sigh in vain'] (DL 90).

52 "*RVF* 70" lines 8-10. ['I beg him again to let me say freely one day among the grass and flowers: it is right and just that I sing and be joyful'] (DL 150).

mercede avrò, ché piú chiara che 'l sole
a Madonna et al mondo è la mia fede.[53]

His "onesto amor" [virtuous love] is supposed to remind us of Dante's relationship
with Beatrice and lend a respectable veneer to Petrarch's relationship with Laura.
Definitions of virtue become a major point of contention between Augustine and
Francesco in the *Secretum* insofar as Petrarch wants to justify his love for Laura as one
that is virtuous and leads to God.

Laura is, of course, at the heart of the *RVF*. Oaths of faithfulness sworn to Laura do
not protect her from criticism, however. While he staunchly defends her against outside critics, the poet himself can criticize his creation and inspiration. It is mostly an
intra-auctorial prerogative and action. He blames her for his suffering, "et la colpa è di
tal che non à cura" ("*RVF* 71," line 45) ['and the fault is hers who does not care' (DL
156)]. "*RVF* 119" illustrates Petrarch's hunger for fame and glory, to which he aspires
after his death, hoping for the assistance of Lady Glory. The theme of fame and glory
is also the focus of "*RVF* 228," which plays on the distinction between Laura and
lauro:

Amor co la man dextra il lato manco
m'aperse, et piantovi entro in mezzo 'l core
un lauro verde, sì che di colore
ogni smeraldo avria ben vinto et stanco.[54]

He ties the green *lauro* in with his pen and the sighs he produces. Laura and the laurel
are at the heart of his literary production, as John Freccero explains, "[t]he poetic lady
created by the poet . . . in turn creates him as poet laureate."[55] The circular pattern
does not refer to anything outside the circle; such a "poetic strategy corresponds, in the
theological order, to the sin of idolatry," Freccero concludes,[56] something which provides ample reason for Petrarch to be self-critical but also illustrates perfect intratextuality. In that same idolatrous vein, Petrarch wishes to eternalize Laura, who will in
return provide immortality for him: "et se mie rime alcuna cosa ponno, / consecrata fra
i nobili intellecti / fia del tuo nome qui memoria eterna."[57] Like Horace in his Canidia
poems, Petrarch emphasizes the poet's ability to create divinity as well as remembrance. In "*RVF* 345," Petrarch comes to terms with the fact that Laura has ascended
to heaven. This poem seems to be the watershed at which the poet has internalized his
vision of Laura and purified it completely.

With the last poem of the *Canzoniere*, Petrarch has completed his circular and intratextual apology structure. As evident from the aforementioned passages, characterized

---

53 "*RVF* 334" lines 1-4. ['If virtuous love can merit mercy and if pity still has all her wonted power,
    I shall find mercy, for brighter than the sun is my faithfulness to my lady and to the world'] (DL
    530).

54 "*RVF* 228" lines 1-4. ['With his right hand Love opened my left side and planted there in the
    midst of my heart a laurel so green that it would surpass and weary any emerald'] (DL 284).

55 John Freccero, "The Fig Tree and the Laurel: Petrarch's Poetics," *Petrarch: Modern Critical
    Views*, ed. Harold Bloom (New York: Chelsea House, 1989) 43-55; here 50.

56 Freccero, "The Fig Tree and the Laurel" 50.

57 "*RVF* 327" lines 12-14. ['and if my rhymes have any power, among noble intellects your name
    will be consecrated to eternal memory'] (DL 514).

by auctorial self-criticism and self-justification in an apologetic framework of such complexity in the *Rime Sparse*, the poet has been struggling with the contemporary philosophy of language and love poetry. The images of women dominate the *Canzoniere*; the body of the work is taken up by Laura—Petrarch's earthly love— while the final poem is dedicated to the Virgin—the female incarnation of heavenly love.[58] Mary—also an earthly woman who has been placed in heaven—through centuries of theology, has been effectively desexualized to become acceptable. The model woman in the medieval Christian cosmos shares little common ground with her medieval earthly sisters in the realm of sexual experience and physical love. Therefore, by bowing humbly to Mary, Petrarch seems to have turned from sexual love (*cupiditas*) embodied by Laura to heavenly love (*caritas*) embodied by Mary. Beginning with "*RVF* 360," the author has been moving his focus away from the earthly towards the heavenly, thereby implying acknowledgment of the end of his life and the termination of being in love and writing love lyrics: "—Non ti nasconder più, tu se' pur vèglio'" ("*RVF* 361," line 4) ['Do not pretend anymore, you are old' (DL 570)]. The poet demonstrates a progression from that statement to the praise of the Virgin.[59] "*RVF* 362" finds him moving towards heaven in his thoughts: "Volo con l'ali de' pensieri al cielo" (line 1) ['I fly with the wings of thought to Heaven' (DL 570)]. Although in "*RVF* 363" a shift toward God is evident—albeit in weariness and self-disgust—only "*RVF* 364" and "*RVF* 365" contain actual prayers, both echoing previous prayers and projecting the final invocation of the Virgin.

The poet's motivation, however, is not altogether salvation-bound in the spiritual sense—Laura is in heaven, and he wishes to join her. His motivation is like Dante's, although Dante is able to separate his earthly and heavenly picture of Beatrice into two works, whereas Petrarch resorts to the intratextual apotheosis of Laura. The poet proclaims:

Omai son stanco, et mia vita reprendo
di tanto error che di vertute il seme
à quasi spento, et le mie parti estreme,
alto Dio, a te devotamente rendo:
pentito et tristo de' miei sí spesi anni,
che spender si deveano in miglior uso,
in cercar pace et in fuggir affanni.[60]

---

58 "In appearance it is the traditional invocation of help with the composition of the poem, in which Christian poets had substituted the Virgin or the Trinity for the Muses, but in essence it is an invocation of spiritual help that the poet may enter the way of the heavenly love. The normal invocation seeks help with the actual writing of the poem; Petrarch is seeking help with the state of his soul which gives rise to the poem but exists apart from it" (Edward Williamson, "A Consideration of "Vergine Bella," *Italica* 29 [1952]: 215-28; here 222-23).

59 Hainsworth asserts that this movement "has no narrative necessity, beyond the need for a conclusion" (*Petrarch the Poet* 64).

60 "*RVF* 364" lines 5-11. ['Now I am weary and I reproach my life for so much error, which has almost extinguished the seed of virtue; and I devoutly render my last parts, high God, to You, repentant and sorrowing for my years spent thus, which ought to have been better used, in seeking peace and fleeing troubles'] (DL 572).

A love- and life-weary Petrarch pronounces these lines, echoing the familiar accusations of other poets that they wasted their life on trifles, disregarding the essential things. The phrase "mie parti estreme" (line 7) can be interpreted both as the last parts of his life and the last parts of this poetic work, especially since the first three hundred fifty-nine were almost devoid of Christian allusions, with classical elements dominating the poetic landscape. Despite professing such devout repentance, the poet has the audacity to blame God for his misery: "Signor che 'n questo carcer m'ài rinchiuso: / tràmene, salvo da li eterni danni, / ch'i' conosco 'l mio fallo, et non lo scuso."[61] This passage also demonstrates that every Petrarchan self-critical statement is somehow modified to make him look more appealing. "RVF 364" and "RVF 365" function more as justifications than self-criticisms.

Petrarch's final and most sudden turn—for ninety-seven poems between "RVF 267" and "RVF 364" are in favor of Laura and defend Petrarch's love for her—to the ultimate woman in the Christian cosmos, Mary, also displays a mixture of auctorial self-criticism and pride. The last seven poems in the collection still mirror the author's wish to follow Laura into death. The contemporary worldview would expect him to progress toward Mary; Dante also ended his *Divina Commedia* with a prayer to the Virgin, the most acceptable woman. Aldo Bernardo does not consider this poem a recantation but a complement to the already existing image of Laura; despite the fact that Petrarch has now lost confidence in his inspirational guide, the human element still dominates the last poem of the *Canzoniere*.[62] It is not surprising that although Petrarch invokes the Virgin with rather traditional epithets and phrases, he often repeats descriptions previously used to sketch Laura. The contrast drawn between Laura and Mary is also evident in, "[c]hè se poca mortal terra caduca / amar con sí mirabil fede soglio, / che devrò far di te, cosa gentile?"[63] This is a back-handed compliment for the Virgin; the passage illustrates how Petrarch, while employing all the conventional vocabulary of praise, still has to demonstrate his intellectual superiority and assure the Virgin that his devotion to her by far outranks his love for Laura.

He furthermore confesses that he has sinned with "parole" [words] ("RVF 366," line 85) and is in need of the Virgin's help in the cleansing process: "Vergine, i' sacro et purgo / al tuo nome et pensieri e 'ngegno et stile, / la lingua e 'l cor, le lagrime e i sospiri."[64] This plea and confession is personal but also heavily literary, since it involves style, tongue and, above all, sighs. Petrarch has now completed the circle and is about to end his collection of poems with the same word he started it with, "sospiri" [sighs] ("RVF 1" line 2; "RVF 366" line 128). The disavowal of his poetry as sighs of his heart is accomplished but again modified. Although admitting his error, he will not shoulder the blame alone but has to reveal his two accomplices, Laura and his

---

61 "RVF 364" lines 12-14. ['Lord who have enclosed me in this prison: draw me from it safe from eternal harm, for I recognize my fault and I do not excuse it'] (DL 572).

62 Aldo Bernardo, *Petrarch, Laura, and the* Triumphs (Albany: State U of New York P, 1974) 301, 157.

63 "RVF 366" lines 121-23. ['for if I am wont to love with such marvelous faith a bit of deciduous mortal dust, how will I love you, a noble thing?'] (DL 582).

64 "RVF 366" lines 126-28. ['Virgin, I consecrate and cleanse in your name my thought and wit and style, my tongue and heart, my tears and my sighs'] (DL 582).

"d'insania" ['insanity'] ("*RVF* 366" line 117)—demonstrating that his poetic inspiration has turned sour on him and led him astray from the path of salvation: "Medusa et l'error mio m'àn fatto un sasso / d'umor vano stillante" ("*RVF* 366" lines 111-12) ['Medusa and my error have made me a stone dripping vain moisture' (DL 582)].[65] The phrasing of line 111 is reminiscent of Ovid's self-accusation "carmen et crimen." Although in "*RVF* 366" Petrarch shows in the Virgin and Laura the dichotomy of the positive and negative female, the real Muse of the *Rime Sparse* is the finally-rejected Laura/Medusa. The initially engendering creative power that Laura could set free has now assumed a destructive side. Fleeing from Medusa, the poet takes refuge with the Virgin, the "vera beatrice" [the one who truly blesses]. The poet draws another comparison between Laura and Mary; Mary has done for humanity what Laura has accomplished for the poet. In the end, Laura's inspirational power still supersedes Mary's for Petrarch.

7.2.2. *Trionfi*

Despite Petrarch's rejection of Laura as a Medusa at the end of the *Canzoniere*, he cannot quite abstain from her. Petrarch is incredibly unsure about giving up Laura and love poetry and rejecting her in favor of salvation, for he rehabilitates her in the last of the *Trionfi*, *Triumphus Eternitatis*. Wilkins affirms that "*RVF* 366" cannot be assigned to a particular period and that Petrarch probably also worked on the *Trionfi* until the end of his life.[66] The *Triumphus Eternitatis* may be the last poem he ever wrote.[67] Since Petrarch rewrote most of his compositions several times, it becomes difficult to decide with certainty which work should be given precedence in the intra-auctorial whole. On the other hand, the works may have been revised and composed side by side, leaving an intentional contradiction representative of the poet's dilemma. Bernardo considers the manifestation of this dilemma "the essential novelty of Petrarch's image of the lady beloved in medieval love poetry" as he desperately tries to retain Laura's "image in his final vision of personal self-fulfillment and salvation."[68] In the last *Triumphus*, he rehabilitates Laura in the chaste image of a heaven-dweller: "Parranno allor l'angeliche divise / e l'oneste parole e i pensier casti / che nel cor giovenil Natura mise."[69] Laura, whom he cursed as Medusa and as the destroyer of

---

65 This phrasing echoes Ovid's dual errors: "duo crimina, carmen et error" (*Tristia* line II.207). Medusa is also mentioned in Petrarch's "Poem 179."

66 Wilkins, *The Making of the* "Canzoniere" 358, 356 and Bergin, *Petrarch* 42.

67 Foster, *Petrarch* 42.

68 Aldo Bernardo, ed. "Laura as a *Nuova Figura*," *Francesco Petrarca, Citizen of the World: Proceedings of the World Petrarch Congress, Washington, DC, April 6-13 1974* (Albany: State U of New York P, 1980) 179-92; here 191.

69 Francesco Petrarch, *Trionfi. Rime e Trionfi*, ed. Ferdinando Neri, 2nd ed. (Turin: Unione Tipografico, 1960) 511-618; *Trionfi Etern.* lines 88-99. ['Then will be manifest the angelic modes, / The honorable words, and the chaste thoughts / That nature set within her youthful

his honor, dignity, and salvation, has now been turned into a chaste creature, much like the Laura in "*RVF* 345." Chastity seems to be the umbrella under which Petrarch can metamorphose earthly love into heavenly love without losing either component. Whereas Dante needs to purge everything physical from his image of Beatrice, Petrarch still stresses that physicality, maybe as a contrast to Dante: "è quella che piangendo il mondo chiama / con la mia lingua e con la stanca penna; / ma 'l ciel pur di verderla intera brama."[70] That stress on her physical beauty proves that he did not succeed in desexualizing Laura and that Thomas Bergin's conclusion, he "sees her precisely as Dante saw Beatrice; an inspiration, a consolation, and a guide, ultimately indeed as a saint"[71] cannot be entirely supported. Although Petrarch constantly attempts to "define Laura as an inspiration fully compatible with the Christian ethic," it is Dante who creates a heavenly vision—Petrarch merely transplants an earthly vision into a heavenly setting.[72]

7.2.3. Secretum

Petrarch's *Secretum* is another intertextual and intra-auctorial monument to his struggle in coming to terms with the contemporary philosophy of language and salvation.[73] Possibly written between 1347 and 1353,[74] the *Secretum* presents in Book III a debate between Petrarch and a fictional Augustine about Petrarch's worldly writings. The *Secretum* addresses the two issues that seem to torment the author most, feminine inspiration (love) and glory, in the form of a trial framework with accusations coming from Augustine and extensive defenses and justifications from Petrarch, for the latter

---

heart'] (Ernest Hatch Wilkins, trans., *The* Triumphs *of Petrarch* [Chicago: U of Chicago P, 1962] 110).

70 Petrarch, *Trionfi Etern.* lines 136-38. ['Is she for whom the world is weeping still, / Calling her with my tongue and weary pen, / But heaven too desires her, body and soul'] (Wilkins, *The* Triumphs *of Petrarch* 112).

71 Bergin, *Petrarch* 151.

72 Bernardo, *Petrarch, Laura, and the* Triumphs 153-54.

73 Robert Pogue Harrison postulates that "Petrarch in the *Secreto conflictu curarum mearum* makes the same confession we hear in the lyric plaints of the *Rime sparse*, the confession of the self's *secretum*. . . . Petrarch's secret is simply the fate of self that, inwardly divided, struggles against itself. The *Canzoniere* is a confession of precisely this secret (the secret, once again, of modernity). The lyric self remains divided, or conflicted, between its desire for peace (which the poet portrays for the last poem) and its failure to will an event of conversion" (*The Body of Beatrice* 107). I contest the notion that Petrarch's inner struggle with self is a sign of modernity. Most of the authors represented in this study demonstrate their intra-auctorial struggle, which is often an inner struggle between their writing and their salvation. This is at any rate as medieval as it is deemed to be modern.

74 Hans Baron, *Petrarch's* Secretum: *Its Making and Its Meaning* (Cambridge: Medieval Academy of America, 1985) 1-18.

never denounces the literary pursuit itself.[75] While he claims that he has renounced love, he still credits Laura with having created him as an unforgettable poet, inspired his talent, and captured the much-desired glory for him. He would rather remain in error than renounce her completely:

> me, quantulumcunque conspicis, per illam esse; nec unquam ad hoc, siquid est, nominis aut glorie fuisse venturum, nisi virtutum tenuissimam sementem, quam pectore in hoc natura locaverat, nobilissimis hec affectibus coluisset. Illa iuvenilem animum ab omni turpitudine revocavit, uncoque, ut aiunt, retraxit, atque alta compulit expectare. . . . Deum profecto ut amarem, illius amor prestitit.[76]

Here the circular referentiality between Laura and *lauro* surfaces again: the poet creates Laura and she creates him as the poet laureate. This creation by Laura then is the antithesis to the detrimental function female influence has on poets in other self-critical instances. Petrarch is furthermore trying to liken Laura to Beatrice by claiming that she leads to God, a notion which the fictional Augustine rejects as an inversion of divine order, as love of the Creator should lead to love of creation and not vice versa. This particular passage presents a strange twist. Since it is presented as a criticism by Augustine and is therefore obviously an issue that bothers Petrarch, it could be seen either as his attempt to give Laura the same status as Beatrice—as a mediatrix between God and the poet—or as a criticism of Dante's view itself.

Petrarch's poison, human glory, for which he could not find any antidote, was due to Laura's direct influence:

> Quid faciam ergo? Labores ne meo interruptos deseram? An accelerare consultius est, atque illis, si Deus annuat, summam manum imponere, quibus curis exutus, espeditior ad maiora proficiscar? Tantum enim ac tam sumptuosum opus vix possum equanimiter medio calle deserere. . . . neque aliam ob causam propero nunc tam studiosus ad reliqua, nisi ut, illis explicitis, ad hec redeam: non ignarus . . . multo michi futurum esse securius studium hoc unum sectari et, deviis pretermissis rectum callem salutis apprehendere. Sed desiderium frenare non valeo.[77]

Several previously discussed elements are mentioned here. On the one hand, there is Petrarch's concern for salvation, coupled with the implication that a literary career is

---

75 Tatham, *Francesco Petrarca, the First Modern Man of Letters, His Life and Correspondence* 2: 248. For a discussion of Petrarch's addiction to fame, see Piero Boitani, *Chaucer and the Imaginary World of Fame* (Totowa, NJ: Barnes & Noble, 1984) 103-24.

76 Petrarch, *Secretum* 1: 182, 186. ['Whatever I am, I owe to her; and I should never have attained the modest name and reputation I have, if she had not fostered, through the power of my noble feelings for her, the feeble seeds of virtue that nature has placed in my heart. It was she who beckoned my youthful soul away from everything base and dragged me back with a hook, as they say, and forced me to have higher expectations. . . . love of her was indeed responsible for my love of God'] (Carozza and Shey, *Petrarch's* Secretum 108, 110).

77 Petrarch, *Secretum* 1: 250, 258. ['What, then, am I to do? Shall I abandon my unfinished works? Or would it be wiser to speed up my work and, with God's help, put the finishing touches on it? Once rid of these worries, shall I not move on to more important matters with a free mind? I can scarcely bear to abandon in mid-course a work that has cost me so much. . . . And now I eagerly hasten to other tasks, so that I can return to these considerations, once they are finished. I am not ignorant, as you were just saying, that it would be a much safer course to tend to the care of my soul and set myself straight on the road to salvation, avoiding the byways. But I cannot restrain my desire for study'] (Carozza and Shey, *Petrarch's* Secretum 140, 144).

contrary to this. On the other hand, the poet states that he not only writes for the sake of writing but also because that particular work could be successful and bring him fame. While he could renounce love with a certain degree of success, he could never sacrifice his yearning for glory and fame, which might be considered the graver offense at that time.

It is not astonishing to discover another letter in which Petrarch seems to answer Boccaccio's own question—which will be discussed later—about his continued literary endeavors. Down-playing the aspect of addiction depicted in the *Secretum*, Petrarch tries to pass his literary efforts off as recreational; he writes, "[l]egere hoc meum et scribere, quod laxari iubes, levis est labor, imo dulcis est requies, que laborum gravium parit oblivionem."[78] Appropriately distinguishing between worldly and heavenly realms, Petrarch makes his final plea for literature as his great love: "Verissime michi videor dicturus: omnium terrestrium delectationum ut nulla literis honestior, sic nulla diuturnior, nulla suavior, nulla fidelior, nulla que per omnes casus possessorem suum tam facili appartu, tam nullo fastidio comitetur."[79] As an answer to the despairing Boccaccio, who has lost all faith in himself as an earthly creator, Petrarch pens the following statement: "optarem—fateor—me, quod aiunt, vita peracta viventem inveniret. Id quia ut sunt res non spero, opto ut legentem aut scribentem vel, si Cristo placuerit, orantem ac plorantem mors inveniat."[80] This passage affirms that Petrarch would only yield up his writing skills if God, the Ultimate Creator, would demand such a thing. His prolonged auctorial activity and complex intra-auctorial web of affirmation and negation is witness to a secure writer who believes in divine sanctioning and can, therefore, safely maneuver through the treacherous waters of contemporary philosophy of language and its impediment to salvation.

7.3. Giovanni Boccaccio

The same is only partially valid for Giovanni Boccaccio (1313-75), who presents a complex intra-auctorial web of literary theory, auctorial self-criticism, and self-justification but who seems to make the transition from the profane to the sacred less smoothly than Dante and yet more severely than Petrarch (who keeps playing both

---

78 Petrarch, "*Sen.* XVII, 2" 866. ['to read–this is what I do–and write, which you bid me let go, is a light effort, or rather a delightful rest which makes me forget heavy labors'] (Bernardo, Levin, and Bernardo, *Francis Petrarch: Letters of Old Age* 2: 653).

79 Petrarch, "*Sen.* XVII, 2" 866-868. ['What I am about to say seems to me very true: of all earthly delights, just as none is more noble than letters, so none is more enduring, none sweeter, none more faithful, none that accompanies its possessor through all vicissitudes with such simple equipment and never with a bad taste'] (Bernardo, Levin, and Bernardo, *Francis Petrarch: Letters of Old Age* 2: 653).

80 Petrarch, "*Sen.* XVII, 2" 868. ['I confess I would wish, as they sat, that it find me living as though my life is done. But since, as things are, I have no hope of that, I wish that death would find me reading or writing, or, if it please Christ, praying and weeping'] (Bernardo, Levin, and Bernardo, *Francis Petrarch: Letters of Old Age* 2: 654).

strings until the very end). Although Boccaccio is equally dependent on female inspiration, he does not create a *donna angelicata* whom he can subsequently exalt to a heavenly position. Although his disillusionment with earthly female inspiration then turns to the Virgin, it assumes the form of antifeminist rejection of earthly ancillas. The *Decameron* establishes the Ladies as Boccaccio's creative handmaidens, whereas the *Corbaccio* destroys that construct. Boccaccio also uses the compiler's defense and his own theory of language to apologize for and defend his *Decameron*. Later intertextual evidence from the *Genealogie deorum gentilium* likewise suggests a change of mind in that respect. Metatextual evidence in the form of correspondence points to a possible extratextual conversion experience that could have influenced Boccaccio's intra-auctorial path in its turn away from secular poetry to Latin writing.

In his most famous and critically acclaimed work, Boccaccio puts forth a great deal of literary theory about writing "cento novelle, o favole o parabole o istorie che dire le vogliamo" designed for the succor and diversion of Ladies in love to provide "diletto" [pleasure] and "utile consiglio"[81] [useful advice], invoking the Horatian requirements for good literature, *utilitas* and *delectatio*. While this literary theory contains merely a token self-critical element that is most defiant and masks a great deal of self-assertion, defense, and flat-out attack against his critics, it is nonetheless necessary to cover it in order to discuss Boccaccio's self-critical writings that oppose this theory and to illustrate the author's change in his perception of his craft. In the *Decameron*, Boccaccio rests his authorship on two pillars: God and the Ladies. His literary theory is expounded in the Proemio, the Introduction to Day IV, and the Conclusione dell'autore; it revolves around the Ladies, the implied audience of the *Decameron*, and is marked by the addresses "Carissime donne" (*Dec.* IV, Intro 459) [Dearest ladies] and "Nobilissime giovane" (*Dec.* Concl. 1254) [Noble young ladies] as well as by Boccaccio's usage of the vernacular language.[82]

---

81 *Dec.* Proemio 9. ['a hundred stories, or fables, or parables, or histories, or whatever you wish to call them'] (MB 3).

82 It is generally assumed that Boccaccio released the first three books of his *Decameron* on a trial basis; obviously some critics—possibly fellow authors—must have given him less-than-favorable reviews, which prompted him to defend himself in the beginning to the fourth day (Francis Macmanus, *Boccaccio* [New York: Sheed, 1947] 197). Even Robert Hastings argues that "for all that, when the narrator of the *Decameron* speaks in the first person to his readers, it is reasonable to assume that Boccaccio expects them to conclude that they are being addressed directly by the author himself and that what he has to say is a reflection (which is not the same as a literal statement) of his own thoughts and experiences" ("To Teach or Not to Teach: The Moral Dimension of the *Decameron* Reconsidered," *Italian Studies* 44 (1989): 19-40; here 25). On the Proemio, Introduction to Day IV, and Conclusione dell'autore, see Cesare De Michelis, *Contraddizioni nel* Decameron (Milano: Guanda, 1983) 60; Robert Fedi, "Il 'regno' di Filostrato: Natura e struttura della Giornata IV del *Decameron*," *Modern Language Notes* 102 (1987): 45-49; Pier Massimo Forni, *Adventures in Speech: Rhetoric and Narration in Boccacio's* Decameron (Philadelphia: U of Pennsylvania P, 1996); Robert Hollander, *Boccaccio's Two Venuses* (New York: Columbia UP, 1977) 106-7 and *Boccaccio's Dante and the Shaping Force of Satire* (Ann Arbor: U of Michigan P, 1997) 89-107; M. Janssens, "The Internal Reception of the Stories within the *Decameron*," *Boccaccio in Europe: Proceedings of the Boccaccio Conference, Louvain, December 1975*, ed. Gilbert Tournoy (Louvain: Leuven UP, 1977) 135-49; Guiseppe Mazzotta,

Like Jean de Meun, Boccaccio charges himself with a number of offenses and appears self-critical towards his own writing, although he immediately justifies his misdeeds and always comes out on top. Boccaccio introduces criticism and then discredits the reprimand by attacking the critic. First, in contrast to some of the medieval French and Spanish examples, Boccaccio is not being accused of misogyny but its opposite: "voi mi piacete troppo e che onesta cosa non è che io tanto diletto prenda di piacervi e di consolarvi e, alcuni han detto peggio, di commendarvi, come io fo."[83] Boccaccio admits: "Le quali cose io apertissimamente confesso, cioè che voi me piacete e che io m'ingegno do piacere a voi" (*Dec.* IV, Intro 466) ['To these accusations I openly confess, that is, that you do please me and I do try to please you' (MB 248)]. His admission of guilt is minimal and serves the sole purpose of reasserting his position and justifying his literary production on the *Decameron* so far, because, as he explains, the Ladies are ancillary to his artistic creation: "senza che le donne già mi fur cagione di comporre mille versi" (*Dec.* IV, Intro 468) ['Furthermore, the fact is that, ladies have already been the reason for my composing these thousands of verses' (MB 248)].[84] Boccaccio's art emphasizes the ladies' ancillary function even more when he states that "[e] già più ne trovarono tralle loro favole i poeti, che molti ricchi tra' loro tresori" (*Dec.* IV, Intro 469) ['And yet, poets have found more of it in their fables than many rich men have in their treasures' (MB 249)]. This passage seems to challenge the Christian world view by challenging the uselessness of fiction. To Luigi Russo, the Ladies are merely a symbol for the worldliness of the new poetry; they are the muses of this world, experts in human vices and values.[85]

While being artistic stimuli, the Ladies also help define the narrative location, as well as the contemporary literary theory, in which they partially also function as scapegoats for Boccaccio. Having made very explicit in the "cornice" of the *Decameron* that the stories were told in gardens, designated spots of pleasure, he feels that nobody should take offense at the tales, since they were not narrated in churches or the schools of philosophers and did not harm anybody. Churches are holy ground and need to be honored, although Boccaccio goes right on the offensive and charges the church with more scandalous writings than his own; both schools of philosophers and churches were domains of men, however, and the stories' immediate and designated audience was women, as was that of most of the storytellers. Since Boccaccio's pen is always a two-edged sword, his turns on the Ladies and uses them as a negative excuse for the facileness of some tales: "Senza che, a avere a favellare a semplici giovinette, come voi il più siete, sciocchezza sarebbe stata l'andar cercando e faticandosi in trovar cose molte esquisite, e gran cura porre di molto misuratamente

---

"The *Decameron*: The Marginality of Literature," *University of Toronto Quarterly* 42 (1972): 64-81; Carlo Muscetta, *Giovanni Boccaccio* (Rome: Laterza, 1974) 156-64, 299-317; Guido di Pino, *La polemica del Boccaccio* (Florence: Vallecchi, 1953) 209-20; and Raffaello Ramat, *Saggi sul Rinascimento* (Florence: La Nuova Italia, 1969) 93-106.

83 *Dec.* IV, Intro 460-61. ['you please me too much and that it is not fitting for me to take so much pleasure from pleasing and consoling you, and, what seems to be worse, in praising you as I do'] (MB 244-45).

84 Also see Bernardo, "Dante, Petrarch, and Boccaccio" 308.

85 Luigi Russo, *Letture Critiche del* Decameron (Bari: Laterza, 1971) 11.

parlare."[86] Since the intended audience is to blame for everything, Boccaccio also exploits his Ladies as a cover against the charge that some stories are too long, for the tales were written for Ladies who had time for leisure, and for nobody else (*Dec.* Concl. 1259).[87]

In his self-assigned role of reporter in the second main element of his literary theory, Boccaccio focuses on the narrators and the readers of the stories. In compliance with that role, he faults the narrators of the stories, the nature of the stories, and their necessary verisimilitude, and then shifts the remainder of literary responsibility onto the readers' corrupt minds.[88] On the one hand, Boccaccio denies the insinuation of having used "troppa licenzia" [too much license] and having subjected the Ladies to unsuitable literature with the claim that no story is "disonesta" [unfitting] as long as it is narrated in "onesti vocabuli" *(Dec.* Concl. 1254-55) [fitting language], implying that language presides over content, signifier over signified.[89] On the other hand, he admits that there might be a few "paroletta" [trifling expressions] that were too "liberale" for the "spigolistra donna" [the prudish women] who prefer "parole" [words] over "fatti" [deeds] (*Dec.* Concl. 1255). Boccaccio concedes that his critics might be right about the unseemliness of certain stories, although he counteracts that with "la qualità delle novelle" (*Dec.* Concl. 1255) [the nature of the story], which needed to be preserved to maintain the verisimilitude of the events narrated. He further cites his use of sexual slang expressions as equivalent to everyday spoken language, which, after all, lends verisimilitude to the writing, since the vernacular is the language of the people.

Boccaccio actively draws the reader into the auctorial triangle of author, text, and reader in order to shirk responsibility and to displace the narrative center. Paralleling to Chaucer, who also employed the rationale that "[l]e quali, chenti che elle si sieno e nuocere e giovar possono, sí come possono tutte l'altre cose, avendo riguardo all'ascoltatore."[90] Boccaccio elaborates on his theory of language. He saddles the readers or listeners with the burden of responsibility: "Niuna corrotta mente intese mai sanamente parola; e così come le oneste a quella non giovano, così quelle che tanto oneste non sono la ben disposta non posson contaminare."[91] In order to substantiate his point, Boccaccio compares his *Decameron* with Scriptures, invoking again that

---

86 *Dec.* Concl. 1258-9. ['moreover in speaking to unassuming young ladies, as most of you are, it would have been foolish to go to about trying to find fancy stories and to take great pains speaking in an extremely formal matter'] (MB 687).

87 See Joy Hambuechen Potter for the argument that Boccaccio claims that women do not count ("Women in the *Decameron*," *Studies in the Italian Renaissance: Essays in Memory of Arnolfo B. Ferruolo*, eds. Gian Paolo Biasin et al [Naples: Società Editrice Napoletana, 1985] 87-103).

88 Claude Cazalé Bérard perceives in the "'thématisation' de l'auteur/ rédacteur" a profound and significant evolution in the process of literary creation and reception ("Propositions pour une approche de la thématique dans l'intratextualité, l'intertextualité et l'extratextualité," *Strumenti Critici* n.s., a. 4 [1989]: 305-20; here 318).

89 See footnote 22 in Chapter 6.

90 *Dec.* Concl. 1256. ['But as they stand, these tales, like all other things, may be harmful or useful depending on who the listener is'] (MB 686).

91 *Dec.* Concl. 1257. ['A corrupt mind never understands a word in a healthy way! And just as fitting words are of no use to a corrupt mind, so a healthy mind cannot be contaminated by words which are not proper'] (MB 686).

acknowledged medieval relationship between God as the Ultimate Creator of the word and the earthly author as the flawed creator of human words. Venturing close to blasphemy, Boccaccio declares that many have been led astray through wrong interpretation of the Bible, implying inherent harmfulness in the perfect Logos of God the Author. He states that:

> Ciascuna cosa in se medesima è buona a alcuna cosa, e male adoperata può essere novica di molte: e cosí dico delle mie novelle. Chi vorrà da quelle malvagio consiglio e malvagia operazion trarre, elle nol vieteranno a alcuno, se forse in sé l'hanno, e torte e tirate fieno a averlo: e chi utilità e frutto ne vorrà, elle nol negheranno.[92]

Thus, according to Boccaccio—and, later, Chaucer—interpretation and the mind of the reader are the culprits. But at the same time, he asserts the profitable potential of his writings, as did Chaucer and Jean de Meun. Boccaccio adds this qualification: "né sarà mai che altro che utile e oneste sien dette o tenute se a que' tempi o a quelle persone si leggeranno per cui e pe' quali state son raccontate."[93] Consequently, the author cleverly can avoid any criticism by assigning his stories a definite audience and locality: Ladies in love, in gardens. If other individuals outside of this prescribed circle read his stories, the author cannot be blamed, since the readers are obviously not in the right frame of mind. Ultimately, like Chaucer later, the author recommends: "Tuttavia chi va tra queste leggendo, lasci star quelle pungono e quelle che dilettano legga" (*Dec.* Concl. 1259) ['However, whoever reads through these stories can leave aside those he finds offensive and read those he finds pleasing' (MB 687)]. Ironically, this warning comes at the very end of the *Decameron* and in order to discover which tales are to be read, one must first read them all. Boccaccio suggests that the reading and writing processes need to be freed from the unilaterality of auctorial responsibility, in which the reader would merely be a victim and never an accomplice in the literary sinning process. He affirms that the reader is as guilty as the author in creating a literary text. Boccaccio's textual and auctorial theory stands as an antithesis to what Roland Barthes calls the "'classical' bourgeois text" that "makes its reader into a passive 'consumer' because it is 'readable' ('lisible') only on the level of representation, where language is assumed to be transparently referential and ideologically innocent" but reinforces Barthes' theory that "the 'writable' ('scriptible') text liberates the reader to participate actively in the 'work' ('travail') or 'production' of literature itself. Each reader 'rewrites' the text by discovering a new arrangement of signification."[94]

---

92 *Dec.* Concl. 1257. ['Everything is, in itself, good for some determined goal, but badly used it can cause a great deal of harm; and I can say the same of my stories. Whoever wishes to derive evil counsel from them or use them for wicked ends will not be prohibited from doing so by the tales themselves if, by chance, they contain such things and are twisted and distorted in order to achieve this end; and whoever wishes to derive useful advice and profit from them will not be prevented from doing so'] (MB 686-87).

93 *Dec.* Concl. 1257. ['nor will these stories ever be described or regarded as anything but useful and proper if they are read at those times and to those people for whom they had been written'] (MB 687).

94 Thaïs E. Morgan, "Is There an Intertext in This Text?" *American Journal of Semiotics* 3 (1985): 1-40; here 19.

Boccaccio, nonetheless, protects himself from charges of unseemliness on both fronts: since both the reader and the sources of the stories are to blame, he pushes responsibility and narrative center into the background. While his medieval contemporaries might have considered him a compiler, Boccaccio poses as a mere scribe and reporter, not a creative author, taking the route of least accountability and greatest literary license, especially when charged with the inclusion of unsuitable tales. Like Jean de Meun and Jean le Fèvre, he incriminates his sources:

> ma io non pote' né doveva scrivere se non le raccontate, e per ciò esse che le dissero le dovevan dir belle e io l'avrai scritte belle. Ma se pur prosuppor si volesse che io fossi stato di quelle e lo 'nventore e lo scrittore, che non fui, dico che io non mi vergognerei che tutte belle non fossero, per ciò che maestro alcun non si truova, da Dio in fuori, che ogni cosa faccia bene e compiutamente.[95]

In the scholastic auctorial hierarchy, he thanks God for His assistance and acknowledges His infallible craft.[96] This gratitude to God appears suspicious when coupled with Boccaccio's acknowledged indebtedness to the Ladies. Serving as a designated audience and supposedly as the source of the stories, they function both as his earthly muses, to whom Boccaccio vows lifelong service, and as symbols of the worldliness of the new poetry. An obviously irreconcilable dichotomy is set up.

In the *Corbaccio* (1355), Boccaccio's last vernacular work he contradicts certain notions of authorship and language expressed in the *Decameron*.[97] In this caustic antifeminist satire—masked as a dream vision to blunt its acerbic impact and to grant more vitriolic license to the author—Boccaccio portrays himself in the embarrassing role of a duped lover. The work is considered a "turning point" in Boccaccio's literary career, "a rejection of the amorous tradition of the earlier works," a *Remedia amoris* to his *Decameron*.[98] More importantly, it is a reflection on Boccaccio's changing view of his literary craft, which now opposes things put forth in the *Decameron*. The change in intended audience, now male, and the substitution of the Virgin for the Ladies in the "Proemio" do not simply constitute a movement from worldly to heavenly matters but a change in Boccaccio's idea of artistic creation and the inspiration of that creation, paying renewed tribute to God as the Supreme Author. He appears to have lost all faith in the capacity of earthly women to inspire positive literary creation.[99] Boccaccio

---

95 *Dec.* Concl. 1258. ['but I could do nothing but write down the tales as they were told, which is to say that had those ladies telling them told them better, I would have written them better. But let us suppose that I was the one who created these stories as well as the one who wrote them down (which I was not). Then, let me tell you that I would not be ashamed if they were not all good, since no artisan, save God Himself, can create everything perfect and complete'] (MB 687).

96 While "Dante's story of course has a highly significant configuration that derives from, or participates in, the master narrative of Christianity" (Harrison, *The Body of Beatrice* 136), Boccaccio writes the "Human Comedy."

97 Salvatore Battaglia, *Le Epoche della letteratura Italiana: Medioevo, Umanesimo, Rinascimento* (Naples: Liguroni, 1965) 368-69; Margo Cottiono-Jones, "The *Corbaccio*: Notes for a Mythical Perspective of Moral Alternatives," *Forum Italicum* 4 (1970): 490-509; Robert Hastings, *Nature and Reason in the* Decameron (Manchester: Manchester UP, 1975) 60.

98 Normand R. Cartier, introduction, *Boccaccio's Revenge*, by Giovanni Boccaccio (The Hague: Martinus Nijhoff, 1977) vii-x; here ix and Hollander, *Boccaccio's Two Venuses* 28.

99 Robert Hollander perceives a change in Boccaccio's writing, attributable to about the time when Boccaccio supposedly met Petrarch in 1350 (*Boccaccio's Two Venuses* 108), which might be

opposes not only the *Decameron* but also Dante's vision of Beatrice as a mediatrix and Petrarch's half-hearted shift from Laura to the Virgin Mary. Having repudiated the source of his literary creation, the author condemns his much-defended novellas as a waste of time: "per non consumare il tempo in novelle"[100] Boccaccio does not repudiate all literary creation, only the one that engulfs the passion of love: "poesia . . . non menoma tra l'altre scienzie." (*Cor*. 28-29) ['poetry . . . not the least among the disciplines' (Cassell 23)]. On three more occasions, he objects to the term "donne" (*Cor*. 30, 31, 45) [ladies], which the "femine" (*Cor*. 30) [women] usurp unrightfully, and recalls that term from the *Decameron*. The antifeminist satire in the *Corbaccio* contradicts Boccaccio's assertion of a lifelong devotion to the Ladies. The contradiction is underscored by the substitution of the Virgin for the Ladies in the Proemio of the *Corbaccio* and the evocation of the Muses, whose company Boccaccio had scorned in the *Decameron* in favor of the Ladies. The supplanting of the Ladies echoes Boethius' *Consolation*, in which Philosophy drives out the whores of the theater: "Mentre tu sarai ne' boschi e ne' remoti luoghi, le Ninfe castalide, alle quali queste malvage femone si vogliono assomigliare, non t'abbandoneranno già mai."[101]

Moreover, Boccaccio seems to betray another favorite concept, truthfulness in literature. In the *Corbaccio* he admits that a writer could and would employ untruth to achieve his purpose, something which the author would not admit in the *Decameron*; there, the fault or truth factor of a tale lay either with the narrator or with the reader: "Se io ho il vero già molte volte inteso, ciascuno che in quello s'è dilettato di studiare o si diletta che tu fai, ottimamente, eziandio mentendo sa cui gli piace tanto famoso e sì glorioso rendere negli orecchi degli uomini."[102] In the *Genealogie deorum gentilium*, Book XIV, Boccaccio reverses his statement about the corrupting potential of literature from the *Decameron* by admitting that the fault lies with the author, not

---

interpreted as a shift from the *dolce stil nuovo* to the New Humanism. Hollander considers the *Decameron* and the *Corbaccio* an Ovidian pair, an *Ars Amatoria* and *Remedia Amoris*, the latter a simultaneous companion piece and "continual correction of the bad doctrines of love" (*Boccaccio's Two Venuses* 114), "not a later recantation of its values" (Hollander, *Boccaccio's Last Fiction* [Philadelphia: U of Pennsylvania P, 1988] 2).

100 Giovanni Boccaccio, *Corbaccio*, ed. Pier Giorgio Ricci (Turin: Guilio Einaudi Editore, 1977) 20. ['so as not to waste time on anecdotes'] (Anthony K. Cassell, trans. and ed., *The Corbaccio or the Labyrinth of Love*, by Giovanni Boccaccio, 2nd rev. ed. [Binghamton, NY: Medieval & Renaissance Texts & Studies, 1993] 16).

101 Boccaccio, *Cor*. 43. ['While you are in the woods and remote places, the Castalian nymphs, with whom these wicked women would compare themselves, will never abandon you'] (Cassell, *The Corbaccio or the Labyrinth of Love* 36). Boccaccio identified with the love-sick ladies of the *Decameron* but now he behaves like a person who has fallen out of love. For a compelling discussion of this issue, see Janet Levarie Smarr, *Boccaccio and Fiammetta: The Narrator as Lover* (Urbana: U of Illinois P, 1986) 158.

102 Boccaccio, *Cor*. 88. ['If I have heard the truth many times in the past, everyone who has delighted and delights in the study of something which you do so excellently, can render even by fiction whom he pleases so famous and so glorious to the ears of men'] (Cassell, *The Corbaccio or the Labyrinth of Love* 72).

with the reader: "Lascivientium quippe ingeniorum culpa hec est."[103] Having thus exonerated both the narrator and the reader, he destroys the carefully raised smoke screen of the compiler, situates the narrative center back within the auctorial mind, and excludes the reader from the creative process.

After the *Corbaccio*, Boccaccio started to pursue Latin writings exclusively. One might even be able to interpret his *De mulieribus claris* as a recantation for the *Corbaccio*. On the extra-literary plane, Boccaccio in his sixties did not recommend his *Decameron* even to a female audience, as he writes to Mainardo Cavalcanti: "Sane, quod inclitas mulieres tuas domesticas nugas meas legere permiseris non laudo, quin imo queso per fidem tuam ne feceris."[104] However, he does not give up writing and staunchly defends literature and poetry in the *Genealogie*; his renewed discovery of and devotion to the ancient writers demonstrates an inverse relationship to Chaucer's auctorial progression: Boccaccio moves from writing in the vernacular, supposedly contemporary reality, to dedicating himself solely to the classical authors, while Chaucer progresses from giving credit to classical authors to creating a vision of contemporary reality.

Metatextual evidence links this change in Boccaccio's writing career with an extratextual event. According to some biographers and critics, and as evidenced from Petrarchan letters to Boccaccio, the author underwent a conversion experience early in 1360, enduring excruciating self-doubt about his more worldly creations. The experience had been induced by a frightful encounter with a Carthusian monk, who claimed to have seen several of Boccaccio's contemporaries suffering in the flames of hell.[105] Through Boccaccio's correspondence with Petrarch, we know that this personal experience caused Boccaccio to question his literary achievement greatly. Though Boccaccio's initial letter is lost, Petrarch's response to it is a valuable source of both his own sentiment and Boccaccio's experience and thus needs to be looked at closely. In "*Sen.* V, 2," Petrarch demonstrates both the intensity of Boccaccio's reaction and of his own love for literature and books by reacting very strongly to Boccaccio's threat to burn his books: "they added this too: that you had burned whatever you once had of vernacular poetry . . . your intention was to redo the ones you had first let loose in your teens and then in your twenties—now that you talent is solid and seasoned . . . even greater was my wonderment at this plan to burn what you wished to revise so that

103 Boccaccio, *Genealogie deorum gentilium Libri*, ed. Vincenzo Romano, 2 vols., Scrittori d'Italia 201 (Bari: Giuseppe Laterza, 1951) 2: 699. ['The fault for such corruption lies in the licentious mind of the artist'] (Charles G. Osgood, trans., *Boccaccio on Poetry*, by Giovanni Boccaccio [Princeton: Princeton UP, 1930] 38).

104 Boccaccio, "A Mainardo Cavalcanti (1373)," *Opere latine minori*, ed. Aldo Francesco Massèra (Bari: Guiseppe Laterza 1928) 209-14; here 211. [I, indeed, do not approve that you allow the renowned women of your household to read my trifles but rather implore you by your faith not to do so].

105 John Addington Symonds, *Giovanni Boccaccio as Man and Author* (London: John C. Nimmo, 1895) 68-70. See also Herbert Thurston, "The Conversion of Boccaccio and Chaucer," *Studies* 25 (1936): 215-25.

there would be nothing left for you to revise."[106] It emerges here that according to Petrarch's sources Boccaccio—much like Augustine in the *Retractations*—had been contemplating rewriting his earlier Italian works, which would be in itself intra-auctorial self-criticism and a form of recantation, although not as severe as the ultimate destruction of his works. It is obvious that Petrarch, consistent with the persona we have already seen, considers the rewriting of poetry a viable undertaking, whereas destruction is abominable to him. At the end of this letter, the author shows some understanding of Boccaccio's position when he writes, "I almost wish I had done with all my works, while it was possible, what I did do [burn] with many of them."[107] Two factors qualify this statement, however. Petrarch only "almost" wished that—and only because he wanted to save his works from ignorant judges; burning his writings would be a protective measure and not a self-critical one. Boccaccio's motivation seems to be more self-critical.

More details about Boccaccio's poetic career, albeit relayed by Petrarch second hand, encapsulate the underlying conclusion of this study that self-criticism is a strategy that perpetuates writing:

> For he tells me that in your early youth, fascinated solely by the vernacular style, you devoted the most time and care to it until, in the course of your research and reading, you came upon the vernacular compositions of my youth in that genre. Whereupon your urge to write grew cool; nor were you subsequently satisfied with not writing any more in that vein—you had to express your hatred for what you had already written; intending not to revise but destroy, you burned them all and deprived yourself and posterity of the fruit of your labors in this genre for no other reason than you judged them inferior to mine.[108]

Boccaccio is portrayed in both an intra-auctorial and an interauctorial fashion. Intra-auctorially, his youthful vernacular creation could endanger his salvation, a fear that has been dismissed by Petrarch as a scare tactic. From the intra-auctorial information, Petrarch draws the interauctorial conclusion that Boccaccio wanted to discard his

---

106 Bernardo, Levin, and Bernardo, *Francis Petrarch: Letters of Old Age* 1: 158. The Latin original is not available to me. See Nathalie Grimes Lawrence for an account of Petrarch's predilection for books. In an interauctorial aside in the *Secretum*, Petrarch demonstrates his abhorrence of book-burning: "Gravi enim morbo correptus viciniam mortis expavi, nichil in eo statu sentiens molestius quam quod *Africam* ipsam semiexplicitam linquebam. Itaque, alienam dedignatus limam, ignibus eam propriis manibus mandare decreveram, nulli amicorum satis fidens, qui post emissum spiritum id michi prestaret; proptereaquod Virgilium nostrum ab imperatore Cesare Augusto hac in re sola non exauditum esse memineram. Quid te moror? Parum affuit quin Africa preter vicini solis ardores, quibus eternum subiacet, ac preter Romanorum faces, quibus ter olim longe lateque perusta est, meis etiam flammis arderet" (*Secretum* 2: 236). ['Once I was stricken with a serious illness and was afraid I was near death, but what bothered me the most then was that I was leaving the *Africa* half-finished. Unwilling for it to receive the finishing touches from another, I determined to burn it myself because I could not trust any of my friends to do it after my death. I recalled that such a request was the only one denied to Vergil by the Emperor Augustus Caesar. But to get to the point, the land of Africa, burnt already by the blazing sun, to which it is eternally exposed, and devastated three times far and wide by Roman torches, almost suffered another conflagration at my hands'] (Carozza and Shey, *Petrarch's* Secretum 136.)

107 Bernardo, Levin, and Bernardo, "*Sen.* V, 2," *Francis Petrarch: Letters of Old Age* 1: 165.

108 Bernardo, Levin, and Bernardo, "*Sen.* V, 2," *Francis Petrarch: Letters of Old Age* 1: 158-59.

poetic activity because he felt inadequate by comparison with Petrarch. Therefore, Petrarch is scolding Boccaccio for not wanting to write anymore, since he himself believes in the inherent salutary worth of literature. To him, writers should not abandon their work out of self-doubt, for they owe it to themselves and the world to show the fruits of their labor. To Petrarch, writing is one of the talents God hands out, and by burying the talent, the writer would act against this God-given gift.[109] Furthermore, Petrarch senses something in Boccaccio's attitude and motivation that generally underlies this entire study. He condemns Boccaccio's action, deems his motive suspect, and voices this final judgment: "I do not know whether it is a self-deprecating humility or a pride, that feels superior to others. . . . I fear, then, that something of pride may be mingled with such great humility"; Petrarch's tactic is to caution Boccaccio not to reject writing completely, and he ends his sermon with the plea, "[h]ave mercy on your works, then, and spare them the flames."[110] This is a reinforcement of the literary nature of both Petrarch's and Boccaccio's recantations.

Dante, Petrarch, and Boccaccio demonstrate through their statements how they coped with their creative power and the role women played therein. Boccaccio seems to have been the one who could divest himself most completely of the influence of female inspiration by abandoning the kind of writing that would necessitate such inspiration. Petrarch does not enlist "eros" enough "in the service of religion" but in the service of his own poetic and human advancement and, therefore, has to grapple much more with the implications the use of a female inspiration conjures up: "The *Canzoniere* is both a confession of sin and an assertion of artistic genius."[111] While Petrarch castigates himself for having been subservient to Laura, and to the world in general, Dante reverses that situation and reproaches himself for not having been faithful to Beatrice.[112] This demonstrates that the poets have set up their premises differently and apply self-criticism accordingly; what seems to us like a contradiction is a mere logical conclusion of the initial strategy. With Boccaccio's initial enslavement to female inspiration, Petrarch's constant wrestling, and Dante's devising a system that combines love of woman and love of God into one powerful force, untouchable by the critics of earthly love, one has to conclude that Johann Wolfgang von Goethe was correct in proclaiming that poets will always be ensnared by femininity: "Das Ewig-Weibliche zieht uns hinan."[113]

---

109 Alistair Minnis claims that poetry "then, for Boccaccio, as for Petrarch, was generally sacral but not sacred . . . Neither of them believed that the poet operated under direct divine influence" (MN 390).

110 Bernardo, Levin, and Bernardo, "*Sen.* V, 2," *Francis Petrarch: Letters of Old Age* 1: 159, 161.

111 Foster, "Beatrice or Medusa" 50 and *Petrarch: Poet and Humanist* 47.

112 Dante Alighieri, *The Divine Comedy*, trans. Charles Eliot Norton (Chicago: Henry Regnery, 1951) *Purgatorio* XXX, 127.

113 Johann Wolfgang von Goethe, *Faust*, ed. Walter Kaufmann (Garden City, NY: Anchor Press, 1962) lines 12110-1.

CHAPTER 8

The British Tradition:
"Blameth nat me if that ye chese amys"[1]

Spanning six hundred years, the British examples of auctorial self-criticism are widely divergent in their genres and content. Although we can distinguish the two main apology strands, to God and to women, the more systematic uniformity achieved by the Latin, German, French, Italian, and Spanish authors is lacking in the English self-critical passages; nevertheless, the English authors invariably emulate the various continental models, such as the early Christian author, the medieval translator and scholastic compiler, the writer accused of antifeminism, and the sinful Christian author. Cynewulf represents the early Christian writer who follows a pattern of pseudo-personal[2] conversion in order to heighten his religious topics. The three Welsh authors included here present themselves as sinful authors in the sight of God. The enigmatic William Langland doubts the value of writing in general in his struggle to understand his auctorial role in God's design. The most complex of all authors, Geoffrey Chaucer, presents us with a canon fraught with self-deprecatory examples ranging from apologies for the unseemliness of language to charges of antifeminist tendencies to a potential disavowal of his entire creative corpus in the face of the Christian Zeitgeist. Furthermore, Thomas Hoccleve both participates in the fifteenth-century pro- and antifeminist debate and imitates Chaucer in his ironic self-chastisement concerning women. Chaucer and Hoccleve illustrate the increasing irony of the convention.[3]

8.1. Old English: Cynewulf

The Anglo-Saxon poet Cynewulf falls into the category of the early Christian writers who enhance their religious works with a pseudo-personal conversion. This is espe-

---

1   Geoffrey Chaucer, GP line 3181.

2   I am using the term "pseudo-personal" because we hardly have any biographical information about most of the authors that would allow us to postulate a personal conversion. Furthermore, the confessions are made in a literary work to which they provide a complementary addition.

3   The anonymous Harley lyric, "The Poet's Repentance," seems to present the apology of a poet for having written satire against women (*The Harley Lyrics: The Middle English Lyrics of MS. Harley 2253*, ed. G. L. Brook [Manchester: Manchester UP, 1954] 33-34). Because of its anonymous nature and slighter self-criticism, this lyric is a special case and will not be treated specifically. For a scholarly discussion, see Daniel J. Ransom, ed., "Antifeminism, Irony, and *The Poet's Repentance*," *Poets at Play: Irony and Parody in* The Harley Lyrics (Norman, OK: Pilgrim Books, 1985) 1-29.

cially evident in Cynewulfian texts with conversion-centered content. Cynewulf connects almost all of his works intertextually using similar penitential semantic patterns in their respective conclusions. The closure Cynewulf provides for his poems—alluding to his own identity, to the ephemerality of life, to his impending death and subsequent punishment for his sins during Judgment—removes them from distant biblical history, places them into a pseudo-personal framework concerning the author, and creates a personal participatory framework for the audience. The author can manipulate this framework to various ends. In *The Fates of the Apostles*, for example, he employs the aforementioned strategy to ask his present and future audience to intercede for him with God, implying that the poet's pleasurable rendition of the poem will bring him, if not salvation, at least prayers in his name. In *Juliana*, the poet uses the pseudo-personal strategy to achieve two different purposes: on the one hand, by asking the future performers of his poem to remember his name, Cynewulf demonstrates a certain confidence in the positive value and longevity of his creation; on the other hand, in accordance with the conventions of medieval *vitae*, and because both this poem and *Elene* sustain the conversion leitmotif,[4] Cynewulf admits his own sinfulness to implore both the future performers of his poetry and St. Elene for intercession.[5]

In the epilogue to his *Elene*, however, Cynewulf links himself intratextually to the main text, making a negative statement about his poetry both to parallel his own pseudo-personal literary conversion with the conversions in the work itself, and to give the audience a good example, much like Hartmann von Aue in his *Gregorius*.[6] Cynewulf wishes to align himself with the converts Constantine, Helena, Symon, and Judas, adding the literary dimension to his penitential stance because the main theme of the poem is the search for Christ's cross, the symbol of the Logos Incarnate on earth. Integrating his poetic craft into the idea of conversion, Cynewulf emphasizes language throughout. He expresses Judas' pre- and post-conversion state with "wordcræft" [skill of words]; both lines 314b and 419a are examples of "'word cræftig" [skilled in words] referring to Judas, who has only a literal but no spiritual

---

4   Allen J. Frantzen, *The Literature of Penance in Anglo-Saxon England* (New Brunswick: Rutgers UP, 1983) 188.

5   Alexandra Hennessey Olsen perceives Cynewulf's naming himself as an act of pride (*Speech, Song, and Poetic Craft: The Artistry of the Cynewulf Canon* [New York: Peter Lang, 1984] 76).

6   This point has been heavily disputed, however. F. Holthausen claims that the ring-receiving Cynewulf mentions would imply that he had been a minstrel in his youth and later converted to composing spiritual poetry (introduction, *Cynewulf's Elene* [Heidelberg: C. Winter, 1905] xii). Other critics object that it is not feasible to draw any autobiographical information from the epilogue to *Elene*. For an overview of the critical positions opposing the autobiographical theory, see Carleton Brown, "The Autobiographical Element in the Cynewulfian Rune Passages," *Englische Studien* 38 (1907): 196-233 and Robert C. Rice, "Cynewulf's *Fates of the Apostles* and Epilogues," *Anglo-Saxon England* 6 (1977): 114. Varda Fish considers the epilogue a "mere appendix" to the poem ("Theme and Pattern in Cynewulf's *Elene*," *Neuphilologische Mitteilungen* 76 [1975]: 1-25; here 22), whereas Jackson J. Campbell supports an autobiographical interpretation ("Cynewulf's Multiple Revelations," *Medievalia et Humanistica* n.s. 3 [1972]: 257-77; here 275—also reprinted in *Cynewulf: Basic Readings*, ed. Robert E. Bjork, Basic Readings in Anglo-Saxon England 4 [New York: Garland, 1996] 229-50).

grasp of language.[7] Alexandra Olsen argues that "wordcræft" connects the poem to the epilogue.[8] In the epilogue, the poet's "wordcræft" (*Elene* line 1237a) [craft of words] becomes the focus because it is, after all, the "poem and the poet's skill" that bring conversion to the audience.[9] The epilogue exhibits the conventional traits of the "sinful youth and wisdom in old age" topos, as the poet stresses his age, "frod" (*Elene* line 1236a) [wise or old], and his own state of sinfulness, "synnum asæled" (*Elene* line 1243a) [fettered by sins], in contrast to God's perfection.[10] Like the Graeco-Roman and Christian authors before him, Cynewulf receives the gift of poetry from a deity, God the Master Author:

ÞUS ic frod 7 fus,   þurh þæt fæcne hus,
wordcræft wæf   7 wundrum læs,
þraȝum þreodude   7 ȝeþanc reodode,
nihtes nearwe;   nysse ic ȝearwe,
be ðære [rode] riht   ær me rumran ȝeþeaht,
þurh ða mæran miht,   on modes þeaht,
wisdom onwreah; . . . .

. . . .

ær me lare onlaȝ   þurh leohtne had,
gamelum to geoce,   gife unscynde
mægencyning amæt . . . .

. . . .

---

7   Cynewulf, *Cynewulf's* Elene, ed. P. O. E. Gradon (Exeter: University of Exeter, 1977). Robert E. Bjork also interprets lines 426-30a as Judas' "wordcræft" ['craft of words'] (*The Old English Verse Saints' Lives: A Study in Direct Discourse and the Iconography of Style*, McMaster Old English Studies and Texts 4 [Toronto: U of Toronto P, 1985] 73, 75).

8   Olsen, *Speech, Song, and Poetic Craft* 44.

9   Frantzen, *The Literature of Penance in Anglo-Saxon England* 192 and Martin Irvine, "Anglo-Saxon Literary Theory Exemplified in Old English Poems: Interpreting the Cross in *The Dream of the Rood* and *Elene*," *Style* 20 (1988): 157-81; here 164-65.

10 It is generally assumed that Cynewulf patterned himself after the author's description (Earl R. Anderson, *Cynewulf: Structure, Style, and Theme in His Poetry* [London: Associated UP, 1983] 17-18) in *The Life of Abraham the Hermit* and utilized the structure of an epilogue attached to a narrative (P. O. E. Gradon, ed., introduction, *Cynewulf's* Elene [Exeter: University of Exeter, 1977] 1-24; here 21-22). Earl R. Anderson further traces the "'aged author'" topos back to Gregory Nazianzenus (329-389): "This topos has three elements: (1) the author claims to be old and sick or near death (2) in the context of disparaging his own weakness or sinfulness, or contrasting his own youthful sinfulness with the religious devotion or piety or penitence of his old age, and further (3) in the context of a concern either for some specific compositional problem, or for compositional problems in general. All three motifs are present in the Basil panegyric, too, but not as fixed rhetorical details. I would suggest that the "aged author" topos developed some time after Gregory Nazianzenus (perhaps inspired by, certainly influenced by, the Basil oration, which was well known), and that the topos was in existence by the sixth century" (*Cynewulf: Structure, Style, and Theme in His Poetry* 18). Anderson's analysis isolates the phenomenon of the "aged author" very well, although there are other examples that emphasize the aspect of literary sins better than either *The Life of Abraham the Hermit* or Gregory's panegyric. According to my research, the first author to use the old age topos in conjunction with writing was Horace in his *Epistles*; see 33-34 in Chapter 2. For the translated *Life of Abraham the Hermit*, see D. G. Calder and Michael J. B. Allen, *Sources and Analogues of Old English Poetry: The Major Latin Texts in Translation* (Cambridge: Brewer, 1976) 68-69.

> leoðucræft onleac þaes ic lustum breac,
> willum in worlde;[11]

Cynewulf's reliance on God's inspiration to help him to correct his writing poses an intra-auctorial problem in conjunction with the age topos. Cynewulf's extant canon is not fraught with worldly writings, and if he did not receive the gift of poetry until he was old, all of his compositions must either be labors of his senectitude or must be considered chaff, not fruit. His nocturnal ruminations demonstrate that he must have been writing before, albeit without taking a sufficiently Christian approach. The incongruity in his canon highlights Cynewulf's literary, not personal, utilization of self-criticism to underline the transforming structure of his poem.

Cynewulf, the fourth protagonist[12] after Constantine, Elene, and Judas, complements this "pseudo-personal" confession of specific literary sins with a general exhortation regarding possible literary sins:

>   sceall æʒhwylc ðær
> reordberendra   riht ʒehyran
> dæda ʒehwylcra   þurh þæs Deman muð
> 7 worda swa same,   wed ʒesyllan
> eallra unsnyttro   ær ʒesprecenra,
> þistra ʒeþonca.[13]

This statement obviously includes the poet and pertains to the author's poetic ability before he received the joyful gift of "wordcraft" blessed by God, as evidenced by the terms "æʒhwylc" (*Elene* line 1281b) [each] and "ær" (*Elene* line 1285b) [formerly]. Varda Fish takes up the topic of intra-auctoriality and argues that the epilogue deals with "the poet's own progress from the confined literalness of the word to a new 'rumran ʒeþeaht' (*Elene* line 1240) [ampler understanding] in which the letter is charged with spiritual meaning"; thus Cynewulf's "poetic conversion" becomes the "spiritualization of his poetic language."[14] This account echoes the conversion of Judas: "þeah ic ær mid dysiʒe þurhdrifen wære / 7 þæt soð to late seolf ʒecneowe" (*Elene* line 707-08) ['although earlier I was imbued with folly and myself recognized the truth too tardily' (Bradley 183)]. In his other judgment accounts, Cynewulf never specifically mentions the sins of words, implying that his literary and pseudo-personal conversion happened intratextually during the compositional process of the poem. In a sinner's psychology, deplorable behavior stands out as such when the person has

---

11 *Cynewulf's* Elene lines 1236a-42a, 1245a-47, 1250a-51a. ['Thus miraculously have I, being old and ready to go because of this fickle carcass, gleaned and woven the craft of words and for long periods pondered and winnowed my thoughts painstakingly by night. I was not entirely aware of the truth about this thing before wisdom, through the sublime Might, discovered to me in the thinking of my mind an ampler understanding. . . . before the mighty King granted me knowledge in lucid form as solace to an old man, meted out his flawless grace . . . and unlocked the art of poesy, which I have used joyously and with a will in the world'] (S. A. J. Bradley, trans., *Anglo-Saxon Poetry* [London: Dent, 1982] 195).

12 Daniel G. Calder, *Cynewulf* (Boston: Twayne, 1981) 134.

13 *Cynewulf's* Elene lines 1281b-86a. ['Each man there shall hear the truth about each one of his deeds and likewise of his words from the Judge's mouth, and will pay the penalty for all things formerly spoken in folly and for all shameless thoughts'] (Bradley, *Anglo-Saxon Poetry* 196).

14 Fish, "Theme and Pattern in Cynewulf's *Elene*" 5, 22.

moved on to another level, that of recognition. This occurrence of conversion presents the reverse situation of the Catalan writer Ramon Llull, whose abstinence from writing amorous poetry led to the revelation of the power of the Incarnate Word and the poet's conversion. The cross is central to both Cynewulf and Llull: with the discovery of the cross, Cynewulf encounters in it "the power of art to transform the soul of the poet and make known to him the wisdom of faith,"[15] whereas for Llull the cross' appearance instills faith in him and demonstrates its power to change the poet's art.[16]

---

15 Calder, *Cynewulf* 137.

16 Although Snorri Sturluson (1179-1241) is geographically far removed from the continent, he is faced with a scenario similar to the early Christian writers in their clash with pagan literature. Sturluson's self-criticism, designed to prevent punishment, is more implicit than explicit and occurs in the *Skáldskaparmál*. Sturluson, who was not a cleric but a Christian with a primarily secular perspective (Anthony Faulkes, introduction, *Edda: Prologue and Gylfaginning*, by Snorri Sturluson [London and Melbourne: Dent, 1987] vii-xx; here xv), undertook the preservation of the art of skaldic poetry that had become increasingly threatened by both the Christian Zeitgeist and the introduction of the dance (Sigurdur Nordal, introduction, *The Prose Edda of Snorri Sturluson: Tales from Norse Mythology*, trans. Jean I. Young [Cambridge: Bowes & Bowes, 1954] 7-15; here 10). Sturluson was treading on thin ice with his *Edda*, for both skalds and saga narrators in the eleventh century took great pains not to refer to pagan deities (Hans Kuhn, "Das Nordgermanische Heidentum in den Ersten Christlichen Jahrhunderten," *Zeitschrift für Deutsches Altertum und Deutsche Literatur* 79 [1942-43]: 133-66; here 134). Since Sturluson's intent was mainly poetic, he wished to preserve the kenningar, indispensable to the repertoire of the practicing skald (Margaret Clunies Ross, *Skáldskaparmál: Snorri Sturluson's Ars Poetica and Medieval Theories of Language* [Odense: Odense UP, 1987] 17). Because most kenningar are impenetrable outside their proper framework, Snorri Sturluson provides the mythological background to the kenningar of the *Skáldskaparmál* in the *Gylfaginning* (Marlene Ciklamini, *Iceland: Snorri Sturluson* [Boston: Twayne, 1978] 60), of which his contemporary young men might either have been unaware or which they might have purposefully avoided (Arthur Gilchrist Brodeur, introduction, *The Prose Edda*, by Snorri Sturluson [New York: The American-Scandinavian Foundation, 1916] ix-xxii; here xvi), although Sturluson makes amply clear in his prologue that the mythological gods are only an aberration of the real faith and stem from a line of humans. For Sturluson's political views, see Theodore M. Andersson, "The Politics of Snorri Sturluson," *Journal of English and Germanic Philology* 93:1 (1994): 55-78.

Analogous to the Christian writer of late antiquity, Sturluson, too, has to contend with the form and content of pagan literature. He wishes to maintain the skaldic poetic forms but cannot justify the content associated with them; therefore, he adjusts the kenningar to a Christian scheme (Faulkes, introduction xxviii). In order to protect himself from the charge of preaching heathenism while getting even with the clergy (Nordal, introduction 12), he admonishes aspiring skalds not to discard the old poetic forms but also not to believe their content: "en eigi skulu kristnir menn trúa á heidin god, ok eigi á sannindi bessar sagnar, annan veg en svá sem hér finnst í upphafi bókar, er sagt er frá atburdum beim, er mannfólkit villtist frá réttri trú" (qtd. in Kurt Schier, "Zur Mythologie der *Snorra Edda*: Einige Quellenprobleme," *Speculum Norroenum: Norse Studies in Memory of Gabriel Turville-Petre*, eds. Ursula Dronke et al. [Odense: Odense UP, 1981] 405-20; here 407 n. 7). ['nor, on the other hand, ought Christian men to believe in heathen gods, nor in the truth of these tales otherwise than precisely as one may find here in the beginning of the book'] (Brodeur, introduction 97). Sturluson's metatextual remark is couched as an admonition to his readers, but it also implies self-criticism and defense. After all, he reported those tales. Therefore, rejecting the content but retaining the form allows him to institute a relationship between pagan mythology and Christian faith (Faulkes, introduction xv). In order to demonstrate the tie between skaldic poetry and Christianity, Sturluson includes among his list

The Welsh Poets

In medieval Welsh literature, auctorial self-criticism appears in lyrical form and only in intertextual contexts. Expressed entirely in apologies to God, except for a smidgen of an apology to women, their self-criticism sustains an interauctoriality that comments on the intra-auctoriality of the authors. The poetry of the Gogynfeirdd, "the Poets of the Princes,"[17] who thrived between the first half of the twelfth and the last half of the fourteenth century, furnishes two of the three Welsh lyrical examples in this study. Gogynfeirdd poetry can be characterized as the eulogizing of patrons, using a rigid form and a limited number of "variations on a few conventional themes."[18] The targets of the eulogies, besides patrons, are saints and God.[19] The poems containing self-criticism have shifted their epideictic purpose from praising earthly rulers to praising God and condemning the poets' own sins. Two of the self-critical poems fit into the Gogynfeirdd subcategory of the *marwysgafn* or deathbed poetry, while the third derives from that form.[20] Since the poets had a deep sense of their despicable sinfulness, at the end of their lives they wrote songs containing a "contrite confession" of their sins, imploring God for forgiveness and reconciliation.[21] The Middle English penitential lyric experienced a similar development. As Simon D. Evans points out, "[w]hile at the time of composition such feelings must have been more imaginary than real, one is occasionally impressed by a note of sincerity."[22] For instance, Bleddyn Fardd (c. 1257-85) and Gruffudd ap Maredudd (c. 1350-90) wrote *marwysgafn*, but

---

kenningar for Christ and cites as an example a half-stanza by Eilífr Godrúnarson, a Norwegian skald of the transitional period (Ross, *Skáldskaparmál* 93). Sturluson emphasizes the connection to Christianity because "skaldic verse in the earlier stages of its development had been closely associated with the heathen religion, in both its subject matter and diction, and many early poets had believed that poetry was the gift of the heathen gods and had originated with them" (Faulkes, introduction xx). By procuring evidence of kenningar for Christ, the author tries to counteract that established belief (Ciklamini, *Iceland: Snorri Sturluson* 62). His strategy sounds similar to Bede's in "Concerning Figures and Tropes" where he proves that certain rhetorical features already exist in the Bible before the classical authors could claim them. Sturluson, however, tries to prove the opposite by asserting that pagan rhetorical devices can be applied to Christian contents and therefore preserved. Thus Sturluson's self-criticism is prevention-oriented, limited to the text and reader, and as far as intra-auctoriality is concerned quite marginal in the scope of this study, but it still illustrates one of the strategies medieval writers busying themselves with pagan literature must resort to in order to express their literary concerns.

17 Thomas Parry, *A History of Welsh Literature*, trans. H. Idris Bell (Oxford: Clarendon, 1955) 44.

18 H. I. Bell, *The Nature of Poetry as Conceived by the Welsh Bards* (Oxford: Clarendon, 1955) 15.

19 Ceri W. Lewis, "The Court Poets: Their Function, Status and Craft," A. O. H. Jarman and Gwilym Rees Hughes, eds., *A Guide to Welsh Literature*, 2 vols. (Swansea: Christopher Davies, 1976) 1: 123-56; here 131.

20 J. E. Caerwyn Williams notes that "[t]he *marwysgafn* reminds us of the *dadolwch*, appeasement song, which the Gogynfardd composed in order to be reconciled with his patron after some estrangement had occurred between them" (*The Poets of the Welsh Princes* [Cardiff: U of Wales P, 1978] 44).

21 Lewis, "The Court Poets" 132.

22 Simon D. Evans, *Medieval Religious Literature*, Writers of Wales (Cardiff: U of Wales P, 1986) 26-27.

174

neither author explicitly refers to his poetic craft.[23] Among the Gogynfeirdd, Meilyr Brydydd and Llewelyn Goch ap Meurig Hen composed *marwysgafn* expressing aucto-

---

23 Cynddelw Brydydd Mawr's *marwysgafn* (1155-1200) functions as a striking counterpiece to Meilyr's. He condemns sinning and asks for forgiveness but does not apply it to himself as a poet. On the contrary, he did not feel his tongue was halting, and the *marwysgafn* serves both as his deathbed poem and his eulogy, composed with undiminished power. Since he venerates his poetic gift as derived from God (J. Lloyd-Jones, "The Court Poets of the Welsh Princes," *Proceedings of the British Academy* 34 [1948]: 167-97; here 172), comparing himself favorably to God the Creator, he displays a great deal of poetic pride, especially for a petitionary poem:
Cyfarchaf i Dduw cyfarchaf
Ceinfolawd ardraethawd iti a draethaf

. . . .
Nid wyf fardd digardd ymdigoned
Ar helw fy nghreawdr llywiawdr lliwed
My Gynddelw geiniad rhad am rhodded

. . . .
Gwledig arbennig pan genais-honawd
Nid ofer draethawd a rydreuthais
Nid eissiwed ced man y cefais
Nid ef ym crews dews diffleis
I wneuthur amhwyll ba thwyll na thrais
Nid ef digrefydd
A gretto Ddofydd

. . . .
Yn ddigabl ar barabl ar ei bariad
Fy ngherdd ith . . .

. . . .
Can wyd athro ym nam eithriad. ("Marwysgafn Cynddelw," *The Myvyrian Archaiology of*
['I salute God, I solicit acclaim   *Wales*, ed. Owen Jones et al [Denbigh: Thomas Gee, 1870]
For the piece I perform   78; lines 16-17, 63-65, 67-73, 85-86, 91)

. . . .
I am a bard, flawlessly fashioned:
In my Creator's hold, legion's Lord,
I Cynddelw the singer, grace I ask

. . . .
Almighty Ruler, when of you I sang,
Not worthless the piece that I performed,
No lack of fine style in His lyric,
No little largesse have I obtained,
Not fashioned was I by changeless God
For devising folly, fraud, or force.

. . . .
Flawless in formation of language,
My song in your praise

. . . .
Since you are my teacher, banish me not.' (Gwyn Jones, trans., "Poem on His Death-bed," by Cynddelw Brydydd Mawr, *The Oxford Book of Welsh Verse in English* [Oxford: Oxford UP, 1977] 27-30). Cynddelw Mawr's positive juxtaposition of his own authorship to God's creatorship provides a good example of a poem which the self-critical poets have emulated in a negative self-referential way.

rial self-criticism. Although Guto'r Glyn does not belong to the Gogynfeirdd, his self-critical poem fits generally in their overall structure. The poems by Meilyr Brydydd, Llewelyn Goch, and Guto'r Glyn demonstrate characteristics evident in the bulk of Welsh religious poetry,[24] and, additionally, their authors make use of intertextual references to entreat God for forgiveness and to acknowledge Him as the superior craftsman. The poets are very cognizant of medieval theories of authorship and language because they make interauctorial comparisons between the creatorship of God—the first Creator with words—and their own faulty creatorship in order to emphasize their own fallibility and need for salvation.

8.2. Meilyr Brydydd

Meilyr Brydydd (c. 1100-37), the earliest of the Gogynfeirdd, uses the eschatological elements of the *marwysgafn* to demonstrate his wish to gain salvation. In that scheme, intertextuality helps to assert the poet's former self, compared to the presently faltering poet in his metamorphosis to the pilgrim. Meilyr Brydydd's alternation of self-accusations with praises of God, Jesus, and Mary functions both as a comparison between divine perfection and earthly imperfection and negative interauctorial comparison with God. The poet actively seeks reconciliation with God, confessing his sins and his lackadaisical approach to religion (lines 4-12). Explicit expressions of impending death or fear of afterworldly retribution indicate the genre of the *marwysgafn* and the poet's rather calculated willingness to reverse course before it is too late, echoing the "better late than never" philosophy first seen in Plato's account of Socrates, Marbod de Rennes, and Peter of Blois: "Gueinnui hagen ym reen ri. / kyn bwyf deyerin diuenynhy."[25] When Meilyr Brydydd mentions his occupation as a court poet and his inspirational Muse, he concedes that God is superior to the "frail princes" and that his poetic ability is either lost or insignificant in light of these eschatological realities:

> Keueis y liaws awr eur a phali.
> gan ureuawl rieu yr eu hoffi.
> Ac wedy dawn awen amgen ynni.
> Amdlawd uyn tauawd ar uyn tewi.
> Mi Veilyr brydyt beryerin y bedyr.[26]

---

24 Lloyd-Jones, "The Court Poets of the Welsh Princes" 183.
25 Meilyr Brydydd, "Marw ysgafyn Veilyr brydyt," *Poetry by Medieval Welsh Bards*, ed. J. Gwenogvryn Evans, 2 vols. (Llanbedrog: Pwllheli, 1926) 2: 182-83, lines 13-14. ['But to my lord king I'll attend me / Before in earth helpless they lay me'] (Tony Conran, trans., "On His Death-bed," by Meilyr Brydydd, *Welsh Verse* [Berkeley: U of California P, 1974] 139-41; here 140).
26 Meilyr Brydydd, "Marw ysgafyn Veilyr brydyt" lines 31-35.
   ['Many times gold and silks in plenty
   For my praise of them, frail princes gave me.
   But after the Muse, a power more mighty—
   My tongue, now it's silent, does but poorly.

The poem bears overtones of the "youth vs. old age" topos when the author refers to his diminishing poetic power with the onset of age. While auctorial self-criticism is implied, Meilyr Brydydd seeks God's help explicitly as a poet, not merely as a human being; that admission and the poet's confidence that the Creator will raise him up (lines 53-56) convey the self-confidence of the poet, who seems to imitate Cynddelw Mawr in his conviction that his poetic creativity was bestowed upon him by God and therefore could not have been completely despicable or vain, despite Meilyr Brydydd's other sins.

8.3. Llywelyn Goch ap Meurig Hen

Because of its technique of alternation between the sins of Llywelyn Goch ap Meurig Hen (1360-90) and the goodness of God, the "I Dduw" [To God] reminds us of the *marwysgafn* of Meilyr Brydydd.[27] The last of the Gogynfeirdd presents this *marwysgafn* as an *awdl gyffes* or 'recantation' for the "Lament for Lleucu Llwyd." The poet's metatextual passages express his self-criticism and gain God's forgiveness before it is too late. Even the forms of the two poems imply a certain self-criticism. The "Lament" is composed in *cywydd* meter, whereas the palinode is written in the *awdl* form; the contemporary *awdlau* demonstrate general confessions to sins as a conventional form.[28] Rachel Bromwich asserts that Llywelyn made a conscientious choice of meter for the respective poems and must have considered the *cywydd* functional "for poetry of a more light and intimate nature," while the *awdl* was reserved primarily for serious formal praise and devotional poetry.[29]

Llywelyn's confession of sins in the "I Dduw" includes both general offenses and specific literary crimes, the latter referring to the offending previous text. The poet's admission of "continual rape" (line 17), combined with the closely following literary sins, may be a reference to his whole literary career. His having "sent messages of love" adumbrates the most heinous crimes:

Gwnaethum ar draethawd guwawd gywydd
Lleucu yn eilfar lliw caen elfydd
Gwnaethum odineb nag ednebydd
Gwnaethost lynn Ebron ai afonydd

As for me, Meilyr the poet, pilgrim to Peter'] (Conran, "On His Death-bed" 140).

27 For Llywelyn Goch ap Meurig Hen's works, see Ifor Williams and Thomas Roberts, *Cywyddau Dafydd ap Gwilym A'I Gyfoeswyr* (Bangor: Argraffwyd gan Evan Thomas, 1914) 96-100.

28 Myrddin D. Lloyd, "The Later Gogynfeirdd," A. O. H. Jarman and Gwilym Rees Hughes, eds., *A Guide to Welsh Literature*, 2 vols. (Swansea: Christopher Davies, 1976) 2: 36-57; here 57.

29 Rachel Bromwich, "The Earlier *Cywyddwyr*: Poets Contemporary with Dafydd ap Gwilym," eds. A. O. H. Jarman and Gwilym Rees Hughes, *A Guide to Welsh Literature*, 2 vols. (Swansea: Christopher Davies, 1979) 2: 144-68; here 161.

Cyffessaf wrthyd byd wybedydd
Cammau a wnaethum cymmen ieithydd.[30]

Since the "Lament" is extant, we can establish the intertextual relationships quite
clearly. For instance, the aspect of adultery is confirmed by the fourth line in the
"Lament" and elaborated on by Iolo Goch, another Welsh poet, who compared
Llywelyn "to David who also was a sinner in love and repented."[31] Although the
"Lament" does not contain a reference to Mary by name, there are numerous references to Lleucu as the perfect maiden. As the cult of the Virgin Mary increased in the
fourteenth century, many authors either substitute the Virgin for earthly women or
indirectly apologize to her, as Llywelyn does. In this case, the Virgin has also conquered another position. The key word "false," usually applied to the pagan fables of
the poets, is used by Llywelyn to praise an earthly woman. Llywelyn imitates the conventional contrast between poetic fables and truthful Logos, namely Christ, with its
equivalent in the feminine realm: the earthly woman contrasted to her heavenly
superior.

We can see Llywelyn's praise for Leucu in the "Lament":

A genais, lugorn Gwynedd,
O eiriau gwawd, eiry ei gwedd,
Llef drioch, llaw fodrwyaur,
Lleucu, moliant fu it, f'aur;
Â'r genau hwn, gwn, ganmawl,
A ganwyf, tra fwyf, o fawl,
F'enaid, hoen geirw afonydd,
Fy nghariad, dy farwnad fydd.[32]

His "life-long" praise in the "Lament" has become "false praise" and constitutes an
abomination to the poet. The author, however, already applies self-criticism in the
"Lament" itself, admitting to falseness of a different kind as well as to his lax religious
performance:

---

30 Llywelyn Goch, "I Dduw," *The Myvyrian Archaiology of Wales*, ed. Owen Jones et al (Denbigh:
    Thomas Gee, 1870) 354, lines 23-29. ['I made in writing a *cywydd* of false praise, comparing
    Lleucu of the snow's hue to the like of Mary; I performed hidden adultery. I confess to Thee, who
    knowest all things, the wrongs that I did, skillful in words'] (Bromwich, "The Earlier
    Cywyddwyr" 164).

31 Bromwich, "The Earlier *Cywyddwyr*" 155.

32 Llywelyn Goch, "Marwnad Lleucu Llwyd," *The Oxford Book of Welsh Verse*, ed. Thomas Parry
    (Oxford: Clarendon, 1962) 43-45, lines 69-76.
    ['All the words, Gwynedd's lantern,
    I've sung, complexion of snow,
    Three groans of grief, gold-ringed hand,
    Lleucu, praised you, my precious.
    With these lips, deft my praise-craft,
    What I'll sing, life-long, in praise,
    My dear, foam's hue on rivers,
    My love, will be your lament'] (Joseph P. Clancy, trans., "Lament for Lleucu Llwyd," *The
    Oxford Book of Welsh Verse in English*, by Llywelyn Goch [Oxford: Oxford UP, 1977] 43-45;
    here 44).

Tydi sydd, mau gywydd gau,
Ar y gwir, rywiog eiriau,
Minnau sydd ieithrydd athrist,
Ar gelwydd tradywydd trist.
Celwyddog wyf, cul weddi.[33]

This passage charts Llywelyn's ambivalent state, accusing Lleucu of lying and then retracting that statement immediately. Intratextually, he accuses himself both of lying in his poetry, alluding to the mandate of truth in poetry, and of lax religious practice. In both poems, he admits that his *cywydd* is false. In the intratextual instance, he apologizes to Lleucu, a woman, for having accused her; then in the "I Dduw," the poet assigns the term "false" a slightly different meaning, now apologizing to God for the entire existence of that poem, and rewriting himself as an author with the help of a semantic change.

The intertext created by the "Lament" and the "I Dduw" also functions on another level that explains the applied auctorial self-criticism in an intratextual and interauctorial framework. In the "I Dduw," Llywelyn treats God in his roles of Creator and Redeemer, a division that is present in inverted form in the "Lament" in regard to the poet's creative powers. In the "Lament," Llywelyn takes on the role of the creator; furthermore, he tries to act as a redeemer and beckons the dead Lleucu to come back to life, an act precedented by Christ and specific to Him:

Cyd bych o fewn caead bedd,
F'enaid, cyfod i fyny,
Egor y ddaearddor ddu,
Gwrthod wely tywod hir,
A gwrtheb f'wyneb, feinir.[34]

The poet has indeed overstepped his bounds and ventured close to blasphemy, since this passage sounds similar to Christ's calling Lazarus back from the dead. In assuming the role of a literary creator, he has infringed upon the role of the Redeemer and taken too much auctorial license. The apology, then, is supposed to restore him to the state of a mere poet.

---

33 Llywelyn Goch, "Marwnad Lleucu Llwyd" lines 41-45.
    ['You are, my cywydd is false,
    Truthful, words sweetly spoken:
    It's I, grief's spilled-out language,
    Who lie in sad harmonies;
    I'm lying, skimping prayer'] (Clancy, "Lament for Lleucu Llwyd" 44).
34 Llywelyn Goch, "Marwnad Lleucu Llwyd" lines 12-16.
    ['Though you are closed in the grave,
    Arise, come up, my dearest,
    Open the dark door of earth,
    Refuse the long bed of sand,
    And come to face me, maiden'] (Clancy, "Lament for Lleucu Llwyd" 43).

8.4. Guto'r Glyn

A poet is what Guto'r Glyn (c. 1435-1493), who was one of the most flamboyant bards of his time and the writer of 95 extant poems, wants to stay.[35] He also deals with the issue of interauctoriality between the poet-creator and the Divine Creator, but whereas Meilyr and Llywelyn appear in a penitential framework, ready to rewrite themselves, Guto'r Glyn struggles with this concept. In his poem "Ystyriaeth Bywyd" [Meditation], the self-criticism constructs a creative interauctorial paradigm and situates Guto'r Glyn and his poetic activity in it. Guto'r Glyn's self-criticism has two main intentions: to appease Guto'r Glyn's patron, the Abbot of Valle Crucis, and to parallel God's positive creation with the poet's own questionable one.[36] In this poem, Guto'r Glyn implements a hierarchical and triangular view of creatorship: on the top is God the infallible, who shaped all creation and is the Master *auctor*, to whom the poet devotes several stanzas. Then follows the poet's patron, a religious poet, who fashions songs (*cywyddau*) about the Virgin for instruction: "A thrwy'r gerdd athro yw'r gwr. / O gwna Dafydd gywydd gwiw, / Ef a'i rhydd i Fair heddiw."[37] At the bottom of the hierarchy, Guto'r Glyn characterizes his own poetic activity as falling outside the acceptable sacramental theory of language, in which only a work with a religious content signifies: "Gwae awyddus gywyddol! / Gwae ni wnaeth gân yn ei ôl!" (lines 7-8) ['Shamed is the greedy poet, / Shamed for not shaping such song' (Clancy 222)]. Judging from this admission, Guto'r Glyn obviously has not always been a religious poet. In fact, both Evans and Caerwyn Williams perceive Guto'r Glyn as hardly a religious man, much less a religious poet, and deny that the poem's sentiments are genuine.[38]

The poet exploits the medieval tension between the corporeal and spiritual to explain why he does not qualify for the accolades due a religious poet. Guto'r Glyn has not been able to make religious poetry because he has been a slave to the world: "Moli bûm ymylau byd, / Malu sôn melys ennyd, / A chablu er yn chweblwydd" (lines 9-11) ['I've sung praise the world over, / Babbling sweet nonsense the while, / Blaspheming since I was six' (Clancy 222)]. Although the pejorative word choice expresses a certain negative intra-auctorial feeling, the poet's underlying passivity and

---

35 For accounts of Guto'r Glyn's poetry, see R. M. Jones, *Guto'r Glyn a'i Gyfnod* (Llandybie: Llyfrau'r Dryw, 1963); Saunders Lewis, "Gyrfa Filwrol Guto'r Glyn," *Ysgrifau Beirniadol* 9 (1976): 80-99; and Enid Roberts, *Y Beirdd a'u Noddwyr ym Maelor* (Awst: Darlith Eisteddfod Genedlaethol Cymru Wrecsam a'r Cylch, 1977) 1-6, 14-19.

36 For an interesting article on Welsh poets and their patrons, see Proinsias Mac Cana, "The Poet as Spouse of His Patron," *Ériu* 39 (1988): 79-85.

37 Guto'r Glyn, "Ystyriaeth Bywyd," *Gwaith Guto'r Glyn*, eds. John Llywelyn Williams and Ifor Williams (Caerdydd: Gwasg Prifysgol Cymry, 1961) 305-07, lines 4-6. ['A teacher through his poems. / If Dafydd shapes a cywydd, / He makes it Mary's that day'] (Joseph P. Clancy, trans., "Meditation," *Medieval Welsh Lyrics* [New York: St. Martin's, 1965] 221-23; here 221).

38 Evans, *Medieval Religious Literature* 27 and J. E. Caerwyn Williams, "Guto'r Glyn," A. O. H. Jarman and Gwilym Rees Hughes, eds., *A Guide to Welsh Literature*, 2 vols. (Swansea: Christopher Davies, 1976) 2: 218-42; here 233.

the fact that the poem was commissioned by Abbot Dafydd[39] open the door for a number of ironic implications:

> Erchis ym eiriach y swydd.
> "Twa," heb hwn, ateb henaint,
> "Tro fal Sawl trwy foli saint."
> Erchi ym a'i orchymyn,
> Foliannu Duw o flaen dyn,
> A rhoi'r gerdd, rhywyr yw'r gwaith,
> I frenin nef ar unwaith.
> Rhannu rhag byrhau einioes.[40]

This passage sends the underlying message that religious literature has redeeming qualities, qualities the poet has purposefully missed so far. The fact that he has to please his patron and that he gives the genesis of this pseudo-religious poem signals that the poet is highly uncomfortable with the subject matter. He seems to experiment with the poetic technique he has been instructed to use. The contrast between his young age and the late hour for repentance as well as the reference to Saul are conventional ploys used to intimidate medieval authors into repentance. It is significant that Guto'r Glyn names Saul, not Paul, as Piccolomini had done, to illustrate that he is still a sinning poet, not a converted one. His choice of the modifier "sweet" for his worldly vanities, coupled with the term "power" for his poetic creativity, albeit waning with age, shows a healthy dose of auctorial pride in his established course of intra-auctoriality. Overall, his passive, almost sluggish response to the requested rewriting of the poet is epitomized by "Gorfod fy mhechod a'm haint, / Gad farw ag edifeiriaint" (lines 53-54) ['Subdue my sin and sickness, / Let me die a penitent' (Clancy 223)]. The poet implies that he is set in his auctorial ways but has not yet reached that penitent state on his own, and therefore he is not ready to write religious poetry.

8.5. Middle English: William Langland

In the fourteenth century, the poet William Langland was just as enigmatic a figure as Cynewulf was in Anglo-Saxon times, although we can gain some insight into his notions of authorship and poetry in *Piers Plowman*. The several extant versions of *Piers Plowman* indicate that the author was dedicated to demonstrating and to revising

---

39 Williams, Guto'r Glyn" 233.
40 Guto'r Glyn, "Ystyriaeth Bywyd" lines 12-19.
     ['He bade me cease such business.
     "Be still," he said, age censured,
     "Change like Saul, by praising saints."
     He begged me and he bade me
     To give God praise before man,
     And to sing, late is the time,
     Now to the King of Heaven'] (Clancy, "Meditation" 222).

an intra-auctorial pattern.[41] Self-criticism comes into play because Langland considers his writing activity as poetic, "which as a mode of life must be justified before God and man."[42] Langland's self-criticism ties in with the issue of the minstrels, with whom he deals differently in all three versions of the text. The author distinguishes between good and bad minstrels in the A- and B-texts:

> And somme merþis to make as mynstralis conne,
> And gete gold wiþ here gle giltles, I trowe.
> Ac Iaperis & iangleris, Iudas children,
> Fonden hem fantasies & foolis hem make,
> And haue wyt at wille to wirche ȝif hem list.
> þat poule prechiþ of hem I dar not proue it here;
> *Qui loquitur turpiloquium* [is] luciferis hyne. [43]

Langland perceives two classes of literary performers and contrasts guiltless minstrels with japers and janglers who practice the art of fables that Paul warns against and of which many self-critical medieval authors accuse themselves.

The B-text contains the preceding passage and additionally demonstrates "a severe judgment against all but the most pious kind of minstrelsy" between Passus X and XIII, "while at the same time tending to disassociate the dreamer from the vocation."[44] The increasingly more negative and damning statements about the japers and janglers exist to set the dreamer/Langland apart from their activity. For instance, japers and janglers are indicted because they perform for money: "Harlotes for hir harlotrie may haue of hir goodes, / And Iaperis and Iogelours and Iangeleris of gestes."[45] Minstrelsy, which was at first more acceptable, is also coming under increased attack: "Theu konne na moore mynstralcie ne Musik men to glade . . . Ac [mynstralcie and murthe] amonges men is noupe / Lecherie, losengerye and losels tales" (B X, lines 44, 49-50). In Passus XII then, Langland employs one form of self-criticism, the dialogue form, in which the self-criticism is expressed as criticism from a third party; in this case Imaginative chides the dreamer for his poetic inclination:[46]

---

41 See also, Charlotte Brewer, "Authorial vs. Scribal Writing in *Piers Plowman,*" *Medieval Literature: Texts and Interpretation,* ed. Tim William Machan (Binghamton, NY: Medieval & Renaissance Texts & Studies, 1991) 59-89 and A. V. C. Schmidt, *The Clerkly Maker: Langland's Poetic Art* (Cambridge: Brewer, 1987).

42 Anne Middleton, "The Audience and Public of Piers Plowman," *Middle English Alliterative Poetry and Its Literary Background: Seven Essays,* ed. David Lawton (Cambridge: Brewer, 1982) 101-23; here 103.

43 William Langland, *Piers Plowman: The A Version,* ed. George Kane, vol. 1 (Rev. ed. London: Athalone Press, 1988) Prologue lines 33-39. The A version is used here because B is identical to A, except for scribal variants.

44 George D. Economou, "Self-Consciousness of Poetic Activity in Dante and Langland," *Vernacular Poetics in the Middle Ages,* ed. Lois Ebin, Studies in Medieval Culture 16 (Kalamazoo, MI: Medieval Institute Publications, 1984) 177-98; here 189.

45 William Langland, *Piers Plowman: The B Version,* eds. George Kane and E. Talbot Donaldson, vol. 2 (Rev. ed. London: Athalone Press, 1988) X, lines 30-31.

46 "The personality thus implicit in the poem is not always adequately distinguished from either supposedly autobiographical reference or the *persona* of the Dreamer" (John Lawlor, *Piers Plowman: An Essay in Criticism* [New York: Barnes & Noble, 1963] 313).

"And þou medlest þee wiþ makynges and myʒtest go sey þi sauter,
And bidde for hem þat ʒyueþ þee breed; for þer are bokes y[n]owe
To telle men what dowel is, dobet and dobest boþe
And prechours to preuen what it is of many a perre freres." (B XII, lines 16-19)

E. Talbot Donaldson theorizes that, at that point, the author had an attack of doubt as to why he was writing; therefore, he can now give his motives for writing in this criticism instigated by Imaginative:[47]

Seide, "Caton conforted his sone þat, clerke þouʒ he were,
To solacen hym som tyme; [so] I do whan I make;
Interpone tuis inderdum gaudia curis.
And of holy men I her[e]," quod I "how þei ouþerwhile
[In manye places pleyden, þe parfiter to ben].
Ac if þer were any wight þat wolde me telle
What were dowel and dobet and dobest at þe laste,
Wolde I neuere do werk, but wende to holi chirche
And þere bydde my bedes but whan ich ete or slepe." (B XII, lines 21-29)

Thus Langland's theory of authorship rests on the two well-known pillars of *utilitas* and *delectatio*. By taking the *delectatio* aspect of his literary task too seriously, the author could jeopardize himself morally.[48] The poet's refusal to quit writing because so far neither all the books available nor their interpreters have been able to give him satisfactory answers to his quest for Dowel, Dobetter, Dobest, presents an actual defiance of the concept of "authority" and affirms that poetry is, indeed, an appropriate activity because it is distinguished from the money-grubbing activity of the japers and janglers.[49]

The appearance of *Activa vita* underscores that point. *Activa vita* makes a point to disassociate himself from the endeavors of the street storytellers:

---

47 E. Talbot Donaldson, *Piers Plowman: The C-Text and Its Poet* (New Haven: Yale UP, 1949) 224-6. George Kane has pointed out the pitfalls of the autobiographical approach: "For all their confidential asides to the audience, their apologies for digression, the dreamers and narrators of Chaucer and Langland are, if I may use jargon, constructs" (*The Autobiographical Fallacy in Chaucer and Langland Studies* [London: University College, 1965] 15). See also George Kane, "Langland and Chaucer: An Obligatory Conjunction," *New Perspectives in Chaucer Criticism*, ed. Donald M. Rose (Norman, OK: Pilgrim Books, 1981) 5-19 and John M. Bowers, *The Crisis of Will in* Piers Plowman (Washington, DC: Catholic U of America P, 1986) 163-89.

48 Kane postulates that by Langland's time a literary convention of moral criticism by self-revelation had developed out of confession formulae. But "there was the overriding question whether the composition of poetry on profane subjects was morally justifiable at all: the discussion, from early Christian times to Chaucer's own day had not produced a generally accepted affirmative answer. Best, if one had not been unable to leave meddling with poetry alone, not to rely on high-flown justifications of the activity to stand at the back of the temple with the publican, or to confess with Langland's dreamer." Kane comments on his point in a footnote: "As far as I know the history of this subject has yet to be written" (*The Liberating Truth: The Concept of Integrity in Chaucer's Writings* [London: Athalone Press, 1980] 14, 21, 32, note 94).

49 David Aers, *Chaucer, Langland and the Creative Imagination* (London: Routledge & Kegan Paul, 1980) 81. See also Theodore L. Steinberg, Piers Plowman *and Prophecy: An Approach to the C-Text*, Garland Studies in Medieval Literature 2 (New York: Garland, 1991) 67-68.

"I am a Mynstrall," quod þat man "my name is *Activa vita*:
Al yde[l] ich hatie for of Actif is my name.
A wafrer, wol ye wite, and serue manye lordes,
[Ac] fewe robes I fonge or furrede gownes.
Couþe I lye [and] do men lauȝe, þanne lacchen I sholde
Ouþer mantel or moneie amonges lordes Mynstrals.
Ac for I can neiþer taboure ne trompe ne telle no gestes,
Farten, ne fiþelen at festes, ne harpen,
Iape ne Iogele ne gentilliche pipe,
Ne neiþer saille ne [sautrie] ne synge with þe gyterne,
I haue none goade gyftes of þise grete lordes. (B XIII, lines 224-34)

But *Activa vita* can also exist as a foil to the japers but also as a more positive model for the dreamer whom poetry has guided to the "exalted service of his God and Maker as His minstrel,"[50] but who is still struggling with his role in the fair field of folk.

In the Prologue to the much-neglected C-text, Langland lumps all minstrels together as questionable, but it is there that, according to Donaldson, we encounter the poet's "conscious assimilation of himself to a minstrel":[51]

And summe murthes to make as mynstrels conneth,
Wolleth neyther swynke ne swete, bote sweren grete othes,
Fyndeth out foule fantasyes and foles hem maketh
And hath wytt at wille to worche yf þei wolde.[52]

In the aforementioned passage in C, the criticism by Imaginative is missing because, as George D. Economou postulates, Reason's criticism of the dreamer's approach to work made it unnecessary because the "rewriting of *Piers Plowman* incorporates poetic activity into the subject matter of the poem."[53] Donaldson interprets that as the poet's resolution of his own self-doubt and self-criticism.[54] But the C-text contains another passage, not found in the B-text, that could be connected to the passage with Imaginative. In Passus VI, the dreamer has to answer Reason's questions about what he does that is productive. After wading through a pool of excuses ranging from physical infirmities to intellectual concerns, the dreamer makes his ultimate confession: "'That ys soth,' ich seide 'and so ich by-knowe, / That ich haue tynt time and tyme mysspended'" (C VI, lines 92-93). The dreamer's misspending of time echoes the professions of many other medieval authors as well as their pleas for redemption and the forgiveness of Christ. In this case, we should be able to apply that statement also to Langland's writing in general and as a commentary on the passage in the B-text. Enigmatic as he may be, Langland gives a rare glimpse of the medieval author revising his work and through revision attaining a self-referential notion of authorship.

---

50   Economou, "Self-Consciousness of Poetic Activity in Dante and Langland" 196.
51   Donaldson, *Piers Plowman* 136.
52   William Langland, *Piers Plowman: An Edition of the C-text*, ed. Derek Pearsall (Berkeley: U of California P, 1978) C Prologue, lines 35-38.
53   Economou, "Self-Consciousness of Poetic Activity in Dante and Langland" 193, 191.
54   Donaldson, *Piers Plowman* 224.

8.6. Geoffrey Chaucer

Chaucer, the uncontested giant of Middle English literature, looms equally large in the apology tradition. Interpretations of Chaucer's Retraction have been especially colored by tenacious claims that the Retraction is the result of Chaucer's alleged deathbed confession at the end of his life and literary career.[55] Naturally, no one should deny Chaucer the comfort of his faith at the time of death, but instead of claiming the Retraction as a unilaterally moral and personal statement, it should be evaluated as a literary expression in the literary context in which it was made. It is evident by now from the foregoing plethora of self-critical authors that the self-criticism inherent in Chaucer's Retraction is neither an isolated incident in European medieval literature nor in the whole of Chaucer's canon, but an integrated one. Chaucer was aware of the apology tradition's two premier strand, apologies to God or the religious establishment and to women, and he makes ample use of their conventions to shirk literary responsibility. Chaucer's metapoetical dialogue, his tactic of portraying himself in a humble

---

55 Both Douglas Wurtele, "The Penitence of Geoffrey Chaucer," *Viator* 11 (1980): 335-59 and James Dean, "Chaucer's Repentance: A Likely Story," *Chaucer Review* 24 (1989): 64-76 interpret Chaucer's Retraction against the backdrop of Thomas Gascoigne's *ex post facto* account of Chaucer's deathbed repentance: "'sicut Chawserus ante mortem suam sepe clamavit, "Ve michi! Ve michi! quia revocare nec destruere jam potero illa que mala scripsi de malo et turpissimo amore hominum ad mulieres, et jam de homine in hominem continuabuntur'" (qtd. in Aage Brusendorff, *The Chaucer Tradition* [London: Oxford UP, 1925] 35) ['just as Chaucer before his death often cried aloud: "Woe is me! Woe is me! because I will now be able neither to call back nor to destroy those evil things that I have written about the evil and most shameful love of men for women, and henceforth they will be passed on from man to man'"] (qtd. in Jon Fyler, *Chaucer and Ovid* [New Haven: Yale UP, 1979] 111). Although Aage Brusendorff doubts Chaucer's alleged repentance, he makes further reference to another work: "A Ballade made by Geffrey Chaucer upon his death-bed lying in his anguish" found in the now destroyed Cottonian MS. Otho A XVIII (*The Chaucer Tradition* 36). Wurtele makes a case for the first part of the Retraction to belong to the Parson, to which the author then appends his own plea ("The Penitence of Geoffrey Chaucer" 340-42). Wurtele, like M. Madeleva (*A Lost Language and Other Essays on Chaucer*, 1951 [New York: Russell & Russell, 1967] 114), concludes that Chaucer's final judgment about his work was not artistic but moral ("The Penitence of Geoffrey Chaucer" 356). James Dean also seconds a deathbed repentance based on Gascoigne ("Chaucer's Repentance: A Likely Story" 64-65). He chides modern readers for not trusting poets' personal statements but rather searching for depersonalizing features, such as literary conventions, rhetorical devices, personae, and above all irony, but concedes that the old-age topos is missing and that Gascoigne might have constructed his account of Chaucer's alleged repentance because of the Retraction ("Chaucer's Repentance: A Likely Story" 70-74). See also Heiner Gillmeister, *Chaucer's Conversion: Allegorical Thought in Medieval Literature*, Aspekte der englischen Geistes- und Kulturgeschichte 2 (Frankfurt: Peter Lang, 1984) and Jameela Lares, "Chaucer's Retractions: A 'Verray Parfit Penitance,'" *Citharia: Essays in the Judeo-Christian Tradition* 34:1 (1994): 18-33. David F. Marshall suggests that if "the Retraction were a separate document illustrating a religious crisis, it would appear in locations other than following the Parson's Tale; there would be manuscripts where it did not appear" ("Unmasking the Last Pilgrim: How and Why Chaucer Used the Retraction to Close *The Canterbury Tales*," *Christianity & Literature* 31 [1982]: 55-74; here 55). Robert M. Estrich also sees no reason to assume a conversion experience ("Chaucer's Maturing Art in the Prologues of the *Legend of Good Women*," *Journal of English and Germanic Philology* 36 [1937]: 326-37; here 329).

light, often deprecating his poetic skills, is part of his masterful manipulation of the concept of the medieval translator, the scholastic compiler, and the sinful author in the Christian cosmos.[56] Chaucer's humble bows to ancient authorities, to contemporary reality, and eventually to Christ, the Master Author, are self-critical elements in *Troilus and Criseyde, The Legend of Good Women, A Treatise on the Astrolabe,* and *The Canterbury Tales,* elements with which Chaucer weaves an intertextual and intra-auctorial tapestry in order to achieve his literary ends and exercise his poetic license.

Just as, on a metatextual level, several classical and medieval authors lead us through almost their entire creative history, critiquing and criticizing their previous compositions, Chaucer employs his metapoetical dialogue to justify his literary creations by providing a statement about his literary interests and how to situate those into his creative cosmos. He begs excuse for three main flaws: the pagan content of the literary material, material celebrating sexuality or proffering sexually explicit content, and questionable language. Chaucer was guilty of all three offenses by using classical sources, by writing about the love of women and thus inherently about sexuality, and by reporting unseemly language. All three of these concerns grow out of the tension between classical antiquity and Christianity that lived on in the *trivium* education of medieval authors. This tension caused an ambiguous environment for writing, as medieval writers are rhetorically trained on classical models, but were instructed to disregard their models' content and were reminded of the medieval sacramental theory of language, in which a text signifies only in an imitation of the Christian master narrative. To be able to steer his literary vessel safely through the treacherous waters of the medieval theory of language, Chaucer never quite wants to don the captain's cap, instead hiding behind the disguise of translator and compiler, and eventually assuming the role of the sinful medieval author. Nevertheless, all of these roles are poetic constructs that allow Chaucer complete artistic license.

8.6.1. *Troilus and Criseyde*

Although some self-deprecating remarks appear in Chaucer's dream-vision poetry, the first work containing the self-critical concepts under scrutiny is *Troilus and Criseyde.*[57] The seemingly oscillating quality of his auctorial stance lies in the fact that

---

56   The following critics have remarked on *The Canterbury Tales* as *compilatio*: Norman D. Hinton, "*The Canterbury Tales* as *compilatio*," *Proceedings of the Illinois Medieval Association* 1 (1984): 28-48; Leonard Michael Koff, *Chaucer and the Art of Storytelling* (Berkeley: U of California P, 1988) 31-32; MN 198-210; and M. B. Parkes, "The Influence of the Concepts of *Ordinatio* and *Compilatio* on the Development of the Book," *Medieval Learning and Literature: Essays Presented to Richard William Hunt,* eds. J. J. G. Alexander and M. T. Gibson (Oxford: Clarendon, 1976) 115-38.

57   The criticism *Troilus and Criseyde* has inspired usually oscillates between the interpretative poles of alleging a sudden and unexpected shift in "philosophical focus" and of confirming an integral dichotomy of worldly and divine love throughout the entire work (Anne Bàrbara Gill, *Paradoxical Patterns in Chaucer's* Troilus: *An Explanation of the Palinode* [Washington, DC:

Chaucer has to do damage control on several fronts, since he is reworking a pagan love story that might be offensive both to women and to the religious sentiments of the Middle Ages. Chaucer's particular preemptive auctorial strategy in *Troilus and Criseyde* is tripartite: he assumes the role of the translator; he apologizes to the women in the audience; and he rejects ancient authorities and simultaneously affirms divine love.

Chaucer's emphasizes his role as translator and his reliance on ancient sources to divert potential blame from himself.[58] Interestingly enough, the intended audience is not stern church representatives but lovers:

Catholic U of America P, 1960] ix). The main arguments in the *Troilus* palinode debate are: *Troilus* demonstrates the irreconcilable differences between the classical/pagan and Christian dichotomy (Charles Dahlberg, *The Literature of Unlikeness* [Hanover: UP of New England, 1988] 131; Gill, *Paradoxical Patterns in Chaucer's* Troilus 11-12; John S. P. Tatlock, "The Epilog of Chaucer's *Troilus*," *Modern Philology* 18 [1921]: 625-59; here 640; and Zacharias Thundyil, "The *Moral* Chaucer," *Christianity and Literature* 20 [1971]: 12-16; here 13); *Troilus* exemplifies the dichotomy between earthly and heavenly love (Gill, *Paradoxical Patterns in Chaucer's* Troilus 105; Gerald Morgan, "The Ending of '*Troilus and Criseyde*,'" *Modern Language Review* 77 [1982]: 257-71; here 258; Karl Young, "Chaucer's Renunciation of Love in *Troilus*," *Modern Language Notes* 40 [1925]: 270-76; here 273); C. S. Lewis, *The Allegory of Love: A Study in Medieval Tradition* (Oxford: Oxford UP, 1935) 179, John M. Steadman, *Disembodied Laughter:* Troilus *and the Apotheosis Tradition* (Berkeley: U of California P, 1972) 144, and Young, "Chaucer's Renunciation of Love in *Troilus*" 271 consider the epilogue to the poem a renunciation of what precedes; the epilogue is not a reversal of philosophy but a culmination of what has gone before (Charles Muscatine, *Chaucer and the French Tradition* [Berkeley: U of California P, 1969] 162; H. L. Rogers, "The Beginning (and Ending) of Chaucer's '*Troilus and Criseyde*,'" *Festschrift for Ralph Farrell* [Bern: Peter Lang, 1977] 185-200; here 196; Steadman, *Disembodied Laughter* 154-55; Bonnie Wheeler, "Dante, Chaucer, and the Ending of *Troilus and Criseyde*," *Philological Quarterly* 61 [1982]: 105-23; here 117); the epilogue represents a repudiation of courtly love and romance (Gill, *Paradoxical Patterns in Chaucer's* Troilus x, 92; Steadman, *Disembodied Laughter* 144); Chaucer condemns the classical past (Wheeler, "Dante, Chaucer, and the Ending of *Troilus and Criseyde*," 116; Peter Dronke, "The Conclusion of *Troilus and Criseyde*," *Medium Aevum* 33 [1964]: 47-52; here 47, 49); Chaucer achieves closure through *contemptus mundi* (Wheeler, "Dante, Chaucer, and the Ending of *Troilus and Criseyde*" 105; James Dean, "Chaucer's *Troilus*, Boccaccio's *Filostrato*, and the Poetics of Closure," *Philological Quarterly* 64 [1985]: 175-84; here 178-79); the epilogue is related to the Retraction (Dahlberg, *The Literature of Unlikeness* 148; Lisa J. Kiser, *Telling Classical Tales: Chaucer and* The Legend of Good Women [Ithaca: Cornell UP, 1983] 153; Steadman, *Disembodied Laughter* 154); Walter C. Curry denies the epilogue the status of an integral part of the drama ("Destiny in Chaucer's *Troilus*," *Publications of the Modern Language Association* 45 [1930]: 129-68; here 167); and G. L. Kittredge argues that the narrator has no other choice of closure (*Chaucer and His Poetry* [Cambridge: Harvard UP, 1915] 142). See also Barbara Nolan, *Chaucer and the Tradition of the Roman Antique* (Cambridge: Cambridge UP, 1992) 198-246.

58 Ann Chalmers Watts writes that the "'I'" at the beginning of *Troilus and Criseyde* is a character whose vision is more limited than the author's; but at the end of the poem narrator and author seem to speak with one voice" ("Chaucerian Selves—Especially Two Serious Ones," *Chaucer Review* 4 [1970: 229-41; here 231). Gale C. Schricker's opinion on the same point is that "the identities of Chaucer and the narrator are undeniably confused at the end of the poem, in a manner that recalls the ambiguity of the attitudes of the personae toward fiction and fact in the

Forwhi to every lovere I me excuse,
That of no sentement I this endite,
But out of Latyn in my tonge it write.

Wherfore I nyl have neither thank ne blame
Of al this werk, but prey yow mekely,
Disblameth me if any word be lame,
For as myn auctour seyde, so sey I. (*TC* II, lines 12-18)

The neutral position of the translator precludes any input on Chaucer's part and allows him to conceal himself conveniently behind the contents of "other books" and his own ignorance, a combination that would absolve him from the guilt of both writing "lame" love poetry and of relating a pagan love story.[59] The poet, however, immediately modifies the auctorial notion he wishes to impress upon the audience and calls into question the stability of both language and auctorial voice early on: "Myn auctour shal I folwen," he vows in his departing prefatory remark, "if I konne" (*TC* II, line 49).

In Book III, he further demonstrates his initial position of faithfully emulating his source:

But sooth is, though I kan nat tellen al,
As kan myn auctour, of his excellence,
Yet have I seyd, and God toforn, and shal
In every thyng, al holly his sentence;
And if that ich, at Loves reverence,
Have any word in eched for the beste,
Doth therwithal right as youreselven leste.

For myne wordes, heere and every part,
I speke hem alle under correccioun
Of yow that felyng han in loves art,
And putte it al in youre discrecioun
To encresse or maken dymynucioun
Of my langage, and that I yow biseche. (*TC* III, lines 1324-36)

At this point, Chaucer admits that he does not have the perspective his "auctour" has but that he maintains the original meaning, which insures that he can gradually increase his license. He does exactly that with his confession of having added to the text; this particular ploy draws an intertextual parallel to a passage in the *Roman de la Rose*, in which Jean de Meun relinquishes the role of the compiler and affirms his own

dream-visions" ("On the Relation of Fact and Fiction in Chaucer's Poetic Endings," *Philological Quarterly* 60 [1981]: 13-25; here 20).

59 Bella Millett postulates that neither the author nor the audience should and would take this translator's defense seriously. Actually Chaucer does not apologize for "pagan beliefs" but for things "heterodox to the God of Love" ("Chaucer, Lollius, and the Medieval Theory of Authorship," *Studies in the Age of Chaucer* 1 [1984]: 93-103; here 96-97). See also Rita Copeland, *Rhetoric, Hermeneutics, and Translation in the Middle Ages* (Cambridge: Cambridge UP, 1991) and Tim William Machan, "Chaucer as Translator," *The Medieval Translator: The Theory and Practice of Translation in the Middle Ages*, ed. Roger Ellis (Cambridge: Brewer, 1989) 55-67.

authorship. Aware of the potential danger of having given away too much of his auctorial strategy, Chaucer immediately counters it by diminishing the linguistic stability even more. In typical Chaucerian fashion, and following a well-known *Exordialtopos*, he pretends to leave the audience in charge of judging his literary effort in the next stanza. Because he is an incompetent lover, he cannot possibly know the most suitable words when dealing with love poetry; the audience, therefore, needs to adjust his language to its level of experience. Language has become a medium of mutability, and the poem has presumably moved further away from a stable central viewpoint: it can run the gamut of love based on the experiences of the readers. Thus, the author is thoroughly relieved of responsibility.

Shirking of responsibility is also evident in Chaucer's emulation of the apology tradition concerning women. Following the ancient and Romance language tradition, Chaucer apologizes to the women in the audience for having had to portray an "unsavory" character like Criseyde:

Bysechyng every lady bright of hewe,
And every gentil womman, what she be,
That al be that Criseyde was untrewe,
That for that gilt she be nat wroth with me.
Ye may hire gilt in other bokes se;
And gladlier I wol write, yif yow leste,
Penolopeës trouthe and good Alceste. (*TC* V, lines 1772-78).

On a narrative and structural level, John Steadman perceives the special function of this apology to be twofold: it points back to "fidelity and infidelity" and adumbrates the final stanzas with their "contrast between true and false love, steadfastness and mutability."[60] This apology comes strategically before the "Go, litel bok, go" passage and the author's exhortation to the "yonge, fresshe folkes." The apology is another phase in Chaucer's strategy to debunk his *auctores* altogether; Chaucer, who has already called into question his own accuracy in representing the sources, nevertheless wants the female audience to subscribe entirely to his claim that he merely faithfully reproduced the Criseyde he found in those sources.

A comparison with Boccaccio's *Filostrato* reveals that Boccaccio did not apologize for his rendition of Criseyde[61] and that Chaucer actually dealt more kindly with his heroine than did Boccaccio. The Italian author finished his work with *contemptus feminae*, indulging in a typical antifeminist accusation of female inconstancy and fickleness, whereas the English poet broadened the spectrum of his final exhortation, elevating it to *contemptus mundi*, forsaking Boccaccio's goal of finding the perfect mistress in favor of focusing on the medieval dichotomy between earthly and heavenly love.[62] The poet's position, however, implies both criticism and condemnation of

---

60 Steadman, *Disembodied Laughter* 118.
61 Steadman, *Disembodied Laughter* 117.
62 Dean, "Chaucer's *Troilus*, Boccaccio's *Filostrato*, and the Poetics of Closure" 175, 179 and Steadman, *Disembodied Laughter* 113-15. According to Bonnie Wheeler, Chaucer assumes a position between Boccaccio's "secular morals" and Dante's *Paradiso* ("Dante, Chaucer, and the Ending of *Troilus and Criseyde*" 112).

Criseyde on two levels:[63] by mentioning Penelope and Alceste as more appropriate pagan women—which is also an intra-auctorial and intertextual adumbration of *The Legend of Good Women*—and by ending the poem with an invocation to Mary. Penelope and Alceste would fit into Chaucer's *Legend of Good Women* as women who deny themselves sexual fulfillment; and although invocations to Mary became increasingly commonplace in the fourteenth century[64] (Chaucer himself implores Mary in both the *Astrolabe* and *The Canterbury Tales*), she is the Christian model of womanhood, an unrealistic but preferable model from which all notions of female sexuality have been drained. Consequently, she is the only female to whom a medieval Christian soul can safely refer without being sexually tempted, making her a fitting and innocuous, albeit afterthought-like, ending to this pagan love story.

In the epilogue to *Troilus and Criseyde*, Chaucer greatly highlights the oscillating nature of his auctorial role, rejecting the same *auctores* he praised only a few lines earlier. He does not repudiate his *Troilus* entirely but puts the pagan tale into a different context and into perspective for a medieval audience while simultaneously exerting his license as an author. *Troilus*, among Chaucer's works, has the greatest share of classical myths. In the first book of *Troilus*, Chaucer evokes both the muse "Thesiphone" (line 6) as well as the "cruwel Furie" (line 9) and dedicates himself as "that God of Loves servantz" (line 15). He connects those classical elements explicitly with the auctorial activity of writing in "as I write" (*TC* I, line 7), in "with which I write" (*TC* IV, line 13), and in "But for that I to writen first bigan / Of his love" (*TC* V, line 1768).[65] In Book II, the poet also casts his lot with the classical world: "O lady myn, that called art Cleo, / Thow be myn speed fro this forth, and my Muse, / To ryme wel this book til I have do" (lines 8-10). In the "Go, litel bok, go" stanza in the epilogue, Chaucer sends off his work and pays rather exuberant homage to classical *literati* by having his book be "subgit . . . to alle poesye; / And kis the steppes where as thow seest pace / Virgile, Ovide, Omer, Lucan, and Stace" (*TC* V, lines 1790-92).

Having thus rooted himself firmly in the ancient tradition, Chaucer launches an intratextual and intra-auctorial attack on that very position:

> Lo here, of payens corsed olde rites!
> Lo here, what alle hire goddes may availle!
> Lo here, thise wrecched worldes appetites!
> Lo here, the fyn and guerdoun for travaille
> Of Jove, Appollo, of Mars, of swich rascaille!
> Lo here, the forme of olde clerkis speche
> In poetrie, if ye hire bokes seche. (*TC* V, lines 1849-55)[66]

Chaucer explicitly discredits the same ancient customs, pagan deities, and pagan literature he has implicitly exalted, a strategy that goes back to the initial conflict between

---

63   Yet Chaucer has been tender towards her in *TC*, V lines 1093-99.

64   Gerald Morgan cites "religious conviction" and an understanding of the *Divine Comedy* as a reason for the last stanza ("The Ending of '*Troilus and Criseyde*'" 269).

65   This passage reminds Jon M. Fyler of Ovid's introduction to the *Amores*; he suggests that maybe Chaucer wishes to imply comically that his choice of subject matter was questionable (*Chaucer and Ovid* 108).

66   This stanza is not in Boccaccio (Steadman, *Disembodied Laughter* 115).

pagan and Christian writing established one thousand years earlier and is characterized by Anne Barbara Gill as an "ambivalent attitude toward literary tradition."[67] At the same time, Chaucer undercuts the ancient literary tradition he has so far hailed and implicitly criticizes himself as a helper to the God of Love as well as an imitator of "olde clerkis speche." This implicit self-criticism is further destabilized by the fact that Chaucer mentions the classical authors as venerable authorities but does not reveal his real sources: Boccaccio, Dante, and Boethius. In both his explicit and implicit self-criticism Chaucer emphasizes his *contemptus mundi* theme and the *cupiditas* rampant in the "wrecched worldes appetites." This fits in his overall exhortatory scheme and the underlying Boethian framework of *Troilus*, which would reject earthly love.

Chaucer's exhortatory scheme has its place in the text and can be explained in the light of his role as translator and the excuse that he makes. Having built up an ambivalent position for narrative responsibility, the poet emphasizes a certain ambiguity in language also, underscoring the issue of earthly mutability:

And for ther is so gret diversite
In Englissh and in writyng of oure tonge,
So prey I God that non myswrite the,
Ne the mysmetre for defaute of tonge; (*TC* V, lines 1793-96)

In typical Chaucerian fashion, the poet makes the reader the agent who imparts meaning—that is the correct meaning—on the text. At the end of the fifth book, the author is faced with his own reliance on classical sources in bequeathing a treacherous pagan love story that resulted in the death of the hero. In the story, great emphasis had been placed on the ambiguity of language; Chaucer, therefore, compounds all of these factors of instability into one focal point, counterbalancing the ambiguity of love and language with the ultimately unwavering and altruistic love of Christ, the Word Incarnate. For Chaucer, this is the logical medieval step to take as well as a clever auctorial *modus operandi* to avoid virtually all responsibility.[68] Although he had himself set up as an imitator of an "olde clerkis speche," Chaucer can now divest himself of any accountability through his own rejection of classical matter. Both his emphasis on the ambiguity of the English language and the dedication of his work to "moral Gower" and "philosophical Strode" (*TC* V, lines 1856-57) serve to cleanse him of all guilt.[69] If Gower and Strode, whom Chaucer entreats to "provide a corrective view for

---

67 Gill, *Paradoxical Patterns in Chaucer's* Troilus 99. Zacharias Thundyil postulates that Chaucer "does not condemn the pagan religion as un-Christian; he simply shows that it would not work even in the pagan world, even though it has great virtues and beauties. Therefore, he argues that the error and incompleteness of rational wisdom and natural love should be removed by the wisdom of faith and the supernatural love of Jesus" ("The *Moral* Chaucer" 13).

68 Wheeler concludes that "all human craft is inevitably flawed," and therefore, a poet "practising his craft carefully, must deny its potential perfection" because "[j]ust as the poet can find reassurance and humility in his formal recognition that God alone is perfect writer, so too can Chaucer's audience find comfort in the poet's generous implication that God is also the only infallible reader" ("Dante, Chaucer, and the Ending of *Troilus and Criseyde*" 120-21).

69 Stephen A. Barney cites a number of references that demonstrate the commonness of a writer's invitation to correct his work (Larry D. Benson, ed. *Riverside Chaucer* 1058). Gill describes Strode as "a Thomist philosopher, who won esteem by his refutation of Wyclif's necessitarian-

those who might mistake its instructive aspects,"[70] were to correct Chaucer's work, then they would be altering the text and thus relieving Chaucer of even more his responsibility. If they were not to change anything, he would be confirmed in the "correctness" of his work and should not be faulted for it. With the Gower invocation, Chaucer again underscores the unreliability of language and places the center of judgment outside the text and outside his own auctorial reach. Much like Hartmann von Aue's apology, Chaucer's disparagement of his own poetry operates as an integral intratextual part of the work to heighten the effect of the mutability of earthly matters and even of writers,[71] as Chaucer needs it to justify his writing about a pagan love story.[72] The mutability issue leads him to exhort the "yonge fresshe folkes" and to stress the *utilitas* of the work by turning it into a moral tale, while still allowing him to exercise his auctorial license to the fullest, as he does in *The Legend of Good Women*.[73]

8.6.2. *The Legend of Good Women*

The Legend of Good Women assumes a unique place both in Chaucer's metapoetical dialogue and his intra-auctorial participation in the medieval apology tradition. For this study, the main interest lies in the extensive prologue, of which we have two versions

---

ism" (*Paradoxical Patterns in Chaucer's* Troilus 107). For further information, see Barney in the *Riverside Chaucer* 1058 n. 1856-59.

70 R. F. Yeager, "'O moral Gower': Chaucer's Dedication of *Troilus and Criseyde*," *The Chaucer Review* 19 (1984): 87-99; here 93.

71 James Dean deduces that Chaucer has "transmogrified from the reverent medieval 'maker' abasing himself before the premier classical poets to the most austere of moralists," who criticizes and "rejects his own poetry to dramatize . . . the instability of even . . . narrative poets" ("Chaucer's *Troilus*, Boccaccio's *Filostrato*, and the Poetics of Closure" 180).

72 This notion might not be as far-fetched as one might think, for William A. Madden considers Boethius the source for Chaucer's apologies and retractions ("Chaucer's Retraction and Medieval Canons of Seemliness," *Medieval Studies* 17 [1955]: 173-84; here 183). Boethius brings on the whores of the theater so that Philosophy can expel them. See also 62 Chapter 3.

73 Chaucer concludes his exhortation with a question: "And syn he best to love is, and most meke, / What nedeth feynede loves for to seke?" (*TC* V, lines 1847-48). According to Wheeler, the gist lies in the term "feynede" ('pretended'): "To argue, however, that the full love of God requires utter repudiation of all earthly loves can only compel assent if the narrator's definition of 'feynede loves' means pretended earthly loves, not all earthly loves. But to damn all worldly love denies any value to the love of Troilus and Criseyde: it repudiates any value the poem itself can claim except the sheerly aesthetic. Even Troilus and the narrator have only condemned the worst of human experience, and then only in comparison to the fullest experience of the divine" ("Dante, Chaucer, and the Ending of *Troilus and Criseyde*" 115). Anthony E. Farnham takes this interpretation a step further into the realm of Chaucerian self-criticism; if, in the face of Christ, one does not need "feynede loves," why does one need to write about it? ("Chaucerian Irony and the Ending of the *Troilus*," *Chaucer Review* 2 [1967]: 207-16; here 215). The conclusion to *Troilus* "integrates several poetic voices in varied stages of transition from the world of the poem to reality, and it prefigures the poetic function of the 'Retraction' as a conclusion to both life and art" (Schricker, "On the Relation of Fact and Fiction in Chaucer's Poetic Endings" 14).

and the only extant evidence of Chaucer's intra-auctorial reworking of his text.[74] The prologue to the *Legend* is a dream vision, whereas the actual stories about the "good women" were supposedly written in an "awakened" state. Although Chaucer often makes self-deprecating comments in the dream visions, none of them contains a literary apology; the distancing effect of the dream vision plays a part in that. In contrast, *Troilus* is a pagan love story that has not been presented as a dream vision, and Chaucer apologizes for it. On an intertextual level, the *Legend* is often considered a palinode to *Troilus* and, in the vein of dream visions, would not itself contain a palinode. Chaucer, however, exploits the construct of the dream vision to the fullest by using it in the *Legend* in conjunction with an apology because of its distancing effect, making the palinode more remote and therefore less damning. The switch to "real time" for writing the actual stories supports that theory. The *Legend* is also the only work in which Chaucer features a partial dream vision. Chaucer capitalizes on the following aspects of the apology tradition: interauctorially he sets up a trial situation, like Machaut in the *Navarre*, in which the author has a third party accuse him of literary improprieties against women; in part of the framework he still relies heavily on the concept of the emulating and innocent translator as mandated in *Troilus*. But the topic of the apology construct focuses on the charge of heresy against the God of Love and of antifeminism, the latter of which Chaucer has touched upon in book V of the *Troilus*.[75] With this dream-vision apology Chaucer points out the dilemma a medieval author could find himself in, serving two masters, the Christian faith and the religion of love. It is furthermore a clever strategy to voice his "final rejection of the court of love"[76] and move on to other literary pastures.

Chaucer's apology and trial structure in the prologue to the *Legend* is governed by a dynamic different from that in the epilogue to his *Troilus*. In *Troilus*, Chaucer apologizes to the female audience for his unavoidable portrayal of Criseyde, constantly

---

74   The general consensus is that G is the revised version of the prologue, which I will use here (Estrich, "Chaucer's Maturing Art in the Prologues of the *Legend of Good Women*" 326; John H. Fisher, "The Revision of the Prologue to the *Legend of Good Women*: An Occasional Explanation," *South Atlantic Bulletin* 43 (1978): 75-84; here 75; Robert O. Payne, "Making His Own Myth: The Prologue to Chaucer's *Legend of Good Women*," *Chaucer Review* 9 [1975]: 197-211; here 93; and Shaner in the *Riverside Chaucer* 1059). See also John C. French, *The Problem of the Two Prologues to Chaucer's* Legend of Good Women (Baltimore: J. H. Furst, 1905) and Robert Worth Frank, *Chaucer and* The Legend of Good Women (Cambridge: Harvard UP, 1972) 11-36.

75   James Wimsatt finds the following similarities between Chaucer and Machaut: "An analogy also exists between the sequences formed by Machaut's two debate poems and by three of Chaucer's works. *Behaigne* is concerned with the tragedies of two lovers; one has suffered a bereavement and the other has been betrayed by a woman who is perfect except that she lacks constancy. Chaucer's *Duchess*, which deals with a bereaved lover, and *Troilus and Criseyde*, which concerns a jilted knight, offer parallels to these tragedies. And just as Machaut's *Navarre* is designed to make amends for the injustices to women performed in *Behaigne*, so Chaucer's *Legend* aims at atonement for *Troilus*. Thus there exists an intriguing coincidence of subject and sequence between the works of the poets" (*Chaucer and the French Love Poets: The Literary Background of the* Book of the Duchess [Chapel Hill: U of North Carolina P, 1968] 96).

76   Donald C. Baker, "Dreamer and Critic: The Poet in the *Legend of Good Women*," *University of Colorado Studies: Series in Language and Literature* 9 (1963): 4-18; here 5.

flaunts his vocation as translator, but then rebukes his pagan sources and indirectly his own literary activity while bowing to Christ, the Master Author. Thus he has complied with the medieval code of literary ethics, but his return to the literary convention of the court of love in the prologue of the *Legend* illustrates both how much control Chaucer has over his material and how much he can manipulate literary conventions in his favor. Chaucer did not need to go this route, but the different dynamic he capitalizes on in the *Legend* serves two purposes: first, it allows him to depict the medieval author in the self-conscious quandary delineated by the dreamer's encounter with the God of Love and his queen Alceste; second, it allows him to make a pagan display of author criticism that is both starkly reminiscent of the first Stesichorean palinode, with its emphasis on divine power and reversal of poetic attitude, and is an ironic and inverted reenactment of what the medieval author should avoid in the Christian cosmos, namely angering God.[77] After all, the prologue evokes notions of authority, patronage, and censorship, concerns that can be dealt with more lightly and ironically in a dream vision with a mythological god than in the religio-political reality of the fourteenth century or in the pagan love story of *Troilus and Criseyde*. Therefore, unlike most medieval authors accused of antifeminism, Chaucer goes back to the Stesichorean pattern of avoiding divine displeasure and offending earthly women.[78]

The Chaucer accused of literary improprieties against women relies heavily on the concept of the emulating and innocent translator, as mandated in *Troilus*. The subject of the apology, however, focuses on the charge of heresy against the God of Love and on antifeminism, the latter of which Chaucer has touched upon in book V of *Troilus*. Cupid finds his self-proclaimed and self-critical "servantz" guilty of heresy against the doctrine of love, especially because of his translation of the *Romance of the Rose*:

> "For thow," quod he, "art therto nothyng able.
> My servaunts ben alle wyse and honourable.
> Thow art my mortal fo and me werreyest,
> And of myne olde servauntes thow mysseyest,
> And hynderest hem with thy translacyoun;
> . . . .
> Thow hast translated the Romauns of the Rose,
> That is an heresye ageyns my lawe." (*LGW* G, lines 246-50, 255-56)

Because it is debatable how a translation of the *Roman*—"the very gospel of love"[79]— could incriminate Chaucer as a disobedient servant of Love, the accusation more aptly demonstrates the ineptitude of the God of Love as a literary critic—he knows less about books than he thinks and his understanding of *translatio* is questionable. Lisa Kiser speculates that Cupid could have been incensed by the way Reason unmasked

---

77 F. N. Robinson claims that the *Legend* "falls at once into the ancient category of palinodes, known in literary history from the time of Stesichorus" (*The Works of Geoffrey Chaucer*, 2nd ed. [Oxford: Oxford UP, 1957] 481). Peter Godman also considers it a "palinode and a legendary in the tradition of Stesichorus, Ovid, Machaut and the Golden Legend" ("Chaucer and Boccaccio's Latin Works," *Chaucer and the Italian Trecento*, ed. Piero Boitani [Cambridge: Cambridge UP, 1983] 269-95; here 281). Robert O. Payne denies that the *Legend* fits into the palinode category ("Making His Own Myth" 197).

78 See 25-26 in Chapter 2 for Helen's special role.

79 Neville Coghill, *The Poet Chaucer* (London: Oxford UP, 1949) 98.

the foolishness resulting from the service of love.[80] Cupid nevertheless exhibits an understanding of *translatio* that is "rudimentary" because he accuses Chaucer for the heresy of his sources.[81] Inherent in this indictment of the God of Love might be an ironic commentary on the ability of the mirrored world—the medieval religio-political establishment—to understand and censor the creative art of a writer.

The second prong of Cupid's accusation points to Chaucer's composition of *Troilus* and his portrayal of Criseyde. Although Chaucer has apologized for that part of *Troilus*, this complaint gives him a suitable lead into the topic he wants to tackle next: stories about good women to contrast with Criseyde:

> "Hast thow nat mad in Englysh ek the bok
> How that Crisseyde Troylus forsok,
> In shewynge how that wemen han don mis?
> But natheles, answere me now to this;
> Why noldest thow as wel [han] seyd goodnesse
> Of wemen, as thow hast seyd wikednesse?
> Was there no good matere in thy mynde,
> Ne in alle thy bokes ne coudest thow nat fynde
> Som story of wemen that were goode and trewe?
> Yis, God wot, sixty bokes olde and newe
> Hast thow thyself, alle ful of storyes grete,
> That bothe Romayns and ek Grekes trete
> Of sundry wemen, which lyf that they ladde,
> And evere an hundred goode ageyn oon badde." (*LGW* G, lines 264-77)

The God of Love does not defend Criseyde but suggests that Chaucer should have chosen a different story, making the appropriate intertextual connection back to *Troilus* V, lines 1777-78, in which Chaucer himself said that he would rather have written about Penelope and Alceste. Cupid's indictment, the main part greatly elaborated on by Chaucer in his G version, is connected to Chaucer's disquisition in the beginning of the prologue on the function of old books in the literary creation process.[82] This orchestration gives the author not only the opportunity to stress and justify his dedication to ancient books and authors that he had self-critically indicted in *Troilus*, but also to show the literary limitations of the God of Love.

In the beginning of the prologue, the author firmly establishes the importance of old books as purports of the literary past and literary fame and shows the crippling effect their absence would have on literary activity:

---

80 Kiser, *Telling Classical Tale* 74. Or it could be considered offensive to women in the way Christine de Pizan takes it.

81 Kiser, *Telling Classical Tales* 81, 75 and Sherron Knopp, "Chaucer and Jean de Meun as Self-Conscious Narrators: The Prologue to the *Legend of Good Women* and the *Roman de la Rose* 10307-680," *Comitatus* 4 (1973): 25-39; here 27.

82 Estrich enumerates Chaucer's expansions in the G version: addition of the poet's indictment by the God of Love and a fifty-line sermon on good women; the modification of Alceste's defense in order to intensify the poet's lack of repentance for his sins and to treat the courtly theme of the poem with broader humor; the omission of line F368 and the reference to Queen Anne ("Chaucer's Maturing Art in the Prologues of the *Legend of Good Women*" 333, 335).

> Thanne mote we to bokes that we fynde,
> Thorugh whiche that olde thynges ben in mynde,
> And to the doctryne of these olde wyse
> Yeven credence, in every skylful wyse,
> And trowen on these olde aproved storyes
> Of holynesse, of regnes, of victoryes,
> Of love, of hate, of othere sondry thynges,
> Of which I may not make rehersynges.
> And if that olde bokes weren aweye,
> Yloren were of remembrance the keye.
> Wel oughte us thanne on olde bokes leve,
> There as there is non other assay by preve.
> And as for me, though that my wit be lite,
> On bokes for to rede I me delyte,
> And in myn herte have hem in reverence,
> And to hem yeve swich lust and swich credence. (*LGW* G, lines 17-32)

Lexical similarities in the treatment of the thought process involved in auctorial activity, such as "fynde" and "mynde," confirm the intratextual connection of this passage to the speech the God of Love addresses to Chaucer dealing with the same subject. The prologue is a far cry from the deprecatory dismissal of "olde clerkis speche" and reverses the previous auctorial self-criticism, both intertextually and intra-auctorially.

Nevertheless, this defense of the *auctoritates* is as necessary and justified in the *Legend* as their dismissal is in *Troilus*. After such a literary disavowal, Chaucer returns to writing about pagan women and their love stories, in much the same way as he contrived to tell the story of *Troilus and Criseyde*. In Chaucer's intra-auctorial strategy, it is appropriate to pay homage again to the classical authors, despite insisting that he would prefer to tell another story. He emphasizes this point in another passage:[83]

> But wherfore that I spak, to yeve credence
> To bokes olde and don hem reverence,
> Is for men shulde autoritees beleve,
> There as there lyth non other assay by preve.
> For myn entent is, or I fro yow fare,
> The naked text in English to declare
> Of many a story, or elles or many a geste,
> As autours seyn; leveth hem if yow leste. (*LGW* G, lines 81-88)

Chaucer sets up his argument carefully: one has to use and to believe in old books because there is no other avenue of past experience; since the sources are by default true, Chaucer, who vouches for the literalness of his translations, cannot possibly be rendering any untruths. These uncharacteristic confirmations of unwavering truth and

---

83 Charles Owen discusses the pagan/Christian dichotomy: "The implicit palinode for a palinode in respect to courtly love, again in reference to the *Troilus*, does not surprisingly impugn the religious commitment at the end of *Troilus*. The two worlds could surely coexist, especially since the story material of his legend material antedates Christianity" (Charles A. Owen, "The Tales of Canterbury: Fictions within a Fiction that Purports Not to Be a Fiction," *Chaucer and the Craft of Fiction*, ed. Leigh A. Arrathoon [Rochester, MI.: Solaris Press, 1986] 179-94; here 183). If one uses that argument, it needs to be noted that the story material of *Troilus* also antedates Christianity.

faltering auctorial center simultaneously contradict the strategies of unstable language and auctorial abilities to convey exactly what the original authors meant; but they also corroborate that very same instability with the conditional phrase "if yow leste," which shifts the center of final judgment once more outside of the text—to the reader—and thereby removes responsibility from the author.

That particular passage also preempts the accusation of the God of Love and challenges his ability as a literary critic long before he appears on the stage. Chaucer's assertions that he translates literally and that everything he writes represents the truth are not inherently contradicted by the God of Love, whose grievance is not whether the poet has rendered the literal truth of *Roman* or *Troilus and Criseyde* accurately, but that Chaucer dared select these topics at all. The God of Love is only interested in stories that further his case, faulting Chaucer for writing the wrong kind of truth and Criseyde for staying alive.[84] The perspective mandated by the God of Love takes on an increasingly more ironic flavor as he defines what kind of women Chaucer should have picked as topics:

> "How clene maydenes and how trewe wyves,
> How stedefaste widewes durynge all here lyves,
>
> . . . .
>
> For to hyre love were they so trewe
> That, rathere than they wolde take a newe,
> They chose to be ded in sondry wyse." (*LGW* G, lines 282-83; 288-90)

Although this list of steadfast women—faithful virgins, wives, and widows, more prone to dying than to loving—directly assaults Criseyde as an inconstant lover, it even more importantly characterizes the God of Love as an increasingly limited antifeminist. His interpretation that the best role for women in the religion of love is to be dead martyrs for the cause of love is coupled with his insistence on notorious antifeminists, like Jerome, as sources for stories about good women. He brings up Ovid as well as Christian and pagan authors, demonstrating once more his literary shortcomings because "to view heathens and Christians as believers in the same ethical code is to misrepresent badly the truth that Chaucer so painstakingly expressed in his *Troilus*—that pagan culture and Christian morality can coexist in a work of art only in a very complicated way."[85]

It is significant that the accusations of the God of Love are partially confirmed and partially countered by his companion Alceste, a woman. The Chaucerian persona has Alceste defend him in the usual characterization of that hardly-conscious, stumbling, definitely unoriginal, emulating, and innocent literary creator whose main task it is to translate:[86]

84　For Chaucer's main sin is bad art; he has to write good poetry in order to atone for the bad poetry, but what is lacking is dictated by Cupid's "moralistic standards" (Robert O. Payne, *The Key of Remembrance: A Study of Chaucer's Poetics* [New Haven: Yale UP, 1963] 98, 99).

85　Kiser, *Telling Classical Tales* 82-3.

86　The "simpleton" character, as Coghill calls him (*The Poet Chaucer* 102).

He may translate a thyng in no malyce,
But for he useth bokes for to make,
And taketh non hed of what matere he take,
Therfore he wrot the Rose and ek Crisseyde
Of innocence, and nyste what he seyde.
Or hym was boden make thilke tweye
Of som persone, and durste it not withseye;
For he hath write many a bok er this.
He ne hath not don so grevously amys
To translate that olde clerkes wryte." (*LGW* G, lines 341-50)

Alceste complements the picture of the uninvolved and blameless translator who produces "bad art" with the additionally exonerating factors of literary patronage—basically Chaucer's was a "court poet" existence[87]—and his previous record with the God
of Love, whose cause Chaucer furthered "Whil he was yong" (*LGW* G, line 400). This
comment certainly evokes the dichotomy so often drawn upon by other self-critical
authors that youth is a time for love, whereas old age is a time for wisdom and
Christian contemplation. This dichotomy signals that Chaucer's days as a love poet
belong to the past, but that he served Cupid when it was his time to do so.[88]

The list of works Alceste cites in Chaucer's defense poses an especially interesting
crux. It appears that Chaucer uses lists of his works several times in self-critical and
self-justifying circumstances: the catalog in this prologue, the list given by the Man of
Law in The Introduction to the Man of Law's Tale, and the enumeration in the
Retraction. Some critics consider the list in the Retraction to be interpolated. That
seems unlikely, however, when the list is juxtaposed with the other lists that showcase
Chaucer's growing canon, lists that help to criticize or to defend him in various ways
against assorted charges and that contribute to the metapoetical dialogue:

"He hath maked lewed folk to delyte
To serven yow, in preysynge of youre name.
He made the bok that highte the Hous of Fame,
And ek the Deth of Blaunche the Duchesse,
And the Parlement of Foules, as I gesse,
And al the love of Palamon and Arcite
Of Thebes, thogh the storye is knowen lite;
And many an ympne for your halydayes,
That highten balades, roundeles, vyrelayes;
And, for to speke of other besynesse,
He hath in prose translated Boece,
And Of the Wreched Engendrynge of Mankynde,
As man may in Pope Innocent yfynde;
And mad the lyf also of Seynt Cecile.
He made also, gon is a gret while,
Orygenes upon the Maudeleyne.
Hym oughte now to have the lesse peyne;
He hath mad many a lay and many a thyng." (*LGW* G, lines 403-20)

---

87   Payne, *The Key of Remembrance* 101, 103.
88   This is also the way Gower presents him at the end of *Confessio Amantis*.

This list contains many of the same works the Retraction does (as well as some not mentioned and considered lost), but uses them for a completely different purpose. In the *Legend*, the author has to curry favor with Cupid for lack of amorous conduct; in the Retraction, he apologizes to the Christian God and the audience for the very same works (including *Troilus*; the *Romaunt* is missing) because of that content. Only the first half of the list, however, demonstrates Chaucer's service to the God of Love. The second half includes works that do not further the cause championed by the God of Love, such as the *Boece*, with which Chaucer tries to placate the Christian God in the Retraction. The list concludes with a phrase similar to the one rounding out the list in the Retraction: "many a lay and many a thyng." One could assume a formulaic usage. If one does not, then Chaucer provides another example of using the same genre to apologize to two different audiences. In the Retraction, he modifies "many a lay" with the pejorative term "leccherous" and places them in the category of the works to be repented. In the *Legend*, the lays follow the non-amorous works. These lists and the discrepancies contained in them elucidate Chaucer's participation in the pervasive dichotomy of love songs and Christian writings long before the Retraction.

Three explanations can be proffered for the indiscriminate inclusiveness of Alceste's list: first, Chaucer wishes to ridicule either Alceste's literary judgment or that of the God of Love; second, he questions the judgment of the potential literary censors in his fourteenth-century religio-political universe; and third, he primarily flaunts his literary fecundity in its entirety, even if the second half of works would need to be rejected by the God of Love more vehemently than the *Romaunt* and *Troilus* were. Chaucer's dichotomous lists illustrate how highly stylized the apology convention was and how expertly Chaucer knew to manipulate it to his own literary ends.

Chaucer resolves the prologue in the same way that Machaut does in the *Navarre*. Chaucer denies any literary guilt and actually justifies his composition with the by now familiar reliance on ancient sources:

"But trewely I wende, as in this cas,
Naught have agilt, ne don to love trespas.
. . . .
Ne a trewe lovere oghte me nat to blame
Thogh that I speke a fals lovere som shame.
They oughte rathere with me for to holde
For that I of Criseyde wrot or tolde,
Or of the Rose; what so myn auctour mente,
Algate, God wot, it was myn entente
To forthere trouthe in love and it cheryce,
And to be war fro falsnesse and fro vice
By swich ensaumple; this was menynge." (*LGW* G, lines 452-53, 456-64)

The poet rightfully points out that he wanted to further truth in love and to warn against vice; unfortunately, the God of Love is not looking for the same kind of truth, and "lewd" works benefit his purpose.[89] Like Machaut and other medieval authors

---

89   Baker, "Dreamer and Critic" 13 and Estrich, "Chaucer's Maturing Art in the Prologues of the *Legend of Good Women*" 330.

accused of having incriminated women, Chaucer readily accepts the typical penance for his literary sin: specifically, continued literary activity.[90] With most self-critical authors, penance is a self-inflicted ritual, but the trial framework requires that penance be inflicted on the literary sinner. In Chaucer's case,

"... yer by yere,
The moste partye of thy tyme spende
In makynge of a gloryous legende
Of goode women, maydenes and wyves,
That were trewe in lovynge al here lyves;
And telle of false men that hem betrayen." (*LGW* G, lines 471-76)

Two important aspects characterize this verdict. Ironically, on the one hand, Chaucer is instructed to write about pagan love stories, an activity highly questioned by medieval Christianity and later by the author himself. On the other hand, the dubious literary judgment and verdict by the God of Love and Alceste, as well as Chaucer's own machinations to switch literary genres, manifest themselves in the actual stories of good women. The legends' purpose of "social corrective" results in a "loss of individuality and diversity" for women as well as "distortion and oversimplification"[91] of their characters and achieves the same caricaturing effect as most medieval antifeminist apologies. As Jon Fyler points out, the "*Legend of Good Women* is no more straightforward than most other literary palinodes" and seems to harbor some of the Ovidian contradiction of the *Remedia Amoris*, in which the poet purports to portray the woman's point of view; Chaucer is supposedly doing so because of the God of Love's unilateral view on women as sufferers for the cause of love.[92] Thus, antifeminist satire can thrive when a defined literary genre is imposed on matter that obviously cannot carry it. The thirteenth- and fourteenth-century *dolce stil nuovo* emphasis on the woman's ability to transform earthly love into heavenly love and thus to lead to God may be a background explanation to the *Legend*, as Kiser so aptly puts it: "The Legend is both an irreverent and a highly comic parody of Dante's contention that ladies symbolize God, and it is an understated confession that what Dante thought was basically right."[93]

The antifeminism is furthermore coupled with Chaucer's desire to "cast off the outgrown shell of courtly love convention in both style and intellectual content,"[94] at whose center women are. Elaine Tuttle Hansen adds that Chaucer must have reached the limits of his portrayal of good men in literature and consequently had to find a new topic.[95] However, the irony inherent in the command to reverse the auctorial design of

---

90 This acceptance "does not suggest that Chaucer was growing more devout and had become displeased with the 'bold analogies between Christian service and the worship of Cupid'" (J. Fisher, "The Revision of the Prologue to the *Legend of Good Women*: An Occasional Explanation" 79-80).

91 Fyler, *Chaucer and Ovid* 107 and Kiser, *Telling Classical Tales* 89.

92 Fyler, *Chaucer and Ovid* 97, 120.

93 Kiser, *Telling Classical Tales* 152.

94 Estrich, "Chaucer's Maturing Art in the Prologues of the *Legend of Good Women*" 337.

95 Elaine Tuttle Hanson, "Irony and the Antifeminist Narrator in the *Legend of Good Women*," *Journal of English and Germanic Philology* 82 (1983): 11-31; here 20.

Troilus with an accolade to good women and a condemnation of treacherous men is evident in *LGW*, the legend of Thisbe:

> And thus are Thisbe and Piramus ygo.
> Of trewe men I fynde but fewe mo
> In all my bokes, save this Piramus,
> And therfore have I spoken of hym thus.
> For it is deynte to us men to fynde
> A man that can in love been trewe and kynde. (lines 916-21)

But this first "legend" does not fulfill the literary penance either. The author does not conform to the instructions and defies Alceste's injunction to tell of true women and false men.

Overall, we encounter in the *Legend* an author who devises a self-critical frame of literary translation to justify what he has written before, to submit to the judgment of a deity—albeit a flawed literary critic—and to subvert that submission into another license to write as he pleases.[96] Ultimately, the prologue to the *Legend* is an ironic microcosmic rendition of the dilemma the medieval author faces. In this mythological dream-vision structure, the poet recreates the archetypal role of the author whose creation is afflicted by censure. He provides the possible scenario and also depicts the only way the author can act: to submit to the constraint of censorship and then to manipulate the circumstances in his favor and to his benefit.[97]

8.6.3. *A Treatise on the Astrolabe*

In the *Astrolabe*, Chaucer assumes the combined role of translator and compiler. First, he categorizes the *Astrolabe* as yet another translation, citing his adherence to "naked wordes in Englissh" (*AS* lines 26-27), as he had done in the *Legend*. Again Chaucer's apology for the unrefined and repetitive writing almost matches the beginning of the Retraction: "Now wol I preie mekely every discret persone that redith or herith this litel tretys to have my rude endityng for excusid, and my superfluite of wordes, for two causes" (*AS* lines 41-44). According to Chaucer, this work was meant for his son Lowys alone, but the apology, which would only be necessary for adult readers who might take offense at its simple style, suggests he aimed at a larger audience. His auctorial pride also manifests itself, illustrating that his position as translator is not neutral—as claimed in the *Troilus*—and even deserves praise:

---

96 In Kiser's opinion "Chaucer expresses confidence in the ultimate truths to be found in his works, recognizing nonetheless that earthly poets like himself may not always succeed in making their doctrines clear, especially to readers who are unfit to receive literature's highest gifts" (*Telling Classical Tales* 154).

97 Lydgate reports that Queen Anne assigned the work to Chaucer, which is of course based on the reference to her in *LGW* F lines 496-97. Constance B. Hieatt subscribes to a topical interpretation of the poems (*The Realism of Dream Visions: The Poetic Exploitation of the Dream-Experience in Chaucer and his Contemporaries* [The Hague: Mouton, 1967] 85); Bertrand H. Bronson opposes that view (*In Search of Chaucer* [Toronto: U of Toronto P, 1960] 54).

> And Lowys, yf so be that I shewe the in my lighte Englissh as trewe conclusions touching this mater, and not oonly as trewe but as many and as subtile conclusiouns, as shewid in Latyn in eny commune tretys of the Astrelabie, konne me the more thank. (*AS* lines 50-55)

Chaucer's alleged translation skills are qualified right away by his claim to the role of mere compiler:

> But considre wel that I ne usurpe not to have founden this werk of my labour or of myn engyn. I n'am but a lewd compilator of the labour of olde astrologiens, and have it translatid in myn Englissh oonly for thy doctrine. And with this swerd shal I sleen envie. (*AS* lines 59-64)

Chaucer reassumes the combined role of the translator and compiler, although Carol Lipson finds that the author only either translated or paraphrased about a fifth of his *Astrolabe* from the known sources of it, such as Messahala or Sacroboso, and that "the treatise is Chaucer's prose handling, and the success or failure of the prose construction rests with Chaucer and not with the sources."[98] Yet, in another self-protective strategy, Chaucer feels compelled to let the "olde" books supposedly speak for themselves.

The passage contains two important elements found in the Retraction. The first one is the reference to Chaucer as a compiler.[99] The only other such reference is found in the last comment of *The Canterbury Tales*: "Heere is ended the book of the tales of Caunterbury, compiled by Geffrey Chaucer, of whos soule Jhesu Crist have mercy. Amen." The second one is the phrase referring to "thy doctrine" or the education of his son. This phrase—or the concept of doctrine—is used to shield Chaucer from blame elsewhere in his work, and he explicitly invokes St. Paul in the Retraction: "For oure book seith, 'Al that is writen is writen for oure doctrine,' and that is myn entente" (RT line 1083). There is a subtle irony here insofar as all of *The Canterbury Tales* narrators make some sort of statement of intent before telling their tale, especially the Miller, who fell short of his stated goal of telling a "legende and a lyf" (MilT line 3141). By choosing the word "entente," Chaucer builds the possibility of failure into the design. By contextualizing all writing as doctrinal in the biblical sense, and therefore as

---

98 Carol Lipson, "'I n'am but a lewd compilator': Chaucer's 'Treatise on the Astrolabe' as Translation," *Neuphilologische Mitteilungen* 84 (1983): 192-200; here 199.

99 Schricker notes that Chaucer only revokes "works of original, thus individual creation" ("On the Relation of Fact and Fiction in Chaucer's Poetic Endings" 24). Tita French Baumlin writes: "Here, then, the narrator's own disclaimers are ultimately resolved, brought to fruition through the author's own acceptance of his moral responsibility—in his own voice as well, through a final shedding of the poetic mask" ("Theology and Discourse in the *Pardoner's Tale*, the *Parson's Tale*, and the *Retraction*," *Renascence* [198]: 127-42; here 140). Millet follows Minnis in her theory of Chaucer's authorship: "Through this parody of the *compilator*'s pose Chaucer implicitly challenges some of the basic values of the 'medieval theory of authorship.' Beneath the disguise of the modest *compilator* deferential to *auctores*, scrupulous in his respect for historical truth, and preoccupied with the moral instruction of his readers, it is possible to glimpse a figure much closer to the modern concept of the 'author'—a writer confident of his own powers of invention and adaptation, untroubled by scruples about the intrinsic value of fiction, and prepared to entertain his readers even at the expense of strict morality" ("Chaucer, Lollius, and the Medieval Theory of Authorship" 103).

utilitas, Chaucer neutralizes any potential criticism.[100] At the same time, he has masterfully united *delectatio* with *utilitas* and justified writing in general. All these possibilities are adumbrated in the *Astrolabe*.

8.6.4. *The Canterbury Tales*

The same strategy is also at the heart of *The Canterbury Tales*. The tales were Chaucer's last big project and have often been valued for their colorful representations of contemporary fourteenth-century life. Chaucer's descriptions of English pilgrims constitute a strategy to make the audience believe in the reality of what will transpire, whereas Chaucer's contemporary pilgrimage framework is as "unrealistic" an auctorial construct as the mostly mythological frames of the dream visions.[101] Although the author still follows the same strategy of avoiding responsibility, he switches roles, moving from the emulating translator of ancient *auctores* closer to the definition of Bonaventure's *compilator*, indeed a mere reporter of supposed contemporary reality expounded by his fellow pilgrims.[102] Nothing has changed in the auctorial approach because the reporter is still as dependent on his verbal sources as the translator is on his written text, and both roles exist to exonerate Chaucer from charges of literary and

---

100 Compare this to Jean de Meun's application of the same strategy in the *Roman* in lines 15203 and in Chapter 6. R. A. Shoaf hesitantly postulates that Chaucer wishes to include his works in that statement (*Dante, Chaucer, and the Currency of the Word: Money, Images, and Reference in Late Medieval Poetry* [Norman, OK: Pilgrim Books, 1983] 242). Theodore Buermann is bolder in asserting that that statement would rid *The Canterbury Tales* of anything sinful ("Chaucer's "Book of Genesis" in *The Canterbury Tales: The Biblical Schema of the First Fragment* [Diss. University of Illinois, 1967] 297). P. B. Taylor, however, perceives the doctrinal issue at face value, "an expression of confidence in words that are ordered for the service in an intent to communicate a moral truth" ("Chaucer's *Cosyn to the Dede*," *Speculum* 57 [1982]: 315-327; here 327). Minnis comments that "St Paul did not say that all that is written is true: he said that all that is written is written is for our doctrine. The onus is therefore placed on the discriminating reader" (MN 205). The discriminating reader is addressed in the same vein at the end of the Nun's Priest's Tale:
But ye that holden this tale a folye,
As of a fox, or of a cok and hen,
Taketh the moralite, goode men.
For Seint Paul seith that al that writen is,
To oure doctrine it is ywrite, ywis;
Taketh the fruyt, and lat the chaf be stille. (lines 3438-44)
101 Morton W. Bloomfield regards the prologue as "an artistic, made-up accessus, not a real one" ("*The Canterbury Tales* as Framed Narratives," *Leeds Studies in English* n.s. 14 [1983]: 44-56; here 46).
102 Katharine S. Gittes postulates that "[s]tanding behind Chaucer the reporter is Chaucer the poet, a figure, who, unlike Petrus Alfonsi, is a manipulator of irony, of details, of structure—the fabricator of a design so inextricable that one can see only some features with certainty while others can only be sensed" (*Framing* The Canterbury Tales: *Chaucer and the Medieval Frame Narrative Tradition* [New York: Greenwood, 1991] 127).

linguistic impropriety.[103] The role of the reporter brings with it an increased emphasis on both the teller and the reader evident in the General Prologue, the Miller's Tale, and the headlink to the Tale of Melibee.

In the apology in the General Prologue, Chaucer's concern concentrates on linguistic and social decorum; that strategy is a calculated and an expected move by Chaucer the pilgrim narrator who is dealing with a motley crew of socially divergent characters.[104] As a presenter of ancient love stories, he frets about the content of his sources; as a reporter presenting a slice of the different fourteenth-century estates, Chaucer is less concerned about content than semantic representation:[105]

> But first I pray yow, of youre curteisye,
> That ye n'arette it nat my vileynye,
> Thogh that I pleynly speke in this mateere,
> To telle yow hir wordes and hir cheere,
> Ne thogh I speke in hir wordes properly.
> For this ye knowen al so wel as I:
> Whoso shal telle a tale after a man,
> He moot reherce as ny as evere he kan
> Everich a word, if it be in his charge,
> Al speke he never so rudeliche and large,

103 According to Minnis, "Chaucer often reacted against literary theory of his day or exploited it in a very unusual way"; Minnis defines an *auctor* as one "who was at once a writer and an authority, someone not only to be read but also to be believed and trusted" ("Chaucer and Comparative Literary Theory," *New Perspectives in Chaucer Criticism*, ed. Donald M. Rose [Norman, OK: Pilgrim Books, 1981] 53-69; here 54, 61).

104 For the "General Prologue," see Judson Boyce Allen and Theresa Anne Moritz, *A Distinction of Stories: The Medieval Unity of Chaucer's Fair Chain of Narratives for Canterbury* (Columbus: Ohio State UP, 1981) 55-56; Ben Kimpel, "The Narrator of *The Canterbury Tales*," *English Literary History* 20 (1953): 77-86; here 81; Thomas A. Kirby, "The General Prologue," *Companion to Chaucer Studies* ed. Beryl Rowland, 2nd ed., 1968 (Oxford: Oxford UP, 1979) 243-70; here 252, 259; William Witherle Lawrence, *Chaucer and* The Canterbury Tales (New York: Columbia UP, 1950) 78-79; John Livingston Lowes, *Geoffrey Chaucer and the Development of His Genius* (Boston: Houghton Mifflin, 1934) 216-17; Barbara Nolan, "'A Poet Ther Was': Chaucer's Voices in the General Prologue to *The Canterbury Tales*, *Publications of the Modern Language Association* 101.1 (1986): 154-69; Paul G. Ruggiers, "The Italian Influence on Chaucer," *Companion to Chaucer Studies*, ed. Beryl Rowland (New York: Oxford UP, 1979) 160-184; here 173-76; J. Swart, "The Construction of Chaucer's General Prologue," *Neophilologus* 38 (1954): 127-36; here 128; Taylor, "Chaucer's *Cosyn* to the *Dede*" 315-27, Derek Traversi, *The* Canterbury Tales: *A Reading* (London: The Bodley Head, 1983) 32-36; and Edward Wagenknecht, *The Personality of Chaucer* (Norman: U of Oklahoma P, 1968) 111-12. For "seemliness," see William A. Madden, "Chaucer's Retraction and Medieval Canons of Seemliness," *Medieval Studies* 17 (1955): 173-84. Robert O. Payne supports the difference between the author and the framing persona; therefore, he claims that "[b]ecause Chaucer's *persona* is comic and not identical with several of his alternative *personae*, we find it hard to correlate with the putative unified personality of a serious 'real Chaucer'" ("Late Medieval Images and Self-Images of the Poet: Chaucer, Gower, Lydgate, Henryson, Dunbar," *Vernacular Poetics in the Middle Ages*, ed. Lois Ebin, Studies in Medieval Culture 16 [Kalamazoo, MI: Medieval Institute Publications, 1984. 249-61; here 250, 253).

105 See Ben Kimpel for connections to the Tale of Sir Thopas ("The Narrator of *The Canterbury Tales*" 81).

Or ellis he moot telle his tale untrewe,
Or feyne thyng, or fynde wordes newe. (GP lines 725-36)

Chaucer's *captatio benevolentiae* is reminiscent of both the *Legend* and Boccaccio's *Decameron*. Posing as a reporter, like Boccaccio masquerading as a mere scribe, Chaucer puts the blame on the teller of the tale and emphasizes the importance of remaining true to the original and not skewing the text to indulge the audience's sense of decorum.[106] His asserted refusal to make any euphemistic linguistic changes has intertextual and interauctorial analogies to both Boccaccio's and Jean de Meun's defense of their use of sexually explicit terms in imitation of everyday vernacular speech. In comparison to the *Legend*, "pleynly speke" corresponds to "the naked text," the unadulterated literal meaning of the text that Chaucer pretends to strive for. As in the *Legend* Chaucer qualifies this promise of the "true" text with the admission that he cannot repeat everything exactly but only as closely as possible. This leaves room for interpretation and linguistic license but still exonerates the author, who after all is only a compiler of stories.

The author enlists further interauctorial and intertextual strategies to make himself look acceptable. Moreover, Chaucer places himself into distinguished company by citing Christ and Plato as models of his own auctorial behavior. Another intertextual parallel exists between Boccaccio and Chaucer in their comparing their literary activity to Christ's word, the Logos Incarnate. Chaucer also ends his self-critical interruption with another confession of social unseemliness, an apology for not following the conventional way of organizing his material by social rank, as well as a generally self-discounting remark, "My wit is short, ye may wel understonde" (GP line 746).[107] This particularly damning statement has actually the opposite effect. After that, nobody should take seriously what Chaucer the pilgrim narrator utters, a strategy that in itself can only increase the author's literary license even as it diminishes his persona. Edward Wagenknecht comments on this self-deprecatory phenomenon: "Chaucer's frequent self-deprecation serves very effectively to keep him in the picture, and sometimes it leaves him in far more undisputed possession of the field than any amount of self-vaunting possibly could."[108]

---

106 See Robert K. Root, "Chaucer and the *Decameron*," *Englische Studien* 44 (1912): 1-7.

107 Swart warns against taking Chaucer seriously on this point ("The Construction of Chaucer's General Prologue" 128).

108 Wagenknecht, *The Personality of Chaucer* 6. For instance, in the *Book of the Duchess*, Chaucer exclaims:
"But which a visage had she thertoo!
Allas, myn herte ys wonder woo
That I ne kan discryven hyt!
Me lakketh both Englyssh and wit
For to undo hyt at the fulle;
And eke my spirites be so dulle
So gret a thyng for to devyse.
I have no wit that kan suffise
To comprehende hir beaute." (lines 895-903)
Passages MerT lines 1736-37, SqT lines 105-06, ProFranT lines 716-27 are often cited as incidents of affected modesty.

The prologue to the Miller's Tale functions as an intratextual reiteration of the apology in the General Prologue.[109] The former actually contains two apologies, one from the Miller and one from Chaucer, who conflates the issue of literary content with the question of linguistic seemliness. Since Chaucer has made a blanket apology for the semantic couching of *The Canterbury Tales*, another statement of literary transgression would actually be superfluous. While the apology in the Miller's Tale is a reiteration of the apology in the General Prologue, it nevertheless surpasses the latter in the scope of the entire tale's framework. The author devises the Miller's drunkenness in order to capitalize on it in his own intratextual stratagem. Neither the Knight's persona nor the Knight's tale required Chaucer to enhance his apology, but both the Miller's persona and the Miller's tale necessitate such a tactic. Coincidentally, both the Miller's and Chaucer's apology attempt to eradicate responsibility and narrative center, as the Miller's admission of his inebriated state expresses: "And therfore if that I mysspeke or seye, / Wyte it the ale of Southwerk, I you preye" (ProMilT lines 3139-40). Additionally, Chaucer levels criticism against the Miller's literary judgment when he announces to relate "a legende and a lyf" (ProMilT line 3141), an amusing thought and a blatant mistake on the Miller's part because the intended saint's life—a genre that is acceptable in the sacramental theory of language—and the proffered *fabliau*—a genre often apologized for by other medieval writers—are on opposite ends of the literary spectrum.

Despite, and because of, the Miller's excuse, Chaucer the reporter needs to make another point:

> M'athynketh that I shal reherce it heere,
> And therfore every gentil wight I preye,
> For Goddes love, demeth nat that I seye
> Of yvel entente, but for I moot reherce
> Hir tales alle, be they bettre or werse,
> Or elles falsen som of my mateere.
> And therfore, whoso list it nat yheere,
> Turne over the leef and chese another tale;
> For he shal fynde ynowe, grete and smale,
> Of storial thyng that toucheth gentillesse,
> And eek moralitee and hoolynesse.

---

109 For the Miller's Tale, see Judson Boyce Allen, *The Ethical Poetic of the Later Middle Ages: A Decorum of Convenient Distinction* (Toronto: U of Toronto P, 1982) 56; Paull F. Baum *Chaucer: A Critical Appreciation* (Durham: Duke UP, 1958) 174; J. Brown, "Chaucer's Double Apology for the *Miller's Tale*," *University of Colorado Studies: Series in Language and Literature* 10 (1966): 15-22; Elton D. Higgs, "'What Man Artow?': Harry Bailly and the 'Elvyssh Chaucer,'" *Mid-Hudson Language Studies* 2 (1979): 28-43; here 31; Kimpel, "The Narrator of *The Canterbury Tales*" 82; Lawrence, *Chaucer and* The Canterbury Tales 80; Donald McGrady, "Chaucer and the *Decameron* Reconsidered," *Chaucer Review* 12 (1977): 1-26; here 2; Beryl Rowland, "Chaucer's Blasphemous Churl: A New Interpretation of the *Miller's Tale*," *Chaucer and Middle English Studies in Honour of Russell Hope Robbins*, ed. Beryl Rowland (London: Allen & Unwin, 1974) 43-55; Shoaf, *Dante, Chaucer, and the Currency of the Word* 163-66; John S. P. Tatlock, "Boccaccio and the Plan of *The Canterbury Tales*," *Anglia* 37 (1913): 69-117; here 113; Traversi, The Canterbury Tales 64-66; and Wagenknecht, *The Personality of Chaucer* 112-13.

Blameth nat me if that ye chese amys.
The Millere is a cherl; ye knowe wel this.
So was the Reve eek and othere mo,
And harlotrie they tolden bothe two.
Avyseth yow, and put me out of blame;
And eek men shal nat maken ernest of game. (MilT lines 3170-86).[110]

Chaucer's self-criticism centers on the truthful emulation of his source and restates both his role as reporter and his regret but also illustrates his own intratextual and intra-auctorial perception of the tales.[111] Giving the audience a choice of various literary types adds content to the list of potential literary offenses and places any literary responsibility into the readers' lap. Thus, the author has twice redeemed himself, since, as a transmitter, he is neither culpable for the content of the stories nor accountable for the readers' selection, which he has actually made for them. Chaucer also mixes a listening audience with a reading audience when he employs "yheere" in connection with "Turne over the leef," a reading-specific situation. This peculiar incident can be explained as a slip-up by the author, who is posing as a pilgrim narrator listening to all these stories and is assigning his audience the same status of "hearing," although the emphasis for him as the author is placed on the actual process of writing, which manifests itself on parchment or paper.[112]

At the same time, the proffered selection and warning reveal the author's concept of the tales at that specific moment; Chaucer divulges that the Reeve will also tell a *fabliau*, but he stops there, although the phrase "othere mo" (MilT line 3183) leaves the possibility open for yet more *fabliaux*. It could mean that Chaucer either had not fixed the order of the tales beyond the Reeve's Tale, because we do have the Cook's Tale, the Shipman's Tale, etc., or that he did not want to go beyond the connective tissue between the Miller and the Reeve. Furthermore, Chaucer sticks to his premise in the General Prologue that he will relate both the words and the "cheere" of the pilgrims. In the case of the Miller and the Reeve, he definitely draws a parallel between the behavior of the personae and the tales they will tell. Since those two characters' narrative skill is limited to ribald tales, Chaucer contextualizes their tales as fun. Thus, Chaucer can exempt their tales from criticism, for if the readers subsequently ignore the jocular framework it is their fault. This intertextual and interauctorial reservation echoes Boccaccio's characterization of the *Decameron* as stories told to women in love in gardens; in fourteenth-century Italy women were discountable and gardens mere places of pleasure. By trivializing his creation and by belittling the audience and context of his tales, Boccaccio manages to divert accountability and serious criticism from himself.[113] Chaucer contrasts the Miller's Tale and Reeve's Tale with the tales

---

110 Root, "Chaucer and the *Decameron*" 3 and J. Brown, "Chaucer's Double Apology for the *Miller's Tale*" 15-17 divide that apology into four subsections: the author's reiteration of his reporter role (MT 3173-75); the choice the reader is presented with (MT 3176-77); the poet's warning to the reader (MT 3181); the poet's categorizing of specific tales as jokes (MT 3186).

111 See also Allen, *The Ethical Poetic of the Later Middle Ages* 55-56.

112 For a discussion of reading in England, see Joyce Coleman, *Public Reading and the Reading Public in Late Medieval England and France* (New York: Cambridge UP, 1996).

113 Compare McGrady, "Chaucer and the *Decameron* Reconsidered" 2 and Root, "Chaucer and the *Decameron*" 1. See also N. S. Thompson, *Chaucer, Boccaccio, and the Debate of Love: A*

containing "moralitee and hoolynesse" in order to demonstrate the dichotomy of the moral and immoral tale, a distinction that becomes blurred again when he categorizes the *fabliaux* as jokes.[114] Overall, however, the question is not whether our modern sense of morality is fulfilled but whether these tales were moral or immoral in the Middle Ages. The pilgrims want "sentence and solaas"; Chaucer, who "adopts a morally neutral stance in judgment of his subject-matter" and merely has to repeat things the way they are, disclaims "responsibility for telling immoral tales" and equally denies having to fulfill the church's teaching of morality—an attitude he reverses in the Retraction.[115]

After the Miller's Tale, Chaucer makes sure to inform the reader that the first audience of the story took it well:

> Whan folk hadde laughen at this nyce cas
> Of Absolon and hende Nicholas,
> Diverse folk diversely they seyde,
> But for the moore part they loughe and pleyde.
> Ne at this tale I saugh no man hym greve
> But it were oonly Osewold the Reve. (ProRvT lines 3855-60)[116]

Although Chaucer states that different literary opinions were voiced, the impression is a favorable one. His pre-tale assurance that the tale is funny becomes true, except for the Reeve, who is insulted professionally. Yet it is that insult that propagates the tales further.

Chaucer fabricates another self-critical situation when it is his turn to tell a tale in the contest. He has the Host stop him from finishing the Tale of Sir Thopas, because his rhyming is so awful. The Host then gives Chaucer the choice between the two literary goals *delectatio* or *utilitas*, in his request for a tale with "some murthe or some doctryne" (ProMel line 935). Chaucer's choice of "a moral tale vertuous" proves the Man of Law wrong in his judgment of Chaucer and also makes Chaucer one for the few characters who can make his literary announcement and its fulfillment congruent. Nevertheless, Chaucer prefaces the Tale of Melibee with an apology similar to the one in the General Prologue and the Miller's Tale in content and phrasing:

Comparative Study of The Decameron *and* The Canterbury Tales (Oxford: Clarendon, 1996) 140-49.

114 According to Madden, the Miller's Tale apology exists because the tale's treatment of marriage violates the medieval view of seemliness ("Chaucer's Retraction and Medieval Canons of Seemliness" 177-78, 181).

115 Derek Brewer, ed., "Gothic Chaucer," *Geoffrey Chaucer* (Athens: Ohio UP, 1975) 1-32; here 2. Taylor sees three important points in Chaucer's insistence on a joke: the still inherent fear of eloquence as the veil for falsehood; the seeming morality of evil intents when they are couched in the right language; and the importance of the audience's role in the narrative process, rather than the subject matter ("*Peynted Confessiouns*: Boccaccio and Chaucer," *Comparative Literature* 34.2 [1982]: 116-29; here 117, 119, 123).

116 J. Brown asserts that "[b]y making the Reeve the prototype of the squeamish reader, Chaucer does much to discredit the argument for turning another leaf as it appears in the formal apology" ("Chaucer's Double Apology for the *Miller's Tale*" 20).

"And though I nat the same wordes seye
As ye han herd, yet to yow alle I preye
Blameth me nat; for, as in my sentence,
Shul ye nowher fynden difference
Fro the sentence of this tretys lyte
After the which this murye tale I write.
And therfore herkneth what that I shal seye,
And lat me tellen al my tale, I preye." (ProMel lines 959-66)

This passage establishes and emphasizes that a given "signified" can be expressed by various "signifiers" expressing it; therefore, Chaucer the poet does not have to use the same signifiers as his source to express the same "sentence."[117] The multitude of nuances in language provides a choice that makes for difference in any given text; but Chaucer presents the audience with a purposefully naive impression, since meaning in language mainly rests on connotation and context. The author lulls the audience into believing that he is reproducing another's "sentence" faithfully without producing different nuances. Furthermore, here Chaucer blends his narrator and author role again. Although the abundant emphasis is on the spoken word, as in "seye," "herd," "herkneth," and "tellen," Chaucer makes specific reference to the process of writing that unmistakably amalgamates the narrator with the author. That reference is especially pertinent because the author invites the audience to listen to his tale, after he asserts that he is writing it, which would work in the court setting as part of the "erzählenden Ichs," but not in the pilgrimage framework of immediate "erlebenden Ichs." Maybe the most intriguing question is why Chaucer gives us another apology so similar to the ones he already proffered. Chaucer supplies this qualifier to his story because he is the teller. The apologies in the General Prologue and the Miller's Tale are both proffered on behalf of the other tellers, whose stories he repeats. The dynamic of the situation is different in the Tale of Melibee, and Chaucer is adjusting to it. As a reporter of his fellow pilgrims' stories, he needs to make sure that he is not condemned for their particular phrasings of content and that it is amply made clear that he is not the source. As the teller of the tale, he suddenly has to be responsible for both the content and the phrasing, so again he cites his faithful emulation of somebody else's "sentence."[118]

---

117 Robert Boenig perceives "[s]imultaneous affirmation and denial" as "a characteristic of mystical theology and medieval language theory. . . . in words denying the validity of words. He [Chaucer] in fact is developing ideas as central to modern literary critical theory as to medieval mysticism—the gap between signifier and signified and the consequent deconstruction of meaning" ("Taking Leave: Chaucer's Retraction and the Ways of Affirmation and Negation," *Studia Mystica* 12 [1989]: 21-34; here 23).

118 In the Nun's Priest's Tale we have an example of a mock-apology in which Chauntecleer is being blamed:
"Wommennes conseils been ful ofte colde;
Wommennes conseil broghte us first to wo
And made Adam fro Paradys to go,
Ther as he was ful myrie and wel at ese.
But for I noot to whom it myght displese,
If I conseil of wommen wolde blame,
Passe over, for I seyde it in my game.

The culmination of Chaucer's self-critical intra-auctorial approach the and most discussed of his apologies is the Retraction at the end of *The Canterbury Tales*.[119] It is

---

Rede auctours, where they trete of swich mateere,
And what they seyn of wommen ye may heere.
Thise been the cokkes wordes, and nat myne;
I kan noon harm of no womman divyne." (NPT lines 3256-66)

This mock-apology follows several topoi of the second apology strand very closely. Citing Eve's role in the dismissal from Paradise is a stock antifeminist argument, which the Priest, being in the Nun's service, cannot really afford to tout. Therefore, he resorts to the same defense as Jean de Meun: the writings of the *auctoritates* (which are cited to be blamed but are in the process proven correct on the topic), his wish not to hurt any woman alive, and his blaming the rooster for the antifeminism. Thus the Nun's Priest imitates Chaucer in this approach and has now added the third level of apology to the work. Hence, there is a triple apology structure in *The Canterbury Tales*: The Nun's Priest excuses himself and blames the rooster; Chaucer excuses himself in the General Prologue, Miller's Tale, and Tale of Melibee and blames the tale tellers; Chaucer excuses and accuses himself in the Retraction. These apologies do not yield a more fixed but a more fluid, less graspable text because the narrative center constantly shifts and with it the responsibility for the text. Chaucer wants the reader to have this illusion even though the author is completely in charge and orchestrates the entire construct.

119 Manuscript evidence demonstrates that the Retraction is not spurious and usually appears with the Parson's Tale, forming an adequate closure to a pilgrimage. Generally, it has been divided into three sections, the initial prayer 1081-84, the "retractatio proper" (list of works) 1085-89, and the final prayer 1090-92. Here is an overview of most of the critical opinions:

Authenticity of the Retraction: Supporters of the spurious nature of the passage are Thomas Hearne, Tyrwhitt, Simon a. a. O., v. Düring (qtd. in Heinrich Spies, "Chaucers 'Retractatio,'" *Festschrift Adolf Dobler* [Geneva: Slatkine Reprints, 1978] 383-94; here 384-85). The early critics Matthew Browne, Furnivall, Bell, A. W. Pollard, W. W. Skeat (qtd. in Spies, "Chaucers 'Retractatio'" 384-85) endorse authenticity, which is now generally accepted (James D. Gordon, "Chaucer's Retraction: A Review of Opinion," *Studies of Medieval Literature in Honor of Professor Albert Croll Baugh*, ed. MacEdward Leach [Philadelphia: U of Pennsylvania P, 1961] 81-94; here 84).

Advocacy of interpolations by monks, especially of the list of works, was popular early on: J. Koch "Chaucer-Schriften." *Englische Studien* 37 (1907): 227-29; v. Düring (qtd. in Spies, "Chaucers 'Retractatio'" 385); yet Minnis postulates that in the framework of a *compilatio*, both the Parson's Tale and the Retraction had been added later by either Chaucer himself or a third party (MN 208).

Advocates of Chaucer's religious conversion are Aers, *Chaucer, Langland and the Creative Imagination* 114; Derek Brewer, *Chaucer* (London: Longman, 1961) 179; Marchette Chute, *Geoffrey Chaucer of England* (New York: Dutton, 1946) 311ff; Helen Storm Corsa, *Chaucer: Poet of Mirth and Morality* (Notre Dame: U of Notre Dame P, 1964) 239, 241; Dean, "Chaucer's Repentance" 74; E. Talbot Donaldson (qtd. in Gordon, "Chaucer's Retraction" 89); v. Düring (qtd. in Spies, "Chaucers 'Retractatio'" 385); Donald Howard, *The Idea of* The Canterbury Tales (Berkeley: U of California P, 1976) 179; P. M. Kean, *Chaucer and the Making of English Poetry: The Art of Narrative*, 2 vols. (London: Routledge & Kegan Paul, 1972) 2: 187; Lares, "Chaucer's *Retractions* 18-33; Lawrence, *Chaucer and* The Canterbury Tales 82-85, 152-59; Thomas R. Lounsbury, *Studies in Chaucer: His Life and Writings*, 3 vols. (London: James R. Osgood, 1892) 3: 40; Madeleva, *A Lost Language and Other Essays on Chaucer* 108-10; Charles Muscatine, *Poetry and Crisis in the Age of Chaucer* (Notre Dame: U of Notre Dame P, 1972) 113; Pollard (qtd. in A. P. Campbell, "Chaucer's 'Retraction': Who Retracted What?" *Humanities Association Bulletin* 16 [1965]: 75-87; here 76); Root, *The Poetry of Chaucer* (Boston: Houghton Mifflin,

at this juncture that the medieval poet Chaucer seems to emerge from behind his assumed personae to acknowledge that he is indeed the creator of his literary works and is therefore responsible for them; it is also at this juncture that some scholars have located his deathbed repentance.[120] Deathbed repentance though it may be, Chaucer's

---

1906) 288; Skeat (qtd. in Gordon, "Chaucer's Retraction" 88); Herbert Thurston, "The Conversion of Boccaccio and Chaucer," *Studies* 25 (1936): 215-25; Watts, "Chaucerian Selves—Especially Two Serious Ones" 238. Manly puts the Retraction in an extraliterary context by pointing out its similarities with the will of Lewis Clifford (Gordon, "Chaucer's Retraction" 84); see also Campbell, "Chaucer's 'Retraction'" 77.

Advocates of the non-conversion theory posit that the Retraction is both a necessary and an integral part of the pilgrimage framework: Allen, *The Ethical Poetic of the Later Middle Ages* 56; Ralph Baldwin, *The Unity of* The Canterbury Tales, Anglistica 5 (Copenhagen: Rosenkilde and Bagger, 1955) 99; Brewer, *Chaucer* 163; Robert S. Knapp, "Penance, Irony, and Chaucer's Retraction," *Assays: Critical Approaches to Medieval and Renaissance Texts* 2 (1982): 45-67; here 47; V. A. Kolve, *Chaucer and the Imagery of Narrative: The First Five Canterbury Tales* (Stanford: Stanford UP, 1984) 370; Traugott Lawler, *The One and the Many in* The Canterbury Tales (Hamden, CT: Archon Books, 1980) 172; Schricker, "On the Relation of Fact and Fiction in Chaucer's Poetic Endings" 13. R. M. Lumiansky follows Manly and Rickert in claiming that neither the Parson's Tale nor the Retraction were actually part of *The Canterbury Tales* (Gordon, "Chaucer's Retraction" 88).

Awakened conscience: Canon Looten (qtd. in Gordon, "Chaucer's Retraction" 89-90).

Decorum: Chaucer wrote the Retraction because he violated the rules of seemliness, for whose upholding the Church was responsible (Madden, "Chaucer's Retraction and Medieval Canons of Seemliness" 173-74).

In conjunction with the Parson's Tale: Baumlin, "Theology and Discourse in the *Pardoner's Tale*, the *Parson's Tale*, and the *Retraction*" 139-40; E. R. Cole, "Chaucer's Retraction and the Parson," *University of Portland Review* 20 (1968): 35-41; Russell Peck, "St. Paul and *The Canterbury Tales*," *Mediaevalia* 7 (1981): 91-117; here 104. E. Talbot Donaldson, *Speaking of Chaucer* (New York: Norton, 1970) 172; R. M. Lumiansky, "Chaucer's Retraction and the Degree of Completeness of *The Canterbury Tales*," *Tulane Studies in English* 6 (1956): 5-13; here 11; and Watts, "Chaucerian Selves—Especially Two Serious Ones" 238 claim that the interpretative link between the Retraction and the Parson's Tale is too restrictive.

For further discussion on the possible genesis of the Retraction as well as the evidence for its authenticity, see Heinrich Spies, "Chaucers 'Retractatio'" 386-92.

For a deconstructionist view, see Victor Yelverton Haines, "Where Are Chaucer's 'Retracciouns'?" *Florilegium* 10 (1988-91): 127-49 and Peter W. Travis, "Deconstructing Chaucer's Retraction," *Exemplaria: A Journal of Theory in Medieval and Renaissance Studies* 3.1 (1991): 135-58.

120 Here are some opinions on the distinction between Chaucer the man, the pilgrim, the artist: Rosemary Woolf states: "Chaucer was writing at a time when there was no tradition of personal poetry in a later Romantic sense: a poet never made his individual emotions the subject-matter of his poetry. Though the personal pronoun 'I' is used frequently in the Medieval narrative and lyric poetry, it is usually a dramatic 'I', that is the 'I' is a character in the poem, bearing no different relation to the poet from that of the other characters, or it expresses moral judgments or proper emotions which belong, or should belong, to everybody. Chaucer's use of an 'I' character in his early poems belongs to the tradition of such characters in dream visions" (150). Thus Woolf supports the interpretation of Chaucer the Pilgrim ("Chaucer as a Satirist in the General Prologue to *The Canterbury Tales*," *Critical Quarterly* 1 (1959): 150-57; here 150-51). Corsa, then, claims that Chaucer the man, not the artist, is confessing his "literary sins" in the Retraction (*Chaucer* 239), and Brewer considers it as breaking "the fictional frame by speaking to us directly and sin-

Retraction may also be viewed as a logical continuation of persistent and pervasive and thoroughly conventional Chaucerian self-criticism. Only this time, the author plays the role of the penitent author, who, in the medieval Christian cosmos based on the sacramentality of language, seems to disavow those of his literary creations that do not express a Christian truth, thereby rejecting pagan and medieval stories of human and sexual love. The self-critical elements evident in the Retraction have intra- and intertextual lexical and semantic connections to his other works—especially the *Astrolabe*—and thus strongly suggest that Chaucer manipulates convention to manipulate his readers.

The first sign of Chaucer's change in role from translator and compiler to Christian author is his conventional invocation to God.[121] The first sentence in the Retraction reads, "Now preye I to hem alle that herkne this litel tretys or rede, that if ther be any thyng in it that liketh hem, that thereof they thanken oure Lord Jhesu Crist, of whom procedeth al wit and al goodnesse" (RT line 1081). The passage pays the customary deference to Christ, the Master Writer, for the pleasing aspects of the work. It is, however, dubious that Chaucer selects *delectatio*, not *utilitas*, as the measuring guide for redeeming literature.[122] He also employs other Christian conventions, modesty and

---

cerely" ("Gothic Chaucer" 3). See also Olive Sayce, "Chaucer's 'Retractions': The Conclusion of *The Canterbury Tales* and Its Place in Literary Tradition," *Medium Aevum* 40 (1971): 230-48; here 231.

121 Sayce lists the following common introductory topoi: *captatio benevolentiae*, addressing the audience, brief exposition, protestations of modesty and incapacity, religious motifs; for conclusions: recapitulation, admonition to sinners, prayers and requests for intercession, mention of the poet's name and the title of the work ("Chaucer's 'Retractions'" 232-33). The Retraction is separated from the Parson's Tale by the rubric header "Heere taketh the makere of this book his leve," which would identify the speaker of the following text as the author. Several critics claim that the first part of the Retraction is actually the end of the Parson's Tale, which would in turn render the rubric header faulty or irrelevant and raise the question what the Parson is apologizing for. His sins surely would not include those the *literati* would commit. The Retraction needs to be treated as a complete and valid utterance by the author and not a hodgepodge of part Parson's Tale and part monkish interpolations. A plethora of similar self-critical examples by other ancient and medieval authors demonstrates, after all, a long-standing convention. Furthermore, Chaucer uses semantic patterns in the Retraction that he has employed in other works, especially in the *Astrolabe*, and which have not been considered in this context. These prove that there is no reason to believe that the words in the Retraction belong to anybody but Chaucer.

122 At the same time, his emphasis on pleasure indicates that the speaker of this passage cannot be the Parson, who stresses *utilitas* and penance in his tale, although he promises "plesaunce" (ProParsT line 41) and a "myrie tale in prose" (ParsT line 46) (see Trevor Whittock, *A Reading of* The Canterbury Tales [Cambridge: Cambridge UP, 1968] 298). The discrepancy between the Parson's promise and his delivery is the typical ironic literary criticism Chaucer levels against most of his storytellers and the Host, who seem to have a rather rudimentary notion of literary genres at best. On the other hand, a comment like the Host's request to hear "a fable anon, for colles bones" from the Parson can cut both ways. First, it is used to indict the Host's literary judgment, for generally the fable genre, associated with a lack of truth, would be ill-matched with the subject of God's bones, the ultimate truth. Second, it might be a clever remark on the Host's part to insinuate that the *vitae* genre was plagued by fable-like untruths as revealed by the Pardoner in his prologue and picked up on by the Host. Nevertheless, the tellers' literary self-perception remains an ironic auctorial characterizing tool. Thus, the Parson's exhortatory tract on penance could hardly

humility, which govern the following passage in the Retraction: "And if ther be any thyng that displese hem, I preye hem also that they arrette it to the defaute of myn unkonnynge and nat to my wyl, that wolde ful fayn have seyd bettre if I hadde had konnynge" (RT line 1082).[123] Chaucer still employs the dichotomy of audience

---

be associated with *delectatio*. Furthermore, Leonard Michael Koff writes: "In general, the modern aesthetic has turned the medieval rhetorical theory on its head: the response of a reader to a story is taken as an index of the 'wholeness' of a work of art, and any defect in the work of art, as the reader perceives it, is said to be a sign that the author has failed in his actual 'vision,' and necessarily in the execution of it. . . . Perhaps this is why the Horatian dictum 'teach and delight,' a rhetorical commonplace in the Middle Ages, is thought to be applicable solely to the author as the standard by which he is judged to have succeeded or failed *as an artist . . .* rather than to the reader as the ground on which he judges himself by judging what is presented to him" (*Chaucer and the Art of Storytelling* 223).

Another point of interpretative contention is the term "litel tretys," which may refer to the Parson's Tale or the entire tale collection. The following critics argue that "tretys" refers to the Parson's Tale: John W. Clark, "'This Litel Tretys' Again," *Chaucer Review* 6 (1971): 152-56; here 156; Howard, *The Idea of* The Canterbury Tales 59; Lawler, *The One and the Many in* The Canterbury Tales 147-72; Lawrence, *Chaucer and* The Canterbury Tales 82; Marshall, "Unmasking the Last Pilgrim" 57; MN 207; James A. Work, "Chaucer's Sermon and Retractations," *Modern Language Notes* 47 (1932): 257-59; here 259. Lumiansky argues against it ("Chaucer's Retraction and the Degree of Completeness of *The Canterbury Tales*" 12). See also Robert M. Jordan, *Chaucer's Poetics and the Modern Reader* (Berkeley: U of California P, 1987) 171-73. Bernard Huppé supports the application of "tretys" to the collective *Canterbury Tales* for the simple reason that Chaucer has no need to feel guilty about the Parson's Tale (*A Reading of* The Canterbury Tales [Albany: State University of New York, 1964] 236), since it is not one of the tales "that sownen into synne." Several other factors endorse Huppé's suggestion. The Retraction is framed by two references to the word "book," which points to a larger literary structure, although those occurrences could be more scribal than auctorial. Chaucer himself, however, has supplied a post-narrative and metafictional device that supports the use of the word "book" as well as the suggested interpretation of "tretys." In the first line, Chaucer does not mix up his narrative and auctorial tasks as he did in the prologue to the Miller's Tale. He speaks of "herkne" and "rede," implying a spoken but also a written narrative. The Parson is the narrator of the Parson's Tale, but his role does not exceed that, and as the narrator he could not be aware that Chaucer the pilgrim would be recording the proffered tales. Therefore, the allusion to "rede" would be inappropriate to the Parson and can only be uttered by Chaucer, who is the actual provider of a written text. Furthermore, the two verbs are in the present tense and also apply to future listeners or readers, not only the current pilgrimage crowd to which the Parson could only speak and would probably do so in the past tense. The last piece of evidence supporting that the speaker is Chaucer can be found both in the prologue to the *Astrolabe* and in the headlink to the Tale of Melibee, where Chaucer uses exactly the same expression, "this litel tretys" (lines 11, 42; 957). This suggests that in the framework of Chaucer's canon, this term is applied to prose texts specific to Chaucer the author, rather than one of his storytellers. It could also imply modesty, as Augustine's and Petrarch's usage of "opuscula mea" for their entire prolific output.

123 Boenig furthermore interprets Chaucer's use of the conventional term "the defaute of myn unkonnynge" as his inability to write any more. I do not agree, however, that we are witnessing the "sad picture of an inert writer who can no longer control his words" (Boenig, "Taking Leave" 27). Chaucer is still in charge, even if he, unlike Boethius, does not recreate himself anymore in writing but merely in reading, giving himself over to the readers' judgment. Taylor, however, claims that Chaucer is hesitant to hand his works over to the judgment of men ("*Peynted Confessiouns*" 128).

approval and audience rejection as the yardstick for his literary creation, and he shirks responsibility once again as he assigns the agreeable parts of his work to God's inspiration—and who is going to argue against divine creation?—and the faulty parts to his inadequacies. As in the apologies in *Troilus*, the *Legend*, the General Prologue, and the prologue to The Miller's Tale, Chaucer's incapabilities absolve him. His propensity to cite lack of talent, however, is restricted to style, not content; he insinuates that the faults found are not in the original source and could have been remedied with better writing. Chaucer presents himself as never doing anything by will or on purpose; his stance here is intertextually as well as intratextually linked to his dependence on ancient sources, patrons' requirements, the rudeness of storytellers, or his lacking talents in the previous Chaucerian examples, forging an invariable intra-auctorial pattern of avoiding accountability.

In the "retractatio proper," Chaucer asks the audience to pray for general forgiveness for his sins and for specific forgiveness for his literary offenses. This admission of literary guilt ties him intertextually to the self-critical pattern of most of the authors in this study. Couching his confession in the framework of an intercession functions as a distancing device that removes the layer of intimacy associated with a direct confession to God:

> Wherfore I biseke yow mekely, for the mercy of God, that ye preye for me that Crist have mercy on me and foryeve me my giltes;/ and namely of my translacions and enditynges of worldly vanitees, the whiche I revoke in my retracciouns:/ as is the book of Troilus; the book also of Fame; the book of the XXV. Ladies; the book of the Duchesse; the book of Seint Valentynes day of the Parlement of Briddes; the tales of Caunterbury, thilke that sownen into synne;/ the book of the Leoun; and many another book, if they were in my remembrance, and many a song and many a leccherous lay, that Crist for his grete mercy foryeve me the synne./ But of the translacion of Boece de Consolacione, and othere bookes of legendes of seintes, and omelies, and moralitee, and devocioun. (RT lines 1084-86)

Once more the catalogue presented by Chaucer raises more questions than it answers.[124] It contains the same dichotomy of literary categories as the prologue to the *Legend*, although it is used in the reversed sense. The works that had been cited as pleasing to Cupid are now being presented in a questionable light for exactly that reason. They are works of worldly vanity, dealing with love of the world and women and therefore suspect on his record before God. For the first time, Chaucer takes responsibility for his translations, which consequently calls into question all his other strategies of eschewing responsibility. At the same time, he admits his unadulterated and true literary authorship, which he had so far only implied and then vehemently denied.

For all the endorsement of Chaucer's sincerity in his literary confession, purposeful and unmitigated vagueness permeates his ostensible repentance and especially the list of works.[125] The first part of the list includes *Troilus*, which has now been apologized

---

124 Alfred David considers the list of works as complete and offered not to literary critics but to "the only judge whose verdict ultimately matters" ("The Man of Law vs. Chaucer: A Case in Poetics," *Publications of the Modern Language Association* 82 [1967]: 217-25; here 224).

125 According to Robert S. Knapp the Retraction is "pious, conventional, and no doubt not ironic in its dominant meaning" ("Penance, Irony, and Chaucer's Retraction" 45) and to Robin Kirkpatrick "modest and self-critical" ("The Wake of the *Commedia*: Chaucer's *Canterbury Tales* and Boccaccio's *Decameron*," *Chaucer and the Italian Trecento*, ed. Piero Boitani [Cambridge:

for four times in Chaucer's canon: in Chaucer's role as translator; in both his indictment of the ancient sources and his confirmation of the Christian Logos; in his apology for the antifeminism in the poem; and finally in the Retraction for the same reason he criticizes the work and himself in the *Troilus*. But the *Romaunt* is entirely missing from this list—strange, considering how instrumental it was in staging the prologue to the *Legend*, identified here as the "book of the XXV. Ladies," although this figure does not coincide with the number of actual legends nor the number given in the prologue to The Man of Law's Tale. It could mean that these divergent numbers reflect different stages in the *Legend*'s conception and completion.[126] Furthermore, Chaucer's intentional ambiguity in not identifying the offensive Tales repeats and imitates the strategy of the prologue to the Miller's Tale, in which he already admits that some stories are going to be ribald and might be avoided by squeamish readers. As before, the burden of choice rests with the readers, who will have to read all of the tales to decide what level of sinfulness they can tolerate or what "sentence" can be found; this strategy results in an indefinite number of different texts of *The Canterbury Tales* because every reader is going to perceive the individual Tales differently. Chaucer insinuates that the reader's set of expectations and prejudices can bear upon the text and remove it further from the author's original meaning, a strategy evident in the self-critical framework of authors like Ovid, Augustine, Gerald of Wales, Piccolomini, Hartmann von Aue, Ulrich von Türheim, Jean de Meun, Juan Ruiz, and Boccaccio. This strategy shifts the emphasis within the auctorial triangle of author, text, reader to the reader and produces in a quadrangle: author, text, reader, new text.[127] Chaucer insinuates that the reader's set of expectations and prejudices can bear upon the text and remove it further from the author's original meaning.

Further inconsistencies exist. The "book of the Leoun" is not extant but believed to be an imitation of either Machaut's or Deschamps' *Dit dou Lyon*, and must have been an amorous work because of its categorization in the Retraction.[128] The author's blanket statement about many other books and lays resembles some authors' general confessions of literary transgression and has the same implausible effect. Aside from the *Romaunt*, all of Chaucer's major works dealing with love are accounted for here, and Chaucer's memory loss is at best suspicious: a poet who stressed both his reliance on the writing of other authors and the importance of memory and remembrance throughout his career cannot now but feign to remember his own compositions. In the *Legend*

Cambridge UP, 1983] 201-230; here 210). Boenig, on the other hand, alleges that the "point is that Chaucer's intratextual allusions that link the Retraction to the work as a whole both affirm and deny simultaneously the meaning of the Retraction" ("Taking Leave" 26).

126 Eleanor Prescott Hammond suggests that the number 25 was Chaucer's estimation in an earlier-composed version of the Retraction, and 19 the number in the Ellesmere group manuscripts. This, then, points to a process in Chaucer's artistic development ("Chaucer's 'Book of the Twenty-Five Ladies,'" *Modern Language Notes* 48 [1933]: 514-16; here 516).

127 See Marshall, "Unmasking the Last Pilgrim" 62 and Knapp, "Penance, Irony, and Chaucer's Retraction" 48. Donald Howard comments on Chaucer's idea of book and the fragmentation of the Tales into acceptable and unacceptable ones: "This must be either because he did not think of it as a book but merely as a collection of tales, or because he intended not to revoke it as a book but only to revoke those tales that 'sownen into sin'" (*The Idea of* The Canterbury Tales 56).

128 V. Langhans, "Chaucers Book of the Leoun," *Anglia* 28 (1952): 113-22; here 113-14.

Chaucer placed the many lays under the category of other works not pleasing to the God of Love. Chaucer's calling attention to his worldly vanities, by a weakness of medieval and modern human nature, was probably quite welcome to his readers. And actually the poet's reputation has not suffered in the slightest by the rejection of any one of them from a place among his writings but instead has benefited partially,[129] perhaps, because those works that he revokes are the ones he is famous for today; listing them by name ensured a reading audience.

The second part of the catalogue—the rejection of the works with a classical bent and an emphasis on earthly love—completes the dichotomy that exists in the Middle Ages in the form of tension between classical training and Christian thought. Since those works at one time helped Chaucer with Cupid but are now being condemned, the author implies that Cupid's charge of antifeminism is the lesser of two evils, an antifeminism that he actually supplants with a more insidious antifeminism at the root of the rejection of the sexual love. But Chaucer is most indeterminate in his enumeration of his redeeming works. Only the *Boece* is cited by name but it is identified as a translation, for which Chaucer, according to his own criteria, should receive "neither thank ne blame" (*TC* II, line 15). Everything else is summed up under an imaginary "etc." of devotional literature. The list in the *Legend* was more specific where it did not need to be and in areas that actually detracted from his achievement in the eyes of Cupid. Here, however, where such a list would be appropriate, there is none. It is noteworthy that Chaucer insists on the term "bookes" for the works that he does not want to revoke, but there are no books extant that fit his description, unless he refers to those parts of *The Canterbury Tales* not found wanting or to the two volumes mentioned in the *Legend*, "Of Wreched Engendrynge of Mankynde" and "Orygenes upon the Maudeleyne." Alceste claims that the latter had been written a long time ago. Chaucer is undercutting his supposed repentance with a touch of irony: first he lumps the avowedly most valuable of his works all together, then provides no guidance, not even a title or a summary, for the reader to find these edifying works.

The most obvious thing Chaucer achieves with the list in the Retraction is the establishment of his canon "through readerly blame and praise."[130] Even theories of interpolation—that either Chaucer himself or a fifteenth-century scribe or editor interpolated the list of works later—would support the intent of establishing Chaucer's canon. Most medieval writers confessing literary sins are fairly cryptic about the actual works to which they are confessing, but some have also used lists for the very same purpose. Bede, Gerald of Wales, Augustine, and Diego de San Pedro follow the classical practice of *de suis libris* and *catalogus brevis*, in which authors compose catalogues of their works in order to provide an exact tally of their accomplishments, ironically undercutting their apologies for these same works. In conjunction with the term "retracciouns" (RT line 1083), which echoes Augustine, the list of works could

---

129 Lounsbury, *Studies in Chaucer* 3: 485.

130 Koff, *Chaucer and the Art of Storytelling* 233. See Brewer, *Chaucer* 96; Knapp, "Penance, Irony, and Chaucer's Retraction" 46; and Schricker, "On the Relation of Fact and Fiction in Chaucer's Poetic Endings" 244-45.

be interpreted in the Augustinian sense as a calling back of the literary works to review them and ultimately to assert their auctorial and literary value.[131]

In the Introduction to the Man of Law's Tale, the Man of Law provides a partial list of Chaucer's literary activity in his attempt to be a literary critic. Like the person manipulating a marionette, Chaucer lets other characters, such as Alceste and the Man of Law, do his work for him, while he keeps himself modestly in the background:

"I kan right now no thrifty tale seyn
That Chaucer, thogh he kan but lewedly
On metres and on rymyng craftily,
Hath seyd hem in swich Englissh as he kan
Of olde tyme, as knoweth many a man;
And if he have noght seyd hem, leve brother,
In o book, he hath seyd them in another.
For he hath toold of loveris up an doun
Mo than Ovide made of mencioun
In his Epistles, that been ful olde.
What sholde I tellen hem, syn they been tolde?
   In youthe he made of Ceys and Alcione,
And sitthen hath he spoken of everichone,
Thise noble wyves and thise loveris eke.
Whoso that wole his large volume seke,
Cleped the Seintes Legende of Cupide,

. . . .

Though I come after hym with hawebake.
I speke in prose, and lat him rymes make." (MLT lines 46-61, 95-96)

This opinion by the Man of Law about Chaucer serves two purposes. First, it is another Chaucerian ploy to satirize the literary judgment of that character, who claims that all the good love stories have been taken by Chaucer.[132] The Man of Law nevertheless announces that he will top Chaucer with his tale in prose—and then proceeds to tell a saint's life in rhyme royal.[133] Once more the character's literary knowledge has been questioned from the start.

---

131 For a discussion of Augustine and Chaucer, see Rosemary Potz McGerr, "Retraction and Memory: Retrospective Structure in *The Canterbury Tales*," *Comparative Literature* 37 (1985): 97-113. Baumlin asserts that Chaucer wished to be known as the sole author of his works and the sole judge ("Theology and Discourse in the *Pardoner's Tale*, the *Parson's Tale*, and the *Retraction*" 140), just as Augustine had been. Koff also postulates that: "Actually the idea of retraction for Chaucer implies both a withdrawal of something because a judgment about it has been made—it is good or harmful—and a withdrawal of something *in order to make* a judgment about it. Moreover, Chaucer uses the word "retraction" as a plural noun ("my retraccions"), which suggests individual reexamination of individual works. For Chaucer to "revoke in my retraccions" (1085) is to invite readers to review his work *with him*—to revoke, as it were, after retraction. Chaucer's retraction constitutes the beginnings of evaluation" (*Chaucer and the Art of Storytelling* 233).

132 See also David, "The Man of Law vs. Chaucer" 224 and Chauncey Wood, "Chaucer's Man of Law as Interpreter," *Traditio* 23 (1967): 149-90; here 156-7.

133 Some critics suggest that Chaucer indeed intended to assign a prose tale to the Man of Law, either the "Wreched Engendrynge of Mankynde" or more likely the Tale of Melibee (see Eberle in the *Riverside Chaucer* 854).

The other purpose is both ironic and self-critical toward Chaucer himself. Chaucer has the Man of Law categorize him as a single-minded love poet whose poetic talents are quite negligible but whose output is nonetheless great. This characterization adumbrates Chaucer's own storytelling. He obliges the Man of Law by starting with the dreadful Tale of Sir Thopas in rhyme, but then switches to the Tale of Melibee in prose. The Man of Law's characterizations of himself and Chaucer as literary creators have both been reversed. On the one hand, the explicit tale-by-tale enumeration of the *Legend* sets up the pagan/Christian dichotomy with Custance, who would be a true "seint" of love, Christian, not pagan.[134] That, on the other hand, would be a real self-criticism on Chaucer's part. Another connection between the introduction to The Man of Law's Tale and the Retraction is the emphasis on Chaucer's literary fecundity, which smacks of bragging in both cases and also helps to keep Chaucer in the picture.

Chaucer ends the Retraction with a conventional prayer, as he and other medieval authors have offered previously:

> that thanke I oure Lord Jhesu Crist and his blisful Mooder, and alle seintes of hevene,/ bisekynge hem that they from hennes forth unto my lyves ende sende me grace to biwayle my giltes and to studie to the salvacioun of my soule, and graunte me grace of verray penitence, confessioun and satisfaccioun to doon in this present lyf,/ thurgh the benigne grace of hym that is kyng of kynges and preest over alle preestes, that boghte us with the precious blood of his herte,/ so that I may been oon of hem at the day of doom that shulle be saved. *Qui cum Patre et Spiritu Sancto vivit et regnat Deus per omnia secula. Amen.* (RT lines 1087-91)

His emphasis on salvation and doomsday contains traditional elements stemming from the early Christian self-critical writers, such as Juvencus and Wandalbert von Prüm. Chaucer voices his prayer in an intercessory manner, expressing his wish to be able to repent and confess his sins and to achieve salvation. These petitions are appropriate and recommended for a medieval Christian and are especially apt in the pilgrimage setting of *The Canterbury Tales*, but they cannot be Chaucer's deathbed repentance because the author's allusion to the end of his life—"from hennes forth unto my lyves ende"—implies that he has not reached it yet.[135] Although that allusion cannot be taken as a completely suitable expression of the "youth vs. age" trope, "to biwayle my giltes and to studie to the salvacioun of my soule" (RT line 1089) comprises the dichotomy set up twice before in the Retraction. Chaucer could bewail his literary guilt but further the salvation of his soul by writing works in the same vein as the ones for which he thanks Christ and Mary.

Furthermore, the syntax of the retraction reinforces its relative indeterminacy even as it seems to affirm its penitent purpose. Chaucer has arranged the first two thirds of the passage in a loose pattern of chiasmus, the rhetorical scheme of the cross, of the Christ he invokes, of Christianity. He mentions works for which readers should thank God, works that may displease although he tried to write them "for oure doctrine,"[136] works that should be forgiven and that he revokes in his "retracciouns," and works for

---

134 Eberle in the *Riverside Chaucer* 854.

135 See Spies, "Chaucers 'Retractatio'" 394 and Hammond, who asserts that "the recantation seems to me neither final nor a death-bed production, but a deliberately-planned conclusion" ("Chaucer's 'Book of the Twenty-Five Ladies'" 515).

136 For parallels to Don Juan Manuel, see also footnote 71 in Chapter 9.

which he thanks "oure Lord Jhesu Crist and his blisful Mooder." The third part of the chiasmus is itself nearly chiastic in nature, beginning as it does with "foryeve me my giltes" and ending with "foryeve me the synne." But Chaucer also begins the whole chiastic pattern with two conditional clauses ("if ther be any thyng in it that lyketh hem . . . if ther be any thyng that displese hem") that serve to destabilize the apparent non-conditionality of the remainder.[137]

Even if Chaucer, in his wrestling with the conflict between pagan and Christian world views, expresses genuine regret, he still wishes his canon to survive: he never advises his readers to ignore his works or suggests his writings should be destroyed. Although Chaucer now behaves like a sinful author in the Christian cosmos, accepting responsibility for his literary actions and deeming them irreversible, the Retraction comes after the fact—the reader has already gone through the entire work before reading it—and Chaucer extends an invitation to the reader to revisit and re-evaluate his writings and thereby to remember him. He has ultimately taken responsibility for writing his works but not for readers reading them. He seems to intend to continue writing, and we cannot infer from anything in the Retraction that he never intends to write again. Usually, self-critical Christian writers promise to redeem their sin of having penned a work celebrating physical love with a didactic work pleasing to God and the religious establishment. Overall, the Retraction transfers the mythological microcosmic aspect and application of the poet's dilemma presented in the *Legend* to the macrocosmic situation of the medieval poet in an all-encompassing Christian universe. Chaucer's encounter with the angry God of Love in the *Legend* serves as his mythological dress rehearsal for the realities of medieval Christianity. The religious Zeitgeist compels him to frame some of his works as sinful and to submit to the constraint of potential censorship. What real repercussions would Chaucer suffer from the God of Love? None, of course. But as Chaucer leaves the literary realm ruled by the God of Love for the new literary landscape of fourteenth-century reality, he changes his allegiance from the God of Love to the God of Salvation and to a scenario that could harm him as an author.

Ultimately, however, Chaucer's use of language is subversive, challenging the monolithic nature of the medieval sacramental theory of language that forces him to discard literary creations celebrating human love and women. Chaucer relished discussing metatextual and intra-auctorial processes and subsequently genuflecting before either the prevailing authority or the one that makes most auctorial sense. For instance, in his various roles as translator, storyteller, and compiler, he asserts the stability of the Christian Logos over the pagan love story in *Troilus*; he bows to the verdict of Alceste and Cupid in the *Legend*, commencing with a new literary form; he gives in to the Host's dislike of his Tale of Sir Thopas and immediately restarts in another literary genre; he still poses as a "lewd compiler," though visibly proud of his translation skills, in the *Astrolabe*; and in the Retraction he fulfills what would be expected of a good Catholic on a pilgrimage. But the Retraction is a literary document mostly concerned with the development of its author. The repentant author is as much Chaucer's personal construct as is the dreamer poet in the *Legend*. How can we trust him to be

---

137 Brewer argues that the Church won a superficial, not a total, victory over Chaucer's creative genius ("Gothic Chaucer" 15).

"sincere" when we have observed his ironic auctorial manipulation of other literary situations? There as here, his self-critical roles are not regressive but progressive strategies central to his creative process. They were central, too, to many another a medieval author who smiled the furtive, humble, knowing smile of Oliver Wendell Holmes, Sr., in recognizing that "[a]pology is only egotism wrong side out."[138]

8.7. Thomas Hoccleve

Chaucer's disciple Thomas Hoccleve emulates his idol in his application of auctorial self-criticism. Hoccleve utilizes the dialogue framework, as seen in Petrarch's *Secretum*, Machaut's *Navarre*, and Chaucer's *Legend*, to demonstrate the conception of a new work. In *Dialogue With a Friend*, Hoccleve fabricates the persona of a friend who, through criticism, guides him to a certain insight into his own intra-auctorial development. The persona of Hoccleve's friend is much more gentle with the author than Petrarch's, Machaut's, and Chaucer's accusers had been and the piece lacks the flavor of the trial structure of its predecessors. Although the self-criticism construct is more equivocal because it manifests itself in the form of good advice, it is nonetheless explicit and demonstrates the forces that can work upon an author's precarious situation. In countering the charge of antifeminism in *Dialogue With a Friend*, Hoccleve evokes both his translator role and the cathartic function of literature.

Since *Dialogue with a Friend* concerns itself with the genesis of literature, the work is rife with overt references to the dynamics of the writing process. Hoccleve is very direct and up-front about his auctorial plans. Because he is fifty-three years old and possibly close to death (lines 246-47), he wishes to set out to translate another work: "in latyn have I sene / a small tretis[e], / whiche 'lerne for to dye' / I-callyd is."[139] His reason is not altruistic, however, and refers both backward and forward. By translating a work dealing with *ars moriendi*, a knowledge of which would be recommended to all medieval people, he wishes to thank God for rescuing him from an illness and to cleanse his soul:

> for where my sowle is / of vertwe all lene,
> and thrwghe my bodyes gilt / fowle & vnclene,
> to clens it / some-what by translation
> of it, shall be / myne occupation. (*Dialogue* lines 214-17)

Hoccleve's cathartic motive for translating an *ars moriendi* work is qualified by two other considerations. He wishes it to be a didactic work that will make other people ponder their sins, but, above all, he admits that it is less his own "devocion" but the ". . . exitynge / and monicion / of a devout man . . ." (*Dialogue* lines 232, 234-35) that would incite him to make the translation. The situation smacks of patronage. Hoccleve is one of the few writers who actually uses the old-age topos in conjunction with giving up writing, whereas most writers employ it in contrast to their youthful literary

---

138 Jonathan Green, *The Cynic's Lexicon* (New York: St. Martin's, 1984) 95.
139 Thomas Hoccleve, *Dialogue with a Friend, Hoccleve's Works*, ed. Frederick J. Furnivall. (London: Oxford UP, 1892. Reprint 1937) 110-39, lines 205-06.

sins, for which they now atone with a more suitable work. Talk of quitting writing completely is scarce.

For the first part of the text, the Friend is actually trying to dissuade the author from writing again. He cites Hoccleve's love of books and writing as the cause of his illness, an argument which Hoccleve refutes as absurd.[140] The Friend finally reconciles himself to Hoccleve's continued literary activity and even gives him complete license: "Do foorth in goddes name / & nat ne woonde / To make and wryte / what thyng þat thee list" (*Dialogue* lines 491-97, 523-24). This granting of license is now immediately modified by the fact that the author still owes his patron, the valorous Duke of Gloucester, a work (*Dialogue* line 532). It had been Hoccleve's feigned intention to devote the *ars moriendi* book to the Duke, but since it would be his last endeavor the dilemma of appropriate subject matter exists. Instead of *utilitas*, which would be given in an *ars moriendi* tract, he wants to opt for *delectatio*, something with which "to glade" (*Dialogue* line 548) the Duke's heart. Therefore, the author considers a translation of ". . . Vegece / Which tretith of the art of Chiualrie" or a chronicle of the Duke's deeds (*Dialogue* line 561-62, 603). The Friend questions the notion of a "purely self-enclosed fiction,"[141] evokes the idea of a literary dialogue, and resurrects the specter of censorship when he cautions Hoccleve to select "good mateer and vertuous" (*Dialogue* line 637) and to consult others before trying to please his august audience.

This account of intra-auctorial ruminations bears fruit in the self-critical pattern the Friend touches off by mentioning Lent, the traditional time for confessing, repenting, and making amends for one's sins (*Dialogue* lines 662-65). Lent ties in intratextually with Hoccleve's earlier intention to cleanse his soul by writing a didactic work. Although his intention is still the same, now the charge is antifeminism:

Thow woost wel / on wommen, greet wyt & lak
Ofte haast thow put / be waar / lest thow be qwit.

. . . .
In hir repreef, mochil thyng haast thow write,
That they nat foryeue haue / ne foryite.

Sumwhat now wryte in honour & preysynge
Of hem / so maist thow do correccioun
Sumdel of thyn offense and mis-berynge.

. . . .
By buxom herte & by submission
To hir graces / yildinge thee coupable /
Thow pardon maist haue, & remission
And do vn-to hem plesance greable.
To make partie / art thow nothyng able;

. . . .

By wordes writen / Thomas, yilde thee;
Euene as thow by scripture hem haast offendid,
Right so / let it be by wrytynge amendid. (*Dialogue* lines 667-68, 671-75, 687-91, 698-700)

---

140 Hoccleve, *Dialogue* lines 302-04, 379-85, 403-06, 424-27.
141 Derek Brewer, *Chaucer: The Poet as Storyteller* (London: Macmillan, 1984) 2.

This passage conjures up several intertextual associations to the other medieval authors' works. It echoes the Augustinian notion of literary atonement for sins committed with words. The charge also harbors a renewed indictment of women, as is usual for most works supposedly battling the charge of antifeminism, such as le Fèvre's *Lamentations* and *Leesce*, as well as many of the Spanish antifeminist authors in the next chapter. Women's anger, justified or not, and unforgiving stance are enlisted to underscore and re-affirm the negative qualities initially attributed to them. Therefore, the Friend also portrays women as conniving and superior enemies against whom Hoccleve has no chance except with his pen and a submissive attitude.

The Friend's motivation for Hoccleve's literary placation is congruent with ancient authors' external motives for making literary apologies—the regaining of love, for instance in Horace's case. The Friend seizes upon the benefits of literary patronage, for if the atoning work were presented to the Duke, himself a ladies' man, it could become instrumental in getting the author back into the ladies' favor. The incentive to regain women's love is ironic within the dynamics of the old-age topos, especially when Hoccleve just admitted to being close to death, which would hardly be the time to return to love poetry. Despite the fact that these strategies should achieve forgiveness for Hoccleve, the Friend advises him not to become too subservient to women and then gives him the chance to bring up the old anti-feminist archetype of Eve's great offense. The entire discussion bears the tone of tolerated evil and forces the conclusion that a writer should not offend women because he has to live with their wrath.

The reason for the women's anger can be found in the *Letter of Cupid*, Hoccleve's translation of Christine de Pizan's *Epistre au dieu d'amours*, a work that "criticized clerical anti-feminism and disrespectful attitudes toward women."[142] This situation contains a similar irony to the *Legend*, in which the *Roman* is attacked on grounds of not being more beneficial to love. According to the Friend, Hoccleve is accused of antifeminism because "'Thow haast of hem / so largeliche said, / That they been swart wrooth / & ful euele apaid'" (*Dialogue* lines 755-56). He indignantly denies but does not recant antifeminism:[143]

Considereth / ther-of / was I noon Auctour;
I nas in þat cas / but a reportour
Of folkes tales / as they seide / I wroot:
I nat affermed it on hem / god woot!

Who so þat shal reherce a mannes sawe,
As þat he seith / moot he seyn & nat varie,
ffor, and he do / he dooth ageyn the lawe
Of trouthe / he may tho wordes nat contrarie.
Who-so þat seith 'I am hir Aduersarie,
And dispreise hir condicions and port,
ffor þat I made of hem swich a report, /

142 Diane Bornstein, "Anti-Feminism in Thomas Hoccleve's Translation of Christine de Pizan's *Epistre au dieu d'amours*," *English Language Notes* 19 (1981): 7-14; here 7.
143 John V. Fleming, "Hoccleve's *Letter of Cupid* and the Quarrel over the *Roman de la Rose*," *Medium Aevum* 40 (1971): 21-40; here 24.

He mis-auysed is / and eek to blame.
Whan I it spak / I spak conpleynyngly;
I to hem thoghte no repreef ne shame.
What world is this / how vndirstande am I?
Looke in the same book / what stikith by?
Who so lookith aright / ther-in may see
þat they me oghten haue in greet cheertee. (*Dialogue* lines 760-77)

Hoccleve imitates Jean de Meun, Jean le Fèvre, Nicole Bozon, Boccaccio, and Chaucer in their application of the translator's defense, the claim of faithful emulation and simple repetition of the source. The source, however, has now become more obscure; instead of the ancient *auctoritates*, less "traceable" folk tales, which also put greater emphasis on the oral tradition, are now being substituted. Moreover, Hoccleve distinguishes his translator role from the role of the creative "Auctour" in Bonaventure's auctorial hierarchy. The translator/poet's indignation over the charge of antifeminism functions again as a gauge and indictment of his accusers' literary judgment, they who know as much about *translatio* as Cupid from Chaucer's *Legend* does.

But how much does Hoccleve know about *translatio* and the role of an *auctor* that the women should thank him for his literary contribution? Opinions on this vary. The editors Skeat and Furnivall admit that Hoccleve's work was a "shortened paraphrase rather than a precise translation."[144] Jerome Mitchell judges the *Letter of Cupid* to be "at least as feminist in outlook as its French source."[145] Mitchell identifies the following passage as a possible offensive part of the *Epistle of Cupid*:

Al-be-hyt that man fynde / o woman nyce,
In-constant, recheles / or varriable,
Deynouse, or proude / fulfilled of malice,
Wythouten feyth or love / and deceyvable,
sly, queynt, and fals / in al vnthrift coupable,
Wikked, and feers / and ful of cruelte,
yt foloweth nat / that swich, al wommen be.[146]

The reasoning here illustrates that, while Hoccleve seems pro-women, he still can choose those negative adjectives for which he might have been scolded. Such a strategy mirrors the concept applied by Le Fèvre in his *Lamentations* and *Leesce* where he apologizes for having to translate such horribly antifeminist literature but repeats the insults word for word.

Diane Bornstein in her comparative study of both Pizan's and Hoccleve's work reaches the conclusion that Hoccleve "subtly introduced an anti-feminist tone . . . by changing the content and style"; according to her, Hoccleve has changed the "serious tone"—previously imitative of the French court and now of the English tavern—to comply with the jester character Cupid, "whose exaggerated defense of women is not

---

144 Bornstein, "Anti-Feminism in Thomas Hoccleve's Translation of Christine de Pizan's *Epistre au dieu d'amours*" 7.

145 Jerome Mitchell, Thomas Hoccleve: A Study in Early Fifteenth-Century English Prose (Urbana: U of Illinois P, 1968) 53.

146 Thomas Hoccleve, *The Letter of Cupid. Hoccleve's Works*, ed. Frederick J. Furnivall (London: Oxford UP, 1892. Reprint 1937) 72-91, lines 148-54.

very trustworthy."[147] Hoccleve subscribes more to direct speech, elaborates on passages unflattering to women, and simply adds parts that are not in the original. Moreover, the increased use of colloquial speech produces a more insulting tone to the woman. Finally, the translator tampers with Pizan's biblical supporting evidence by omitting the argument "that woman was formed in Paradise, whereas man was not" and by modifying Pizan's perception of Mary as a "natural woman" and mother of Jesus into a "role as a saintly intercessor between man and God." Bornstein concludes that Hoccleve's translation made a mere "parody of feminism" out of a "judicious, courtly defense of women."[148]

It is difficult to discern for which reasons Hoccleve offers this translator's excuse. Is it because women before Bornstein have discovered the modification in his translation; or because his foremost goal is to rekindle a popular medieval topic and to bring part of the *Querelle de Roman de la Rose* to England; or because he wishes to demonstrate the intra-auctorial genesis of a literary text; or because this is an interesting way to move into his next literary endeavor? Hoccleve's Friend still has to push him into accepting literary penance and prod him with literary supervision and censure until he resolves to write for the women:

> Though I my wordes can nat wel portreye /
> Lo, heer the fourme / how I hem obeye.
> . . . .
>
> But I your freend be . . . .
>
> But nathelees / I lowly me submitte
> To your bontees / as fer as they han place
> In yow / vn-to me, wrecche, it may wel sitte
> To axe pardoun / thogh I nat trespace;
> Leuer is me / with piteous cheere & face,
> And meek spirit, do so / than open werre
> yee make me / & me putte atte werre.
> A tale eek / which I in the Romayn deedis
> Now late sy / in honur & plesance
> Of yow, my ladyes . . . .
> . . . .
> Wole I translate / and þat shal pourge, I hope,
> My gilt / as cleene / as keuerchiefs dooth sope. (*Dialogue* lines 804-05, 810, 813-22, 825-26)

This passage evokes the cleansing function of an apology á la Stesichorus. But, unlike Machaut and Chaucer, who readily accept their penance without admitting guilt, Hoccleve very explicitly affirms his innocence, although he might be the most devious of those authors in the process. One irony is that Hoccleve's protestations of good will toward women and their hostility toward him serve to indict the women once again as unreasonable creatures. His penance is dubious, for he professes his own lack of verbal

---

147 Bornstein, "Anti-Feminism in Thomas Hoccleve's Translation of Christine de Pizan's *Epistre au dieu d'amours*" 7-8.
148 Bornstein, "Anti-Feminism in Thomas Hoccleve's Translation of Christine de Pizan's *Epistre au dieu d'amours*" 8-10, 12-14.

skill and then announces another translation of a pagan work meant to endear him to the ladies. Given his track record in translating profeminist works, his strategy is highly ironic. His self-critical construct has an additional function: the dialogue structure and the prodding friend provide a shield for him, in case anybody would accuse him, at his advanced age, of indulging in more literature dealing with women instead of *ars moriendi*, as initially planned. At any rate, the self-criticism has at least engendered a promise of more composition and has, therefore, retrospective and progressive referentiality.

Overall, the English examples by themselves represent a microcosmic delineation of the apology. Cynewulf and Langland both concern themselves with their literary creation in the eyes of God: Cynewulf in the dichotomy between pagan/Christian literature; Langland in the dichotomy between his role as an author and other medieval professions, which either encroach on that role or give him a bad reputation. The three Welsh poets display a homogeneity in their poems that stems from the genre of the praise poem and indicates a pattern of composition. In a mixture of intertextuality and interauctoriality, the Welsh poets contrast God's impeccable creative record with their own fallible creatorship and exercise auctorial self-criticism in order to please the religious establishment and the deity. Llywelyn's Goch's explicit dealing with the female element in his poetry is a sample of the increased attention women will receive in the apology tradition. Furthermore, Guto'r Glyn's reference to the poet's enslavement by worldliness parallels the sentiments and strategies of the German epic and lyric poets who make extensive use of the arising *contemptus mundi* theme in their self-critical works. Chaucer still deals with all of these issues but has a markedly higher level of irony in his apologies and their literary context. He is indeed a master at exploiting all of the nuances of the convention. In Hoccleve's *Dialogue*, salvation concerns become more covert as auctorial concerns become more overt. Irony is rife. The tradition had always been characterized by ironical elements, but at the close of the Middle Ages irony becomes the foremost concern in the apology tradition. This is evidenced by the Spanish apology tradition, especially in its exploitation of apologies to women.

CHAPTER 9

The Spanish Tradition:
Troubadour's Apology and Misogynist's Excuse

Both apologies to God and women culminate in the Spanish apology tradition, which is characterized by the generally late appearance of vernacular literature. Because of the century-long delay in the blooming of Spanish vernacular literature, many influences from other European apology traditions can be seen in it. What is most striking about both the Spanish troubadour's apology and the misogynist's excuse is their overt focus on women. For the latter that focal point is, of course, built into the design, but for the former it has been more insinuated than openly expressed after classical times. The early Christian and early medieval authors' emphasis on youthful errors in the vein of classically-influenced compositions—vain, empty, and devoid of Christian truth—has always included, as Gascoigne has Chaucer exclaim, "the evil and most shameful love of men for women."[1] It is not until the Spanish tradition, however, that these implicit love compositions fully take the place of untruthful pagan fables. Thus the immorality of illicit love becomes the center of the apologies to God, culminating in the dichotomy of *cupiditas* and *caritas*. These tendencies can be seen in other traditions. For instance, Ibn Hazm and Guibert de Nogent allude to carnal aspects of love; Llywelyn's "I Dduw" specifically regrets his poem about Lleucu; Walther von der Vogelweide and Neidhart von Reuenthal couch their *contemptus mundi* in the "Dame World" metaphor; the Italian poets treat woman both as creative inspiration and physical being. For Chaucer the topic is highly pertinent as well. It is the Spanish apology tradition, however, in which that strange *cupiditas/caritas* dichotomy culminates in the self-critical poets' dilemma of either composing love poetry, thus offending the contemporary Christian Zeitgeist, and then repenting their literary sins, or writing antifeminist tracts, thus outraging women, and then apologizing to them. Ramon Llull, Juan Ruiz, Juan Rodríguez del Padrón, and Diego de San Pedro are caught on the salvation-seeking side of the dichotomy, with its emphasis on the religious correctness of repentance, *contemptus mundi et feminae*, and literary atonement, whereas Alfonso Martínez de Toledo, Pere Torroella, Juan de Tapia, and Hernán Mexía participate in the pro- and antifeminist debate of the fifteenth century, with its overt irony inherent in its outrageously blatant blanket condemnations and praises.[2]

---

1   Jon M. Fyler, *Chaucer and Ovid* (New Haven: Yale UP, 1979) 111.

2   For a discussion of post-1500 (c. 1500 is the cut-off line for this study) examples of Spanish recantations, see Otis H. Green, *Spain and the Western Tradition: The Castilian Mind in Literature from* El Cid *to* Calderón (Madison: U of Wisconsin P, 1963) 1: 264-99. Green, furthermore, enumerates pre-1500 Spanish recantation examples in *The Literary Mind of Medieval & Renaissance Spain* (Lexington: UP of Kentucky, 1970) 71-74. I am indebted to his list but have to qualify his approach. Green includes any kind of statement that indicates the

author's turning from love, whereas I try to discuss only examples explicitly stating a change in the intra-auctorial paradigm. For instance, the example of Mosén Fenollar (fifteenth century) is too vague to define the author's service to Cupid as literary or personal only:

Pésame que t'e seguido,
engañado hast' aqui;
qu'en auerte conoscido
y de ti ya despedido,
lloro el tiempo que perdí.
  Lloro, no tu despedida,
mas lloro que tarde fue;
lloro, no perder la vida,
mas lloro mi poca fe;
lloro, no a ti, Cupido,
mas lloro que te seruî;
lloro, no de ti vencido,
aunque fui tan sometido,
mas lloro que me vencí.

['I grieve for having followed you in my blindness until now; having known you for what you are and taken leave of you, I weep for the time that I lost. I weep, not because I leave you, but rather that this came late; I weep, not at the thought of death, but over my lack of faith. I weep not for you, oh Cupid, but rather because I served you; I weep, not vanquished by you, though you held me in subjection, but rather because I allowed myself to be defeated'] (qtd. in Green, *Spain and the Western Tradition* 1: 285-86).

Another liminal poet, Juan del Encina (c. 1468-1529), should be mentioned because of his similar utilization of the traditional auctorial apology for worldly sins. In his work describing his pilgrimage to Jerusalem, *Viaje y peregrinación a Jerusalén*, he regrets his former vanities and demonstrates the religiously correct time to repent:

Can Fe protestando mudar de costumbre,
dexando de darme a cosas livianas,
y a componer obras del Mundo ya vanas: (qtd. in Green, *The Literary Mind of Medieval &*
. . . .   *Renaissance Spain* 73)
Y guarde no menos silencio la lengua
si no se ocupare en Oración santa:
palabras ociosas, en edad ya tanta,
es liviandad much y discreción poca. (qtd. in Green, *Spain and the Western Tradition* 1: 287)
[With Faith protesting my usual custom,
and ceasing to dedicate myself to trivial things,
and to compose works both worldly and vain:

. . . .

'Let my tongue likewise keep silent except to engage in holy prayer; idle words, at so advanced an age, show frivolity and little discretion'] (Green, *Spain and the Western Tradition* 287, n. 62).

Furthermore, M. R. Lida de Malkiel considers Juan de Mena's (1404-60) passage a close imitation of Boethius' prose and his rejection of the profane poetry of his youth (*Juan de Mena, poeta del prerrenacimiento español* [Mexico City, 1950] 112):

Venid, lisongeras canas,
que tardays demasiado;
tirad presumpciones vanas
al tiempo tan mal gastado; ("Coplas que fizo el famoso Juan de Mena contra los pecados
[Come, flattering gray hair   mortales," Cancionero *Castellano del siglo XV*,
You waited too long.   ed. R. Foulché-Delbosc, 2 vols. [Madrid: Bailly-
Throw away your vain presumption   Balliére, 1912] 1: 120-52; here 120).

9.1. Ramon Llull

The earliest Spanish example by the Catalan theologian and philosopher Ramon Llull (1232-1316), of whom about two hundred and forty-three, mostly didactic, works are extant,[3] delineates in his possibly autobiographical vita an alleged conversion experience. Because Llull is primarily considered a Catalan author, he is featured in this chapter, although the text of the *Vita coetanea* is in Latin. Thematically, that work also fits better here because this metatextual and meta-auctorial account tries to rationalize and explain his intra-auctorial shift from a troubadour to a religious writer as well as to demonstrate the connection between writing and salvation. The *Vita* identifies Llull as a follower of the traditional court life with its amorous exploits and cultivation of the troubadour lyric, implying that he had been a "womanizing troubadour."[4] Externally that impression gains credibility, for James the Conqueror, Llull's lord, had a predilection for Provençal troubadour poetry.[5] Starting in June 1263, however, Llull underwent a profound religious conversion, although Llull's biographer, J. N. Hillgarth, provides evidence that the *Vita* might have been touched up by its anonymous monastic author.[6] The second paragraph of the *Vita* demonstrates the intertwined state of writing and salvation:

. Raymundus senescallus mense regis Maioricarum, dum iuvenis adhuc in vanis cantillenis seu carminibus componendis et aliis lasciviis seculi deditus esset nimis, sedebat nocte quadam iuxta lectum suum paratus ad dictandum et scribendum in suo vulgari unam cantilenam de quadam domina, quam tunc amore fatuo diligebat. Dum igitur cantilenam predictam inciperet scribere, respiciens a dextris vidit dominum Iesum Christum tanquam pendentem in cruce; quo viso timuit, et relictis que habebat in manibus, lectum suum, ut dormiret, intravit.[7]

The text lays bare two essential points important to this study. First, the author's love song compositions are explicitly tied to his youth and fit into the topos of youth vs.

---

to your misspent youth]. While this passage follows the "youth vs. age" dichotomy, it is not specific enough to the author's writing career.

3   Paul Russell-Gebbett, ed., "Medieval Catalan Literature," *Spain: A Companion to Spanish Studies* (London: Methuen, 1977) 247-63; here 250.

4   Mark D. Johnston, *The Spiritual Logic of Ramon Llull* (Oxford: Clarendon, 1987) 10.

5   Erhard W. Platzeck, ed., introduction, *Das Leben des seligen Raimund Llull, dei Vita coetanea und ausgewählte Texte aus seinen Werken und Zeitdokumenten* (Düsseldorf: Patmos Verlag, 1964) 1-35; here 146.

6   Johnston, *The Spiritual Logic of Ramon Llull* 10 and J. N. Hillgarth, *Ramon Lull and Lullism in Fourteenth-Century France* (Oxford: Clarendon, 1971) 1, 46 n. 2.

7   Ramon Llull, *Vita coetanea, Das Leben des seligen Raimund Llull, dei Vita coetanea und ausgewählte Texte aus seinen Werken und Zeitdokumenten*, ed. Erhard W. Platzeck (Düsseldorf: Patmos Verlag, 1964) 145-80; here 145-46. [Ramon had been seneschal of the king of Mallorca. He was still young and had been dedicating himself quite a bit to the writing of vain lays or love songs and other all-too-facile poems. Thus one night he was sitting at his bed ready to compose and write a lay in his vernacular to a lady with whom he was then passionately in love. And as he started to write the lay, he looked to his right and saw the Lord hanging on the cross. At this sight he was afraid, and he dropped what he held in his hands and went to bed to sleep]. The *Vita coetanea* exists in two forms, Latin and Catalan. I am working from the Latin text of Baudouin de Gaiffier because it has been established as the original, with the Catalan a somewhat inept translation (Hillgarth, *Ramon Lull and Lullism in Fourteenth-Century France* 46, fn 2).

writings are solely identified as love songs employed in Llull's amorous exploits. Second, the appearance of the Logos Incarnate shames the poet into stopping his own imperfect creation with words, an activity that is incompatible with Christ's teaching and underscores the medieval dichotomy of *cupiditas* and *caritas*.

The next paragraph in the *Vita* shows how the anti-love-song atmosphere escalates:

> In crastino vero surgens, et ad vanitates solitas rediens, nichil de visione illa curabat, immo cito quasi per octo dies postea, in loco quo prius, et quasi hora eadem, iterum se aptavit ad scribendum et perficiendum cantilenam suam predictam; cui Dominus iterum in cruce apparuit, sicut ante; ipse vero tunc territus plus quam primo, lectum suum intrans, ut alias, obdormivit; sed adhuc crastino apparitionem negligens sibi factam, suam lasciviam non dimisit; immo post paululum suam cantilenam nitebatur perficere incoatam, donec sibi tertio et quarto successive diebus interpositis aliquibus Salvator in forma semper, qua primitus, appareret.[8]

The *Vita* labels the undertakings of the author "vanitates" [vain dealings] and "suam lasciviam" [his lascivious intentions], with which the Logos Incarnate is being contrasted repeatedly. The repetitiveness of the situation establishes two points: first, it exhibits both the stubbornness of the author in his wish to finish his vernacular love song and the increasing difficulty he has with that endeavor; second, it shows that Christ is insistent in breaking a sinner of his habit because Christ as Logos has the power and will to redeem human language. The Christian word lures souls to Christ, whereas the troubadour word lures women away from *caritas* to bed and therefore to illicit love, *cupiditas*. And the soul, of course, is always feminine.

In the next passage, the targeted sinner finally makes the connection between the direction of his creative ability and his salvation:

> In quarta ergo vel etiam quinta vice, sicut plus creditur, eadem apparitione sibi facta territus nimium lectum suum intravit, secum tota illa nocte cogitando tractans quidnam visiones iste tociens iterate significare deberent. Hinc sibi quandoque dictabat consciencia, quod apparitiones ille nichil aliud pretendebant, nisi, quod ipse mox relicto mundo domino Jesu Christo ex tunc integre deserviret; illinc vero sua consciencia ream se prius et indignam Christi servitio acclamat; sicque super hiis nunc secum disputans, nunc attentius Deum orans, laboriosam noctem illam duxit insompnem. Denique, dante Patre luminum, consideravit Christi mansuetudinem, patientiam ac misericordiam, quam habuit et habet circa quoslibet peccatores; et sic intellexit tandem certissime Deum velle quod Raymundus mundum relinqueret Christoque corde ex tunc integre deserviret.[9]

---

8   Llull, *Vita coetanea* 146-47. [Next morning, however, he got up and went about his usual vain dealings without thinking further about the vision. Then eight days later, at the same spot as before, almost at the same hour, he attempted once more to write down and finish said lay. The Lord appeared again on the cross as before. Thus he went to bed again and fell asleep, but more scared than before. The day after that, he did not think about the vision that had been revealed to him anymore and did not let go of his lascivious intentions. But a little later he tried to finish the lay he had begun, until the Savior appeared a third and fourth time within a few days, in the same form as the first time].

9   Llull, *Vita coetanea* 147. [There, the fourth or more likely the fifth time that the apparition was given, he went to bed greatly frightened and mused the entire night about what these repeated visions could mean. On the one hand, his conscience was telling him loudly and clearly that these apparitions could not mean anything else but that he should soon leave this world behind in order to serve the Lord Jesus Christ entirely from now on. But on the other hand, his conscience proclaimed itself burdened with guilt and not worthy to serve Christ. And thus, now disputing these things with himself, now attentively praying to God, he spent this troublesome night sleepless.

The *contemptus mundi* and implicitly *contemptus feminae* conclusion of the author smacks of the atmosphere of repentance that, for example, frightened Boccaccio. Boccaccio's response to the prediction by the Carthusian monk was an emotional one, whereas the *Vita coetanea* shows that it takes Ramon Llull intensive intellectual thought to reach that resolution, and that he needs a lot of prompting to get there. As one might suspect, none of his troubadour lyrics has survived, and Wolfgang Schleicher even suggests that Llull might have destroyed the missing troubadour lyrics himself,[10] although there is really no definitive statement of literary guilt in the *Vita*. Erhard W. Platzeck, however, asserts that as a troubadour, Llull had seen much and said much in his verses that should not have been said.[11] As evident from the rest of the *Vita* and Llull's prolific extant literary production, the goal was not to make him stop writing but rather to shift his focus. The *Vita* reveals that his ardent wish and atonement had been to write a book to convert the infidels; thus the conversion of the author and the redemption of his linguistic capabilities is essential to his writing a work inducing heathens to conversion. As a matter of fact, the *Vita* continues to give many accounts of Llull's post-conversion writing activity, trying to explain his intra-auctorial path by recounting a conversion experience more elaborate than those found in the usual auctorial professions of a sinful youth.[12] Still he changes his auctorial direction in his youth, and his subsequent religious works function as the required atonement.

9.2. Juan Ruiz

Because fourteenth-century author Juan Ruiz also perceives his amatory writing as endangering his salvation, he uses intratextual self-criticism to exonerate himself from the charge. His famous work *El Libro de buen amor* (1343) ['The Book of Good Love'] may be separated into two parts, with the first part an *Ars Amatoria* in the Ovidian sense and the second part the dark side of the force, "the sinfulness of love and its ephemeral nature."[13] These opposites constitute the central medieval

---

Finally, illuminated by the gift of the father of light, he considered the condescension, patience, and mercy Christ showed, and still shows toward each sinner, and eventually came to the conclusion that God wanted Raymond to forsake the world and serve Christ from now on with his whole heart and devotion].

10   Arthur Terry, *A Literary History of Spain: Catalan Literature* (New York: Barnes & Noble, 1972) 12 and Wolfgang Schleicher, *Ramon Lulls* Libre de Evast et Blanquerna, Kölner Romanistische Arbeiten 12 (Geneva: Librairie E. Droz, 1958) 13.

11   Platzeck, introduction, *Das Leben des seligen Raimund Llull, dei Vita coetanea und ausgewählte Texte aus seinen Werken und Zeitdokumenten* 11.

12   See also Roberto J. González-Casanovas, "The Writer and Preacher as *Juglar de Déu*: Literary Conversion in Ramon Llull," *Romance Languages Annual* 1 (1989): 460-63.

13   Colbert I. Nepaulsingh, *Towards a History of Literary Composition in Medieval Spain* (Toronto: U of Toronto P, 1986) 127.

dichotomy of earthly and spiritual love. The Archpriest of Hita tries to bridge this gulf in two ways. First, he intimates that his book contains "deep allegorical value":[14]

> Non tengades que es libro neçio de devaneo,
> nin creades que es chufa algo que en él leo,
> ca, segund buen dinero yaze en vil correo,
> ansí en feo libro está saber non feo.[15]

This intratextual strategy is obviously supposed to keep Ruiz's readers interested, to avert any judgment that his book is facile in content and negligible, and to establish the supremacy of the signified over the signifier. Ruiz achieves this with already-known methods involving *delectatio* and *utilitas*. Although he rejects the notion that his verses are foolish, Ruiz immediately contextualizes them as jests, thus *delectatio*, which is what Chaucer does in the prologue to the Miller's Tale in order to avert responsibility. Ruiz, however, is quick to assert that the readers should not judge the book by its cover alone but should make the effort to find the *utilitas* inherent in the work. In doing so, he echoes Jean de Meun in the *Roman*, asserting that the pagan poets hide truth in their fables.

His second method is to provide a palinode more than halfway through the book. Otis Green considers the following prayer to Saint Mary of Ford as a "recantation of the sinful":[16]

> Santiago apóstol diz *que* todo bien conplido
> e todo don muy bueno de *Dios* bien' escogido.
> E yo, desque salí de todo aqueste rroído,
> torné rrogar a Dios que me non diese a olvido.[17]

Ruiz's preoccupation with salvation occurs after the raunchy encounter with the wanton *serranas* and might, as Green suggests, be an apology for the immoral aspects of the work so far; John Esten Keller, however, doubts the sincerity of the recantation and attributes it instead to the parodistic nature of the entire work.[18] Ruiz simply augments this claim that the work is allegorical with the expected repentance of his autobiographical amatory exploits, although his work actually concentrates on "el amor

---

14 John Esten Keller, introduction, *The Book of Good Love*, trans. Elisha Kent Kane (Chapel Hill: U of North Carolina P, 1968) xix-lv; here li.

15 Juan Ruiz, *Libro de buen amor*, ed. G. B. Gybbon-Monypenny (Madrid: Editorial Castalia, 1988) copla 16:
   ['Don't think that this is a foolish book replete with giddy verse,
   Nor hold the jests therein contained as something even worse;
   For oft, as goodly money lies within a filthy purse,
   A messy book may likewise hold much wisdom sound and terse'] (Elisha Kent Kane, trans., *The Book of Good Love*, by Juan Ruiz [Chapel Hill: U of North Carolina P, 1968] 7).

16 Green, *Spain and the Western Tradition* 71.

17 Ruiz, *Libro de buen amor* copla 1043:
   ['Saint James, the blest apostle, says that every perfect gift
   And every good descends from God who ne'er deserts His shift;
   Wherefore, as soon as I got through my amatory rift,
   I turned to pray to God on high to cast me not adrift'] (Kane, *The Book of Good Love* 150).

18 Green, *Spain and the Western Tradition* 71 and Keller, introduction, *The Book of Good Love* li.

sexual"[19] nonetheless. Ruiz can thus exercise as much license as he pleases, is also supported by his skirting around the contemporary philosophy of language: "No ha mala palabra si non es a mal tenida" (copla 64, 2) ['No word is wicked in itself unless it's wrongly taken'(Kane 15)]. Ruiz joins Ovid, Jean de Meun, Boccaccio, Chaucer et al. in their strategy of partially unburdening themselves of their auctorial task— imparting meaning on a text—by granting the reader equal creative power and therefore literary responsibility.

9.3. Juan Rodríguez del Padrón

Juan Rodríguez del Padrón (1390-c. 1450), a writer of courtly love poetry and later a priest, participates in the troubadour's repentance but grapples heavily with his auctorial pride, lending an overt sense of irony to the apology. The author, who supposedly had written "Fuego del divino rayo" ['The fire of the divine ray'] in the monastery of Herbón that he founded, imitates the German and French epic poets as well as his fellow Spanish troubadours in their insistence on *contemptus mundi* coupled with a rejection of their profane works and an emphasis on timely repentance.[20] The desire to atone with another work, however, is conspicuously absent:

La falsa gloria del mundo
y vana prosperidad
contemplé;
con pensamiento profundo
el centro de su maldad
penetré.
. . . .
Así yo, preso de espanto,
que la divina virtud
offendí,
comienço me triste planto
fazer en mi juventud
desde aquí;
los desiertos penetrando,

---

19 G. B. Gybbon-Monypenny, ed., introduction, *Libro de buen amor* (Madrid: Editorial Castalia, 1988) 7-78; here 40.

20 Cesar Hernandez Alonso, introduction, *Obras completas*, by Juan Rodríguez del Padrón (Madrid: Editora Nacional, 1982) 9-136; here 89. The following scholarly interpretation by Martin S. Gilderman exemplifies the fragmented and discipline-bound knowledge of the history of the palinode: "In the early fifteenth century, it was not uncommon for a poet who had spent his early years writing verses to his lady to repent his actions and claim that his former life was sin and folly. Thus there arose the subgenre known as the *palinodio* ("palinode"), in which the poet would bid a final fond farewell to the court and worldly pleasures, and promise to lead a saintly, ascetic life in order to find salvation lest it be too late (*Juan Rodríguez de la Cámara* [Boston: Twayne, 1977] 63). Although Gilderman is generally correct, the palinode is, for one thing, not a fifteenth-century invention. Second, Rodríguez stresses that his repentance is being implemented in his youth. Third, not all such disavowals are on the surface as amiable as this one.

do con esquivo clamor
pueda, mis culpas llorando,
despedirme sin temor,
de falso plazer e honor.[21]

Like Llull, Juan Rodríguez moves from the conscientious intellectual contemplation of *vanitas vanitatis* to its obvious rejection. The author's offense with the word in writing love songs is contrasted to Christ's linguistically redeeming function and points up the dichotomy between *cupiditas* and *caritas* again. In the "youth vs. age" debate, Juan Rodríguez portrays himself as one of the authors who wants to repent while young; this strategy is as much preventative as is the claim of the "old" author that vain poetry was a fact of his youth, because asserting that one is still young and writing love poetry affirms that the poet has not yet left the only "acceptable" space for said activity.

And blatant intratextual discrepancy surfaces when stanza three and four are juxtaposed. The trembling fear of the repentant poet is being neutralized by the outright pride he displays in the writings he renounces:

Adiós, real resplandor
que yo serví et loé
con lealtat;
adios, que todo el favor
e cuanto de amor fablé
es vanidat.
Adiós, los que bien amé;
adiós, mundo engañador;
adiós, donas que ensalçé
famosas, dignas de loor,
orad por mí pecador![22]

The petition for intercession is a typical medieval *captatio benevolentiae* gesture like Boccaccio's petitioning the ladies for intercession at the end of the *Decameron*. Juan Rodríguez' intratextual repudiation of the ladies and his request that they pray for the well-being of his soul, however, is incongruous at best. Other semantic choices underscore the incongruity between the supposed repentance and the obvious pride. That the ladies were famous and worthy of praise is inherently a positive statement and Horatian in nature, for it insinuates that his poetry made them famous. He served the fickle, mundane elements of love and fortune "loyally." The anaphoric use of the term

---

21 Juan Rodríguez del Padrón, "Fuego del diuino rayo," *Obras Completas*, ed. Cesar Hernandez Alonso (Madrid: Editora Nacional, 1982) 340-41; stanzas 2 and 3. ['I have contemplated the false glory and vain prosperity of the world, and with profound thinking have penetrated the core of its evil. Thus I, gripped with fear, I who have offended the divine virtue, do begin to make my sad lament now, in my youth? So that I, entering the deserts may with secret cries bemoan my guilt and depart, without fear, from false pleasure and honor'] (Gilderman, *Juan Rodríguez de la Cámara* 63-64).

22 Rodríguez, "Fuego del diuino rayo" stanza 4. ['Farewell, royal splendor which I loyally served and praised. Farewell, for whatever I spoke of love and good fortune is vanity. Farewell, you whom I loved well. Farewell, deceitful world; farewell, you ladies whom I exalted, famous ladies, worthy of praise, pray for me, your sinner'] (Gilderman, trans., *Juan Rodríguez de la Cámara* 64).

"adios," charged with a positive, regretful connotation, compounds the ironic tone of an expected renunciation of the world and supports Martin S. Gilderman's interpretation "that the finale, rather than giving the reader a sense of true repentance, seems to be the author's way of boasting about his accomplishments."[23]

9.4. Diego de San Pedro

Diego de San Pedro presents an especially interesting metatextual and intra-auctorial case because he is most Chaucerian in his ambivalence, discussing the pitfalls of medieval writing and his reasons for self-criticism, and later recanting all of his amorous compositions, one by one establishing a very clear intertextual and intra-auctorial relationship. In *Cárcel de Amor* ['Prison of Love'], San Pedro employs notions of audience and patronage to exonerate himself:

> Aunque me falta sofrimiento para callar, no me fallesce conoscimiento para ver quánto me estaría mejor preciarme de lo que callase que arepentirme de lo que dixiese; y puesto que assí lo conozca, aunque veo la verdad, sigo la opinión; y como hago lo peor nunca quedo sin castigo, porque si con rudeza yerro, con vergüença pago.[24]

The poet is caught in the dilemma between abstaining from writing or composing with impending punishment, echoing the passage in Matthew about being judged by one's words. Like Socrates, however, San Pedro has a calculated recourse to make amends for his sin. The difference between them lies in their audiences: Socrates refers to a divine audience, whereas San Pedro refers to the worldly patron who requested the literary composition. Furthermore, the author also demonstrates an intellectual quality in his apology that can be found in Llull and Juan Rodríguez del Padrón.

Like Chaucer, however, San Pedro qualifies his modest stance with a number of mitigating defense mechanisms that divert blame and guilt from himself:

> Verdad es que en la obra presente no tengo tanto cargo, pues me puse en ella más por necesidad de obedescer que con voluntad de escrevir. Porque de vuestra merced me fue dicho que devía hazer alguna obra del estilo de una oración que enbié a la señora doña Marina Manuel . . . y en fin escogí lo más dañoso para mi vergüença y lo más provechoso para lo que devía. Podré ser reprehendido si en lo que agora escrivo tornare a dezir algunas razones de las que en otras cosas he dicho.[25]

---

23 Gilderman, *Juan Rodríguez de la Cámara* 65.

24 Diego de San Pedro, *Cárcel de Amor*, ed. Carmen Parilla (Barcelona: Critica, 1995) 3. ['Although I may be wanting in the self-restraint to hold my tongue, I do not lack the wit to see how much better it would be for me to be able to pride myself on what I refrained from saying than to have to rue what I have written. But although I know this to be so, even while I perceive this truth, I pursue my fantasy; and since I have chosen the worse course, I shall surely not go unpunished, for if through my ignorance I go astray, through my humiliation I shall pay for it'] (Keith Whinnom, trans., *Prison of Love*, by Diego de San Pedro [Edinburgh: Edinburgh UP, 1979] 3).

25 San Pedro, *Cárcel de Amor* 3-4. ['In truth, so far as the present work is concerned, I am the less to blame in that I embarked upon it more because of my duty of obedience than because of my desire to write; for it was your lordship who told me that I should compose some work in the style of a discourse which I sent to the Lady Marina Manuel . . . and in the end I chose the course most

Aside from his purported ignorance, the poet's most placatory device is the claim that the work had been commissioned and the poet did not want to appear disobedient toward either his master or his lady. Forgetfulness joins ranks with the other exonerating factors in his claim that he does not intentionally insult people but forgets what he had said before that might have found disfavor. All of these are *captatio benevolentiae* and exoneration strategies in the Chaucerian vein that signal the poet's unlimited license, now that he has made all the possible disclaimers. He furthermore gives the reader a glimpse of the medieval writer's psyche when he postulates that because of all the defects in his writing "yo estava determinado de cesar ya en el metro y en la prosa, por librar mi rudeza de juizios y mi espíritu de trabajos" (*Cárcel* 81) ['I was determined to compose nothing more either in verse or prose, so that I should not subject my poor talent to harsh criticism and might spare my spirit mortification' (Whinnom, *Prison* 4)]. The author prefers self-criticism to outside criticism, a strategy that is equally ironic and bolsters the author's power over his own auctorial fate.

San Pedro did not stop writing, despite his threat. How creative he actually was is illustrated in a seemingly negative and self-critical way in his *Desprecio de la Fortune* [Contempt of Fortune]. In an emulation of Chaucer's Retraction, he accuses himself of vain and profane works, now answering to a different authority, namely God, whose power over him would be much greater than the power of his earthly patrons. Nevertheless, the intra-auctorial picture contains elements of auctorial pride in his works. According to Keith Whinnom, several external factors converged to bring about his repentance for frivolous writings. In advanced years, San Pedro accompanied his master, Juan Tellez-Giron, into exile from court, a circumstance that might have led to serious contemplation of life's purpose and vicissitudes. Furthermore, influenced by San Pedro's reading of Boethius, the *Desprecio* targets the new subject of fortune, a subject appropriate for the aging Count.[26] Whinnom likewise supports a biographical reading highlighting San Pedro's isolated state and keen awareness of his age, which incites him to turn his thoughts toward the nether world and become vexed by the way he has spent his talents:[27]

> Mi seso lleno de canas,
> de mi consejo engañado,
> hasta aquí con obras vanas
> y en escrituras livianas
> siempre anduvo desterrado.
> Y pues carga ya la edad
> donde conosco mi yerro,
> afuera la liviandad,
> pues que ya mi vanidad
> ha complido su destierro.[28]

---

likely to cause me humiliation and that most indicated by my duty. It may be that I shall be censured if, in what I now write, I repeat some of the notions and phrases which I have already used in other works'] (Whinnom, *Prison of Love* 3-4).

26 Keith Whinnom, *Diego de San Pedro* (New York: Twayne, 1974) 27, 128-29.

27 Whinnom, *Diego de San Pedro* 128.

28 Diego de San Pedro, *Desprecio de la Fortuna, Obras completas*, eds. Dorothy S. Severin and Keith Whinnom, 5 vols. (Madrid: Unigraf, 1979) 3: 275-97, stanza 1. [My head is full of gray

Indeed, like other authors in the apology tradition, San Pedro capitalizes on the familiar dichotomy of gray hair and youthful errors. His frivolous works have, so far, separated him from true communion with God and have now, in a truly Petrarchan way, been confined to his youth, the time in which they can still be forgiven. The tone of the passage expresses a conscientious thought process leading to the decision that it is time to give up on the vanities of youth and poetry. Simultaneously, in the prose preface to the poem, the poet exonerates himself again with the patronage ploy: "Mas por servicio de Vuestra Señoria y de algunos señores grandes de quien me fue mandado que no passasse la vida en silencio" (*Desprecio* 273) [But for the service to your Lordship and the other great lords, who made it mandatory for me that I did not pass my life in silence]. He thereby assigns his poetic activity solely to the realm of court patronage and denies it personal intent. Whereas in the *Cárcel* the patronage excuse glosses over his possible poetic shortcomings, in the *Desprecio* he uses it to apologize for having composed poetry at all.

Whinnom attributes the love poetry repudiated in the *Desprecio* to the period during which San Pedro entertained the queen and court members, approximately 1480-1492.[29] The list of poems—reminiscent of the book lists of the ancient authors, as well as those of Bede, Gerald, and Chaucer—led by the *Cárcel*, represents an explicit rejection of earthly love:

> Aquella Cárcel de Amor
> que assí me plugo ordenar,
> ¡qué propria para amador,
> qué dulce para sabor,
> qué salsa para pecar!
> Y como la obra tal
> no tuvo en leerse calma,
> he sentido por mi mal
> cuán enemiga mortal
> fue la lengua para el alma.[30]

In the poet's description of the positive and negative effects of the *Cárcel* lies a certain ambivalence, a certain pride, almost nostalgic in tone. The *Cárcel* is explicitly identified as a manual for sinning and, because of that, it has become detrimental to the poet's salvation. He does not take all the responsibility, however, as he indicts the readers, who did not read it calmly and let it ignite the fires of passion in them.

Structurally, San Pedro's introductory apology stanzas are based on a trial-and-judgment pattern. In the first stanza, he acknowledges his sinful creative activity; in the second stanza, he establishes a connection between that activity and salvation; and in the third stanza, he identifies God as the Judge:

---

hair, of my mistaken counsel. Until now I have always gone banished with vain works and in licentious writings. And since I reached an age in which I recognize the errors of my youth, moreover the frivolity, since then my vanity has completed its exile].

29 Whinnom, *Diego de San Pedro* 121.

30 San Pedro, *Desprecio de la Fortuna* stanza 2. [That Prison of Love, which I so let command me, how suitable for the lover, how sweet for pleasure, desirable for sinning! And because the work was not read calmly, I have experienced the harm, how mortal an enemy was the tongue for the soul].

Y los yerros que ponía
en un Sermón que escreví,
como fue el amor la guía
la ceguedad que tenía
me hizo que no los vi.
Y aquellas cartas de amores
escriptas de dos en dos,
¿qué serán, dezí, señores,
sino mis acusadores
para delante de Dios?[31]

Almost sounding like a lawyer's plea, his rejection of the *Sermon*, another lovers' guide, harbors a rhetorical question, which could at least give the reader the chance to protest and offer a different answer than a plain affirmative sentence. The poet employs the rhetorical question to soften the preceding statements.

These discouraging-sounding disavowals of his works end with a repetition of a rhetorical question and retain their judgment structure by identifying parts of his literary production as material his accusers could use against him:

Y aquella copla y canción
que tú, mi seso, ordenavas
con tanta pena y passión
por salvar el coraçón
con la fe que allí le davas;
y aquellos romances hechos
(por mostrar el mal allí)
para llorar mis despechos,
¿qué serán sino pertrechos
con que tiren contra mí?[32]

The poet's emphasis on his literary efforts reminds us of the nostalgic, ambivalent, and proud tone of stanza 2. It is furthermore naturally suspicious that he claims to be the author of only one verse and one song, implying that not all of his lyric poetry would imperil his salvation. That also leads to the missing *La Pasión trovada* [The Versified Passion]; unfortunately, we cannot glean any chronological information from the work—namely whether it was written later. According to Whinnom, *La Pasión* had been printed several times before the *Desprecio* (it might actually have been his earliest work), but obviously, because of its content, it would not be included among the sinful works.[33] Such a separation of the wheat from the chaff, the dichotomy between *caritas* and *cupiditas*, echoes Chaucer, who presents the duality of his canon with the same, if not greater, ambivalence and ambiguity.

---

31 San Pedro, *Desprecio de la Fortuna* stanza 3. [And the errors that I have put in a Sermon which I have written, how love was the guide to ignorance, what happened that I did not see it. And those love letters, written by couples; what are they, my lords, if not my accusers in the sight of God?].

32 San Pedro, *Desprecio de la Fortuna* stanza 4. [And that verse and song, that you, my brain, have asserted with great pain and passion in order to save the heart with the belief that you gave him; and those romances made (to show the harm there) to lament my sins; what are they if not defense equipment that will be used against me?].

33 Whinnom, *Diego de San Pedro* 35, 36.

San Pedro's one-by-one enumeration of his works also serves to establish his canon of works cultivating love, as the poet never explicitly says that he no longer agrees with their contents but instead reveals both underlying pride and regret about this stage of his career. His moralistic judgment might hinge on his denominational affiliation (he converted from Judaism to Catholicism) in two ways: intra-auctorially he portrays himself as an old man who has overcome the lure of love poetry; intratextually the *Desprecio* expounds on the advantage of a serene denouncement of earthly delights.[34] Because the work he is about to write does not have a love interest, he invokes God's assistance before embarking on the new theme:

> Mas Tú, Señor eternal,
> me sey consuelo y abrigo
> con tu perdón general,
> que sin gracia divinal
> no sabré lo que me digo.
> Y pues Tú, me Dios Sagrado,
> de bondages eres fuente,
> plégate, Señor, de grado
> absolverme en lo passado
> y ayudarme en lo presente.[35]

Like others before him, the poet presents himself in a passive state in need of God's grace. He furthermore invokes the medieval auctorial hierarchy. God, who is at the top of the hierarchy and therefore is the disseminator of literary creativity, is asked to redeem the poet's language. That request also implies a certain exoneration of the poet since, because of his unredeemed state, he cannot compose works of *caritas* but only of *cupiditas*. The focus on the self-critical aspects of the *Desprecio* in the list of San Pedro's amorous works reveals that, although rejected by the poet from a moral standpoint, he obviously considers them valuable enough intra-auctorial documents deserving extensive individual attention and preservation for future audiences.[36]

On the other side of the Spanish apology tradition, the pro- and antifeminist debate raged. Half of the "convicted" antifeminists in the Spanish apology tradition are part of this chapter because they ironically rewrite themselves intra-auctorially. Some of the profeminists, Juan Rodríguez del Padrón, Juan de Mena, Diego de San Pedro, as well as Juan del Encina, a fence-straddler, have been represented in the first part of this chapter because they felt their allegiance to women and love did not align with the Christian master narrative and jeopardize their salvation.[37] Of the three categories of

---

34 Regula Langbehn-Rohland, *Zur Interpretation der Romane des Diego de San Pedro*, Studia Romanica 18 (Heidelberg: C. Winter, 1970) 24-25.

35 San Pedro, *Desprecio de la Fortuna* stanza 5. [But my eternal Lord, console and shelter me with your general forgiveness, since without your divine grace, I cannot understand what you tell me. And then, my Holy God, you take me out of the fetters, Lord, absolve me in the future and help me in the present].

36 Langbehn-Rohland, *Zur Interpretation der Romane des Diego de San Pedro* 25.

37 For a list of the participants in "El Debate," see Augustín Boyer, *Estudio descriptivo del* Libro de las virtuosas e claras mugeres *de Don Alvaro de Luna: fuentes, género y ubicación en la debate feminista del siglo XV* (Diss. Berkeley: U of California, 1988); Jacob Ornstein, "La Misoginía y el

French antifeminist authors, only one applies to the Spanish authors. The compiler or translator persona and the trial structure are conspicuously absent from the Spanish tradition; the lyrical "poet" persona is the only full-fledged representative of the earlier French models, a shift one might explain with the theory that the Spanish antifeminist strand was not influenced by the French sources but rather by Juvenal and Boccaccio.[38] Alfonso Martínez de Toledo, Pere Torroella, Juan de Tapia, and Hernán de Mexía, however, participate in "El Debate" to some extent and in that stylized form of discourse employ irony to its fullest in order to assert women's negative side after all.[39]

9.5. Alfonso Martínez de Toledo

The irony in Alfonso Martínez de Toledo's (1397/8-1468) work *Arçipreste de Talavera o Corbacho* (1438) is inherent in its structure, which deals with women's role in human love in the prologue, four books and an epilogue, called *demanda*.[40] The first part, a large *Ars Amatoria*, actually functions like a *Remedia Amoris*, in which earthly love is rejected through the author's pointing out all its pitfalls. Consequently, in the second part theoretical arguments against love are concretized and applied to the objects of earthly love, women. There the author repeats and asserts such stock antifeminist arguments as, for instance, that women are the main cause of man's perdition. In a typical antifeminist manner, the Archpriest exempts a particular group of women in order not to portray himself as completely narrow-minded (as Jean de Meun had done with his claim not to want to offend any women *alive*): "E por quanto, al presente algunos viçios de mal bevir declararé en parte de mugeres; esto se entienda

---

profeminismo en la literatura castellana," *Revista de Filologia Hispanica* 3 (1941): 219-32; here 220-21; and Kenneth R. Scholberg, *Sátira e invectiva en la España medieval* (Madrid: Editorial Gredos, S. A., 1971) 272-80.

38 Ornstein, "La Misoginía y el profeminismo en la literatura castellana" 221. The *Corbaccio*'s influence was extensive in Spain and definitely applies to the Archpriest of Talavera. Boccaccio, however, served both sides in "El Debate," a fact that is often overlooked and explains the literary conventions inherent in these diatribes for and against women. For instance, "Queen, Doña María, was greatly incensed at the brutal and villainous attack of Talavera. She called upon defenders to uphold woman's honor, and several of the noblest of her courtiers and some poets sallied forth as the paladins of the superior sex, battling as knights in a tournament for their incomparable Dulcineas and Lauras" (Barbara Matulka, *The Novels of Juan de Flores and Their European Diffusion: A Study in Comparative Literature* [Geneva: Slatkine Reprints, 1974] 13). One of the poets singing women's praises was Mosen Diego de Valera, who wrote the *Tratado en deffension de virtuosas mugeres*, which patterns itself after Boccaccio's *De Claris Mulieribus* (Matulka, *The Novels of Juan de Flores and Their European Diffusion* 14) and thus uses Satan to drive out Beelzebub.

39 Torroella actually cites Alain de Chartier's *La Belle dame sans mercy* "to confirm his own sentiments on the tyranny of love" (Hoffman 57, n. 12).

40 He was a chaplain at the court of Juan II (Matulka, *The Novels of Juan de Flores and Their European Diffusion* 9).

de aquellas que viçios e mal usar de sí partir sería imposible, las virtuosas, honestas e buenas como oro de escoria apartando: que si lo malo non fuese reprovado, lo bueno non sería loado."[41] This passage functions both as a feeble apology and a strong justification of what is to come as well as a clever ploy capitalizing on human nature, as most women in the audience would not automatically associate themselves with the wicked but the virtuous group and therefore would not accuse the Archpriest.

In Book II, the Archpriest does not contrast good and bad women but women and men. He defends Book III intratextually: "E por quanto el intento de la obra principalmente de reprobación de amor terrenal, el amor de Dios loando, e porque fasta aquí el amor de las mugeres fue reprovado, conviene quel amor de los ombres non se loado . . . E por quanto comúnmente los omnres no son comprehendidos como las mugeres so reglas generales—esto por el seso mayor e más juizio que alcançan— conviene, puea, particularmente fablar de cada uno segund su qualidad."[42] An analysis of Book III proves that the Archpriest's attempt at achieving parity by describing men's nature and qualities is again only a badly disguised slap in the face for women since all of the examples of reproachable male conduct can be attributed to the intervention of a bad woman.[43] Thus the Archpriest's attempts to camouflage his antifeminist sentiments by attacking men with the same accusations are "formulaic" as well as highly ironic, and often resemble "afterthoughts."[44]

In the epilogue, the *demanda*, Martínez retracts his previous attacks on women. Unfortunately, there is some controversy over the authenticity of the *demanda*. for only the printed editions, not the manuscript, contain the epilogue, in form of a letter.[45] Erich von Richthofen thinks it is genuine; Martín de Riquer, Mario Penna, and Christine Whitbourn assume that it is apocryphal, because, as Whitbourn points out, "it would constitute a complete denial of everything Martínez has been at pains to establish in the rest of his work."[46] This is exactly why the work becomes interesting

41 Alfonso Martínez de Toledo, *Arçipreste de Talavera o Corbacho*, ed. Michael Gerli (Madrid: Ediciones Cátedra, 1979) 144. ['Let it be understood, since I shall presently explain some of the vices and evil-living of women, that I speak only of those who find it impossible to put away their vices and wicked ways, refining out, as gold from dross, the virtuous, the honest, and the good, for if evil is not reproved, virtue is not praised'] (Lesley Byrd Simpson, trans., *Little Sermons on Sin: The Archpriest of Talavera*, by Alfonso Martínez de Toledo [Berkeley: U of California P, 1959] 100).

42 Alfonso Martínez de Toledo, *Arçipreste de Talavera o Corbacho* 204. ['Since the purpose of this book is the reprobation of worldly love and praise of the love of God, and since up to this point I have reproved the love of women, it would be not fitting for me to praise the love of men. . . . And, since men are not commonly reproved in this as women are—this because of their greater sense and judgment—it will be fitting, then, to speak of each man according to his nature'] (Simpson, *Little Sermons on Sin* 164).

43 Michael Gerli, ed., introduction, *Arçipreste de Talavera o Corbacho*, by Alfonso Martínez de Toledo (Madrid: Ediciones Cátedra, 1979) 15-57; here 24.

44 Michael Gerli, *Alfonso Martínez de Toledo* (Boston: Twayne, 1976) 30.

45 Per Nykrog, "Playing Games with Fiction: *Les Quinzes Joyes de Mariage, Il Corbaccio, El Arçipreste de Talavera*," *The Craft of Fiction: Essays in Medieval Poetics*, ed. Leigh A Arrathoon (Rochester, MI: Solaris Press, 1984) 423-51; here 443.

46 Erich F. von Richthofen, "Fünfzig Jahre *Arçipreste-de-Talavera-Studien*: ein Überblick," *Zeitschrift für Romanische Philologie* 104 (1988): 13-19; here 19 and Christine J. Whitbourn, *The*

to this study; but the claim that it denies everything prior to it cannot be maintained when we examine Martínez's strategy in the *demanda*, which divulges the ironic nature of the entire work.

The *demanda* echoes the literary fate of Euripides, who was attacked by an angry mob of women, as depicted in Aristophanes' play *Thesmophoriazousae*. Having fallen asleep while thinking about his work, Martínez dreams he is being attacked by a furious bunch of women demanding an apology for the misogyny in his treatise on love. Like Euripides, Martínez placates the women. The difference between Euripides and Martínez lies in the dream construct, which brings the *demanda* closer to Chaucer's *Legend of Good Women*. As in the *Legend*, the *demanda* is divided into a dream and a "waking" part; the charges of misogyny are leveled against the authors in the dream part, whereas the atonement happens in the waking state, a strategy that helps to assert the literariness of these constructs. The ironic nature of Martínez's palinode is most striking in that the author devotes about half of the *demanda* to the description of the women abusing him both physically and verbally, leaving him basically no other choice but to recant. Thus when he wakes up terrified, he sighs and responds to the female coercion with "[m]as, con arrepentimiento demando perdón dellas, e me lo otorguen o que quede el libro y yo sea mal quisto para mientra biva de tanta linda dama, o que pena cruel sea" (*demanda* 306) [But with repentance I ask forgiveness from the ladies, and grant it to me or leave the book so I will not be welcome in my life in front of all these beautiful ladies, oh what a cruel pain]. If one were to look at this apology independently, it could very well contradict what has been expounded in the main part of the text. If one takes into consideration the literary construct erected for this purpose, however, as has been suggested by Michael Gerli, the apology is blatantly ironic and does not really retract anything because in the process of apologizing for having done women wrong, Martinez uses the very same devastating arguments in the treatise against them by showing their viciousness and brutality.[47] Therefore, his initially antifeminist position is confirmed and the retraction is, at best, the author's ironic footnote to a misogynist work, appearing to be an apology on its surface only.

"Arçipreste de Talavera" and the Literature of Love, Occasional Papers in Modern Languages 7 (Hull: U of Hull P, 1970) 60. In a stylistic comparison both the main part of the book and the *demanda* show "frequent use of exclamations; colloquial speech; and form of familiar address directed at the reader" (Gerli, *Alfonso Martínez de Toledo* 33). The differences are that the "tone is sportive and gallant, and the writer mockingly uses religious terminology" in the *demanda* (Gerli, *Alfonso Martínez de Toledo* 34). Whitbourn disputes Alfonso's authorship of the *demanda*: "Moreover, the acceptance of the *demanda* as the work of Martínez would imply that he himself regarded his work as anti-feminist, whereas he seems to have made a real attempt to emphasize its didactic nature and to keep a balance in his treatment of the two sexes. It would be surprising, therefore, if he had added an epilogue in which he recognized his responsibility for an anti-feminist treatise" (*The "Arçipreste de Talavera" and the Literature of Love* 62). I disagree with Whitbourn insofar as the treatment seems decidedly unbalanced and slanted in favor of men, and as the work fits in the mold of an antifeminist work complete with an ironic recantation.

47   Gerli, introduction, *Arçipreste de Talavera o Corbacho* 27-28. Richthofen speculates that the author might have really been attacked by women (although mainly verbally) after the publication of his book, which might have prompted him to write his apology ("Alfonso Martínez de Toledo und sein *Arçipreste de Talavera*, ein kastilisches Prosawerk des 15. Jahrhunderts," *Zeitschrift für romanische Philologie* 61 (1941): 417-537; here 464, n. 1).

As Colbert Nepaulsingh concludes, "the epilogue, therefore, is artistically essential to the *Corbacho* as a whole, especially because it explains the book's existence as a cautious example of the vice the book itself condemns. It is by no means an unexpected ending, nor is it a joke or a retraction of what the rest of the book stands for."[48] Because the *demanda* is consciously and blatantly a part of the *Corbacho*, not a detachable appendage that can be construed either as a sincere repentance or as a literary device, it further develops the apology tradition.

9.6. Pere Torroella

In contrast to Alfonso Martínez de Toledo's misogynist diatribe, the offense committed by Pere Torroella, a bilingual Catalan and Castilian writer prospering between 1436 and 1486, appears to be petty and undeserving of the outrageous reaction it received.[49] Retraction becomes integral to Torroella's work also, albeit in an intertextual and not intratextual fashion, as he is a lyric poet dabbling in the highly stylized and ironic pro- and antifeminist debate, which necessitates a retraction as part of the

---

48 Nepaulsingh, *Towards a History of Literary Composition in Medieval Spain* 159. Some critics have drawn intertextual and interauctorial parallels between Alfonso Martínez de Toledo's *Arçipreste de Talavera, o Corbacho* and both Boccaccio's *Corbaccio* and, in its title, *Reprobación del amor*, the third book of Andreas Capellanus' *De amore* (Gerli, introduction, *Arçipreste de Talavera o Corbacho* 20). On an intertextual and interauctorial level, Gerli also considers the *demanda* in the *Arçipreste de Talavera* an ironic imitation of the retraction in the third book of Andreas Capellanus's *De amore*, (introduction, *Arçipreste de Talavera o Corbacho* 45), a work it was proven to use as a source (Richthofen, "Fünfzig Jahre *Arçipreste-de-Talavera-Studien* 15). This interpretation allows for two reactions. On the one hand, it contradicts the previous point both in that the *demanda* is not out of line with the ideology of the work it is attached to and in that the *Arçipreste* never makes a positive case for human love, as the *De amore* does in its first two books. Thus, the *De amore* represents two different views of love, while the *Arçipreste de Talavera* stays on a single track in its denial of noble human love. On the other hand, because of the sustained negative ethos of Talavera's work and the lack of anything counterbalancing it, unlike Ovid's and Andreas' works, which are tempered by their respective Books III, the apology provided by the Archpriest could in its surface meaning alone function as that moderating, albeit "scherzendes" [jocular], element (Richthofen, "Fünfzig Jahre *Arçipreste-de-Talavera-Studien* 17). Although Richthofen also acknowledges the *demanda* as a "natural" counterpart to the main body of the work, in the vein of the *Reprobatio* and the *Remedia Amoris*, harboring the central medieval poles of "'buen amor'" and "'amor mundano'" and their extensions, profeminism and antifeminism ("Fünfzig Jahre *Arçipreste-de-Talavera-Studien* 19), he too fails to notice that the Arçipreste rejects human love in most of its forms. The author cannot help concluding his work with yet another jibe at women: "Pero ¡guay del cuitado que siempre solo duerme con dolor de axaqueca e en su casa rueca nunca entra todo el año! Este es el pejor daño" (*demanda* 306) [But how about the wretched man who sleeps alone with a headache and does not enter his spouse's bedroom all year long. That is the worst ever].

49 Peter Cocozzella, "Pere Torroella: Poet of the Catalan Pre-Renaissance," *Hispanófila* 86 (1986): 1-14; here 4; Boyer, *Estudio descriptivo del* Libro de las virtuosas e claras mugeres *de Don Alvaro de Luna* 273; and Whitbourn, The *"Arçipreste de Talavera" and the Literature of Love* 30.

literary game. Torroella's literary career was spent mostly in writing love poetry exalting the virtues of women; the incident that turned him into medieval Spain's worst woman-hater occurred when he wrote "Maldezir de mugeres" [Diatribe Against Women], which Peter Cocozzella characterizes as "a spiritless assemblage of stock-in-trade motifs derived from a long line of misogynist diatribes."[50] This twelve-stanza poem against women, considered a literary game and Torroella's exploitation of a contemporary literary topic in Spain, fueled both the slogans of misogynists and the anger of woman-defenders.[51] The "Maldezir" became the pivotal point of a literary battle of the sexes, with one camp viewing Torroella as the defender of men and the other seeing him as the vilest offender of women. His reputation was so bad that the fifteenth-century author Juan Flores chose to make him and his poetic exercise a central part of his novel *Grisel y Mirabella*.[52] As evident from other auctorial examples, Torroella was not alone in writing such a work, as misogynist literature had been developing for many centuries from its roots in ancient literature. His work merely happened to get embroiled in the antifeminist climate of fifteenth-century Spain, which was itself a counteroffensive against the glorification of women in the troubadour lyrics, Marian cult, and *dolce stil nuovo*. Although Torroella unleashes a vicious assault on women in general, he makes the obligatory exceptions by excluding both his own lover and "good women," ironically exonerating them on creative grounds. The statement that "Muger es un animal" [woman is an animal] leads the author to conclude that therefore "E, pues les son naturales / Quando se demuestran tales, / Que son sin culpa concluyo."[53] This conclusion is naturally deceptive and actually enhances the accusation of woman's animal nature.

The "Razonamiento . . . en deffensión de las donas" stands as a protracted and pedantic intertextual example opposing the views expressed in the "Maldezir." Forgotten is the animal nature and invoked is the "pietat, beniuolencia, suauidat er verguensa"[54] [piety, benevolence, gentleness, and modesty] of women. Here we find Torroella's apology for writing "las coplas aquéllas que de mugeres mal dizen" (296) [those stanzas that cursed women]. His apology is founded on the excuse that the passion of love made him write the "Maldezir": "con desatiento de enamorada passion . . . e a venjança sin injura" (296) [with worry of enamored passion . . . and a revenge without harm]. As Barbara Matulka points out, the author had addressed his disillu-

---

50 Cocozzella, "Pere Torroella: Poet of the Catalan Pre-Renaissance" 5.

51 Charles V. Aubrun, *Le Chansonnier espagnol d'Herberay des Essarts* (Bordeaux: Feret, 1951) XLVIII, XLIX; Scholberg, *Sátira e invectiva en la España medieval* 275; and Gilderman, *Juan Rodríguez de la Cámara* 108.

52 For a comprehensive account, see Matulka, *The Novels of Juan de Flores and Their European Diffusion*, especially 111ff.

53 Pere Torroella, "Maldezir de mugeres," *The Works of Pere Torroella: A Catalan Writer of the Fifteenth Century*, ed. Pedro Bach y Rita (New York: Instituto de las Españas, 1930) 199-215, stanza IXa. [And then they are natural when they prove like that; I conclude that they are blameless].

54 Pere Torroella, "Razonamiento de Pere Torroella e deffensión de las donas contra los maldizientes por satisfacción de unas coplas que en dezir mal de aquéllas compuso," *The Works of Pere Torroella: A Catalan Writer of the Fifteenth Century*, ed. Pedro Bach y Rita (New York: Instituto de las Españas, 1930) 296-306; here 297.

sionment with love, passion, and women in previous love poems; his initial attack on women fuses a personal animosity with the impersonal hostility found in the writers before him, since most of his diatribe and motivation is common to other authors as well.[55] In the vein of other medieval misogynists, his remedy consists of singing women's praises: "E por que, senyoras, creays al juzio que tantos bienes de vosotras percibe si no obsegado de passión consentiera a la lengua refferir el contrario, vos suplico queraes ver las razones qu'en deffenzión vuestra contra los mal dizientes me occorren."[56]

In the "Razonamiento," Pere Torroella practices contradictory intertextuality by unearthing the "most commonplace and tritest arguments which the feminist debate had offered"[57] and employing them in his defense of women. With academic pedantry, he inquires whether the women-slanderers cursed women in general, or one in particular. Applying the principle of equality, he condones the slandering of a particular woman as justified, for both men and women possess evil traits. Women-hating across the board is a more serious offense, however, and needs to be examined physiologically to decide whether evil dwells in women's souls or their bodies. Since the physiological argument does not hold water, he brings out as positive criteria mental qualities, such as piety, benevolence, gentleness, and modesty, which are considered more distinctively feminine. The highlight of the recantation and the most direct ironic contradiction to the "Maldezir" lie in the debate about who is more perfect: Eve or Adam. He comes to exactly the opposite conclusion from the "Maldezir": "Adam rustiferoçe, peloso, a la naturaleza de los animales brutos parasciendo; a Eua, blanca, suaue, delicada e lisa, más angélica ydea que forma vmana representado."[58] Now he has almost meticulously reversed the textuality of his first text, and the women no longer possess an evil nature but instead develop reprehensible traits. He furthermore ironically inverts the common allegory that Eve represents the senses, whereas Adam represents the intellect. (Senses subvert the intellect and overturn reason.) Simultaneously, though, he bemoans women's having been barred from intellectual life. Other blatant ironies are the author's claim that he and other misogynists must have had personal reasons for their diatribes and his citing a few negative female role models among his enumeration of famous good women.

Torroella's almost clinical approach and his use of irony both point to the author's participation in the literary pro- and antifeminist battle and to his execution of an academic exercise. His retraction exudes a tone of erudition lacking in his antifeminist writings. For a retraction, it is "heavy-footed and impersonal"; Matulka presents three theories explaining the recantation:

---

55 Matulka, *The Novels of Juan de Flores and Their European Diffusion* 115.
56 Torroella, "Razonamiento de Pere Torroella e deffensión de las donas contra los maldizientes" 296. [And in order that you, Ladies, may believe the mind that could perceive so many virtues in you—if blinded by passion, it would not allow the tongue to say otherwise—I pray you to consider the reasons that occur to me in your defense against the slanderers].
57 Matulka, *The Novels of Juan de Flores and Their European Diffusion* 117.
58 Torroella, "Razonamiento de Pere Torroella e deffensión de las donas contra los maldizientes" 297. [Adam, coarse and ferocious, hairy, by nature among the brutish animals; Eve a white, soft, more angelic idea represented by human shape].

1. Torrellas was sincere but uninspired and unintelligent in his defense of woman, whereas he had been vigorous and brilliant in his attack. 2. Torrellas was insincere in his "Retraction,"—and this exactly what Juan de Flores suggests in his novel . . . and the very impersonality of his trite arguments would then betray his lack of conviction. 3. Torrellas was writing a mock-earnest parody of the Arguments of Defense.[59]

Given the ironic nature of the second apology strand and the imitative nature of "El Debate," I advocate the third explanation, since parodies abound in the literary battle of the sexes. No matter what the real reason for the recantation, Pedro Bach y Rita claims that it was futile and that Torroella could never quite shake his infamy,[60] as evidenced by Juan Flores' representing him as the incarnation of a misogynist.

9.7. Juan de Tapia

Two other Spanish writers who imitate Torroella's apologetic method support and extend the parody theory. The first one is Juan de Tapia, a writer at the court of Alfonso V de Aragón,[61] who provides a commentary, "La Glosa," on one of Torroella's short poems, "Yerra con poco saber." In that fifteen-stanza commentary, a combination of intertextuality and interauctoriality, Tapia lets the venom of his misogynistic pen spew out, but at the end of the poem he hastens to add that he is not to blame for its contents: "Ha sallido de la Glosa, y despídese de la dama que le mandó glosar la cancion, y muestra cómo lo hizo más con gana de obedescer, que con intencion de publicar la verdad."[62] The poet tries to excuse himself with the pretense of patronage. In that, he raises three important concerns. First, the lady might have requested a gloss, but did she expect a barrage of antifeminist slurs? Second, why would a woman commission an antifeminist piece? Third, the poet remarks on his strategy of obeying the lady's wish rather than publishing the truth, which revives the "truth in poetry" concern. In this case, he seems to imply that what he wrote might not have been the truth, but his patroness made him compose it, which in turn charges the lady with antifeminism and releases him.

The last stanza supports that highly ironic strategy:

Veys aquí, dama hermosa,
la canción que vos glosastès;
no digo que la trobastes,

59 Matulka, *The Novels of Juan de Flores and Their European Diffusion* 118-19.

60 Pedro Bach y Rita, ed. *The Works of Pere Torroella: A Catalan Writer of the Fifteenth Century* (New York: Instituto de las Españas, 1930) 51.

61 Francisca Vendrell Gallostra, *La corte literaria de Alfonso V de Aragón y tres poetas de la misma* (Madrid: Archivos, 1933) 5. For new autobiographical data, see José Carlos Rovira, "Nuevos documentos para la biografía de Juan de Tapia," *Anales de Literatura Española* 5 (1986-87): 437-60.

62 Juan de Tapia, "La Glosa," *Cancionero General de Hernando del Castillo*, 2nd ed., 2 vols. (Madrid: La Sociedad de Bibliofilos Españoles, 1882) 2: 70-72; here 72. [You have finished the parody, said goodbye to the lady who sent it to you, and show that you did it more to obey than with the intention of making the truth public].

mas que hezistes la glosa,
pues que vos me los mandastes,
c'os den la pena, señora,
pues tenés la culpa della,
y con vos mal la hechora
tengan todas la querella
y á mi déxenme sin ella.[63]

To the obvious reason for Tapia's protecting himself, namely not to fall out of favor with his lady, Matulka adds that his excuse could have served as a precaution not to be considered a disciple of Torroella and thus become an obvious target of the profeminist camp.[64] Another possibility, as suggested by Hernán Mexía in the next poem, might be that in Spain women also participate in the parodying of the literary quarrel that raged through the fifteenth century. This dimension would definitely heighten the ironic intention of these antifeminist apologies even more.

9.8. Hernán Mexía

The second imitator of Pere Torroella, Hernán Mexía, who was also generally an advocate of women in his literary endeavors, employs the same excuse and the same intertextual and interauctorial ploy as Juan de Tapia. He claims to have composed the "Otras suyas en que descubre los defectos de las condiciones de las mugeres, por mandado de dos damas," a satire on women, only after having been prompted to by lady friends of his. Thus the poet prefaces his work with an apology to the women responsible for his creativity, delineating in a patronage excuse that he does not actually subscribe to the ideas expounded in the poem:

Porfiays, damas, que diga
al reues de quanto dixe,
induziendo que persiga
aquella seta enemiga
la qual por vos contradixe;
pero no tanto vos teme,
consintiendo vuestro ruego
mi lengua, porque sse atreue
a tocar, quemar, ni queme
muchas buenas con su fuego.[65]

---

63   de Tapia, "La Glosa" stanza 15. [You see here, beautiful lady, the song which you had parodied; I do not say that you wrote it, but that you did parody it when you sent it to me. You should be sorry, my lady, and the fault is yours, and you must accept the credit for its qualities, leaving me without blame].

64   Matulka, *The Novels of Juan de Flores and Their European Diffusion* 121.

65   Hernán Mexía, "Otras suyas en que descubre los defectos de las condiciones de las mugeres, por mandado de dos damas," *Cancionero Castellano del siglo XV*, ed. R. Foulché-Delbosc, 2 vols. (Madrid: Bailly-Bailliére, 1912) 1: 280-85, stanza 1. [Be stubborn, ladies, and say the opposite of what I said, inducing one to pursue that poisonous mushroom, which is contradicted by you; but I

The poet wants to insure that his intentions will not be mistaken and that he will not be branded as a one-sided poet.

In this intratextual apology, the poet warns the reader of what is to come partly because apologies both at the outset and the end possess the forcefulness of a cyclic structure; Mexía reiterates his commissioned state again at the end of the poem. Furthermore, an apology at the beginning has the added advantage of being an advance warning, a safety valve for angry readers:

> Pero por satisfazer
> vuestra causa principal,
> que es querer, saber y ver
> quanto mi flaco saber
> sabe bien dezir de mal;
> de vuestro mando vencido,
> de vuestra gracia rogado,
> plazeme con tal partido
> que en publico ni encondido
> no se impute a mi el pecado.[66]

In this self-absolution, Mexía emphasizes the author/patron relationship as a means of escaping accountability. He had good reason to apologize for what was to come. Mexía calls Torroella's writings as "verdad como Euangelio" [true as the Gospel] and then invokes on antifeminist *auctoritates*, such as Boccaccio. Matulka concludes that Mexía's attack on women surpasses Torroella's vitriolic satire and was part of a courtly literary game, one in which women obviously took part.[67] The delicacy of the matter and the great quarrel it had brought on all over Europe, however, force the poet to make it amply clear that the presented views are not his, as other writers have used the ancient sources; he can both criticize and exonerate himself for having written an antifeminist piece.

Despite these extended and repeated self-exonerations, Mexía did not seem to feel comfortable in his role, since he addresses this topic again interauctorially in order to shift the blame even farther away from himself. In the "Pensado que unas coplas que halló en vn cancionero de mal dezir de mugeres eran suyas," Mexía attempts to implicate his friend J. Alvarez Gato in the authorship of his "Otras suyas":[68] "no fue, no, de cauallero / dezir tan mal de mugeres."[69] He accuses Gato of having wanted to curry

---

do not fear so much consenting to the use of my tongue, because it dares to feel and burn, but does not burn the good with its fire].

66 Mexía, "Otras suyas en que descubre los defectos de las condiciones de las mugeres, por mandado de dos damas" stanza 3. [But in order to satisfy your main cause, which is to desire, to know and to see how much my feeble knowledge knows to speak well of evil; conquered by your order, implored by your gentility, it pleases me with great interest that it is neither concealed from the public nor that one can accuse me of a sin].

67 Matulka, *The Novels of Juan de Flores and Their European Diffusion* 125.

68 Bach y Rita, *The Works of Pere Torroella* 67.

69 Hernán Mexía, "Pensado que unas coplas que halló en vn cancionero de mal dezir de mugeres eran suyas," *Cancionero Castellano del siglo XV*, ed. R. Foulché-Delbosc, 2 vols. (Madrid: Bailly-Bailliére, 1912) 1: 276-77; here 276. [No "caballero" should ever speak so badly about women].

favor with Torroella: "gane las gracias Torrellas / de obra tan enemiga" ("Pensado" 276) [again Torroella's favors with a work so hostile]. Mexía finally blames Gato of having given in to perverse pleasures and done much harm:

asy las coplas y versos
de mal dezir quescreuistes
por vnos autos peruersos
y por otros mas diuersos
dañaron quanto hezistes.[70]

Because of these lines, a literary quarrel ensued between Gato and Mexía. The abundance of material that sprung up in the fifteenth century in favor of and against women testifies to the immense interest the pro- and antifeminist debate aroused, but it also suggests that the "repentant antifeminists" in the Spanish apology tradition participated in it. Consequently, their literary pro- and antifeminist writings are both highly ironic.

In summary, the Spanish apology tradition centers on women, both in their negative role as the cause of troubadours' veering from the course of the Christian master narrative, and in their role as recipients of ironic apologies for auctorial antifeminism. Ramon Llull exemplifies the troubadour's redirection of his creative effort to Christian subjects using a redeemed language. Juan Ruiz, Juan Rodríguez del Padrón, and Diego de San Pedro all repent amatory writings but also display a healthy portion of auctorial pride in their works, which ironically assert their authorship despite the self-criticism.[71] The other Spanish authors, Alfonso de Martínez de Toledo, Pere Torroella,

---

70 Mexía, "Pensado que unas coplas que halló en vn cancionero de mal dezir de mugeres eran suyas" 276-77. ['Thus the stanzas and verses of bad-mouthing, which you wrote for perverse reasons and others more diverse, harmed everything you wrote].

71 Because of its slight self-criticism, I am not discussing the prologue to Don Juan Manuel's fourteenth-century Spanish story collection, *Count Lucanor*; I am including a passage here, however, possibly to compare to Chaucer's similar passage in the Retraction (see page 212ff. in Chapter 8): "Et Dios, que es complido et compildoi de todoo lot buenos [fechos], por la su merçed et por la su piadat, quiera que los que este libro leyeren, que se aprovechen dél a serviçio de Dios et para salvamiento de sus almas et aprovechamiento de sus cuerpos; asî commo Él sabe que yo, don Iohan, lo digo a essa entención. et lo que y fallaren que non es tan bien dicho, non pongan culpa a la mi entençión, mas pónganla a la mengua del mio entendimiento. Et si alguna cosa fallaren bien dicha o aprovechosa, gradéscanlo a Dios, ca Él es aquél por quien todos los buenos dichos et fechos se dizen et se fazen" (Don Juan Manuel, *El Conde Lucanor*, eds. Carlos Alvar and Pilar Palanco [Barcelona: Planeta, 1984] 8). ['And may God, Who is the Author and Maker of all good deeds, wish by His Grace and Holiness that those who read this book profit from it in God's service to the salvation of their souls and the good of their bodies, just as He knows that I, Don Juan, speak with this intention. And whatever they find therein that is not well said, let it not be blamed upon my intent, but rather on the weakness of my understanding. And if they find something well said or profitable, let them thank God for it, as He is the One through Whom all good sayings and deeds are spoken and done'] (John E. Keller, L. Clark Keating, and Barbara E. Gaddy, trans., *The Book of Count Lucanor and Patronio: A Translation of Don Juan Manuel's* El Conde Lucanor [New York: Peter Lang, 1993] 52. Both Don Juan Manuel's and Chaucer's passages present the typical *captatio benevolentiae* strategies of medieval authors. For a comparative study on Don Juan Manuel and Chaucer, see Jesus Serrano-Reyes, *Didactismo y moralismo en Geoffrey Chaucer y Don Juan Manuel: Un estudio comparativo textual* (Cordoba, Spain: U of Cordoba, 1995).

Juan de Tapia, and Hernán Mexía, participate in the pro- and antifeminist debate of the fifteenth century, creating an intertextual, interauctorial, and intratextual pattern of affirmation and rejection of women in the most outrageously ironic way. Blanket condemnations and praises attest to the character of their works as literary games. This leads us back to the claim in the introduction that the Stesichorean Ur-apology was one in which writing prompted a reaction from gods or women, which in turn led authors to write an apology for personal safety or fear of damnation. In the later Middle Ages, apologies firmly developed into an increasingly more literary, and therefore more ambiguous and ironic, concept having broader political, theological, philosophical, and literary ramifications. In the concluding chapter we will encounter a group that so far did not fit into the mostly-male apology paradigms: women writers and their apology strategies.

CHAPTER 10

Conclusion: Gender Differences and General Ruminations

This study has outlined the history and anatomy of the European apology tradition from the sixth century BCE to 1500, encompassing the apologies of more than sixty male authors—but only one woman: Proba, a new late-antiquity convert to Christianity. Why this dearth of women participating in this literary phenomenon? Feminist critic Elaine Showalter claims that men and women read differently because of the way they are socialized; men and women also write differently in the European apology tradition. The concepts of intertextuality and intratextuality were among the theoretical parameters for studying these self-critical authors. Most of the male authors apologize intertextually in a work in atonement for a previous literary offense and thus provide examples of *post-culpam* apologies. Medieval women writers, however, have a different *modus operandi*, apologizing intratextually during the literary creation. Both forms of auctorial self-criticism are progressive tactics that do not retard but rather engender literary creation, as they allow the authors to situate themselves within the creative cosmos, a cosmos differentiated by gender, however. Although men call themselves sinners, guilty of literary offenses, they do not feel they have to apologize for their gender. Instead, they pass the blame onto women. Female authors trying to appease male censors cannot pass the blame onto men, at least not overtly—so, in a highly sagacious manner, they criticize themselves because of their gender and then often authorize themselves with the help of God, the Master Author. These tactics are seen in Baudonivia of Poitiers, Dhuoda of Uzès, Hugeberc von Hildesheim, Hrotswitha von Gandersheim, Hildegard von Bingen, Mechthild von Magdeburg, and Teresa de Cartagena.

A summary of the authors discussed so far shows that during the Graeco-Roman period self-critical authors apologize mainly to divinities and women, primarily in *post-culpam* attempts to alleviate or avert punishment. Most of the apologies to women are ironic and antifeminist. These elements of irony and antifeminism temporarily vanish as the apology tradition moves into the early Christian realm, in which apologies are prompted by a theological concern about the place of one's literary works in the sight of God. These apologies are primarily addressed to God and secondarily to a general Christian audience, and combine Christian humility with Latin rhetorical devices. The tension between classical antiquity and Christianity lived on in the *trivium* education of medieval authors, causing a schizophrenic environment for writing and culminating in the medieval theory that language signifies only as an imitation of the Christian master narrative and the hierarchical medieval view of authorship. These notions express a medieval philosophical concern about language and its role, and therefore the role of the author, in cosmic history.

Most medieval apologies belong to the first and second strands, apologies to God for secular works and apologies to women, which are tied together by the specifically misogynistic treatment of women. The first apology strand develops in the Middle Ages from a concept tied to the contrast between pagan fables and Christian truth to the inherently medieval dichotomy of earthly love and spiritual love, accompanied by the trappings of *contemptus mundi*, the "youth vs. old age" topos, and *contemptus feminae*. Several authors of both the first and second strands shroud their auctorial activity in translator's, compiler's, or scribe's robes to mislead the audience as to their place in the auctorial hierarchy.

Medieval apologies to women appear in highly ironic contexts and are mainly insincere and often as misogynistic as the works for which they repent, because the antifeminist treatment is part of the game. These apologies for misogyny provide a highly overt outlet for misogynistic views; in contrast, apologies to God contain a more deeply-rooted and insidious antifeminism that can be traced to biblical precedents.

Recantation of a youthful secular work initially implicitly and later explicitly denotes a rejection of love poetry, which has at its center—at least for the most part—women. A repudiation of love therefore implies a rejection of woman; woman became the literary "other," a "persona non grata" who had to be removed from the literary creation in order for the author to achieve spiritual union with divinity. Women were literally written out of the text. Even though the first apology strand issues apologies to God, its repudiation of women and love lets me conclude that almost the entire apology is unified through its underlying antifeminist inter- and subtext. Apologies to women, even ironic ones, were possible in the Graeco-Roman world because women were part of the religious mythology of their cultures, whereas in the Judeo-Christian realm, God is represented as male. This male-privileging creation text, coupled with Jewish and early Christian patriarchal structures, as well as with Gnostic influences, branded the feminine as utterly undesirable in the production of text, even as a topic, and forms the beginning of an ingrained theory of creation that has ramifications for medieval authors. The second apology tradition is basically dormant from late antiquity to the high Middle Ages, but then resurfaces in highly stylized and ironic form in the wake of *Minnesang*, troubadour lyric, Marian cult, and *dolce stil nuovo*.

In the apology tradition youthful poetry dealing with women was disavowed because of its threat to the authors' salvation. Examples of this can be seen in many of the authors discussed, such as Marbod de Rennes' recantation of his juvenilia, Hartmann von Aue's apology in the penitent and world-negating *Gregorius* for writing courtly romances, and Chaucer's Retraction, in which he disavows his works dealing with human/sexual love—to name only a few. Ultimately, then, in the Middle Ages, women had to be rebuked for their connection to the non-rational. The prevailing medieval theological view was that Adam possessed a rational mind and Eve did not; therefore, Adam's and subsequently all men's ties to the Logos were greater and all men's claims to logocentric authorship were more justifiable than those of women. As daughters of Eve, women were suspect both as the subjects of male writers, whom they undoubtedly enticed to write amorous verse, and as writers—claimants to logocentricity. Women in the Middle Ages were excluded from the divine because they were viewed as a sexual threat, as given to the passions of the flesh without the saving grace of rational thought. By removing the feminine from male writing, medieval patriarchy in essence wanted to remove the female body, practicing a narrow form of *contemptus mundi* in *contemptus feminae*. The only exception to this is Dante, but only because he spiritualizes Beatrice and removes all physical and earthly impurity from her image.

Given these patriarchal constraints in the literary creation process in the Middle Ages, and the process' connections to authority, authorship claims of women were considered even more dangerous than those of men. To avoid censure or worse, women authors took great pains to secure patriarchal approval before and during the process of their literary creation, instead of presenting after-the-fact, injury-preventing apologies. This proactive tactic makes their self-censure intratextual rather than inter-textual, the preferred format for male writers. Just like the male medieval writers of apologies, some female authors pepper their self-critical passages with notions of self-justification, in effect questioning and undermining the philosophy that forces them to adopt this self-critical stance in the first place.[1]

10.1. Baudonivia of Poitiers

Medieval women writers use several humility strategies in their writings. First, like men, they often mention that a patron requested the work to be composed. Second, they claim that they are illiterate or uneducated, which men also sometimes claim. Third, they admit that they are in violation of their gender's permitted role in society. The early-seventh-century nun Baudonivia of Poitiers engages the first two topoi in her preface to *The Life of St. Radegund*. Addressing the commissioner of the saint's life, the abbess Dedimia, Baudonivia strikes a humble pose and expounds on her auctorial mission:

> This task you have assigned me of writing the life of the Lady St. Radegund is like attempting to touch heaven with a fingertip. It is our duty to say the best possible things of her. But it is a task that ought to be given to those who have within them the fount of eloquence. For when such a thing is enjoined upon those eloquent persons, they are able to expound with fluency and refreshing song. On the contrary, those limited in their ideas and lacking the articulate flow can neither provide refreshment for others nor relieve their own dryness. Such persons would never attempt to write of their own accord and, if asked to write, are exceedingly fearful. I recognize myself to be this kind of person, humble of spirit and possessing few expressive ideas. . . .Although I myself am the most humble of all the humble . . . I am able to discourse briefly, not fully, but at least incorporating some part of the immeasurable benefits I received from her [Radegund's] example. To this end, as long as I continue publicly to commend her glorious life to the ears of her flock, I am ready

---

1   For some studies on medieval women writers, see Jane Chance, ed., *Gender and Text in the Later Middle Ages* (Gainesville: UP of Florida, 1996) and Joan Ferrante, *To the Glory of Her Sex: Women's Roles in the Composition of Medieval Texts* (Bloomington: Indiana UP, 1997).

to obey your most benevolent will, with an eloquence that is as devoted as it is unworthy. Full of devotion, though lacking in erudition, I beg you for your prayers.[2]

Baudonivia's protests of ineptitude still reflect the earliest Christian writers' stylistic insecurity, which contrasts with the assurance of more eloquent pagan rhetoricians. At the same time, her claim of lack of erudition actually signals her knowledge of classical sources.[3] This passage, however, is surprisingly devoid of gender-based self-deprecation. Instead, she draws distinctions between eloquent and uneloquent people, emphasizing both her public and commissioned role as an author.

10.2. Dhuoda of Uzès

Even though Dhuoda of Uzès' ninth-century self-criticism does not loom large in her writings, it illustrates several evolving aspects of women's apology strategies within the framework of an unusual literary piece—a mother's instruction manual to her son:

> Things that are obvious to many people often escape me. Those who are like me lack understanding and have dim insight, but I am even less capable than they. Yet always there is he at my side who *opened the mouths of the dumb, and made the tongues of infants eloquent.* I, Dhuoda, despite my weakness of mind, unworthy as I am among worthy women—I am still your mother, my son William, and it is to you that I now address the words of my handbook.[4]

Addressing herself to her young warrior son, Dhuoda hints at her own womanly inferiority. Although she does not specify who exactly the people with dim insight are, one can assume she implies women with the lack of intellectual acuity that was customarily attributed to them in the Middle Ages. Despite her humility, however, Dhuoda identifies two sources of authority that shore up her qualification for authorship: her status as a mother, and God, who can inspire eloquence in the most unlikely vessel. This co-opting of God as an ally became a popular strategy in the authorizing process of later medieval women writers.

10.3. Hugeberc von Hildesheim

Medieval women were severely affected by the biblical, classical, and Christian antifeminism that hardened into an institutionalized marginalization of the feminine. But self-critical women authors also had to became accomplices in the antifeminist mindset, at least superficially, since their main criticism of themselves is that they are

---

2   Marcelle Thiébaux, trans., *The Life of St. Radegund by Baudonivia of Poitiers, The Writings of Medieval Women: An Anthology*, 2nd ed. (New York: Garland, 1994) 106-20; here 106-7. The original text was not available to me.

3   Thiébaux, *The Writings of Medieval Women* 93.

4   Dhuoda, *Handbook for William: A Carolingian Woman's Counsel for Her Son*, trans. Carol Neel (Lincoln and London: U of Nebraska P, 1991) Prologue 4. The original text was not available to me.

female. Because of their transgression into the forbidden realm of the symbolic order usually created and controlled by men, they have to become the self-censured (to expand the term from Irigaray) and focus on their gender's unworthiness and their inadequate education. For instance, Hugeberc von Hildesheim, the English-born eighth-century Benedictine nun and writer of *The Hodoeporicon of St. Willibald*, demonstrates this self-critical focus in the preface to that work:

> To the venerable priests, deacons, abbots and brethren beloved in Christ . . . I, an unworthy sister of Saxon origin, last and least in life and manners, venture to write for the sake of posterity and present to you who are religious and preachers of the Gospel a brief account of the early life of the venerable Willibald. Although I lack the necessary experience and knowledge because I am but a weak woman, yet I would like, as far as lies in my power, to gather together a kind of nosegay of his virtues and give you something by which you may remember them. And here I repeat that I am not urged on through presumption to attempt a task for which I am so ill fitted. It is your authority and kindness and God's grace which has prompted me to describe the scenes where the marvels of the Incarnate Word were enacted . . . I know that it may seem very bold on my part to write this book when there are so many holy priests capable of doing better, but as a humble relative I would like to record something of their deeds and travels for future ages. In the hope, then, that you will excuse me and kindly grant me your indulgence.[5]

With Hugeberc surfaces an interesting contrast with male authors: she differentiates her in audience and directs her apology to men, not to women or to God. It is obvious that Hugeberc feels that she has to be authorized by the male ecclesiastical hierarchy, not by God, because in God ideally there are no gender distinctions. Gender distinctions are man-made, and in a subliminal way, these women writers seem to imply they practice self-censure, indeed "auto-antifeminism," because of the patriarchal rules, not because of a divine command. Hugeberc also tempers her authorship by mentioning her status as a relative of the saint.

10.4. Hrotswitha von Gandersheim

The aristocratic tenth-century Benedictine nun Hrotswitha von Gandersheim (935-1001) wrote saints' lives, plays, and epics. She displays a strong authorial personality but employs some humility formulas typically found in medieval prefaces, especially in the prefaces to her legends and her dramas. In her legend prologue, she first admits to writing in an unornate style ("parvo ullius decoris cultu ornatum")[6] and to having made metrical errors—reminiscent of Wandalbert von Prüm, who also worried about his versification. Second, Hrotswitha chalks off content errors to her ignorance ("error ignorantiae" [Praefatio 3]) as well as to her youth. The classical strategy of asking for correction from the more learned audience becomes her third topos, although she

---

5   C. H. Talbot, trans., *The Hodoeporicon of St. Willibald*, by Hugeberc of Hildesheim, *Medieval Women's Visionary Literature*, ed. Elizabeth Alvilda Petroff (Oxford: Oxford UP, 1986) 92-106; here Preface 106. The original text was not available to me.

6   *Hrotsvithae Opera*, ed. H. Homeyer (Munich: Ferdinand Schöningh, 1970) 1. Praefatio 1. For a study on Hrotswitha's overall auctorial persona, see Katharina M. Wilson, *Hrotsvit of Gandersheim: The Ethics of Authorial Stance* (Leiden: Brill, 1988).

restricts her critics to the following: "qui erranti non delectantur derogare, sed magis errata corrigere" (Praefatio 1) [those who do not delight in scolding the person making the mistakes but who actually want to correct the errors]. Despite these bristly humility formulas, Hrotswitha also engages in auto-antifeminism, but she remarks that her feminine weaknesses be remedied by God's grace, as she embarks on her metrically-challenging mission: "Quamvis etiam metrica modulatio femineae fragilitati difficilis et ardua" (Praefatio 8) [even if the metrical rhythm of female weakness is difficult and arduous].

Although the preface and letter to her plays contain still more self-derogatory statements, parts of the pieces have a distinctly defensive flavor and are often phrased in the conditional mode:[7]

> Non enim dubito, mihi ab aliquibus obici, quod huius vilitas dictationis / multo inferior, / multo contractior / penitusque dissimilis / eius, quem proponebam imitari, sit sententiis. / Concedo; / ipsis tamen denuntio, / me in hoc iure / reprehendi non posse, / quasi his vellem abusive assimilari, / qui mei inertiam / longe praecesserunt in scientia sublimiori.[8]

Hrotswitha also stresses her humble and devoted heart, along with her worthlessness and rustic, inelegant style. She calls her other works trifling, always re-emphasizing that it is God's grace that alleviates her worthlessness.

10.5. Hildegard von Bingen

The audience dichotomy between male ecclesiastics and God is most obvious in the work of female mystical authors, who often apologize to a male clerical audience but enlist God in support of their auctorial endeavors. Three pertinent examples of this duality are the German mystics Hildegard von Bingen, Mechthild von Magdeburg, and the Spanish nun Teresa de Cartagena. Just as some apologies by male writers contain a healthy dose of self-justification, so do those of these three women. Hildegard of Bingen employs three facets of self-censure: the use of a male scribe, her supposed

---

7   An example of a more feisty defense can be seen in the epilogue to Marie de France's *Fables*:
    Marie ai num, si sui de France.
    Put cel estre que clerc plusur
    Prendreient sur eus mun labur.
    Ne voil que nul sur li le die!
    ['I am from France, my name's Marie is.
    And it may hap that many a clerk
    Will claim as his what is my work.
    But such pronouncements I want not!'] (Marie de France, *Fables*, ed. and trans. Harriet Spiegel [Toronto: U of Toronto P, 1987] Epilogue lines 4-7).

8   *Hrotsvithae Opera* 2. Praefatio 6. ['Doubtlessly some will berate the worthlessness of this composition as much inferior, much humbler, on a much smaller scale, and not even comparable to the language of him whom I set forth to imitate. I concede to that; but I say this to my critics: they cannot in fairness reprehend me for considering myself presumptuously yearning / to be the equal of those who by far are my betters in learning'] (Katharina Wilson, trans., *The Plays of Hrotsvit of Gandersheim* [New York: Garland, 1989] 3-4).

lack of education, and God's command to write. Her scribe Volmar helped with her first rite of passage into authorship. Many medieval women writers, even if they themselves could write, employed scribes for two reasons. First, a male scribe—usually a cleric—lent credence to a female author[9] and could speed her acceptance, since through this method a male member of the Church would at least implicitly sanction what she had created. Second, scribes allowed women to maintain the appearance of illiteracy, as part of the scheme to appear humble and less threatening to the symbolic order controlled by men. In a letter to Bernard of Clairvaux, Hildegard emphasizes her need for ecclesiastical confirmation due to her self-proclaimed "elementary" literacy and understanding:

> Scio enim in textu interiorem intelligentiam expositionis Psalterii et Euangelii et aliorum uoluminum, que monstrantur mihi de hac uisione, que tangit pectus meum et animam sicut flamma comburens, docens me hec profunda expositionis. Sed tamen non docet me litteras in Teutonica lingua, quas nescio, sed tantum scio in simplicitate legere, non in abscisione textus. Et de hoc responde mihi, quid tibi inde uideatur, quia homo sum indocta de ulla magistratione cum exteriori materia, sed intus in anima mea sum docta.[10]

From manuscript illuminations and from her works, we know that Hildegard was highly educated and could also write in Latin.

Another passage from her first theological work, the *Scivias*, relates what the heavenly voice said about Hildegard's mission:

> Sed quia timida es ad loquendum et simplex ad exponendum et indocta ad scribendum ea, dic et scribe illa non secundum os hominis nec secundum intellectum humanae adinuentionis nec secundum uoluntatem humanae compositionis, sed secundem id quod ea in caelestibus desuper in mirabilibus Dei uides et audis, ea sic edisserendo proferens, quemadmodum et auditor uerba praeceptoris sui percipiens, ea secundum tenorem locutionis illius, ipso uolente, ostendente et preacipiente propalat. Sic ergo et tu, o homo, dic ea quae uides et audis; et scribe ea non secundum

---

9 See I. S. Johnson: "Hildegard thus underlines her authority as both author and seer, an authority manifested through Volmar, who does not attempt to impose his will upon her words, . . . Both the miniature [showing Hildegard passing along the words of the Living Light to Volmar] and Hildegard's account of Volmar seem to hint that an author's authority is in some measure enhanced by the presence of a scribe. . . . Since St. Augustine, St. Gregory, and St. Bernard had composed 'through' a secretary, Hildegard explicitly claimed her right to compose and asserted her status as an author. This authority she traces directly to divine inspiration, which allowed an 'unlearned' woman to understand exegetical and theological matters for which she was not trained. Hildegard's special understanding is then further verified by the scribe, who transcribes in a more permanent form the wax tablets he receives from the author" ("The Trope of the Scribe and the Question of Literary Authority in the Works of Julian of Norwich and Margery Kempe," *Speculum* 66 [1991]: 820-838; here 823-4).

10 Hildegard von Bingen, *Epistolarium*, ed. L. van Acker, 2 vols. *Corpus Christianorum Continuatio Medievalis* 91 and 91:A (Turnholti: Brepols, 1991, 1993) "Epist." I, lines 17-25. ['Through this vision which touches my heart and soul like a burning flame, teaching me profundities of meaning, I have an inward understanding of the Psalter, the Gospels, and other volumes. Nevertheless, I do not receive this knowledge in German. Indeed, I have no formal training at all, for I know how to read only on the most elementary level, certainly with no deep analysis. But please give me your opinion in this matter, because I am untaught and untrained in exterior material, but am only taught inwardly, in my spirit'] (J. L. Baird and R. K. Ehrman, trans., *The Letters of Hildegard of Bingen* [New York: Oxford UP, 1994] 1: 28).

te nec secundum alium hominem, sed secundum uolentatem scientis, uidentis et disponentis omnia in secretis mysteriorum suorum.[11]

This passage paints Hildegard as humble and unpolished, a reluctant Moses-like medium who assumes the risky task of authorship only after the repeated command from God the Master Author and, as she relates later, only after she refused and was subsequently struck down by God with illness. This stance, of course, served to release her from potential criticism by the patriarchal hierarchy. The fact that Hildegard was a cloistered nun who authorized herself with these self-critical gestures, garnering the support of such ecclesiastical eminencies as Bernard of Clairvaux and Pope Eugenius III, helped make her a powerful writer, an author who was later unafraid to criticize the same churchmen who had valorized her.

10.6. Mechthild von Magdeburg

For Mechthild von Magdeburg (1207-1282), a Beguine, the scenario is both more difficult and more bold.[12] Because of her status as a Beguine[13] and her visionary ideas, Mechthild was more vulnerable than a cloistered nun. In her book, *Flowing Light of the Divinity*, we encounter an author both highly critical of her auctorial activity and greatly defiant of submission to patriarchy. She admits to not knowing Latin, the accepted language of the Church, and calls herself "ein tore, ein súndig und ein arm mensche bin an libe und an sele."[14] Mechthild cleverly sets herself up for auctorial

---

11 Hildegard von Bingen, *Scivias*, ed. A. Führkötter, 2 vols. *Corpus Christianorum Continuatio Medievalis* 43 and 43:A (Turnholti: Brepols, 1978) 1, lines 10-21. ['But since you are timid in speaking, and simple in expounding, and untaught in writing, speak and write these things not by a human mouth, and not by the understanding of human invention, and not by the requirements of human composition, but as you see and hear them on high in the heavenly places in the wonders of God. Explain these things in such a way that the hearer, receiving the words of his instructor, may expound them in those words, according to that will, vision and instruction. Thus therefore, O human, speak these things that you see and hear. And write them not by yourself or any other human being, but by the will of Him Who knows, sees and disposes of all things in the secrets of His mysteries'] (C. Hart and J. Bishop, trans., *Hildegard of Bingen: Scivias* [New York: Paulist Press, 1990] 59)

12 For an overview of Mechthild, see Frank Tobin, *Mechthild von Magdeburg: A Medieval Mystics in Modern Eyes* (Columbia, SC: Camden House, 1995).

13 Beguines attracted some disagreeable attention because "their conspicuousness and their lack of affiliation . . . [made] them vulnerable to accusations of mendicancy and vagabondage, even heresy. In 1273 Gilbert Bishop of Tournai sent a report to Pope Gregory X: 'There were among us women called beguines, some of whom blossom forth in subtleties and rejoice in novelties. They have interpreted in vernacular French idiom the mysteries of Scripture which are scarcely accessible to experts in divine writings. They read aloud in common irreverently and boldly, in conventicles and public squares'" (Thiébaux, *The Writings of Medieval Women* 386). Mechthild in her claim to know more than learned clerics would equally fit into this description.

14 Mechthild von Magdeburg, *Das fließende Licht der Gottheit*, ed. Hans Neumann and Gisela Vollmann-Profe (Munich: Artemis Verlag, 1990) 2,3 line 48 and 4,2 line 119. ['a fool, and a sin-

self-criticism, only to vindicate herself by her visionary experience of God. Bemoaning her shortcomings, Mechthild is told by God that if she is truly obedient to him, she will do what he wills, which is an implicit sanctioning of her writerly activity—and what clergyman would want to argue with that authority? In fact, she relates that her confessor approved of her divine experience and encouraged her to do what God had ordered, that "eim snoeden wibe hies us gottes herzen und munt dis buch schriben. Alsust ist dies buch minnenklich von gotte har komen und ist us menschlichen sinnen nit genomen" (4,2 lines 132-34) [a wretched woman should have been commanded to write this book straight from the heart and mouth of God" (Galvani 100)].

Mechthild's auctorial strategies oscillate between use of the "poor woman" topos and statements of justification for her authorship. In order to shore up her credibility, she tries to demonstrate her spiritual worthiness:

> Alle mine lebtage e ich dis buches began und eb sin von gotte ein einig wort in min sele kam, do was ich der einvaltigosten menschen eines, das ie in geistlichem lebende erschein. Von des túfels bosheit wiste ich nit, der welte krancheit kante ich nit, geistlicher lúte valscheit was mir och unkúndig. Ich mus sprechen got ze eren und och durch des buches lere: Ich unwirdigú súnderin wart gegruesset von dem heligen geiste in minem zwoelften jare also vliessende sere, do ich was alleine, das ich das niemer mere moechte erliden, das ich mich zu einer grossen teglichen súnde nie mohte erbieten.[15]

Despite protestations of her sinful nature—as a human, not specifically as a woman— Mechthild virtually declares herself sinless in this passage. At the same she insinuates that other spiritual people, possibly clerics, are really liars who are leading the flock astray. Therefore, Mechthild has to step in and rectify this deplorable state of affairs. It is highly significant that she claims the Holy Spirit visited her, because the Holy Spirit is directly related to the Pentecostal call to evangelization. The Holy Spirit is said to bring the gifts of "healing, prophecy, wisdom, knowledge, the working of miracles, speaking in tongues, and the interpretation of tongues."[16] In Book 4,13, she reconfirms her commission by the Holy Spirit: "Ich enkan noch mag nit schriben, ich sehe es mit den ogen miner sele und hoere es mit den oren mines ewigen geistes und bevinde in allen liden mines lichamen die kraft des heiligen geistes" [I cannot nor do I wish to write; I see it with the eyes of my soul, and hear it with the ears of my eternal spirit and feel it in all the members of my body: the power of the Holy Spirit].[17] According

---

ful and poor being in body and soul'] (Christiane Mesch Galvani, trans., *Flowing Light of the Divinity*, ed. Susan Clark [New York: Garland, 1991] 99).

15 Mechthild, *Das fließende Licht der Gottheit* 4,2 lines 4-11. ['All the days of my life, before I began this book and before one single word of it came from God into my soul, I was the simplest of all creatures who have ever appeared in spiritual life. I knew nothing of the Devil's wickedness; I did not know the sickness of the world; I was unaware of the duplicity of spiritual people. I must speak out for the glory of God and through the instruction of this book. In my twelfth year, I, unworthy sinner, was greeted in such an overwhelming way by the Holy Spirit when I was alone, that I can never again tolerate giving in to any great daily sin'] (Galvani, *Flowing Light of the Divinity* 96).

16 Linwood Urban, *A Short History of Christian Thought* (Rev. ed. Oxford: Oxford UP, 1995) 317.

17 This is my own translation, as Galvani's does not capture the passage's mystical Augustinian categories.

to the Augustinian scale of visionary experience, Mechthild claims the second highest level of mystical experience, even though she does allow for a visceral sensation of the Holy Spirit.[18]

Ultimately, Mechthild contends for a prophetic position in a society she considers corrupt and effeminate (see 3,15; 5,34; 6,3; and 6,21): "Meister Heinrich, úch wundert sumenlicher worten, die in disem buche gescriben sint. Mich wundert, wie úch des wundern mag. Mer: mich jamert des von herzen sere sid dem male, das ich súndig wip schriben mus" (5,12 lines 2-4) ['Master Heinrich, you are amazed at the masculine style of this book? That surprises me. I am far more concerned about the fact I, a sinful woman, must write that' (Galvani 140)]. The masculinization of women because of a moral vacuum left by men is a recurring topos with a number of visionaries (see Hildegard von Bingen and Jean d'Arc), and here she ties it directly to the gift of the Holy Spirit, who after all, also empowered biblical cowards such as Moses and Daniel (5,12).

Another instance illustrates that Mechthild, despite her employment of self-critical strategies, felt highly empowered and went on the offensive. She must have been criticized for her revelations, a criticism she here brings before God:

> Ich wart vor diesem buche gewarnet, und wart von menschen also gesaget: Wolte man es nit bewaren, da moechte ein brant úber waren. . . . "Eya herre, . . . so hastu mich verleitet, wan du hies mich es selber schriben." Do offenbarte sich got zehant miner trurigen sele und hielt is buch in siner vordern hant und sprach: "Lieb minú, betruebe dich nit ze verre, die warheit mag nieman verbrennen."[19]

Where many male authors fear God as the judge of their literary creation, for Mechthild God has clearly become the ally of the female author—has, in fact, revived

---

18 The three Augustinian categories of vision experiences in descending order of validity are "intellectuale," "spiritale," and "corporale" (*Augustine, De genesi ad litteram libri duodecim*, trans. P. Agaësse and A. Signac [Paris: Desclée de Brouwer, 1972] line 12.7.16). The purest intellectual visions employ neither the eyes of the body nor those of the soul (*De genesi* line 12.10.21). In a spiritual vision, the mystic sees with the interior eyes of the soul, while a corporeal vision utilizes the external eyes and is thus the least viable as a mystical experience (*De genesi* line 12.7.17). Voices, too, can be grouped into a corresponding system: the "inarticulate voice," one that leaves more of an impression than definite words; the "distinct interior voice," which speaks in clear words but is recognized as being inside the mind; and "the exterior voice, which appears to be speaking externally to the subject and to be heard by the outward ear" (E. Underhill, *Mysticism: A Study in the Nature and Development of Man's Spiritual Consciousness* [New York: E. P. Dutton, 1911] 273).

19 Mechthild, *Das fließende Licht der Gottheit* 2,26 lines 2-9.
['I was warned about this book and was told by men
That it should not be preserved
But destroyed by fire.

. . . .
"You have misled me
In making me write this book."
At that God immediately revealed Himself
To my sad soul, holding this book in His right hand
And said: "My love, do not upset yourself too much;
The truth cannot be burned by anyone.'] (Galvani, *Flowing Light of the Divinity* 56-57)

Jesus' command to Mary Magdalen to spread the good news and has confirmed her in both her visionary and auctorial work. Further dialogue with God reveals that Mechthild is going to practice auto-antifeminism in order to orchestrate God's vindication of her:

"Eya herre, were ich ein geleret geistlich man, und hettistu dis einig grosse wunder an im getan, so moehtistu sin ewige ere enpfahen. Wie sol man dir nu des getrúwen, das du in den unvletigen pful has ein guldin hus gebuwen und wonest da werlich inne mit diner muter und mit allen creaturen und mit allem dinem himelschem gesinde? Herre, da kan dich dú irdensche wisheit nit gevinden."[20]

Aware of the privileging of the ordained male over the lay female in the medieval church, Mechthild cleverly requests that God shed some light on her having been chosen despite her obvious gender shortcomings. Her word choice of "earthly wisdom" adumbrates how God's explanation will contradict the accepted antifeminist attitudes of the male church hierarchy:

"Tohter, es verlúret manig wise man sin túres golt von verwarloesi in einem grossen herwege, da er mitte ze hoher schule moehte varen; das mus ieman vinden. Ich habe von nature daz getan manigen tag, wa ich ie sunderliche gnade gap, da suchte ich ie zu die nidersten, minsten, heimlichosten stat. . . . Man vindet manigen wisen meister an der schrift, der an im selber vor minen ogen ein tore ist. Und ich sage es noch me: Das ist mir vor inen ein gros ere und sterket die heligen cristanheit an in vil sere, das der ungelerte munt die gelerte zungen von minem heligen geiste leret."[21]

---

20 Mechthild, *Das fließende Licht der Gottheit* 2,26 lines 18-23.
   ['Alas, Lord, were I a learned [clergy] man
   And You had worked this miracle in me
   It would forever bring You glory.
   But how can anyone believe
   That you have built a golden house
   In this filthy slough,
   To live here with Your Mother
   And all creatures
   As well as Your heavenly servants?
   Lord, I cannot find earthly wisdom in that.'] (Galvani, *Flowing Light of the Divinity* 56)
21 Mechthild, *Das fließende Licht der Gottheit* 2,26 lines 24-33.
   ['Daughter, many a wise man has lost his precious gold
   Through carelessness on the big highway,
   Hoping to come to higher learning;
   Someone else will find it.
   I have by nature done that many a day.
   Whenever I bestowed a special grace
   I always sought for the lowest,
   The least, the best concealed place.
   . . . .
   You find many a wise master, learned in the scripture
   Who himself is a fool in My eyes.
   And I will tell you more:
   It is a great honor for Me
   And strengthens Holy Christianity significantly
   That the unlearned mouth teaches
   The erudite tongues about My Holy Spirit.'] (Galvani, *Flowing Light of the Divinity* 56-57)

God turns Mechthild's auto-antifeminism into triumph, as he criticizes the scholastic learnedness of the medieval church. This passage proves that medieval women writers were painfully aware of the dichotomy inherent in the practices of the church concerning women. One the one hand, the church regarded women as inferior, basing this belief on classical and medieval sources. On the other hand, the Bible claims that there is neither male nor female in Christ. It is this equality, even superiority in Mechthild's case, that medieval women writers exploit, drawing a clear distinction between the misogyny of men and the gender-neutral wisdom of God. Women vanquish misogynists with the very weapon, God's word, that they had used to subjugate women.

10.7. Teresa de Cartagena

The fifteenth-century Spanish nun Teresa de Cartagena, presents a unique case in this study, since her self-criticism occurs intertextually, not intratextually as in the works of the other women writers. In response to criticism of her work *Grove of the Infirm* [*Arboleda de los enfermos*], Teresa composed *Wonder at the Works of God* [*Admiraçión operum Dey*] to explain her theory of composition and theodicy, making this entire twenty-five-page work a metatextual statement, an *apologia* in the vein of the early Christian apologists who were defending Christianity against paganism. Although she employs modesty formulas and assures her audience that offending anybody is the farthest thing from her intention, the piece is both a defense of her authorship and a defense against the charge of plagiarism in *Grove of the Infirm*. I chose to discuss her here because Teresa confirms the importance of women writers and rejects the expected auto-antifeminism and thereby the patriarchal dominion over women's literary creation. In addition, Dayle Seidenspinner-Núñez situates this text within the pro- and antifeminist debate in fifteenth-century Spain, a debate we have already encountered from a male perspective in Chapter 9.

Even as she sprinkles her defense with self-deprecatory humility formulas, Teresa employs the same strategy as Mechthild, claiming God as her ally and protector, a superior substitution for a male clerical patron. The title *Wonder at the Works of God* sums up the core of her argument that God can achieve exceptional feats, even if humans do not understand their purpose. Declaring herself to be a "small piece of dirt" and a "fool," she nonetheless asserts that God is "scattering His abundant grace over this dry and sterile land, so that a sinful woman removed from virtue may know how to form her words in praise and glory of the most Holy and Lord of virtues."[22] We can gather that a charge of plagiarism seems to hang over her, as she states "Many times, virtuous lady, I have been informed that some prudent men and also discreet women have marveled at a treatise that, with divine grace directing my weak and womanly understanding, was written by my hand" (*Wonder* 87). Teresa declares her authorship of her "womanly text of little substance" without the help of a scribe, as she was deaf

---

22 Teresa de Cartagena, *Wonder at the Works of God, The Writings of Teresa de Cartagena*, trans. Dayle Seidenspinner-Núñez (Cambridge: Brewer, 1998) 86-112; here 88, 86, 87. The original text was not available to me.

and sickly (much of the subject matter of *Grove of the Infirm*), but she immediately seizes upon that double handicap—being a woman and an invalid—as the impetus for her critics' attacks:[23] "my offense is clear, since apparently their awe does not result from the merits of my text but from the defects of its author . . . but because of me and my justly deserved adversities and increased suffering" (*Wonder* 88, 87).

Teresa focuses mercilessly on the real reasons for her critics' consternation, her gender, and gives an overview of medieval antifeminism:

> I think, most virtuous lady, that the reason that men marvel that a woman has written a treatise is because this is not customary in the female condition but only in the male. For men have had the practice of writing books and learning and applying their learning since such ancient times that apparently this is assumed to be the natural course of things, and therefore no one wonders. But since women have not had this custom nor have acquired learning, and since their understanding is not as perfect as men's, it is considered a marvel. Yet it is no greater marvel nor less easy for God's omnipotence to do one more than the other, for He who could infuse the understanding of men with knowledge can thus infuse the understanding of women, even though our understanding may be imperfect or not as able or sufficient to receive and retain knowledge as that of males. For God's divine greatness can readily repair this imperfection and small insufficiency and even remove it completely and give perfection and ability to female understanding just as to male, for the sufficiency that men have they did not acquire on their own but because God gave it to them. Of this the Apostle says, "Not that we are sufficient to think anything of ourselves, as of ourselves: but our sufficiency is from God [2 Cor. 3:5]. For if the sufficiency of men comes from God and God give to each one according to the measure of His gift, why should we women not receive the same when He judges it necessary and appropriate.[24]

The lady Teresa keeps addressing is the patroness who urged her to pen this defense, commonly considered to be Juana de Mendoza.[25] The refreshingly honest tone of this passage might be attributed to her assuredly female audience, but it probably also demonstrates Teresa's boldness in going against general opinion. She pillories male superiority, calling into question men's accepted supremacy by arguing that it is based merely on custom and assumption. Effectively challenging and rejecting the foundations of antifeminism, Teresa argues that males are not inherently superior in their essence, an idea that had been championed by patristic and scholastic authors alike, but that their knowledge is a gift from God. Teresa's argument turns the tables on her male critics, as she enlists biblical exegesis, the same weapon misogynistic writers had used against women. Teresa's claims of divine grace and inspiration that infuse her with understanding, not necessarily in the same way that they do as men, constitute an early example of Kristeva's notion of *écriture féminine*. While many female medieval writers emulate men to gain acceptance in the male symbolic order, Teresa seems to advocate women-specific authorship, apart from men. And while male authors in the apology tradition situate themselves in violation of Christian truth, the women claim their writings to be absolute Christian truth, valorized by the highest authority.

---

23 Dayle Seidenspinner-Núñez adds Teresa's *conversa* status as a third objection for her critics (introduction, *The Writings of Teresa de Cartagena* [Cambridge: Brewer, 1998] 1-21; here 3). See also Alan Deyermond's seminal article, "The Works of Teresa de Cartagena," *Journal of Hispanic Philology* 1 (1976): 19-29.

24 Teresa de Cartagena, *Wonder at the Works of God* 89-90.

25 Seidenspinner-Núñez, introduction, *The Writings of Teresa de Cartagena* 12.

This brief overview of women's participation in the medieval apology tradition is by no means complete, as new texts become available every day. The gender-based differences among self-critical writers in the Middle Ages illustrate that it is often not enough to classify self-critical passages simply as examples of the humility topos without examining the philosophical underpinnings of this literary phenomenon. Some general differences between the genders can be highlighted. Women authors primarily apologize intratextually, and often resort to auto-antifeminism to placate the male hierarchies. While male writers apologize because of their fear of God, women unabashedly enlist God as their champion and ally in a move of supreme resistance against the male monopoly on both God and authorship. God the Master Author personally authorizes these women. The closer we get to the end of the Middle Ages, the more ironic the apologies of male writers become, as apologies have become part of a literary convention or game. For women, the picture is different. While they become more combative as the Middle Ages decline, writing can still bring into real and sometimes imminent danger. Granted, the women authors who fit into the constraints of this discussion were primarily religious figures and thus were generally somewhat privileged in their societies, but some others who have not been discussed here, were not so fortunate. Women writers who did not succumb to ecclesiastical rules, did not practice auto-antifeminism, did not become like men (as Isotta Nogarola was told), might not always fare so well. Spanish mystics Sor María and Madre Juana[26] enjoyed some tolerance from the hierarchy, but neither woman ever committed her experiences to paper, nor claimed to be educated, in essence did not impinge on the male domain too much. Marguerite de Porete, on the other hand, addressed her book, *The Mirror of Simple Souls*, exclusively to a female audience and omitted any auto-antifeminist remarks. Jean d'Arc behaved different from their gender's norms and did not seek the validating stamp of the Church for her saintly voices: both of them were burned at the stake.

10.8. General Ruminations

Aside from the outline of the apology tradition and its connective feminist subtext discussed in the first part of this chapter, several other concluding remarks can be offered for this diverse and complex topic. Although individual examples of the negative-sounding strategy of auctorial self-criticism might not evoke these conclusions, the sheer number of self-critical examples demonstrates that this literary tactic strikes at the heart of medieval language and literature. Ultimately, auctorial self-criticism centers on the usage of language, questioning linguistic signs and signifiers. We can see this in the modern terminology applied to self-criticism, the establishment of literary tradition, intertextuality, and canon formation, all of which are significant to this tradition as well as medieval literature.

---

26   See also Luis Miguel Vicente Garcia, "La defensa de la mujer como intelectual en Teresa de Cartagena y Sor Juana Inés de la Cruz," *Mester* 18.2 (1989): 95-103.

The equivocal linguistic nature of the phenomenon of auctorial self-criticism is evident from terminology problems in the modern literary discussion. Three technical terms crystallized during antiquity and are employed rather interchangeably today: palinode, recantation, and retraction. In general, the much broader, more comprehensive, and more accommodating term "apology" proves more flexible, meaning both a literary defense, explanation or excuse, in which no "admission of wrongdoing or expression of regret is involved" and as a "defense of a writer's reasoning . . . associated with guilt," denoting "a work expressing sorrow or regret."[27] The ancient authors themselves had to invent terms to accommodate their literary *faux pas*. For example, a modern definition of Stesichorus' "palinode" explains it as "a poem in which a writer retracts or counter-balances a statement made in an earlier poem."[28] *The Oxford English Dictionary* (*OED*) defines a palinode as a "singing over again, repetition, *esp.* recantation . . . of an ode or song." Horace takes the ode-and-song quality of Stesichorus' term into account when he invents the expression *recantation* because he needs a word for the untranslatable Greek "Palinodia."[29] The *OED* sheds further light on the term; it defines the verb "to recant" as "to withdraw, retract, or renounce (a statement, opinion, belief, etc.) as erroneous, and *esp.* with formal or public confession of errors in matters of religion," although one subdefinition does not stress the requirement of religious themes. The third term, "retraction," derives from the Latin *retractatio* ("the action of handling or going over again . . . re-examination, reconsideration") (*Oxford Latin Dictionary*), which took on the meaning of "withdrawal or recantation of an opinion, statement, etc., with admission of error" in modern English (*OED*). According to the definitions, there is an incongruity between the modern "retraction" and the ancient and medieval "retractationes," derived from Augustine's *Retractations*. As evident from Augustine's work, he did not retract anything in the modern sense but merely corrected his previous errors and published his emendations. Most medieval authors titling their apology with anything resembling "retractatio" generally refer to Augustine's example and include the third strand, the less significant discussion of questionable literary practices along with examples of the first. So, our modern notion of retraction as medieval needs revision.

Furthermore, this study attempted to establish auctorial self-criticism as a literary tradition, fueled by both announced and unannounced intertextuality. This diachronic examination of literary apologies comprises more than seventy authors and an even greater number of their works, but it cannot make the claim to be exhaustive. Other examples in various languages remain to be discovered. Nevertheless, over seventy authors over a period of two thousand years participating in an intertextual literary topos are hardly negligible, and fit Ernst Robert Curtius' definition of a literary topos as well as Claudio Guillén's theory about literary traditions:

> One encounters a phenomenon which appears to mean little or nothing. If it recurs constantly, it has a definite function. . . . When we have isolated and named a literary phenomenon, we have estab-

---

27 Hugh C. Holman, *A Handbook to Literature*, 5th ed. (New York: Macmillan, 1986) 33 and Jack Myers and Michael Simms, *Longman Dictionary and Handbook of Poetry* (New York: Longman, 1985) 21.

28 J. A. Cuddon, *A Dictionary of Literary Terms* (Garden City, NY: Doubleday, 1977) 466.

29 Eduard Fraenkel, *Horace* (Oxford: Clarendon, 1957) 209.

lished one fact. At that one point we have penetrated the concrete structure of the matter of literature. We have performed an analysis. If we get at a few dozen or a few hundred such facts, a system of points is established. They can be connected by lines; and this produces figures. If we study
and associate these, we arrive at a comprehensive picture. . . . Through our analysis of texts we
were led to understand that the Middle Ages must be seen in its continuity not only with Antiquity
but also with the Modern period.[30]

Since the apology tradition is rooted in antiquity, flourishes in the Middle Ages, and
continues from the Renaissance to the twentieth century, a second volume could trace
the history and anatomy of the apology tradition, with its basic tenets, nuances, and
contexts, from 1500 to the present.

Guillén proffers the following theory about literary traditions:

Traditions tend to be conventions laid out as sequences (conventions, one might say, with a past).
When A occurs a reasonable number of years after B and C, we are inclined to state that we have
encountered a tradition. Diachrony plays here, it seems to me, the most perfunctory of roles. In the
case of either a convention or a tradition, what is at stake is not the unusual trait, the single impact,
the inventive individual, or the concrete shape of a historical process, but a collective usage. . . .
Conventions and traditions are "fields" or "systems" where the main unifying factor is accepted
usage. . . . Significant influences are usually unmediated, one-to-one relationships—not distant
kinships by association.[31]

Curtius and Guillén provide useful definitions; both, however, stress the system too
much and completely neglect the author in their attempts to define "topos" and
"tradition." Curtius assumes that a recurring motif serves a definite function, but the
history and anatomy of the apology possesses a certain fluidity and individuality. Not
to overemphasize diachrony, but chronological consideration does demonstrate
changes and progressions in the apology tradition. Curtius' and Guillén's definitions of
"topos" and "tradition," as well as these terms' partial applicability to the apology
genre, suggest that the apology cannot be limited in definition to either "topos" or
"tradition." Instead, the auctorial apology takes elements from the definitions for
"topos" and "tradition" and combines them with the specific context the author provides. Helmut Beumann proposes that topoi are not only constants in a tradition but
variables which can be functionally combined to serve individual expressions,[32] and
then applied to intra-auctorial situations.

Both literary traditions and topoi leading to individual expressions are grounded in
intertextuality. But most medieval self-critical authors' use of language is subversive,
challenging the monolithic nature of the medieval sacramental theory of language that
forces them to disavow their literary creations. Most of the self-critical examples further illustrate that, throughout two millennia, auctorial self-criticism has often been
intermixed with self-defense and specifically reveals the medieval authors' awareness
of their craft, an awareness that has so often been denied them by modern critics. By
creating an inter- and intratext, the authors weave a web of interauctoriality by refer-

---

30 Ernst Robert Curtius, *European Literature and the Latin Middle Ages*, trans. Willard R. Trask,
    Bollingen Series 36 (New York: Pantheon Books, 1953) 382-83.
31 Claudio Guillén, *Literature as System: Essays Toward the Theory of Literary History* (Princeton:
    Princeton UP, 1971) 60.
32 Helmut Beumann, "Topos und Gedankengefüge bei Einhard," *Archiv für Kulturgeschichte* 33
    (1951): 337-50; here 349.

ring to other participants in the tradition, but they can, more importantly, map out their own creative history with an intra-auctorial diagram. Consequently, an author's apology functions simultaneously as an assertion of the power of language and literature and, paradoxical, of the power and self-assertion of the authors. These authors participate in the medieval tension between the corporeal and the eternal, but undermine the conventionally-expected one-dimensional role of the Christian author in particular and literature in general.

This expected monolithic role of the Christian author stems from the restrictive sacramental theory of language; an excursion into modern intertextuality theory points to connections with medieval sign theory. Julia Kristeva postulates that "the text organizes a frontal attack on the 'logocentric reader' by destabilizing the signifier and pluralizing through an endless series of intertextual signifieds."[33] Some of the authors in the apology tradition have done exactly that, staged an attack on the "logocentric reader"; more importantly, though, the self-critical authors have questioned the concept of the logocentric writer, which means breaking out of the accepted mainstream. Their apologies would then confirm them as logocentric writers and return them to the mainstream, a process that would conform to Kristeva's interpretation of intertextuality as "a complex *procès de rejet multipliant la position du language et du sujet*" ('process of rejection that multiplies the position of language and of the subject'), a 'negativity' ('*negativité*') that destroys old texts in order to create new texts."[34]

But do medieval author also destroy their texts? In his 1984 article entitled "Palinodes and Palindromes," Stan Fogel discusses postmodern writers' use of the palinode as a purely narratological vehicle of "erasure," of writing "both something and nothing."[35] This interpretation of a palinode sounds congruous with the piece of literature that gave it its name, Stesichorus' "Palinodia," with its attempt to "erase" his "Helen" poem. The majority of the self-critical medieval authors, however, admit that the text cannot be erased, that the word uttered cannot be recalled, and that the "negativity" Kristeva perceives in intertextuality does not destroy the texts but contextualize them within the intra-auctorial system. Therefore, pre-modern intertextuality is not limited to Barthes' and Kristeva's notion of a "revolutionary gesture directed by the modern text against the closure of the signifier in bourgeois or representational discourse"; on the contrary, since Michael Riffaterre and Gérard Genette claim that "intertextuality is the normal *modus operandi* for all literature, classical and contemporary alike,"[36] medieval auctorial self-criticism is a vehicle for the creation of both a new text and a new author, as well as a tool for the assertion of an already existing text and author.

Intertextuality helps to paint a "meaningful" picture by drawing lines between the various points of literary reference, as Curtius suggests, but it draws more than one picture. There is the "big picture," sketching the entire tradition; within that, there are

---

33 Thaïs E. Morgan, "Is There an Intertext in This Text?" *American Journal of Semiotics* 3 (1985): 1-40; here 24.

34 Morgan, "Is There an Intertext in This Text?" 22.

35 Stan Fogel, "Palinodes and Palindromes," *International Fiction Review* 11 (1984): 51-54; here 53-54.

36 Morgan, "Is There an Intertext in This Text?" 24.

many smaller inter- and intra-auctorial pictures. The intratextual examples furthermore create an analogy to the rhetorical device "occupatio," "the summary mention of a thing while professing to omit it."[37] "Occupatio" mostly applies to the intratextual examples because they remain within the boundaries of one text, which provides the framework for the author to negate and affirm the text within one given audience setting. Since this rhetorical device would not be as effective spread over two works. Boccaccio's first story for the first day in the *Decameron* serves as an intratextual example of a kind of "occupatio" that encapsulates and confirms the entire apology tradition in its ironic context.

Boccaccio starts his one-hundred-story marathon work with the outrageously virtuous and false confession of the confirmed liar and sinner Ser Cepperello, who is canonized after his confession and subsequent death because his unknowing confessor believes the outrageous lies. Ser Cepperello, a metaphor for both Boccaccio and the quintessential medieval author, exemplifies the microcosmic strategy an author has to follow in order to escape earthly judgment. As Boccaccio points out, this is a tale concerned with the judgment of men—not God, a comment that wishes to anchor literary creation in the earthly realm and which constitutes a strategy to rebel against the medieval theories of language and auctorial hierarchy. Panfilo, the narrator, ushers in his story with the remarks that this will be a story about one of God's marvelous works—he who is immutable. The miracle of Ser Cepperello is not a miracle of God's doing but one achieved by Cepperello's creative literary power—which would normally descend from God, although the irony in that would have bordered on blasphemy in medieval times. In the hands of the author—who, faced with the medieval requirement of Christian truth, has to become what he should shun, a liar, in order to be accepted by the Zeitgeist and allowed into the sanctuary of medieval linguistic theory—language becomes mutable, and therefore, unreliable. The earthly author plays his own game of God, creating a saint while using false signs. This strategy of authorization is also reflected in the medieval women writers' confident assurance of God's request and thereby implied approval of their authorship.

Misleading signs in the story of Ser Cepperello also function on another level very essential to this study: they question medieval as well as modern notions of literary canon. Not only does Boccaccio present an ironic treatment of the medieval author as the quintessential liar, but he also satirizes the notion of canon, since Ser Cepperello was canonized. Because the word "canon" is also used to identify the books accepted as part of the Bible, and because Ser Cepperello's confession was a lie, Boccaccio was mocking both the canonizing of saints and the canonizing of literature. The medieval notion of canon could also illuminate our current grappling with the notion of what a canon is. Current opinion is striving to include the "margins" in the mainstream, if not substituting the "margin" for the mainstream, or creating two canons alongside of each other. The self-critical medieval authors also work with canons, their own individual ones and one accepted by the religious establishment. They also create two canons alongside each other, as, for instance, Chaucer does in his Retraction: the acceptable one and the unacceptable one. Ironically, it is largely the then-unacceptable canon that

---

37 Qtd. in A. H. Kelly, "*Occupatio* as Negative Narration: A Mistake for *Occultatio/ Praeteratio*," *Modern Philology* (1977): 311-15; here 315.

we read and teach today, and barely anyone deals with Chaucer's translation of Boethius. Further irony surfaces when we look at Chaucer's other attempts at delineating his canon in *The Legend of Good Women* and the headlink to the Man of Law's Tale. He cites the later "unacceptable" part of his work as conforming to the canon the God of Love wishes to see. Chaucer was extremely aware of contemporary notions of canon and satirizes them. He marginalizes his own creation in order to look acceptable to the mainstream.

We can now return to the introductory comments of Milan Kundera's surgeon. The surgeon's opinion about retractions as antiquated medievalism mirrors modern perceptions of medieval culture and literary creation as simpleminded and uncritical. What he made sound so simple and medieval, so self-negating and even expected, turns out to be highly complex and self-asserting. Even though Kundera's surgeon assumes that medieval retractions mute the text, they actually relish the creation of new text. Medieval authors work within a restrictive system, in which their apology strategies assure that they prevail. Thus, the apology tradition characterized by inter-auctoriality, intertextuality, and intratextuality, enables self-critical authors to refer not only backward but also—primarily—forward, making the medieval apology a progressive strategy that engenders new literature. What may sound like an arcane topic illuminates many central linguistic, literary, religious, and philosophical issues of the Middle Ages and allows us to travel deep into medieval minds, minds no less complex or intellectual than ours.

BIBLIOGRAPHY

This bibliography lists only the works referred to in this study and in no way claims to be exhaustive. Multiple articles in essay collections are cross-referenced.

PRIMARY TEXTS

Alfonso Martínez de Toledo. *Arçipreste de Talavera o Corbacho*. Ed. Michael Gerli. Madrid: Ediciones Cátedra, 1979.

———. *Little Sermons on Sin. The Archpriest of Talavera*. Trans. Lesley Byrd Simpson. Berkeley: U of California P, 1959.

Andreas Capellanus. *De Amore*. Ed. E. Trojel. Munich: Eidos Verlag, 1964.

——. *The Art of Courtly Love*. Trans. John Jay Parry. New York: Frederick Ungar, 1964.

Anonymous. "The Poet's Repentance." *The Harley Lyrics: The Middle English Lyrics of MS. Harley 2253*. Ed. G. L. Brook. Manchester: Manchester UP, 1954. 33-34.

Apuleius, Lucius. *Metamorphoseon oder Der Goldene Esel*. Ed. and trans. Rudolf Helm. 6th ed. Schriften und Quellen der Alten Welt 1. Berlin: Akademie-Verlag, 1970.

Arator. "Epistle to Parthenius." *Arator's* On the Acts of the Apostles (De Actibus Apostolorum). Trans. Richard J. Schrader et al. Atlanta: Scholars Press, 1987. 101-03.

——. "Epistola ad Parthenium." Ed. J. P. Migne. *Patrologiae Cursus Completus* 68. Turnholti: Brepols, 1963. 245-52.

——. "Epistola ad Vigilium." Ed. J. P. Migne. *Patrologiae Cursus Completus* 68. Turnholti: Brepols, 1963. 71-82.

Aristophanes. *The Thesmophoriazusae*. Trans. Benjamin Bickley Rogers. Cambridge: Harvard UP, 1955. 130-241.

Augustine, Saint. *Confessionum Libri XIII*. Ed. Lucas Verheijen. *Corpus Christianorum Series Latina* 27. Turnholti: Brepols, 1981.

——. *De civitate Dei*. Ed. Johann Divjak. 5th ed. Stuttgart: Teubner, 1981.

——. *De genesi ad litteram libri duodecim*. Trans. P. Agaësse and A. Signac. Paris: Desclée de Brouwer, 1972.

——. *Retractationum Libri II*. Ed. Almut Mutzenbecher. *Corpus Christianorum Series Latina* 57. Turnholti: Brepols, 1984.

——. *Saint Augustine Confessions*. Trans. Vernon J. Bourke. The Fathers of the Church 21. Washington, DC: Catholic U of America P, 1953.

——. *The Retractations*. Trans. Mary Inez Bogan. The Fathers of the Church 60. Washington, DC: Catholic U of America P, 1968.

Baudonivia of Poitiers. *The Life of St. Radegund by Baudonivia of Poitiers*. Trans. Marcelle Thiébaux. *The Writings of Wedieval Women: An Anthology*. 2nd ed. New York: Garland, 1994. 106-120.

Bede. *Commentary on the Acts of the Apostles*. Trans. Lawrence T. Martin. Cistercian Studies 117. Kalamazoo, MI: Cistercian Publications, 1989.

——. "Concerning Figures and Tropes." Trans. Gussie Hecht Tannenhaus. *Readings in Medieval Rhetoric*. Eds. Joseph M. Miller, Michael H. Prosser, and Thomas W. Benson. Bloomington: Indiana UP, 1973. 96-122.

——. *De Arte Metrica et De Schematibus et Tropis*. Eds. C. B. Kendall and M. H. King. *Corpus Christianorum Series Latina* CXXIII A. Turnholti: Brepols, 1975. 60-171.

——. *De Temporum Ratione*. Ed. Ch. W. Jones. *Corpus Christianorum Series Latina* CXXIII B. Turnholti: Brepols, 1977.

——. *Expositio Actuum Apostolorum et Retractatio*. Ed. M. L. W. Laistner. The Medieval Academy of America Publication 35. 1939. New York: Kraus Reprint, 1970.

Boccaccio, Giovanni. "A Mainardo Cavalcanti (1373)." *Opere latine minori*. Ed. Aldo Francesco Massèra. Bari: Guiseppe Laterza, 1928. 209-14.

——. *Boccaccio on Poetry*. Trans. Charles G. Osgood. Princeton: Princeton UP, 1930.

——. *Corbaccio*. Ed. Pier Giorgio Ricci. Turin: Guilio Einaudi Editore, 1977.

——. *Decameron*. Ed. Vittore Branca. Turin: Guilio Einaudi Editore, 1980.

——. *Genealogie deorum gentilium Libri*. Ed. Vincenzo Romano. 2 vols. Scrittori d'Italia 201. Bari: Giuseppe Laterza, 1951. Vol 2.

——. *The Decameron*. Trans. Mark Musa and Peter Bondanella. New York: Norton, 1982.

——. *The Corbaccio or the Labyrinth of Love*. Trans. and ed. Anthony K. Cassell. 2nd rev. ed. Binghamton, NY: Medieval & Renaissance Texts & Studies, 1993.

Boethius, Anicius Manlius Severinus. *Philosophiae Consolatio*. Ed. Ludwig Bieler. Turnholti: Brepols, 1984.

——. *The Consolation of Philosophy*. Trans. Richard Green. New York: Macmillan, 1986.

Bozon, Nicole. *Char d'Orgueil. Deux Poemes de Nicholas Bozon*. Göteborg: Elanders, 1905. 3-60.

——. *De la Bonté des femmes. Les contes moralisés de Nicole Bozon*. Eds. Lucy Toulmin Smith and Paul Meyer. Reprint. Paris: Librairie de Firmin Didot, 1968. xxxiii-xli.

Callimachus. *Aetia*. Trans. C. A. Trypanis. Cambridge: Harvard UP, 1975. 1-99.

Catullus, Gaius Valerius. "Poem 42." *The Poems of Catullus*. Trans. Horace Gregory. New York: Covici-Friede, 1931. 100-01.

Chartier, Alain. *The Poetical Works of Alain Chartier*. Ed. J. C. Laidlaw. London: Cambridge UP, 1974.

Chaucer, Geoffrey. *The Riverside Chaucer*. Ed. Larry D. Benson. Boston: Houghton Mifflin, 1987.

Cixous, Hélène. "Sorties." *New French Feminisms: An Anthology*. Eds. Elaine Marks and Isabelle de Courtivron. New York: Schocken Books, 1980. 90-98.

Cynddelw Brydydd. Mawr. "Marwysgafn Cynddelw." *The Myvyrian Archaiology of Wales*. Ed. Owen Jones et al. Denbigh: Thomas Gee, 1870. 78.

——. "Poem on His Death-bed." Trans. Gwyn Jones. *The Oxford Book of Welsh Verse in English*. Oxford: Oxford UP, 1977. 27-30.

Cynewulf. *Cynewulf's* Elene. Ed. P. O. E. Gradon. Exeter: University of Exeter, 1977.

——. *Elene. Anglo-Saxon Poetry*. Trans. S. A. J. Bradley. London: Dent, 1982. 165-97.

Dante Alighieri. *Dante's Vita Nuova: A Translation and an Essay*. Trans. Mark Musa. Bloomington: Indiana UP, 1973.

——. *The Divine Comedy*. Trans. Charles Eliot Norton. Chicago: Henry Regnery, 1951.

——. *Vita Nuova*. Ed. Vittorio Cozzoli. Milan: EDIS Edizione Culturali, 1995.

Dhuoda. *Handbook for William: A Carolingian Woman's Counsel for Her Son*. Trans. Carol Neel. Lincoln and London: U of Nebraska P, 1991.

Diego de San Pedro. *Cárcel de Amor*. Ed. Carmen Parilla. Barcelona: Critica, 1995.

——. *Desprecio de la Fortuna. Obras completas*. Eds. Dorothy S. Severin and Keith Whinnom. 5 vols. Madrid: Unigraf, 1979. 3: 275-97.

——. *Prison of Love*. Trans. Keith Whinnom. Edinburgh: Edinburgh UP, 1979.

Don Juan Manuel. *El Conde Lucanor*. Eds. Carlos Alvar and Pilar Palanco. Barcelona: Planeta, 1984.

——. *The Book of Count Lucanor and Patronio: A Translation of Don Juan Manuel's* El Conde Lucanor. Trans. John E. Keller, L. Clark Keating, and Barbara E. Gaddy. New York: Peter Lang, 1993.

Dracontius, Blossius Aemilius. *De laudibus Dei*. Ed. Friedrich Vollmer. Berlin: Weidmann, 1905.

——. *Dracontii Satisfactio*. Trans. M. Margaret. Diss. Philadelphia: U of Pennsylvania, 1936.

Gerald of Wales. "Retractationes." *Opera*. Ed. J. S. Brewer. 6 vols. London: Longman, 1861. 1: 425-27.

Goch, Llywelyn. "I Dduw." *The Myvyrian Archaiology of Wales*. Ed. Owen Jones et al. Denbigh: Thomas Gee, 1870. 354.

——. "Lament for Lleucu Llwyd." Joseph P. Clancy. *The Oxford Book of Welsh Verse in English*. Oxford: Oxford UP, 1977. 43-45.

——. "Marwnad Lleucu Llwyd." *The Oxford Book of Welsh Verse*. Ed. Thomas Parry. Oxford: Clarendon, 1962. 43-45.

Goethe, Johann Wolfgang von. *Faust*. Ed. Walter Kaufmann. Garden City, NY: Anchor Press, 1962.

Green, Jonathan. *The Cynic's Lexicon*. New York: St. Martin's, 1984.

Guibert de Nogent. *A Monk's Confession: The Memoirs of Guibert of Nogent*. Trans. Paul J. Archambault. University Park: Pennsylvania State UP, 1996.

——. *Autobiographie*. Ed. and trans. Edmond-René Labande. Paris: Société d'Édition Les Belles Lettres, 1981.

Guillaume le Clerc de Normandie. *Le Besant de Dieu*. Ed. Pierre Ruelle. Université Libre de Bruxelles 54. Bruxelles: Editions de l'Université de Bruxelles, 1973.

Guto'r, Glyn. "Meditation." Trans. Joseph P. Clancy. *Medieval Welsh Lyrics*. New York: St. Martin's, 1965. 221-23.

——. "Ystyriaeth Bywyd." *Gwaith Guto'r Glyn*. Eds. John Llywelyn Williams and Ifor Williams. Caerdydd: Gwasg Prifysgol Cymry, 1961. 305-07.

Hartmann von Aue. *Gregorius*. Ed. Hermann Paul. 13th ed. Tübingen: Max Niemeyer, 1984.

Hildegard von Bingen. *Epistolarium*. Ed. L. van Acker. 2 vols. *Corpus Christianorum Continuatio Medievalis* 91 and 91:A. Turnholti: Brepols, 1991, 1993.

——. *Hildegard of Bingen: Scivias*. Trans. C. Hart and J. Bishop. New York: Paulist Press, 1990.

——. *Scivias*. Ed. A. Führkötter. 2 vols. *Corpus Christianorum Continuatio Medievalis* 43 and 43:A. Turnholti: Brepols, 1978.

——. *The Letters of Hildegard of Bingen*. Trans. J. L. Baird and R. K. Ehrman. Vol. 1. New York: Oxford UP, 1994.

Hoccleve, Thomas. *Hoccleve's Works*. Ed. Frederick J. Furnivall. Reprint 1937. London: Oxford UP, 1892.

Horace. *Q. Horatius Flaccus: Oden und Epoden*. Ed. A. Kiessling. 4th ed. 2 vols. Berlin: Weidmann, 1901.

——. *Horace: The Complete Odes and Epodes and the Centennial Hymn*. Trans. W. G. Shepherd. Harmondsworth: Penguin, 1983.

——. *Horaz: Satiren und Episteln*. Ed. and trans. Otto Schönberger. Schriften und Quellen der Alten Welt 33. Berlin: Akademie-Verlag, 1976.

Hrotswitha von Gandersheim. *Hrotsvithae Opera*. Ed. H. Homeyer. Munich: Ferdinand Schöningh, 1970.

——. *The Plays of Hrotsvit of Gandersheim*. Trans. Katharina Wilson. New York: Garland, 1989.

Hugeberc von Hildesheim. *The Hodoeporicon of St. Willibald*. Trans. C. H. Talbot. *Medieval Women's Visionary Literature*. Ed. Elizabeth Alvilda Petroff. Oxford: Oxford UP, 1986. 92-106.

Ibn Hazm. *The Ring of the Dove: A Treatise on the Art and Practice of Arab Love*. Trans. A. J. Arberry. London: Luzac, 1953.

Isidore of Seville. *Isidore of Seville on the Pagan Gods* (Origines *VIII.11*). Ed. Katherine Nell MacFarlane. Philadelphia: The American Philosophical Society, 1980.

Irigaray, Luce. *The Irigaray Reader*. Ed. Margaret Whitford. Oxford: Blackwell, 1991.

Jean de Meun. *Le Testament*. Ed. Aimee Celest Bourneuf. Diss. New York: Fordham University, 1956.

——, and Guillaume de Lorris. *Le Roman de la Rose*. Ed. Félix Lecoy. 3 vols. Paris: Librairie Honoré Champion, 1968.

——. *Le Roman de la Rose*. Ed. Ernest Langlois. 5 vols. Paris: Librairie Ancienne Edouard Champion, 1912.

——. *The Romance of the Rose*. Trans. Charles Dahlberg. 1971. Hanover: UP of New England, 1986.

Jean le Fèvre. *Les Lamentations des Matheolus et le Livre de Leesce*. Ed. A. G. van Hamel. 2 vols. Paris: Librairie Émile Bouillon, 1905.

Juan de Mena. "Coplas que fizo el famoso Juan de Mena contra los pecados mortales." *Cancionero Castellano del siglo XV*. Ed. R. Foulché-Delbosc. 2 vols. Madrid: Bailly-Balliére, 1912. 1: 120-52.

Juan Rodríguez del Padrón. "Fuego del diuino rayo." *Obras Completas*. Ed. Cesar Hernandez Alonso. Madrid: Editora Nacional, 1982. 340-41.

Juvencus. "Praefatio." *Early Christian Latin Poets from the Fourth to the Sixth Century*. Ed. and trans. Otto J. Kuhnmuench. Chicago: Loyola UP, 1929. 18-19.

Konrad von Fußesbrunnen. *Die Kindheit Jesu*. Eds. Hans Fromm and Klaus Grubmüller. Berlin: Walter de Gruyter, 1973.

Kundera, Milan. *The Unbearable Lightness of Being*. Trans. Michael Henry Heim. New York: Harper & Row, 1984.

Langland, William. *Piers Plowman: The A Version*. Ed. George Kane. Rev. ed. Vol. 1. London: Athalone Press, 1988.

——. *Piers Plowman: The B Version*. Eds. George Kane and E. Talbot Donaldson. Rev. ed. Vol. 2. London: Athalone Press, 1988.

——. *Piers Plowman: An Edition of the C-text*. Ed. Derek Pearsall. Berkeley: U of California P, 1978.

Llull, Ramon. *Vita coetanea. Das Leben des seligen Raimund Llull, dei Vita coetanea und ausgewählte Texte aus seinen Werken und Zeitdokumenten*. Ed. Erhard W. Platzeck. Düsseldorf: Patmos Verlag, 1964. 145-80.

Lucian. *Apology for the "Salaried Posts in Great Houses."* Trans. K. Kilburn. Loeb Classics. 7 vols. Cambridge: Harvard UP, 1959. 6: 191-213.

——. *Philosophies for Sale*. Trans. A. M. Harmon. Loeb Classics. 7 vols. New York: Macmillan, 1915. 2: 449-511.

——. *The Fisherman. Selected Satires of Lucian*. Ed. and trans. Lionel Casson. Chicago: Aldine Publishing, 1962. 334-363.

Machaut, Guillaume de. "Le Lay de Plour." *The Judgment of the King of Navarre*. Ed. and trans. R. Barton Palmer. Garland Library of Medieval Literature A45. New York: Garland, 1988. 190-213.

——. *The Judgment of the King of Bohemia*. Ed. and trans. R. Barton Palmer. Garland Library of Medieval Literature A9. New York: Garland, 1984.

——. *The Judgment of the King of Navarre*. Ed. and trans. R. Barton Palmer. Garland Library of Medieval Literature A45. New York: Garland., 1988.

Marbod de Rennes. *Liber decem capitulorum*. Ed. Rosario Leotta. Rome: Herder, 1984.

Marie de France. *Fables*. Ed. and trans. Harriet Spiegel. Toronto: U of Toronto P, 1987.

Mechthild von Magdeburg. *Das fließende Licht der Gottheit*. Ed. Hans Neumann and Gisela Vollmann-Profe. Munich: Artemis Verlag, 1990.

——. *Flowing Light of the Divinity*. Ed. Susan Clark. Trans. Christiane Mesch Galvani. New York: Garland, 1991.

Meilyr Brydydd. "Marw ysgafyn Veilyr brydyt." *Poetry by Medieval Welsh Bards*. Ed. J. Gwenogvryn Evans. 2 vols. Llanbedrog: Pwllheli, 1926. 2: 182-83.

——. "On His Death-bed." Trans. Tony Conran. *Welsh Verse*. Berkeley: U of California P, 1974. 139-41.

Mexía, Hernán. "Otras suyas en que descubre los defectos de las condiciones de las mugeres, por mandado de dos damas." *Cancionero Castellano del siglo XV*. Ed. R. Foulché-Delbosc. 2 vols. Madrid: Bailly-Bailliére, 1912. 1: 280-85.

——. "Pensado que unas coplas que halló en vn cancionero de mal dezir de mugeres eran suyas." *Cancionero Castellano del siglo XV*. Ed. R. Foulché-Delbosc. 2 vols. Madrid: Bailly-Bailliére, 1912. 1: 276-77.

Neidhart von Reuental. *Die Lieder Neidharts*. Ed. Siegfried Beyschlag. Darmstadt: Wissenschaftliche Buchgesellschaft, 1975.

The New American Bible. Wichita: Catholic Bible Publishers, 1983.

Otloh von Emmeram. *Das Buch von seinen Versuchungen*. Ed. and trans. Wilhelm Blum. Aschendorff Münster: Aschendorffsche Buchdruckerei, 1977.

Ovid. *Amores*. Ed. E. J. Kenney. Oxford: Clarendon, 1961. 1-107.

——. *Ars Amatoria*. Ed. E. J. Kenney. Oxford: Clarendon, 1961. 113-200.

——. *Metamorphoses*. Ed. and trans. Georges Lafaye. 3 vols. Paris: Société d'Édition "Les Belles Lettres," 1985.

——. *Ovid:* Amores *Text, Prolegomena and Commentary*. Ed. J. C. McKeown. 2 vols. ARCA Classical and Medieval Texts, Papers and Monographs 22. Leeds: Francis Cairns Ltd., 1989.

——. *Ovid: Tristia. Ex Ponto*. Trans. Arthur Leslie Wheeler. 2nd ed. Loeb Classics. 6 vols. Cambridge: Harvard UP, 1988. Vol. 6.

——. *Remedia Amoris*. Ed. A. A. R. Henderson. Edinburgh: Scottish Academic Press, 1979.

——. *The Love Poems*. Trans. A. D. Melville. Oxford: Oxford UP, 1990.

The Oxford English Dictionary. 2nd ed. Oxford: Clarendon, 1989.

The Oxford Latin Dictionary. Oxford: Clarendon, 1982.

Paulinus of Nola. "Carmen XII." *Corpus Scriptorum Ecclesiasticorum Latinorum* 29. Vindobonae: F. Tempsky, 1894. 186-93.

——. "Poem 22." *The Poems of St. Paulinus of Nola*. Trans. P. G. Walsh. New York: Newman Press, 1975. 202-08.

Peter of Blois. "XVII ['A new leaf']." *The Virgin and the Nightingale: Medieval Latin Poems*. Trans. Fleur Adcock. Newcastle: Bloodaxe Books Ltd., 1983. 70-71.

Petrarch, Francesco. *Canzioniere*. Ed. Gianfranco Contini. Turin: Giulio Einaudi, 1964.

——. *Epistole*. Ed. Ugo Dotti. Turin: Unione Tipografico, 1978.

——. *Francis Petrarch: Letters of Old Age:* Rerum senilium libri I-XVIII. Trans. Aldo S. Bernardo, Saul Levin, and Reta A. Bernardo. 2 vols. Baltimore: Johns Hopkins UP, 1992.

——. *Francesco Petrarca: Letters on Familiar Matters:* Rerum familiarium libri XVII-XXIV. Trans. Aldo S. Bernardo. Baltimore: Johns Hopkins UP, 1985.

——. *Petrarch's Lyric Poems. The* Rime Sparse *and Other Lyrics.* Trans. Robert M. Durling. Cambridge: Harvard UP, 1976.

——. *Petrarch's* Secretum *with Introduction, Notes,and Critical Anthology.* Trans. Davy A. Carozza and H. James Shey. American University Studies. New York: Peter Lang, 1989.

——. *Secretum. Opere latine.* Ed. Antonietta Bufano et al. 2 vols. Turin: Unione Tipografico, 1975. 1: 44-259.

——. *The* Triumphs *of Petrarch.* Trans. Ernest Hatch Wilkins. Chicago: U of Chicago P, 1962.

——. *Trionfi. Rime e Trionfi.* Ed. Ferdinando Neri. 2nd ed. Turin: Unione Tipografico, 1960. 511-618.

Piccolomini, Aeneas Sylvius (Pius II). "Bulla Retractationum." *Opera Omnia.* Reprint. Frankfurt: Minerva, 1967. 1-8.

——. *De Gestis Consilii Basiliensis Commentariorum Libri II.* Eds. and trans. Denys Hay and W. K. Smith. Oxford: Clarendon, 1967.

——. *The Goodli History of the Ladye Lucres of Scene and of her Lover Eurialus.* Ed. E. J. Morrall. Eearly English Texts Society 308. Oxford: Oxford UP, 1996.

Piramus, Denis. *La Vie Seint Edmund le rei: Poème anglo-normand du XIIe siècle.* Ed. Hilding Kjellman. Geneva: Slatkine Reprints, 1974.

Plato. *Phaedrus. Great Books of the Western World.* Trans. Benjamin Jowett. Chicago: Encyclopedia Brittanica, Inc., 1952. 7: 115-41.

Proba, Faltonia Betitia. *Probae Cento.* Trans. Elizabeth A. Clark and Diane F. Hatch. *The Golden Bough, The Oaken Cross: The Vergilian Cento of Faltonia Betitia Proba.* Chico, CA: Scholars Press, 1981. 12-95.

Rudolf von Ems. *Barlaam und Josaphat.* Ed. Franz Pfeiffer. Berlin: Walter de Gruyter, 1965.

Ruiz, Juan. *Libro de buen amor.* Ed. G. B. Gybbon-Monypenny. Madrid: Editorial Castalia, 1988.

——. *The Book of Good Love.* Trans. Elisha Kent Kane. Chapel Hill: U of North Carolina P, 1968.

Rutebeuf. "La repentance de Rutebeuf." *Rutebeuf: Oeuvres complètes.* Paris: Bordas, 1989. 1: 298-303.

Sedulius. *Paschale Carmen. Sedulii opera omnia*. Ed. Johannes Huemer. *Corpus Scriptorum Ecclesiasticorum Latinorum* 10. 1-146.

Serlo of Wilton. *Serlon de Wilton: Poèmes latins*. Ed. Öberg, Jan. Stockholm: Almqvist and Wiskell, 1965.

Sidonius, Apollonaris. *Poems and Letters*. Trans. W. B. Anderson. 2 vols. Cambridge: Harvard UP, 1965.

Stehling, Thomas, trans. *Medieval Latin Poems of Male Love and Friendship*. Garland Library of Medieval Literature, Series A. Vol. 7. New York: Garland, 1984.

Stesichorus. "Helen and Klytaimnestra." Trans. Richmond Lattimore. *Greek Lyrics*. 2nd ed. Chicago: U of Chicago P, 1960. 37.

Sturluson, Snorri. *The Prose Edda*. Trans. Arthur Gilchrist Brodeur. New York: The American-Scandinavian Foundation, 1916.

Tapia, Juan de. "La Glosa." *Cancionero General de Hernando del Castillo*. 2nd ed. 2 vols. Madrid: La Sociedad de Bibliofilos Españoles, 1882. 2: 70-72.

Teresa de Cartagena. *The Writings of Teresa de Cartagena*. Trans. Dayle Seidenspinner-Núñez. Cambridge: Brewer, 1998.

Thomasin of Zirclaere. *Der Wälsche Gast*. Ed. Heinrich Rückert. Quendlinburg and Leipzig 1852.

Torroella, Pere. "Maldezir de mugeres." *The Works of Pere Torroella: A Catalan Writer of the Fifteenth Century*. Ed. Pedro Bach y Rita. New York: Instituto de las Españas, 1930. 199-215.

—. "Razonamiento de Pere Torroella e deffensión de las donas contra los maldizientes por satisfacción de unas coplas que en dezir mal de aquéllas compuso." *The Works of Pere Torroella: A Catalan Writer of the Fifteenth Century*. Ed. Pedro Bach y Rita. New York: Instituto de las Españas, 1930. 296-306.

Ulrich von Türheim. *Rennewart*. Ed. Alfred Hübner. Deutsche Texte des Mittelalters. Berlin: Weidmann, 1964.

Walther von der Vogelweide. *Walther von der Vogelweide: Leich, Lieder, Sangsprüche*. Eds. Karl Lachmann and Christoph Cormeau. 14th ed. Berlin: Walter de Gruyter, 1996.

Wandalbert von Prüm. *Martyrologium*. Ed. J. P. Migne. *Patrologiae Cursus Completus* 121. Turnholti: Brepols, 1963. 567-622.

Watriquet de Couvin. *Dits de Watriquet de Couvin*. Ed. August Scheler. Brussels: Victor Devaux, 1868.

William of Aquitaine. "Pos de chantar m'es pres talentz." *The Medieval Lyric. Anthology 1*. Mount Holyoke College: 1988. 42-43.

SECONDARY TEXTS

Adolf, Helen. "Walther von der Vogelweide and the Awakening of Personality." *Germanic Studies in Honor of Edward Henry Sehrt*. Eds. Frithjof Andersen Raven et al. Coral Gables, FL: U of Miami P, 1968. 1-13.

Ady, Cecilia M. *Pius II (Aeneas Silvius Piccolomini the Humanist Pope)*. London: Methuen, 1913.

Aers, David. *Chaucer, Langland and the Creative Imagination*. London: Routledge & Kegan Paul, 1980.

Ahsan, M. M., and A. R. Kidwai, eds. *Sacrilege versus Civility: Muslim Perspectives on the Satanic Verses Affair*. Markfield, UK: Islamic Foundation, 1991.

Alexander, William Hardy. *Horace's Odes and Carmen Saeculare*. Berkeley: U of California P, 1947.

Allen, Judson Boyce. *The Ethical Poetic of the Later Middle Ages: A Decorum of Convenient Distinction*. Toronto: U of Toronto P, 1982.

——, and Theresa Anne Moritz. *A Distinction of Stories: The Medieval Unity of Chaucer's Fair Chain of Narratives for Canterbury*. Columbus: Ohio State UP, 1981.

Alonso, Cesar Hernandez. Introduction. *Obras completas*. By Juan Rodríguez del Padrón. Madrid: Editora Nacional, 1982. 9-136.

Amory, Frederic. "The Confessional Superstructure of Guibert of Nogent's *Vita*." *Classica et Medieavalia* 25 (1964): 224-40.

Anderson, Earl R. *Cynewulf: Structure, Style, and Theme in His Poetry*. London: Associated UP, 1983.

Andersson, Theodore M. "The Politics of Snorri Sturluson." *Journal of English and Germanic Philology* 93.1 (1994): 55-78.

Annas, Julia. "Classical Greek Philosophy." *The Oxford History of the Classical World*. Eds. John Broadman, Jasper Griffin, and Oswyn Murray. Oxford: Oxford UP, 1986. 234-53.

Arberry, A. J. Preface. *The Ring of the Dove*. By Ibn Hazm. London: Luzac, 1953. 7-14.

Arbusow, Leonid. *Colores Rhetorici: Eine Auswahl rhetorischer Figuren und Gemeinplätze als Hilfsmittel für akademische Übungen an mittelalterlichen Texten*. Göttingen: Vandenhoeck & Ruprecht, 1948.

Aubrun, Charles V. *Le Chansonnier espagnol d'Herberay des Essarts*. Bordeaux: Feret, 1951.

Baca, Albert A. "Enea Silvio Piccolominis Verteidigung der Literatur." *Antike und Abendland* 17 (1971): 162-72.

——. Introduction. *Selected Letters of Aeneas Silvius Piccolomini*. Trans. Albert R. Baca. Northridge, CA: San Fernando Valley State College, 1969. xi-xiv.

Bach y Rita, Pedro. *The Works of Pere Torroella: A Catalan Writer of the Fifteenth Century*. New York: Instituto de las Españas, 1930.

Badel, Pierre-Yves. Le Roman de la Rose *au XIV siècle: Étude de la réception de l'oeuvre*. Geneva: Librairie Droz, 1980.

Baker, Donald C. "Dreamer and Critic: The Poet in the *Legend of Good Women*." *University of Colorado Studies: Series in Language and Literature* 9 (1963): 4-18.

Baldwin, John W. "The Image of the *Jongleur* in Northern France around 1200." *Speculum* 72.3 (1997): 635-63.

Baldwin, Ralph. *The Unity of* The Canterbury Tales. Anglistica 5. Copenhagen: Rosenkilde and Bagger, 1955.

Barchiesi, Alessandro. *The Poet and the Prince: Ovid and Augustan Discourse*. Berkeley: U of California P, 1997.

Bardenhewer, Otto. *Geschichte der altkirchlichen Literatur*. Vol. 4. Darmstadt: Wissenschaftliche Buchgesellschaft, 1962.

Barney, Stephen A. "Notes on *Troilus and Criseyde*." Benson 1020-58.

Baron, Hans. *Petrarch's* Secretum: *Its Making and Its Meaning*. Cambridge: Medieval Academy of America, 1985.

Barsby, John A. *Ovid*. Oxford: Clarendon, 1978.

Barthes, Roland. "The Death of the Author." *Falling into Theory: Conflicting Views on Reading Literature*. Ed. David H. Richter. Boston: Bedford, 1994. 222-6.

Bartlett, Robert. *Gerald of Wales 1146-1223*. Oxford: Clarendon, 1982.

Battaglia, Salvatore. *Le Epoche della letteratura Italiana: Medioevio, Umanesimo, Rinascimento*. Naples: Liguroni, 1965.

Baum, Paull F. *Chaucer: A Critical Appreciation*. Durham: Duke UP, 1958.

Baumlin, Tita French. "Theology and Discourse in the *Pardoner's Tale*, the *Parson's Tale*, and the *Retraction*." *Renascence* (1989): 127-42.

Beer, Jeanette M. A. *Narrative Conventions of Truth in the Middle Ages*. Geneva: Librairie Droz, 1981.

Bell, H. I. *The Nature of Poetry as Conceived by the Welsh Bards*. Oxford: Clarendon, 1955.

Benson, Larry D., ed. *The Riverside Chaucer*. 3rd ed. Boston: Houghton Mifflin, 1987.

Benton, J. F. *Culture, Power and Personality in Medieval France*. Ed. Thomas N. Bisson. London: Hambledon, 1991.

Bérard, Claude Cazalé. "Propositions pour une approche de la thématique dans l'intratextualit', l'intertextualité et l'extratextualité." *Strumenti Critici* n.s., a. 4 (1989): 305-20.

Bergin, Thomas G. *Petrarch*. New York: Twayne, 1970.

Bernardo, Aldo S. "Dante, Petrarch, and Boccaccio." Corrigan 270-317.

——. "Laura as a *Nuova Figura*." *Francesco Petrarcha, Citizen of the World: Proceedings of the World Petrarch Congress, Washington, DC, April 6-13 1974*. Ed. Aldo S. Bernardo. Albany: State U of New York P, 1980. 179-92.

——. *Petrarch, Laura, and the* Triumphs. Albany: State U of New York P, 1974.

Beumann, Helmut. "Topos und Gedankengefüge bei Einhard." *Archiv für Kulturgeschichte* 33 (1951): 337-50.

Bjork, Robert E, ed. *Cynewulf: Basic Readings*. Basic Readings in Anglo-Saxon England 4. New York: Garland, 1996.

——. *The Old English Verse Saints' Lives: A Study in Direct Discourse and the Iconography of Style*. McMaster Old English Studies and Texts 4. Toronto: U of Toronto P, 1985.

Blamires, Alcuin. *The Case for Women in the Medieval Culture*. Oxford: Clarendon, 1997.

Blanc, P. "Petrarca ou la poétique de l'ego: elements de psychopoétique Pétrarchienne." *Revue des Études Italiennes* 29 (1983): 122-69.

Bloom, Harold, ed. *Petrarch*. Modern Critical Views. New York: Chelsea House, 1989.

Bloomfield, Morton W. "*The Canterbury Tales* as Framed Narratives." *Leeds Studies in English* n.s. 14 (1983): 44-56.

Blumenfeld-Kosinski, Renate. "Jean le Fèvre's *Livre de Leesce*: Praise or Blame of Women?" *Speculum* 69.3 (1994): 705-25.

Blumenthal, Amy. "New Muses: Poetry in Boethius's *Consolatio*." *Pacific Coast Philology* 21 (1986): 25-29.

Boenig, Robert. "Taking Leave: Chaucer's Retraction and the the Ways of Affirmation and Negation." *Studia Mystica* 12 (1989): 21-34.

Bogan, Mary Inez. Introduction. *The Retractations*. By St. Augustine. The Fathers of the Church 60. Washington, DC: Catholic U of America P, 1968. xiii-xxi.

Boitani, Piero. *Chaucer and the Imaginary World of Fame*. Totowa, NJ: Barnes & Noble, 1984.

Bolgar, R. R. "The Teaching of Rhetoric in the Middle Ages." *Rhetoric Revalued: Papers from the International Society for the History of Rhetoric*. Ed. Brian Vickers. Binghamton, NY: Center for Medieval & Early Renaissance Studies, 1982. 79-86.

Bolton, W. F. *A History of Anglo-Latin Literature 597-1066*. Princeton: Princeton UP, 1967.

Boor, Helmut de. *Die höfische Literatur: Vorbereitung, Blüte, Ausklang, 1170-1250*. 9th ed. Munich: C. H. Beck, 1974.

Bornstein, Diane. "Anti-Feminism in Thomas Hoccleve's Translation of Christine de Pizan's *Epistre au dieu d'amours*." *English Literary Notes* 19 (1981): 7-14.

Boulting, William. *Aeneas Silvius (Enea Silvio de' Piccolomini-Pius II) Orator, Man of Letters, Statesman, and Pope*. London: Archibald Constable, 1908.

Boutière, J., and A. H. Schutz. *Biographies des Troubadours: Textes Provencaux des XIII et XIV Siècles*. Paris: A. G. Nizet, 1964.

Bowers, John M. *The Crisis of Will in* Piers Plowman. Washington, DC: Catholic U of America P, 1986.

Bowra, C. M. *Greek Lyric Poetry: From Alcman to Simonides*. 2nd ed. Oxford: Clarendon, 1961. 74-129.

Boyer, Augustín. *Estudio descriptivo del* Libro de las virtuosas e claras mugeres *de Don Alvaro de Luna: fuentes, género y ubicación en la debate feminista del siglo XV*. Diss. Berkeley: U of California, 1988.

Böhm, H. *Walther von der Vogelweide*. Stuttgart: Köhler, 1949.

Branham, Bracht R. *Unruly Eloquence: Lucian and the Comedy of Traditions*. Cambridge: Harvard UP, 1989.

Bray, Gerald. "Explaining Christianity to Pagans: The Second-Century Apologists." *The Trinity in a Pluralistic Age: Theological Essays on Culture and Religion*. Ed. Kevin J. Vanhoozer. Grand Rapids, MI: Eerdman, 1997. 9-25.

Brehaut, Ernest. *An Encyclopedist of the Dark Ages: Isidore of Seville*. New York: Burt Franklin, 1964.

Brewer, Charlotte. "Authorial vs. Scribal Writing in *Piers Plowman*." *Medieval Literature: Texts and Interpretation*. Ed. Tim William Machan. Binghamton, NY: Medieval & Renaissance Texts & Studies, 1991. 59-89.

Brewer, Derek. *Chaucer*. London: Longman, 1961.

——. *Chaucer: The Poet as Storyteller*. London: Macmillan, 1984.

——, ed. "Gothic Chaucer." *Geoffrey Chaucer*. Athens: Ohio UP, 1975. 1-32.

Bright, David F. *The Miniature Epic in Vandal Africa*. Norman: U of Oklahoma P, 1987.

Brincken, Anna-Dorothee von den. "Geschichtsbetrachtung bei Vincenz von Beauvais: Die *Apologia Actoris* zum *Speculum Maius*." *Deutsches Archiv für Erforschung des Mittelalters* 34 (1978): 410-99.

Brodeur, Arthur Gilchrist. Introduction. *The Prose Edda*. By Snorri Sturluson. New York: The American-Scandinavian Foundation, 1916. ix-xxii.

Broich, Ulrich. "Formen der Markierung von Intertextualität." *Intertextualität: Formen, Funktionen, anglistische Fallstudien*. Eds. Ulrich Broich and Manfred Pfister. Konzepte der Sprach- und Literaturwissenschaft 35. Tübingen: Max Niemeyer, 1985. 31-47.

Bromwich, Rachel. "The Earlier *Cywyddwyr*: Poets Contemporary with Dafydd ap Gwilym." Eds. A. O. H. Jarman and Gwilym Rees Hughes. *A Guide to Welsh Literature*. 2 vols. Swansea: Christopher Davies, 1979. 2: 144-68.

Bronson, Bertrand H. *In Search of Chaucer*. Toronto: U of Toronto P, 1960.

Brown, Carleton. "The Autobiographical Element in the Cynewulfian Rune Passages." *Englische Studien* 38 (1907): 196-233.

Brown, George Hardin. *Bede the Venerable*. Boston: Twayne, 1987.

Brown, J. "Chaucer's Double Apology for the *Miller's Tale*." *University of Colorado Studies: Series in Language and Literature* 10 (1966): 15-22.

Brown, Peter. *The Body and Society: Men, Women and Sexual Renunciation in Early Christianity*. New York: Columbia UP, 1988.

Browne, G. F. *The Venerable Bede*. New York: Pott, Young, 1879.

Brownlee, Kevin. *Poetic Identity in Guillaume de Machaut*. Madison: U of Wisconsin P, 1984.

Brunhölzl, Franz. *Geschichte der lateinischen Literatur des Mittelalters*. Munich: Wilhelm Fink, 1975.Vol. 1.

Brusendorff, Aage. *The Chaucer Tradition*. London: Oxford UP, 1925.

Buermann, Theodore Barry. *Chaucer's "Book of Genesis" in* The Canterbury Tales: *The Biblical Schema of the First Fragment*. Diss. U of Illinois. 1967.

Bulst, Walther. "Studien zu Marbods *Carmina varia* und *Liber decem capitulorum*." *Nachrichten von der Gesellschaft der Wissenschaften zu Göttingen* (1939): 173-241.

Burdach, Konrad. "Walthers Aufruf zum Kreuzzug Kaiser Friedrichs II." *Walther von der Vogelweide*. Ed. Siegfried Beyschlag. Wege der Forschung 112. Darmstadt: Wissenschaftliche Buchgesellschaft, 1971. 117-39.

Burke, Séan. *The Death and Return of the Author: Criticism and Subjectivity in Barthes, Foucault and Derrida*. Edinburgh: Edinburgh UP, 1992.

Busse, Eberhard Kurt. *Ulrich von Türheim*. Palaestra 121. Berlin: Mayer & Müller, 1913.

Cairns, Francis. "The Genre Palinode and Three Horatian Examples: *Epode*, 17; *Odes*, I, 16; *Odes*, I 34." *L'Antiquite Classique* 47 (1978): 546-52.

——. *Tibullus: A Hellenistic Poet at Rome*. Cambridge: Cambridge UP, 1979.

Calder, Daniel G. *Cynewulf*. Boston: Twayne, 1981.

——, and Michael J. B. Allen. *Sources and Analogues of Old English Poetry: The Major Latin Texts in Translation*. Cambridge: Brewer, 1976.

Calin, William. *A Poet at the Fountain: Essays on the Narrative Verse of Guillaume de Machaut.* Lexington: UP of Kentucky, 1974.

Calomino, Salvatore. *From Verse to Prose: The Barlaam and Josaphat Legend in Fifteenth-Century Germany*. Scripta Humanistica 63. Potomac, MD: Scripta Humanistica, 1990.

Camargo, Martin. "Rhetoric." Wagner 96-124.

Cameron, Alan. "The First Edition of Ovid's *Amores*." *Classical Quarterly* 18 (1968): 320-33.

Campbell, A. P. "Chaucer's 'Retraction': Who Retracted What?" *Humanities Association Bulletin* 16 (1965): 75-87.

Campbell, Jackson J. "Cynewulf's Multiple Revelations." *Medievalia et Humanistica* n.s. 3 (1972): 257-77.

Cartier, Normand R., trans. Introduction. *Boccaccio's Revenge*. By Giovanni Boccaccio. The Hague: Martinus Nijhoff, 1977. vii-x.

Chance, Jane, ed. *Gender and Text in the Later Middle Ages*. Gainesville: UP of Florida, 1996.

Cheney, C. R. *Hubert Walter*. Leaders of Religion. London: Nelson, 1967.

Chute, Marchette. *Geoffrey Chaucer of England*. New York: Dutton, 1946.

Ciklamini, Marlene. *Iceland: Snorri Sturluson*. Boston: Twayne, 1978.

Clark, Elizabeth A., and Diane F. Hatch. *The Golden Bough, The Oaken Cross: The Vergilian Cento of Faltonia Betitia Proba*. Chico, CA: Scholars Press, 1981.

Clark, John W. "'This Litel Tretys' Again." *Chaucer Review* 6 (1971): 152-56.

Cocozzella, Peter. "Pere Torroella: Poet of the Catalan Pre-Renaissance." *Hispanofila* 86 (1986): 1-14.

Coghill, Neville. *The Poet Chaucer*. London: Oxford UP, 1949.

Cohn-Sherbok, Dab, ed. *The Salman Rushdie Controversy in Inter-Religious Perspective*. Lewiston: Mellon, 1990.

Cole, E. R. "Chaucer's Retraction and the Parson." *University of Portland Review* 20 (1968): 35-41.

Coleman, Joyce. *Public Reading and the Reading Public in Late Medieval England and France*. New York: Cambridge UP, 1996.

Colish, Marcia L. *The Mirror of Language: A Study in the Medieval Theory of Knowledge*. Lincoln: U of Nebraska P, 1983.

Comreau, Christoph. *Hartmanns von Aue* Armer Heinrich *und* Gregorius: *Studien zur Interpretation mit dem Blick auf die Theologie zur Zeit Hartmanns*. Munich: C. H. Beck, 1966.

Copeland, Rita. *Rhetoric, Hermeneutics, and Translation in the Middle Ages*. Cambridge: Cambridge UP, 1991.

Corrigan, Beatrice, ed. *Italian Poets and English Critics, 1755-1859: A Collection of Critical Essays*. Patterns of Literary Criticisms. Chicago: U of Chicago P, 1969.

Corsa, Helen Storm. *Chaucer: Poet of Mirth and Morality*. Notre Dame: U of Notre Dame P, 1964.

Cottiono-Jones, Margo. "The *Corbaccio*: Notes for a Mythical Perspective of Moral Alternatives." *Forum Italicum* 4 (1970): 490-509.

Crabbe, Anna. "Literary Design in the *De Consolatione Philosophiae*." *Boethius: His Life, Thought and Influence*. Ed. Margaret Gibson. Oxford: Blackwell, 1981. 237-74.

Cuddon, J. A. *A Dictionary of Literary Terms*. Garden City, NY: Doubleday, 1977.

Cuilleanain, Cormac O. *Religion and the Clergy in Boccaccio's* Decameron. Letture di Pensiero e d'Arte. Rome: Edizione di Storia e Letteratura, 1984.

Curry, Walter C. "Destiny in Chaucer's *Troilus.*" *Publications of the Modern Language Association* 45 (1930): 129-68

Curtius, Ernst Robert. *European Literature and the Latin Middle Ages*. Trans. Willard R. Trask. Bollingen Series 36. New York: Pantheon Books, 1953.

Dahlberg, Charles. *The Literature of Unlikeness*. Hanover: UP of New England, 1988.

David, Alfred. "The Man of Law vs. Chaucer: A Case in Poetics." *Publications of the Modern Language Association* 82 (1967): 217-25.

Davies, W. S. "Giraldus Cambrensis: *De Invectionibus*." *Y Commrodor. The Magazine of the Honorable Society of Cymmrodorion* 30 (1920) 16.

Davison, J. "Stesichorus and Helen." *From Archilochus to Pindar*. New York: St Martin's, 1968. 196-225.

De Michelis, Cesare. *Contraddizioni nel* Decameron. Milano: Guanda, 1983.

Dean, James. "Chaucer's Repentance: A Likely Story." *Chaucer Review* 24 (1989): 64-76.

——. "Chaucer's *Troilus*, Boccaccio's *Filostrato*, and the Poetics of Closure." *Philological Quarterly* 64 (1985): 175-84.

Deyermond, Alan. "The Works of Teresa de Cartagena." *Journal of Hispanic Philology* 1 (1976): 19-29.

Donaldson, E. Talbot. *Piers Plowman: The C-Text and Its Poet*. New Haven: Yale UP, 1949.

——. *Speaking of Chaucer*. New York: Norton, 1970.

Doria, Charles, and Harris Lenowitz, eds. and trans. *Origins: Creation Texts from the Ancient Mediterranean*. Garden City, NY: Anchor Books, 1976.

Dronke, Peter. "The Conclusion of *Troilus and Criseyde*." *Medium Aevum* 33 (1964): 47-52.

——. *Medieval Latin and the Rise of European Love-Lyric*. 2nd ed. 2 vols. Oxford: Clarendon, 1968.

——. "Peter of Blois and the Poetry at the Court of Henry II." *Mediaeval Studies* 38 (1976): 184-235.

Dubois, Jacques. "Le martyrologe métrique de Wandelbert: ses sources, son originalité, son influence sur le martyrologe d'Usard." *Analecta Bollandiana* 79 (1961): 257-93.

Duckett, Eleanor Shipley. *Anglo-Saxon Saints and Scholars*. New York: Macmillan, 1947.

Dyson, M. "Horace: Odes I 16." *Journal of the Australian Universities' Modern Language Association* 30 (1968): 169-79.

Eberle, Patricia. "Notes to the Man of Law's Tale." Benson 854-63.

Economou, George D. "Self-Consciousness of Poetic Activity in Dante and Langland." *Vernacular Poetics in the Middle Ages*. Ed. Lois Ebin. Studies in Medieval Culture 16. Kalamazoo, MI: Medieval Institute Publications, 1984. 177-98.

Ehrismann, Gustav. *Studien über Rudolf von Ems: Beiträge zur Geschichte der Rhetorik und Ethik im Mittelalter*. Sitzungsberichte der Heidelberger Akademie der Wissenschaften 8. Heidelberg: C. Winter, 1919.

Eller, Meredith F. "The *Retractationes* of Saint Augustine." *Church History* 18 (1949): 172-83.

Enk, P. J. "A Propos d'Apulee." *Acta Classica* (1958): 85-91.

Easterman, Daniel. *New Jerusalems: Reflections on Islam: Fundamentalism and the Rushdie Affair*. London: Grafton, 1992.

Estrich, Robert M. "Chaucer's Maturing Art in the Prologues of *The Legend of Good Women*." *Journal of English and Germanic Philology* 36 (1937): 326-37.

Evans, Harry B. *Publica Carmina: Ovid's Books from Exile*. Lincoln: U of Nebraska P, 1983.

Evans, Simon D. *Medieval Religious Literature*. Writers of Wales. Cardiff: U of Wales P, 1986.

Faral, Edward. *Jongleurs en France au Moyen Age*. 2nd ed. Paris: Librairie Honoré Champion, 1964.

Farnham, Anthony E. "Chaucerian Irony and the Ending of the *Troilus*." *Chaucer Review* 2 (1967): 207-16.

Faulkes, Anthony. Introduction. *Edda: Prologue and Gylfaginning*. By Snorri Sturluson. London: Dent, 1987. vii-xx.

Fedi, Robert. "Il 'regno' di Filostrato: Natura e struttura della Giornata IV del *Decameron*." *Modern Language Notes* 102 (1987): 45-49.

Ferrante, Joan M. *To the Glory of Her Sex: Women's Roles in the Composition of Medieval Texts*. Bloomington: Indiana UP, 1997.

Fichte, Joerg O. *Chaucer's 'Art Poetical': A Study in Chaucerian Poetics*. Tübingen: Gunter Narr, 1983.

Finke, Laurie A. and Martin B. Shichtman. "Introduction: Critical Theory and the Study of the Middle Ages." *Medieval Texts & Contemporary Readers*. Ithaca: Cornell UP, 1987. 1-11.

Fish, Varda. "Theme and Pattern in Cynewulf's *Elene*." *Neuphilologische Mitteilungen* 76 (1975): 1-25.

Fisher, John H. "The Revision of the Prologue to *The Legend of Good Women*: An Occasional Explanation." *South Atlantic Bulletin* 43 (1978): 75-84.

Fischer, Karl-Hubert. *Zwischen Minne und Gott: Die geistesgeschichtlichen Voraussetzungen des deutschen Minnesangs mit besonderer Berücksichtigung der Frömmigkeitsgeschichte*. Frankfurt: Peter Lang, 1985.

Fleming, John V. "Hoccleve's *Letter of Cupid* and the Quarrel over the *Roman de la Rose*." *Medium Aevum* 40 (1971): 21-40.

——. *The* Roman de la Rose: *A Study in Allegory and Iconography*. Princeton: Princeton UP, 1969.

Fogel, Stan. "Palinodes and Palindromes." *International Fiction Review* 11 (1984): 51-54.

Forni, Pier Massimo. *Adventures in Speech: Rhetoric and Narration in Boccacio's* Decameron. Philadelphia: U of Pennsylvania P, 1996.

Foscolo, Ugo. "An Essay on the Poetry of Petrarch." Corrigan 78-97.

Foster, Kenelm. "Beatrice or Medusa." *Italian Studies Presented to E. R. Vincent*. Eds. C. P. Brand, K. Foster, and U. Limentani. Cambridge: W. Heffer, 1962. 41-56.

——. *Petrarch: Poet and Humanist*. Edinburgh: Edinburgh UP, 1984.

Fraenkel, Eduard. *Horace*. Oxford: Clarendon, 1957.

Frank, Robert Worth, Jr. *Chaucer and* The Legend of Good Women. Cambridge: Harvard UP, 1972.

Frantzen, Allen J. *The Literature of Penance in Anglo-Saxon England*. New Brunswick, NJ: Rutgers UP, 1983.

Fränkel, Hermann. *Ovid: A Poet Between Two Worlds*. Sather Classical Lectures 18. Berkeley: U of California P, 1945.

Freccero, John. "The Fig Tree and the Laurel: Petrarch's Poetics." Bloom 43-55.

French, John C. *The Problem of the Two Prologues to Chaucer's* Legend of Good Women. Baltimore: J. H. Furst, 1905.

Fromm, Hans, and Klaus Grubmüller. Introduction. *Die Kindheit Jesu*. By Konrad von Fußesbrunnen. Berlin: Walter de Gruyter, 1973. 1-70.

Fyler, Jon M. *Chaucer and Ovid*. New Haven: Yale UP, 1979.

Gärtner, Kurt. "Zur neuen Ausgabe und zu neuen Handschriften der '*Kindheit Jesu*' Konrads zu Fußesbrunnen." *Zeitschrift für deutsches Altertum und deutsche Literatur* 105 (1976): 11-53.

Gallostra, Francisca Vendrell. *La corte literaria de Alfonso V de Aragón y tres poetas de la misma*. Madrid: Archivos, 1933.

Garcia, Luis Miguel Vicente. "La defensa de la mujer como intelectual en Teresa de Cartagena y Sor Juana Inés de la Cruz." *Mester* 18.2 (1989): 95-103.

Gerli, Michael. *Alfonso Martínez de Toledo*. Boston: Twayne, 1976.

——. Introduction. *Arçipreste de Talavera o Corbacho*. By Alfonso Martínez de Toledo. Ed. Michael Gerli. Madrid: Ediciones Cátedra, 1979. 15-57.

Ghellinck, J. de. "Les Rétractations de Saint Augustin examen de conscience de l'ecrivain." *Nouvelle Revue Theologique* 57 (1930): 481-500.

Ghosh, Bishnupriya. "Feminist Critiques of Nationalism and Communalism from Bangladesh and India." *Interventions: Feminist Dialogues on Third World Literature and Film*. Ed. Bishnupriya Ghosh and Brinda Bose. New York: Garland, 1997. 135-62.

Gilderman, Martin S. *Juan Rodríguez de la Cámara*. Boston: Twayne, 1977.

Gill, Anne Barbara. *Paradoxical Patterns in Chaucer's* Troilus: *An Explanation of the Palinode*. Washington, DC: Catholic U of America P, 1960.

Gillmeister, Heiner. *Chaucer's Conversion: Allegorical Thought in Medieval Literature*. Aspekte der englischen Geistes- und Kulturgeschichte 2. Frankfurt: Peter Lang, 1984.

Gittes, Katharine S. *Framing* The Canterbury Tales: *Chaucer and the Medieval Frame Narrative Tradition*. New York: Greenwood, 1991.

Godman, Peter. "Chaucer and Boccaccio's Latin Works." *Chaucer and the Italian Trecento*. Ed. Piero Boitani. Cambridge: Cambridge UP, 1983. 269-95.

Gomez, Emilio Garcia. Introduction. *El Collar de la Paloma*. By Ibn Hazm. 2nd ed. Madrid: Sociedad de Estudios y Publicaciones, 1967. 31-83.

González-Casanovas, Roberto J. "The Writer and Preacher as *Juglar de Déu*: Literary Conversion in Ramon Llull." *Romance Languages Annual* 1 (1989): 460-63.

Gordon, James D. "Chaucer's Retraction: A Review of Opinion." *Studies of Medieval Literature in Honor of Professor Albert Croll Baugh*. Ed. MacEdward Leach. Philadelphia: U of Pennsylvania P, 1961. 81-94.

Gradon, P. O. E., ed. Introduction. *Cynewulf's* Elene. Exeter: University of Exeter, 1977. 1-24.

Green, Otis H. *Spain and the Western Tradition: The Castilian Mind in Literature from* El Cid *to Calderón*. Madison: U of Wisconsin P, 1963.

——. *The Literary Mind of Medieval & Renaissance Spain*. Lexington: UP of Kentucky, 1970.

Gregorovius, Ferdinand. *History of the City of Rome in the Middle Ages*. Trans. Annie Hamilton. 4th ed. 8 vols. New York: AMS, 1967.

Grimal, Pierre. "L'originalité des Metamorphoses d'Apulée." *L'Information Littéraire* 9 (1957): 156-62.

Grosse, Siegfried. "Beginn und Ende der erzählenden Dichtungen Hartmanns von Aue." *Hartmann von Aue*. Eds. Hugo Kuhn and Christoph Cormeau. Wege der Forschung 359. Darmstadt: Wissenschaftliche Buchgesellschaft, 1973. 172-94.

Guillén, Claudio. *Literature as System: Essays Toward the Theory of Literary History*. Princeton: Princeton UP, 1971.

Gunn, Alan. *The Mirror of Love: A Reinterpretation of* The Romance of the Rose. Lubbock: Texas Tech P, 1952.

Gybbon-Monypenny, G. B. Introduction. *Libro de buen amor*. Madrid: Editorial Castalia, 1988. 7-78.

Haight, Elizabeth Hazelton. *Apuleius and His Influence*. New York: Longman, Green, 1927.

Haines, Victor Yelverton. "Where Are Chaucer's 'Retracciouns'?" *Florilegium* 10 (1988-91): 127-49.

Hainsworth, Peter. *Petrarch the Poet: An Introduction to the* Rerum vulgarium fragmenta. London: Routledge, 1988.

Hallenstein, S. *Nachbildung und Umformung der Bekenntnisse Augustins in der Lebensgeschichte Guiberts*. Diss. Hamburg, 1935.

Hammond, Eleanor Prescott. "Chaucer's 'Book of the Twenty-Five Ladies.'" *Modern Language Notes* 48 (1933): 514-16.

Hansen, Elaine Tuttle. "Irony and the Antifeminist Narrator in *The Legend of Good Women.*" *Journal of English and Germanic Philology* 82 (1983): 11-31.

Harnack, Adolf. "Die *Retractationen* Augustin's." *Sitzungsberichte der Königlichen preussischen Akademie der Wissenschaften* 53 (1905): 1096-1131.

Harriott, Rosemary. *Poetry and Criticism before Plato.* London: Methuen, 1969.

Harrison, Robert Pogue. *The Body of Beatrice.* Baltimore: Johns Hopkins UP, 1988.

Hastings, Robert. *Nature and Reason in the* Decameron. Manchester: Manchester UP, 1975.

——. "To Teach or Not to Teach: The Moral Dimension of the *Decameron* Reconsidered." *Italian Studies* 44 (1989): 19-40.

Hasty, Will. *Adventures in Interpretation: The Works of Hartmann von Aue and Their Critical Reception.* Columbia, SC: Camden House, 1996.

Haubrichs, Wolfgang. *Die Kultur der Abtei Prüm zur Karolingerzeit: Studien zur Heimat des althochdeutschen Georgsliedes.* Bonn: Ludwig Röhrscheid, 1979.

Haug, Walter. *Literaturtheorie im Deutschen Mittelalter von den Anfängen bis zum Ende des 13. Jahrhunderts: Eine Einführung.* Darmstadt: Wissenschaftliche Buchgesellschaft, 1985.

Haxo, Henry. "Denis Piramus: La Vie Seint Edmunt." *Modern Philology* 12 (1914): 345-66.

Heidel, Alexander. *The Babylonian Genesis: The Story of Creation.* 2nd ed. Chicago: U of Chicago P, 1951.

Henkel, Nikolaus. *Deutsche Übersetzungen lateinischer Schultexte: Ihre Verbreitung und Funktion im Mittelalter und in der frühen Neuzeit.* Munich: Artemis Verlag 1988.

Herrmann, Léon. "L'Ane d'or et le christianisme." *Latomus* 12 (1953): 188-91.

Herzog, Reinhart. *Die Bibelepik der lateinischen Spätantike: Formgeschichte einer erbaulichen Gattung.* Munich: Wilhelm Fink, 1975. Vol. 1.

Hexter, Ralph J. *Ovid and Medieval Schooling. Studies in Medieval School Commentaries on Ovid's* Ars Amatoria, Epistulae ex Ponto, *and* Epistulae Heroidum. Munich: Arbeo-Gesellschaft, 1986.

Hicter, M. "L'Autobiographie dans l'âne d'or d'Apulée." *L'Antiquite Classique* 13 (1944-45): 61-68, 95-111.

Hieatt, Constance B. *The Realism of Dream Visions: The Poetic Exploitation of the Dream-Experience in Chaucer and his Contemporaries.* The Hague: Mouton, 1967.

Higgs, Elton D. "'What Man Artow?': Harry Bailly and the 'Elvyssh Chaucer.'" *Mid-Hudson Language Studies* 2 (1979): 28-43.

Hillgarth, J. N. *Ramon Lull and Lullism in Fourteenth-Century France*. Oxford: Clarendon, 1971.

Hinton, Norman D. "*The Canterbury Tales* as *compilatio.*" *Proceedings of the Illinois Medieval Association* 1 (1984): 28-48.

Hoffman, Edward Joseph. *Alain Chartier: His Work and Reputation*. Geneva: Slatkine Reprints, 1975.

Hollander, Robert. *Boccaccio's Dante and the Shaping Force of Satire*. Ann Arbor: U of Michigan P, 1997.

——. *Boccaccio's Last Fiction*. Philadelphia: U of Pennsylvania P, 1988.

——. *Boccaccio's Two Venuses*. New York: Columbia UP, 1977.

Holman, Hugh C. *A Handbook to Literature*. 5th ed. New York: Macmillan, 1986.

Holthausen, F., ed. *Cynewulf's* Elene. Heidelberg: C. Winter, 1905.

Howard, Donald R. *The Idea of* The Canterbury Tales. Berkeley: U of California P, 1976.

Huntsman, Jeffrey F. "Grammar." Wagner 58-95.

Huot, Sylvia. *From Song to Book: The Poetics of Writing in Old French Lyric and Lyrical Narrative Poetry*. Ithaca: Cornell UP, 1987.

Huppé, Bernard. *A Reading of* The Canterbury Tales. Albany: State U of New York, 1964.

Hutchinson, G. O. *Hellenistic Poetry*. Oxford: Clarendon, 1988.

Irvine, Martin. "Anglo-Saxon Literary Theory Exemplified in Old English Poems: Interpreting the Cross in *The Dream of the Rood* and *Elene.*" *Style* 20 (1988): 157-81.

Iwand, Käthe. *Die Schlüsse der mittelhochdeutschen Epen*. Berlin: Emil Ebering, 1922.

Jackson, W. T. H. "The Ambivalent Image in the Poetry of Walther von der Vogelweide." *Spectrum Medii Aevi. Essays in Early German Literature in Honor of George Fenwick Jones*. Ed. William C. McDonald. Göppingen: Kümmerle, 1983. 157-76.

Janson, Tore. *Latin Prose Prefaces: Studies in Literary Conventions*. Stockholm: Almqvist & Wiksell, 1964.

Janssens, M. "The Internal Reception of the Stories within the *Decameron.*" *Boccaccio in Europe: Proceedings of the Boccaccio Conference, Louvain, December 1975*. Ed. Gilbert Tournoy. Louvain: Leuven UP, 1977: 135-49.

Jarman, A. O. H., and Gwilym Rees Hughes, eds. *A Guide to Welsh Literature*. 2 vols. Swansea: Christopher Davies, 1976.

Jeffrey, David L., and Brian J. Levy. Introduction. *The Anglo-Norman Lyric: An Anthology*. Toronto: Pontifical Institute of Mediaeval Studies, 1990.

Jenkins, Claude. "Bede as Exegete and Theologian." *Bede: His Life, Times, and Writings*. Ed. A. Hamilton Thompson. New York: Russell & Russell, 1966. 152-200.

Johnson, L. S. "The Trope of the Scribe and the Question of Literary Authority in the Works of Julian of Norwich and Margery Kempe." *Speculum* 66 (1991): 820-838.

Johnson, Phyllis, and Brigitte Cazelles. *Le Vain Siecle Guerir: A Literary Approach to Sainthood through Old French Hagiography of the Twelfth Century*. North Carolina Studies in the Romance Languages and Literatures 205. Chapel Hill: U of North Carolina P, 1979.

Johnston, Mark D. *The Spiritual Logic of Ramon Llull*. Oxford: Clarendon Press, 1987.

Jones, Paul John. *Prologue and Epilogue in Old French Lives of Saints Before 1400*. Philadelphia: Pennsylvania University Publications, 1933.

Jones, R. M. *Guto'r Glyn a'i Gyfnod*. Llandybie: Llyfrau'r Dryw, 1963.

Jong, J. C. de. *Hartmann von Aue als Moralist in seinen Artusepen*. Amsterdam: Wed. G. van Soest N. V., 1964.

Jordan, Robert M. *Chaucer's Poetrics and the Modern Reader*. Berkeley: U of California P, 1987.

Jubinal, Achille. *Nouveau Recueil de contes, dits, fabliaux et autres pièces inédites des XIII, XIV, et XV siècles I-II*. Geneva: Slatkine Reprints, 1975.

Jungbluth, Günther. "Walthers Abschied." *Walther von der Vogelweide*. Ed. Siegfried Beyschlag. Wege der Forschung 112. Darmstadt: Wissenschaftliche Buchgesellschaft, 1971. 514-38.

Kambylis, Athanasios. "Der Vollzug der Dichterweihe bei Kallimachos." *Kallimachos*. Ed. Aristoxeneos D. Skiadas. Darmstadt: Wissenschaftliche Buchgesellschaft, 1975. 81-99.

Kane, George. "Langland and Chaucer: An Obligatory Conjunction." *New Perspectives in Chaucer Criticism*. Ed. Donald M. Rose. Norman, OK: Pilgrim Books, 1981. 5-19.

——. *The Autobiographical Fallacy in Chaucer and Langland Studies*. London: University College, 1965.

——. *The Liberating Truth: The Concept of Integrity in Chaucer's Writings*. London: Athalone Press, 1980.

Kean, P. M. *Chaucer and the Making of English Poetry: The Art of Narrative*. 2 vols. London: Routledge & Kegan Paul, 1972.

Keller, John Esten. Introduction. *The Book of Good Love*. Trans. Elisha Kent Kane. Chapel Hill: U of North Carolina P, 1968. xix-lv.

Kelly, A. H. "*Occupatio* as Negative Narration: A Mistake for *Occultatio/ Praeteratio*." *Modern Philology* (1977): 311-15.

Kelly, Douglas. *Medieval Imagination: Rhetoric and the Poetry of Courtly Love*. Madison: U of Wisconsin P, 1978.

Kenney, E. J. Introduction. *Ovid: The Love Poems*. Trans. A. D. Melville. Oxford: Oxford UP, 1990. viii-xxix.

Kerth, Thomas, ed. Introduction. *Tristan*. By Ulrich von Türheim. Altdeutsche Textbibliothek 89. Tübingen: Max Niemayer, 1979. vii-xvi.

Kimpel, Ben. "The Narrator of *The Canterbury Tales*." *English Literary History* 20 (1953): 77-86.

Kirby, Thomas A. "The General Prologue." *Companion to Chaucer Studies*. Ed. Beryl Rowland. 2nd ed. 1968. Oxford: Oxford UP, 1979. 243-70.

Kirkpatrick, Robin. "The Wake of the *Commedia*: Chaucer's *Canterbury Tales* and Boccaccio's *Decameron*." *Chaucer and the Italian Trecento*. Ed. Piero Boitani. Cambridge: Cambridge UP, 1983. 201-230.

Kiser, Lisa J. *Telling Classical Tales: Chaucer and* The Legend of Good Women. Ithaca: Cornell UP, 1983.

Kittredge, G. L. *Chaucer and His Poetry*. Cambridge: Harvard UP, 1915.

Klemm, Elisabeth. "Die Regensburger Buchmalerei des 12. Jahrhunderts." *Regensburger Buchmalerei: Von frühkarolingischer Zeit bis zum Ausgang des Mittelalters*. Munich: Prestel-Verlag, 1987. 39-58.

Klopsch, Paul. *Einführung in die Dichtungslehren des lateinischen Mittelalters*. Darmstadt: Wissenschaftliche Buchgesellschaft, 1980.

Knapp, Robert S. "Penance, Irony, and Chaucer's Retraction." *Assays: Critical Approaches to Medieval and Renaissance Texts* 2 (1982): 45-67.

Knopp, Sherron. "Chaucer and Jean de Meun as Self-Conscious Narrators: The Prologue to *The Legend of Good Women* and the *Roman de la Rose* 10307-680." *Comitatus* 4 (1973): 25-39.

Koch, J. "Chaucer-Schriften." *Englische Studien* 37 (1907): 227-29.

Koff, Leonard Michael. *Chaucer and the Art of Storytelling*. Berkeley: U of California P, 1988.

Kolve, V. A. *Chaucer and the Imagery of Narrative: The First Five Canterbury Tales*. Stanford: Stanford UP, 1984.

König, Bernhard. "Das letzte Sonett des *Canzoniere*: Zur 'architektonischen' Funktion und Gestaltung der *Ultime Rime* Petrarcas." *Interpretation: Das Paradigma der europäi-*

schen Renaissance-Literatur. Festschrift für Alfred Noyer-Weidner zum 60. Geburtstag. Eds. Klaus Hempfer and Gerhard Regn. Wiesbaden: Franz Steiner, 1983. 239-57.

——. "Die Anordnung der Gedichte des *Canzoniere* als Problem der Literaturkritik und der Petrarca-Editionen des 15. bis 19. Jahrhunderts." *Romanistisches Jahrbuch* 44 (1993): 124-38.

Kuhn, Hans. "Das Nordgermanische Heidentum in den Ersten Christlichen Jahrhunderten." *Zeitschrift für Deutsches Altertum und Deutsche Literatur* 79 (1942-43): 133-66.

Kuhnmuench, Otto J. *Early Christian Latin Poets from the Fourth to the Sixth Century.* Chicago: Loyola UP, 1929.

La Bonnardière, Anne-Marie. "La lettre à Proba." *Saint Augustine et la Bible.* Ed. Anne-Marie la Bonnardière. Paris: Beauchesne, 1986. 181-88.

Laistner, M. L. W. "Bede as a Classical and Patristic Scholar." *Transactions of the Royal Historical Society* 16 (1933): 67-94.

——. Introduction. *Expositio Actuum Apostolorum et Retractatio.* By the Venerable Bede. The Medieval Academy of America Publication 35. 1939. New York: Kraus Reprint, 1970. xi-xlv.

——. *Thought and Letters in Western Europe.* London: Methuen, 1931.

Landor, Walter Savage. "Francesco Petrara." Corrigan 156-78.

Langbehn-Rohland, Regula. *Zur Interpretation der Romane des Diego de San Pedro.* Studia Romanica 18. Heidelberg: C. Winter, 1970.

Langhans, V. "Chaucers Book of the Leoun." *Anglia* 28 (1952): 113-22.

Langlois, Charles V. *La Vie en France au Moyen Age.* Paris: Librairie Hachette, 1925.

Langosch, Karl. *Lyrische Anthologie des lateinischen Mittelalters.* Darmstadt: Wissenschaftliche Buchgesellschaft, 1968.

Lares, Jameela. "Chaucer's *Retractions*: A 'Verray Parfit Penitance.' *Citharia: Essays in the Judeo-Christian Tradition* 34:1 (1994): 18-33.

Lawler, Traugott. *The One and the Many in* The Canterbury Tales. Hamden, CT: Archon Books, 1980.

Lawlor, John. *Piers Plowman: An Essay in Criticism.* New York: Barnes & Noble, 1963.

Lawrence, Nathalie Grimes. "Petrarch's Other Love." *Carrell* 4 (1963): 1-6.

Lawrence, William Witherle. *Chaucer and* The Canterbury Tales. New York: Columbia UP, 1950.

Leclercq, Jean. *The Love of Learning and the Desire for God: A Study of Monastic Culture.* Trans. Catharine Misrahi. 2nd ed. New York: Fordham UP, 1977.

Lefkowitz, Mary R. *The Lives of the Greek Poets*. Baltimore: Johns Hopkins UP, 1981.

Legge, Dominica M. *Anglo-Norman Literature and Its Background*. Oxford: Clarendon, 1963.

Lehmann, Paul. "Autobiographies of the Middle Ages." *Transactions of the Royal Historical Society*. 5th Series. 3 (1953): 41-52.

Lerer, Seth. *Boethius and Dialogue: Literary Method in the* Consolation of Philosophy. Princeton: Princeton UP, 1985.

——. "Transgressio studii: Writing and Sexuality in Guibert of Nogent." *Stanford French Review* 14:1-2 (1990): 243-66.

Levy, Leonard W. *Blasphemy: Verbal Offense against the Sacred from Moses to Salman Rushdie*. New York: Knopf, 1993.

Lewis, C. S. *The Allegory of Love: A Study in Medieval Tradition*. Oxford: Oxford UP, 1935.

Lewis, Ceri W. "The Court Poets: Their Function, Status and Craft." Jarman and Hughes 1: 123-56.

Lewis, Saunders. "Gyrfa Filwrol Guto'r Glyn." *Ysgrifau Beirniadol* 9 (1976): 80-99.

Lida de Malkiel, M. R. *Juan de Mena, poeta del prerrenacimiento español*. Mexico City, 1950.

Lieser, Ludwig. *Vinzenz von Beauvais, Kompilator und Philosoph: Untersuchung seiner Seelenlehre im* Speculum Maius. Leipzig: Felix Meiner, 1928. 76-96, 194-200.

Lipson, Carol. "'I n'am but a lewd compilator': Chaucer's 'Treatise on the Astrolabe' as Translation." *Neuphilologische Mitteilungen* 84 (1983): 192-200.

Lloyd, Myrddin D. "The Later Gogynfeirdd." Jarman and Hughes 2: 36-57.

——. "The Poets of the Princes." Jarman and Hughes 1: 157-88.

Lloyd-Jones, J. "The Court Poets of the Welsh Princes." *Proceedings of the British Academy* 34 (1948): 167-97.

Lounsbury, Thomas, R. *Studies in Chaucer: His Life and Writings*. 3 vols. London: James R. Osgood, 1892.

Lowes, John Livingston. *Geoffrey Chaucer and the Development of His Genius*. Boston: Houghton Mifflin, 1934.

Lumiansky, R. M. "Chaucer's Retraction and the Degree of Completeness of *The Canterbury Tales*." *Tulane Studies in English* 6 (1956): 5-13.

Lusignan, Serge. *Préface au* Speculum Maius *de Vincent de Beauvais: Réfraction et Diffraction*. Montreal: Bellarmin, 1979.

Lutz, Eckart Conrad. *Rhetorica Divina: Mittelhochdeutsche Prologgebete und die rhetorische Kultur des Mittelalters*. Berlin: Walter de Gruyter, 1984.

Mac Cana, Proinsias. "The Poet as Spouse of His Patron." *Ériu* 39 (1988): 79-85.

Machan, Tim William. "Chaucer as Translator." *The Medieval Translator: The Theory and Practice of Translation in the Middle Ages*. Ed. Roger Ellis. Cambridge: Brewer, 1989. 55-67.

MacKay, L. A. "The Sin of the Golden Ass." *Arion* 4 (1965): 474-80.

Macmanus, Francis. *Boccaccio*. New York: Sheed, 1947.

Madden, William A. "Chaucer's Retraction and Medieval Canons of Seemliness." *Medieval Studies* 17 (1955): 173-84.

Madeleva, M. *A Lost Language and Other Essays on Chaucer*. 1951. New York: Russell & Russell, 1967.

Manitius, Max. *Geschichte der Lateinischen Literatur des Mittelalters*. 3 vols. 1911, 1931. Reprint. Munich: C. H. Beck, 1974.

Mann, Jill. *Apologies to Women.* Cambridge: Cambridge UP, 1991.

Margaret, M. Introduction. *Dracontii Satisfactio*. Diss. Philadelphia: U of Pennsylvania, 1936. 1-27.

Marshall, David F. "Unmasking the Last Pilgrim: How and Why Chaucer Used the Retraction to Close *The Canterbury Tales*." *Christianity & Literature* 31 (1982): 55-74.

Martin, Ernst. Introduction. *Le Besant de Dieu*. By Guillaume le Clerc de Normandie. Geneva: Slatkine Reprints, 1975. i-xlviii.

Martin, Lawrence T., trans. Introduction. *Bede's Commentary on the Acts of the Apostles*. Cistercian Studies 117. Kalamazoo, MI: Cistercian Publications, 1989. xv-xxxv.

Masser, Achim. *Bibel- und Legendenepik des Deutschen Mittelalters*. Grundlagen der Germanistik 19. Berlin: Erich Schmidt, 1976.

Matulka, Barbara. *The Novels of Juan de Flores and Their European Diffusion: A Study in Comparative Literature*. Geneva: Slatkine Reprints, 1974.

Mazzaro, Jerome. *The Figure of Dante. An Essay on the* Vita Nuova. Princeton Essays in Literature. Princeton: Princeton UP, 1981.

Mazzotta, Guiseppe. "The *Canzoniere* and the Language of Self." Bloom 57-78.

——. "The *Decameron*: The Marginality of Literature." *University of Toronto Quarterly* 42 (1972): 64-81.

——. *The Worlds of Petrarch*. Durham: Duke UP, 1993.

McDonald, William C. *German Medieval Literary Patronage from Charlemagne to Maximilian I: A Critical Commentary with Special Emphasis on Imperial Promotion of Literature.* Amsterdam: Rodopi, 1973.

McGerr, Rosemarie Potz. "Retraction and Memory: Retrospective Structure in *The Canterbury Tales*." *Comparative Literature* 37 (1985): 97-113.

McGrady, Donald. "Chaucer and the *Decameron* Reconsidered." *Chaucer Review* 12 (1977): 1-26.

Menocal, Maria Rosa. *The Arabic Role in Medieval Literary History: A Forgotten Heritage*. Philadelphia: U of Pennsylvania P, 1987.

Merk, Josef. *Die Literarische Gestaltung der altfranzösischen Heiligenleben bis Ende des 12. Jahrhunderts*. Diss. Zurich: Zurich University, 1946.

Mertens, Volker. *Gregorius Eremita: Eine Lebensform des Adels bei Hartmann von Aue in ihrer Problematik und ihrer Wandlung in der Rezeption*. Munich: Artemis Verlag, 1978.

Middleton, Anne. "The Audience and Public of Piers Plowman." *Middle English Alliterative Poetry and Its Literary Background: Seven Essays*. Ed. David Lawton. Cambridge: Brewer, 1982. 101-23.

Miller, Jacqueline T. *Poetic License: Authority and Authorship in Medieval and Renaissance Contexts*. Oxford: Oxford UP, 1986.

Millett, Bella. "Chaucer, Lollius, and the Medieval Theory of Authorship." *Studies in the Age of Chaucer* 1 (1984): 93-103.

Minnis, Alistair J. "Chaucer and Comparative Literary Theory." *New Perspectives in Chaucer Criticism*. Ed. Donald M. Rose. Norman, OK: Pilgrim Books, 1981. 53-69.

——. *Medieval Theory of Authorship: Scholastic Literary Attitudes in the Later Middle Ages*. 2nd ed. Philadelphia: U of Pennsylvania P, 1988.

Minois, Georges. *History of Old Age from Antiquity to the Renaissance*. Trans. Sarah Hanbury Tenison. Oxford: Polity Press, 1989.

Misch, Georg. *Geschichte der Autobiographie*. 4 vols. Bern: A. Francke, 1949-69.

Mitchell, Jerome. *Thomas Hoccleve: A Study in Early Fifteenth-Century English Prose*. Urbana: U of Illinois P, 1968.

Mitchell, R. J. *The Laurels and the Tiara: Pope Pius II 1458-1464*. Garden City, NY: Doubleday, 1962.

Morgan, Gerald. "The Ending of '*Troilus and Criseyde*.'" *Modern Language Review* 77 (1982): 257-71.

Morgan, Thaïs E. "Is There an Intertext in This Text?" *American Journal of Semiotics* 3 (1985): 1-40.

Morris, Colin C. *The Discovery of the Individual, 1050-1200*. New York: Harper & Row, 1973.

Morrison, Karl E. "Incentives for Studying the Liberal Arts." Wagner 32-57.

Murgia, Charles E. "Influence of Ovid's *Remedia Amoris* on *Ars Amatoria 3* and *Amores 3*." *Classical Philology* 8 (1986): 203-220.

Muscatine, Charles. *Chaucer and the French Tradition*. Berkeley: U of California P, 1969.

——. *Poetry and Crisis in the Age of Chaucer*. Notre Dame: U of Notre Dame P, 1972.

Muscetta, Carlo. *Giovanni Boccaccio*. Rome: Laterza, 1974.

Myers, Jack, and Michael Simms. *Longman Dictionary and Handbook of Poetry*. New York: Longman, 1985.

Nepaulsingh, Colbert I. *Towards a History of Literary Composition in Medieval Spain*. Toronto: U of Toronto P, 1986.

Nethercut, William. "Apuleius' Metamorphoses: The Journey." *Agon* 3 (1969): 97-134.

Nisbet, R. G. M., and Margaret Hubbard. *A Commentary on Horace: Odes Book 1*. Oxford: Clarendon, 1970.

Nolan, Barbara. "'A Poet Ther Was': Chaucer's Voices in the General Prologue to *The Canterbury Tales*. *Publications of the Modern Language Association* 101.1 (1986): 154-69.

——. *Chaucer and the Tradition of the Roman Antique*. Cambridge: Cambridge UP, 1992.

Nordal, Sigurdur. Introduction. *The Prose Edda of Snorri Sturluson: Tales from Norse Mythology*. Trans. Jean I. Young. Cambridge: Bowes & Bowes, 1954. 7-15.

Norwood, Francis. "The Magic Pilgrimage of Apuleius." *The Phoenix* 10 (1956): 1-12.

Nykl, A. R. Introduction. *A Book Containing the Risala Known As the Dove's Neck-Ring: About Love and Lovers*. By Ibn Hazm. Paris: Librairie Orientaliste Paul Geuthner, 1931. xiii-cxxiv.

Nykrog, Per. "Playing Games with Fiction: *Les Quinzes Joyes de Mariage, Il Corbaccio, El Arçipreste de Talavera*." *The Craft of Fiction: Essays in Medieval Poetics*. Ed. Leigh A Arrathoon. Rochester, MI: Solaris Press, 1984. 423-51.

Olsen, Alexandra Hennessey. *Speech, Song, and Poetic Craft: The Artistry of the Cynewulf Canon*. New York: Peter Lang, 1984.

Ornstein, Jacob. "La Misoginía y el profeminismo en la literatura castellana." *Revista de Filologia Hispanica* 3 (1941): 219-32.

Owen, Charles A., Jr. "The Tales of Canterbury: Fictions within a Fiction that Purports not to Be a Fiction." *Chaucer and the Craft of Fiction*. Ed. Leigh A. Arrathoon. Rochester, MI: Solaris Press, 1986. 179-94.

Owen, Henry. *Gerald the Welshman*. London: David Nutt, 1904.

Palmer, R. Barton, ed. and trans. Introduction. *The Judgment of the King of Navarre*. By Guillaume de Machaut. Garland Library of Medieval Literature A45. New York: Garland, 1988. xi-l.

——. "Transtextuality and the Producing-I in Guillaume de Machaut's Judgement Series." *Exemplaria: A Journal of Theory in Medieval and Renaissance Studies* 5:2 (1993): 282-304.

Palmier, M. "Etude sur l'etat des connaissances au milieu du XIIIe siècle: Nouvelles recherches sur la genèse du *Speculum maius* de Vincent de Beauvais." *Spicae: cahiers de l'atelier Vincent de Beauvais*. Paris: Centre National de la Recherche Scientifique, 1978. 91-121.

Parkes, M. B. "The Influence of the Concepts of *Ordinatio* and *Compilatio* on the Development of the Book." *Medieval Learning and Literature: Essays Presented to Richard William Hunt*. Eds. J. J. G. Alexander and M. T. Gibson. Oxford: Clarendon, 1976. 115-38.

——. Introduction. *The Art of Courtly Love*. By Andreas Capellanus. New York: Frederick Ungar, 1964. 3-24.

Parry, Thomas. *A History of Welsh Literature*. Trans. H. Idris Bell. Oxford: Clarendon, 1955.

Payen, Jean-Charles. *Le Motif du repentir dans la littérature française médiévale (dès origines à 1230)*. Geneva: Librairie Droz, 1967.

Payne, Robert O. "Late Medieval Images and Self-Images of the Poet: Chaucer, Gower, Lydgate, Henryson, Dunbar." *Vernacular Poetics in the Middle Ages*. Ed. Lois Ebin. Studies in Medieval Culture 16. Kalamazoo, MI: Medieval Institute Publications, 1984. 249-61.

——. "Making His Own Myth: The Prologue to Chaucer's *Legend of Good Women*." *Chaucer Review* 9 (1975): 197-211.

——. *The Key of Remembrance: A Study of Chaucer's Poetics*. New Haven: Yale UP, 1963. 91-111.

Peck, Russell. "St. Paul and the *Canterbury Tales*." *Mediaevalia* 7 (1981): 91-117.

Pfister, Manfred. "Konzepte der Intertextualität." *Intertextualität: Formen, Funktionen, anglistische Fallstudien*. Eds. Ulrich Broich and Martin Pfister. Konzepte der Sprach- und Literaturwissenschaft 35. Tübingen: Max Niemeyer, 1985. 1-30.

Phelps, Ruth Shepard. *The Earlier and Later Forms of Petrarch's* Canzoniere. Chicago: U of Chicago P, 1925.

Phillippy, Patricia Berrahou. *Love's Remedies: Recantation and Renaissance Lyric Poetry*. Lewisburg: Bucknell UP, 1995.

Pino, Guido di. *La polemica del Boccaccio*. Florence: Vallecchi, 1953.

Pipes, Daniel. *The Rushdie Affair: The Novel, the Ayatollah, and the West*. New York: Carol Pub. Group, 1990.

Platzeck, Erhard W., ed. Introduction. *Das Leben des seligen Raimund Llull, dei Vita coetanea und ausgewählte Texte aus seinen Werken und Zeitdokumenten*. Düsseldorf: Patmos Verlag, 1964. 1-35.

"Police in Rushdie Alert." *The European* 13-20 Sept. 1991: 7.

Potter, Joy Hambuechen. "Women in the *Decameron*." *Studies in the Italian Renaissance: Essays in Memory of Arnolfo B. Ferruolo*. Eds. Gian Paolo Biasin et al. Naples: Società Editrice Napoletana, 1985. 87-103.

Pratt, Karen. "Analogy or Logic; Authority or Experience? Rhetorical Strategies for and against Women." *Literary Aspects of Courtly Culture*. Eds. Donald Maddox and Sara Sturm-Maddox. Cambridge: Brewer, 1994. 57-66.

Priskil, Peter. *Taslima Nasrin: Der Mordaufruf und seine Hintergründe*. Ahriman Flugschrift 7, 1994.

Pucci, Robert Gregg. "The Metaphorical Rose: Mythology, Language and Poetics in the *Roman de la Rose*." *DA* 34 (1974): 7323A. Brown U.

Puelma, Mario. "Kallimachos-Interpretationen II: Der Epilog zu den *Aitien. Kallimachos*. Ed. Aristoxeneos D. Skiadas. Darmstadt: Wissenschaftliche Buchgesellschaft, 1975. 43-69.

Raby, F. J. E. *A History of Christian-Latin Poetry from the Beginning to the Close of the Middle Ages*. 2nd ed. Oxford: Clarendon, 1966.

——. *A History of the Secular Latin Poetry in the Middle Ages*. 2nd ed. 2 vols. Oxford: Clarendon, 1957.

Ramat, Raffaello. *Saggi sul Rinascimento*. Florence: La Nuova Italia, 1969.

Rand, Edward Kennard. *Founders of the Middle Ages*. 1928. New York: Dover Publications, 1957.

Ransom, Daniel J. ed. "Antifeminism, Irony, and *The Poet's Repentance*." *Poets at Play: Irony and Parody in* The Harley Lyrics. Norman, OK: Pilgrim Books, 1985. 1-29.

Regalado, Nancy Freeman. *Poetic Patterns in Rutebeuf: A Study in Noncourtly Poetic Modes of the Thirteenth Century*. New Haven: Yale UP, 1970.

Reinsch, Robert. *Die Pseudo-Evangelien von Jesu und Maria's Kindheit in der romanischen und germanischen Literatur*. Halle: Max Niemeyer, 1879.

Rice, Robert C. "Cynewulf's *Fates of the Apostles* and Epilogues." *Anglo-Saxon England* 6 (1977): 114.

Richter, Michael. "Gerald of Wales: A Reassessment on the 750th Anniversary of His Death." *Traditio* 29 (1973): 379-90.

Richthofen, Erich F. von. "Alfonso Martínez de Toledo und sein *Arçipreste de Talavera*, ein kastilisches Prosawerk des 15. Jahrhunderts." *Zeitschrift für romanische Philologie* 61 (1941): 417-537.

——. "Fünfzig Jahre *Arçipreste-de-Talavera-Studien*: ein Überblick." *Zeitschrift für Romanische Philologie* 104 (1988): 13-19.

Rigg, A. G. "Serlo of Wilton: Biographical Notes." *Medium Aevum* 65:1 (1996) 96-99.

Riley, Henry T., trans. *The Heroides or Epistles of the Heroines, Amours, Art of Love, Remedy of Love, and Minor Works*. By Ovid. London: George Bell, 1879.

Ritter, Richard. *Die Einleitungen der deutschen Epen*. Bonn: Carl Georgi, 1908.

Roberts, Enid. *Y Beirdd a'u Noddwyr ym Maelor*. Awst: Darlith Eisteddfod Genedlaethol Cymru Wrecsam a'r Cylch, 1977.

Robinson, F. N., ed. *The Works of Geoffrey Chaucer*. 2nd ed. Oxford: Oxford UP, 1957.

Rogers, H. L. "The Beginning (and Ending) of Chaucer's '*Troilus and Criseyde*.'" *Festschrift for Ralph Farrell*. Bern: Peter Lang, 1977. 185-200.

Rohde, Erwin. *Kleine Schriften*. Tübingen: J. C. B. Mohr, 1901. 2: 43-74.

Root, Robert K. "Chaucer and the *Decameron*." *Englische Studien* 44 (1912): 1-7.

——. *The Poetry of Chaucer*. Boston: Houghton Mifflin, 1906.

Ross, Margaret Clunies. *Skáldskaparmál: Snorri Sturluson's ars poetica and Medieval Theories of Language*. Odense: Odense UP, 1987.

Rovira, José Carlos. "Nuevos documentos para la biografía de Juan de Tapia." *Anales de Literatura Española* 5 (1986-87): 437-60.

Rowland, Beryl. "Chaucer's Blasphemous Churl: A New Interpretation of the *Miller's Tale*." *Chaucer and Middle English Studies in Honour of Rossell Hope Robbins*. Ed. Beryl Rowland. London: Allen & Unwin, 1974. 43-55.

Rubino, Carl. "Literary Intelligibility in Apuleius' *Metamorphoses*." *The Classical Bulletin* 5 (1966): 65-69.

Ruggiers, Paul G. "The Italian Influence on Chaucer." *Companion to Chaucer Studies*. Ed. Beryl Rowland. New York: Oxford UP, 1979. 160-184.

Rupp, Heinz. "Rudolfs von Ems *Baarlam und Josaphat*." *Dienendes Wort: Eine Festschrift für Ernst Bender zum 70. Geburtstag*. Ed. Walter Franke. Karlsruhe: Braun, 1959. 11-37.

Rushdie, Salman. "My Decision." *Index on Censorship* 2 (1991): 34.

——. "I Did Not Want to Gibber." *The Arizona Republic* 14 Feb. 1993: C2-3.

Russell-Gebbett, Paul. "Medieval Catalan Literature." *Spain: A Companion to Spanish Studies*. Ed. P. E. Russell. London: Methuen, 1977. 247-63.

Russo, Luigi. *Letture Critiche del* Decameron. Bari: Laterza, 1971.

Ruthven, Malise. *A Satanic Affair: Salman Rushdie and the Rage of Islam*. London: Chatto & Windus, 1990.

——. *A Satanic Affair: Salman Rushdie and the Wrath of Islam*. London: Hogarth, 1991.

Salholz, E. "Rushdie Embraces the Faith." *Newsweek* 17 Jan. 1991: 52.

Sardar, Ziauddin and Merryl Wyn Davies. *Distorted Imagination: Lessons from the Rushdie Affair*. London: Grey Seal, 1990.

Sayce, Olive. "Chaucer's 'Retractions': The Conclusion of the *Canterbury Tales* and Its Place in Literary Tradition." *Medium Aevum* 40 (1971): 230-48.

——. "Prolog, Epilog und das Problem des Erzählens." *Probleme Mittelhochdeutscher Erzählformen*. Eds. Peter F. Ganz and Werner Schröder. Berlin: Erich Schmidt, 1972. 63-72.

Scaglione, Aldo. "Classical Heritage and Petrarchan Self-Consciousness in the Literary Emergence of the Interior 'I'." Bloom 125-37.

——. *Nature and Love in the Late Middle Ages*. Berkeley: U of California P, 1963.

——. "The Structure of the *Canzoniere* and Petrarch's Method of Composition." *Francesco Petrarca, Citizen of the World: Proceedings of the World Petrarch Congress, Washington, DC, April 6-13, 1974*. Ed. Aldo S. Bernardo. Albany: State U of New York P, 1980. 301-13.

Schabert, Ina. "Interauktorialität." *Deutsche Vierteljahresschrift für Literaturwissenschaft und Geistesgeschichte* 57 (1983): 679-701.

Schauwecker, Helga. *Otloh von St. Emmeram: Ein Beitrag zur Bildungs- und Frömmingkeitsgeschichte des 11. Jahrhundert*. Munich: Verlag der Bayer. Benediktiner-Akademie, 1964.

Scherer, W. *A History of German Literature*. Trans. F. C. Conybeare. Ed. F. Max Müller. Vol. 1. New York: Haskell House, 1971.

Schier, Kurt. "Zur Mythologie der *Snorra Edda*: Einige Quellenprobleme." *Speculum Norroenum: Norse Studies in Memory of Gabriel Turville-Petre*. Eds. Ursula Dronke et al. Odense: Odense UP, 1981. 405-20.

Schleicher, Wolfgang. *Ramon Lulls* Libre de Evast et Blanquerna. Kölner Romanistische Arbeiten 12. Geneva: Librairie E. Droz, 1958.

Schmidt, A. V. C. *The Clerkly Maker: Langland's Poetic Art*. Cambridge: Brewer, 1987.

Schmitt, Alfred. *Matheus von Boulogne:* "Lamentationes Matheoluli" *(Kommentierte und kritische Edition der beiden ersten Bücher)*. Diss. Bonn: Rheinisch Friedrich-Wilhelm-University, 1974.

Schnapp, Jeffrey T. "Reading Lessons: Augustine, Proba, and the Christian Detournement of Antiquity." *Stanford Literature Review* 9.2 (1992): 99-123.

Schneider, J. "Recherches sur une encyclopédie du XIIIe siècle: Le *Speculum Majus* de Vincent de Beauvais." *Comptes Rendus de L'Académie des Inscriptions*. Paris: Klincksieck, 1976. 174-89.

Schnell, Rüdiger. *Rudolf von Ems: Studien zur inneren Einheit seines Gesamtwerkes*. Basler Studien zur deutschen Sprache und Literatur 41. Bern: A. Francke, 1969.

Scholberg, Kenneth R. *Sátira e invectiva en la España medieval*. Madrid: Editorial Gredos, S. A., 1971.

Schricker, Gale C. "On the Relation of Fact and Fiction in Chaucer's Poetic Endings." *Philological Quarterly* 60 (1981): 13-25.

Schupp, Volker. "Gregorius-*der guote sündaere* unter Rittern, Mönchen und Devoten." *Bild und Gedanke: Festschrift für Gerhart Baumann zum 60. Geburtstag*. Eds. Günter Schnitzler et al. Munich: Wilhelm Fink, 1980. 165-86.

Schwarz, Birgit. "Outspoken and in Hiding: Writer Decries Abuse of Women." *The Phoenix Gazette* 18 July 1994: B5.

Schweikle, Günther. *Neidhart*. Realien zur Literatur 253. Stuttgart: J. B. Metzler, 1990.

Schwietering, Julius. *Die Demutsformel mittelhochdeutscher Dichter*. Berlin: 1921.

——. "The Origins of the Medieval Humility Formula." *Publications of the Modern Lanuage Association* 69 (1954): 1279-91.

Senior, Diane Hichwa. "The Politics of Self and Dante's *Vita Nuova*." *NEMLA Italian Studies* 18 (1994): 5-12.

Seroni, Adriano. *Apologia di Laura e Altri Saggi*. Milan: Bompiani, 1948.

Serrano-Reyes, Jesus. *Didactismo y moralismo en Geoffrey Chaucer y Don Juan Manuel: Un estudio comparativo textual*. Cordoba, Spain: U of Cordoba, 1995.

Shaner, M. C. E. "Notes to *The Legend of Good Women*." Benson 1059-75.

Shaw, I. P. "Giraldus Cambrensis and the Primacy of Canterbury." *The Church Quarterly Review* 148 (1949): 82-101.

Shoaf, R. A. *Dante, Chaucer, and the Currency of the Word: Money, Images, and Reference in Late Medieval Poetry*. Norman, OK: Pilgrim Books, 1983.

Sievers, Eduard. "Zur inneren und äußeren Chronology der Werke Hartmanns von Aue." *Festgabe Philipp Strauch*. Eds. Georg Baesecke und Ferdinand Joseph Schneider. Halle: Max Niemeyer, 1932. 53-66.

Simon, Eckehard. *Neidhart von Reuental*. Boston: Twayne, 1975.

Singleton, Charles S. *An Essay on the* Vita Nuova. Cambridge: Harvard UP, 1958.

Smarr, Janet Levarie. *Boccaccio and Fiammetta: The Narrator as Lover*. Urbana: U of Illinois P, 1986.

Smith, Lucy Toumlin, and Paul Meyer, eds. Introduction. *Les contes moralisés de Nicole Bozon*. Reprint. Paris: Librairie de Firmin Didot, 1968. i-lxxiv.

Southern, Richard W. *Medieval Humanism and Other Studies*. Oxford: Blackwell, 1970.

Sparnaay, H. *Hartmann von Aue. Studien zu einer Biographie*. 2 vols. Darmstadt: Wissenschaftliche Buchgesellschaft, 1975.

Spearing, A. C. *Medieval Dream-Poetry*. Cambridge: Cambridge UP, 1976.

Spies, Heinrich. "Chaucers 'Retractatio.'" *Festschrift Adolf Dobler*. Geneva: Slatkine Reprints, 1978. 383-94.

Springer, Carl P. E. *The Gospel as Epic in Late Antiquity. The* Paschale Carmen *of Sedulius*. Supplements to Vigiliae Christianae II. Leiden: Brill, 1988.

Stammler, Wolfgang. *Die Deutsche Literatur des Mittelalters: Verfasserlexikon*. Berlin: Walter de Gruyter, 1933-55.

Steadman, John M. *Disembodied Laughter:* Troilus *and the Apotheosis Tradition*. Berkeley: U of California P, 1972.

Steinberg, Theodore L. Piers Plowman *und Prophecy: An Approach to the C-Text*. Garland Studies in Medieval Literature 2. New York: Garland, 1991.

Stotz, Peter. "Dichten als Schulfach—Aspekte mittelalterlicher Schuldichtung." *Mittellateinisches Jahrbuch* 16 (1981): 1-16.

Sturm, Sara. "The Poet-Persona in the *Canzoniere*." *Francis Petrarch Six Centuries Later: A Symposium*. Ed. Aldo Scaglione. Chapel Hill: U of North Carolina, 1975. 192-212.

Suchomski, Joachim. *Delectatio und Utilitas: Ein Beitrag zum Verständnis mittelalterlicher komischer Literatur*. Bibliotheca Germanica 18. Bern: A. Francke, 1975.

Swan, John C. "The *Satanic Verses*, the *Fatwa*, and Its Aftermath: A Review Article." *Library Quarterly* 61:4 (1991): 429-43.

Swart, J. "The Construction of Chaucer's General Prologue." *Neophilologus* 38 (1954): 127-36.

Symonds, John Addington. *Giovanni Boccaccio as Man and Author*. London: John C. Nimmo, 1895.

Syndikus, Hans Peter. *Catull: Eine Interpretation*. Impulse der Forschung 46. Darmstadt: Wissenschaftliche Buchgesellschaft, 1984.

Taheri, Amir. "Reflections on an Invalid *Fatwa*." *Index on Censorship* 4 (1990): 14-16.

Tatham, Edward H. R. *Francesco Petrarca, the First Modern Man of Letters, His Life and Correspondence: A Study of the Early Fourteenth Century (1304-1347)*. 2 vols. London: Seldon Press, 1925.

Tatlock, John S. P. "Boccaccio and the Plan of *The Canterbury Tales*." *Anglia* 37 (1913): 69-117.

——. "Chaucer's *Retractions*." *Publications of the Modern Language Association* 21 (1913): 521-529.

——. "The Epilog of Chaucer's *Troilus*." *Modern Philology* 18 (1921): 625-59.

Taylor, P. B. "Chaucer's *Cosyn to the Dede*." *Speculum* 57 (1982): 315-327.

——. "*Peynted Confessiouns*: Boccaccio and Chaucer." *Comparative Literature* 34.2 (1982): 116-29.

Terry, Arthur. *A Literary History of Spain: Catalan Literature*. New York: Barnes & Noble, 1972.

Thibault, John C. *The Mystery of Ovid's Exile*. Berkeley: U of California P, 1964.

Thompson, N. S. *Chaucer, Boccaccio, and the Debate of Love: A Comparative Study of* The Decameron *and* The Canterbury Tales. Oxford: Clarendon, 1996.

Thompson, W. H. *Phaedrus of Plato with English Notes and Dissertations*. London: Whittaker, 1868.

Thundyil, Zacharias. "The *Moral* Chaucer." *Christianity and Literature* 20 (1971): 12-16.

Thurston, Herbert. "The Conversion of Boccaccio and Chaucer." *Studies* 25 (1936): 215-25.

Tobin, Frank J. Gregorius *and* Der Arme Heinrich. *Hartmann's Dualistic and Gradualistic Views of Reality*. Stanford German Studies 3. Bern: Peter Lang, 1973.

Tobin, Frank. *Mechthild von Magdeburg: A Medieval Mystics in Modern Eyes*. Columbia, SC: Camden House, 1995.

Traversi, Derek. The Canterbury Tales: *A Reading*. London: The Bodley Head, 1983.

Travis, Peter W. "Deconstructing Chaucer's Retraction." *Exemplaria: A Journal of Theory in Medieval and Renaissance Studies* 3.1 (1991): 135-58.

Trypanis, C. A. *Greek Poetry from Homer to Seferis*. Chicago: U of Chicago P, 1981.

Ullmann, Walter. *The Individual and Society in the Middle Ages.* Baltimore: Johns Hopkins Press, 1966.

Underhill, E. *Mysticism: A Study in the Nature and Development of Man's Spiritual Consciousness.* New York: E. P. Dutton, 1911.

Urban, Linwood. *A Short History of Christian Thought.* Rev. ed. Oxford: Oxford UP, 1995.

van Hamel, A. G. Introduction. *Les Lamentations des Matheolus et le Livre de Leesce.* Ed. A. G. van Hamel. 2 vols. Paris: Librairie Émile Bouillon, 1905. 2: xxvii-ccxxvi.

Vising, Johan. Introduction. *Deux Poemes de Nicholas Bozon.* Göteborg: Elanders, 1919. iv-xxii.

Voorbij, J. B. "The *Speculum Historiale*: Some Aspects of Its Genesis and Manuscript Tradition." *Vincent of Beauvais and Alexander the Great: Studies on the* Speculum Maius *and Its Translations Into Medieval Vernaculars.* Eds. W. J. Aerts, E. R. Smits, and J. B. Voorbij. Groningen: Egbert Forsten, 1986. 11-55.

Voretzsch, Karl. *Introduction to the Study of Old French Literature.* Geneva: Slatkine Reprints, 1976.

Vries, G. J. *A.* de. *Commentary on the* Phaedrus *of Plato.* Amsterdam: Hakkert, 1969.

Vürtheim, J. *Stesichoros' Fragmente und Biographie.* Leiden: A. W. Sijthoff's Uitgevers-maatschappij N. V., 1919.

Wagenknecht, Edward. *The Personality of Chaucer.* Norman: U of Oklahoma P, 1968.

Wagner, David L., ed. *The Seven Liberal Arts in the Middle Ages.* Bloomington: Indiana UP, 1983.

——. "The Seven Liberal Arts and Classical Scholarship." Wagner 1-31.

Waller, Marguerite R. *Petrarch's Poetics and Literary History.* Amherst: U of Massachusetts P, 1980.

Walsh, P. G. "Lucius Madaurensis." *Phoenix* 22 (1968): 143-57.

Walshe, M. O'C. "The Prologue to Hartmann's *Gregorius.*" *London Mediaeval Studies* 2 (1951): 87-100.

Ward, Benedicta. *The Venerable Bede.* London: Geoffrey Chapman, 1990.

Watts, Ann Chalmers. "Chaucerian Selves—Especially Two Serious Ones." *Chaucer Review* 4 (1970): 229-41.

Weatherby, William J. *Salman Rushdie: Sentenced to Death.* New York: Carroll & Graf Publishers, 1990.

Weaver, Mary Anne. "A Fugitive from Injustice." *The New Yorker* Sept 12, 1994: 48-60.

Webster, Michael. *A Brief History of Blasphemy: Liberalism, Censorship and* "The Satanic Verses." Southwold, Suffolk: Orwell Press 1990.

Wechssler, Eduard. *Das Kulturproblem des Minnesangs: Studien zur Vorgeschichte der Renaissance.* 2 vols. Halle: Max Niemeyer, 1909.

Wehrli, Max. "Die Elegie Walthers von der Vogelweide." *Walther von der Vogelweide.* Ed. Siegfried Beyschlag. Wege der Forschung 112. Darmstadt: Wissenschaftliche Buchgesellschaft, 1971. 190-209.

Weidmann, Walter. *Studien zur Entwicklung von Neidharts Lyrik.* Basler Studien zur deutschen Literatur 5. Basel: Benno Schwabe, 1947.

Wentzlaff-Eggbert, F. W. *Kreuzzugsdichtung des Mittelalters: Studien zu ihrer geschichtlichen und dichterischen Wirklichkeit.* Berlin: Walter de Gruyter, 1960.

Werner, Karl. *Beda der Ehrwührdige und seine Zeit.* Vienna: Wilhelm Braunmüller, 1881.

Westphal-Schmidt, Christa. *Studien zum "Rennewart" Ulrichs von Türheim.* Frankfurt/Main: Haag & Herchen, 1979.

Wheeler, Arthur Leslie. Introduction. *Tristia. Ex Ponto.* By Ovid. 2nd ed. Loeb Classics. 6 vols. Cambridge: Harvard UP, 1988. 6: vii-xxxviii.

Wheeler, Bonnie. "Dante, Chaucer, and the Ending of *Troilus and Criseyde.*" *Philological Quarterly* 61 (1982): 105-23.

Whinnom, Keith. *Diego de San Pedro.* New York: Twayne, 1974.

——. "The *Historia de Duobus Amantibus* of Aeneas Sylvius Piccolomini (Pope Pius II) and the Development of Spanish Golden-Age Fiction." *Essays on Narrative Fiction in the Iberian Penisula in Honour of Frank Pierce.* Ed. R. B. Tate. Valencia: Dolphin Book, 1982. 243-55.

Whitbourn, Christine J. *The "Arçipreste de Talavera" and the Literature of Love.* Occasional Papers in Modern Languages 7. Hull: U of Hull P, 1970.

Whittock, Trevor. *A Reading of* The Canterbury Tales. Cambridge: Cambridge UP, 1968.

Wilkins, Charles. *History of the Literature of Wales From the Year 1300 to the Year 1650.* Cardiff, 1884.

Wilkins, Ernest Hatch. *Studies on Petrarch and Boccaccio.* Ed. Aldo S. Bernardo. Padua: Editrice Antenore, 1978.

——. *The Making of the* "Canzoniere" *and other Petrarchan Studies.* Storia E Letteratura Raccolta di Studi e Testi 38. 1955. Rome: Folcroft, 1977.

Williams, J. E. Caerwyn. "Guto'r Glyn." Jarman and Hughes 2: 218-42.

——. *The Poets of the Welsh Princes.* Cardiff: U of Wales P, 1978.

Williams, E. A. "A Bibliography of Giraldus Cambrensis." *Cylchgrawn Llyfrgell Genedlaethol Cymru: The National Library of Wales Journal* 12 (1961): 97-140.

Williams, Ifor, and Thomas Roberts. *Cywyddau Dafydd ap Gwilym A'I Gyfoeswyr*. Bangor: Argraffwyd gan Evan Thomas, 1914.

Williamson, Edward. "A Consideration of "Vergine Bella." *Italica* 29 (1952): 215-28.

Wilson, Katharina M. *Hrotsvit of Gandersheim: The Ethics of Authorial Stance*. Leiden: Brill, 1988.

Wimsatt, James. *Chaucer and the French Love Poets: The Literary Background of the* Book of the Duchess. Chapel Hill: U of North Carolina P, 1968.

Wimsatt, James I., and William W. Kibler. Introduction. *Le Jugement du Roy de Behaigne* and *Remede de Fortune*. By Guillaume de Machaut. Athens: U of Georgia P, 1988. 3-57.

Winkler, John J. *Auctor & Actor. A Narratological Reading of Apuleius's* Golden Ass. Berkeley: U of California P, 1985.

Wlosok, Antonie. "Zur Einheit der Metamorphosen des Apuleius." *Philologus* 113 (1969): 68-84.

Wolterbeek, Marc. *Comic Tales of the Middle Ages: An Anthology and Commentary*. Contributions to the Study of World Literature 39. New York, Greenwood, 1991.

Wood, Chauncey. "Chaucer's Man of Law as Interpreter." *Traditio* 23 (1967): 149-90.

Woolf, Rosemary. "Chaucer as a Satirist in the General Prologue to *The Canterbury Tales*." *Critical Quarterly* 1 (1959): 150-57.

Work, James A. "Chaucer's Sermon and Retractations." *Modern Language Notes* 47 (1932): 257-59.

Wright, F. A., and T. A. Sinclair. *A History of Later Latin Literature: From the Middle of the Fourth to the End of the Seventeenth Century*. New York: Macmillan, 1931.

Wright, Neil. "Arator's Use of Caelius Sedulius: A Re-Examination." *Eranos* 87.1 (1989): 51-61.

Wulff, August. *Die Frauenfeindlichen Dichtungen in den Romanischen Literaturen des Mittelalters bis zum Ende des XIII Jahrhunderts*. Romanische Arbeiten 4. Halle: Max Niemeyer, 1914.

Wurtele, Douglas. "The Penitence of Geoffrey Chaucer." *Viator* 11 (1980): 335-59.

Yeager, R. F. "'O moral Gower': Chaucer's Dedication of *Troilus and Criseyde*." *The Chaucer Review* 19 (1984): 87-99.

Young, Charles R. *Hubert Walter: Lord of Canterbury and Lord of England*. Durham: Duke UP, 1968.

Young, Karl. "Chaucer's Renunciation of Love in *Troilus*." *Modern Language Notes* 40 (1925): 270-76.

Zink, Michel, ed. Introduction. *Rutebeuf: Oeuvres complètes*. Paris: Bordas, 1989. 1: 1-40.

——. *Medieval French Literature: An Introduction*. Trans. Jeff Rider. Binghamton, NY: Medieval & Renaissance Texts & Studies, 1995.

Zöller, Sonja. *Kaiser, Kaufmann und die Macht des Geldes: Gerhard Unmaze von Köln als Finanzier der Reichspolitik und der "Gute Gerhard" des Rudolf von Ems*. Munich: Wilhelm Fink, 1993.

GENERAL INDEX

Alceste 198, 199, 200, 217

Alfonso Martínez de Toledo 240
    Arçipreste de Talavera o Corbacho
    240-43
    demanda 240-42

Andreas Capellanus
    De Amore 72 fn 5

Andronicus 47

antifeminism 45, 113, 118, 126, 164, 215,
    220, 221, 254

Apuleius 39, 40, 41
    Apologia 39
    Metamorphoseon 39, 40

architextuality 19

Arator 61 fn 55

Aristophanes 28, 41, 242
    Thesmophoriazousae 28, 41, 242

ars moriendi 221

auctor 63, 66, 113, 119

auctores 47 fn 8, 118, 189, 203

auctoritates 66, 76, 122, 123, 187, 223

Augustine 20, 52-56, 66, 68, 74, 76, 81,
    83, 85, 90, 142, 152, 215-16, 265
    Confessions 52, 71, 79, 83, 90, 96, 142
    De Academicis 55
    De Genesi ad litteram liber I
    imperfectus 55
    De inmortalitate animae liber I 55
    De uera religione 55
    Retractationes 18, 52, 53, 54, 55, 56, 68,
    75, 90, 265

auto-antifeminism 69, 255-56, 261-62

aventure 113, 116

awdl 177

Babylonian creation myth 45

Barthes, Roland 11, 38, 162, 267

Baudonivia of Poitiers 253
    The Life of St. Radegund 253

Beatrice 139, 149, 152-53, 157

Bede 49, 73-77, 81, 216, 237
    De Arte Metrica et De Schematibus et
    Tropis 49, 74, 77
    Expositio Actuum Apostolorum et
    Retractatio 73-76

Beguines 258 fn 13

Bernard of Clairvaux 257-58

Boccaccio, Giovanni 38, 158-66, 189, 191,
    205, 207, 215, 223, 231, 233, 268

Corbaccio 164, 243 fn 48
Decameron 159, 160, 162-65, 205, 234,
268
De mulieribus claris 165
Genealogie deorum gentilium 159, 164-
65
Il Filostrato 189

Boethius 61-62, 111, 164, 191, 236
    De Consolatione Philosophiae 61

Bonaventure 66, 223

Bozon, Nicole 125, 223
    Char d'Orgueil 125-27
    De la Bonté des femmes 125
    La Plainte d'Amour 126
    Les femmes a la pie 125

Callimachus 29, 86, 151
    Aetia 29

canon 216, 268

captatio benevolentiae 120, 205, 234, 236

caritas 22, 153, 227, 230, 234, 238

Catullus 30, 32

censorship 12

Chartier, Alain 134-35
    La Belle dame sans mercy 134

Chaucer, Geoffrey 32, 38, 40, 121, 147,
    161, 162, 165, 185-219, 223, 232-33,
    237, 268
    Astrolabe 202, 212
    Book of the Duchess 205 fn 108
    The Canterbury Tales 18, 203-19
    General Prologue 204, 207, 209
    The Man of Law's Tale 218
    Miller's Tale 206, 208, 209
    The Legend of Good Women 192-94,
    201, 220, 242
    Nun's Priest's Tales 209-10 fn 118
    "Of Wreched Engendrynge of
    Mankynde" 216
    "Orygenes upon the Maudeleyne" 216
    Parson's Tale 212-13 fn 122
    Retraction 18, 121, 124, 198, 199, 210-
    19, 236, 265, 268
    Reeve's Tale 207
    Tale of Melibee 208, 209, 218
    Troilus and Criseyde 186-94, 197

chiasmus 218

Cixous, Hélène 68

commentator 66

compilator 66, 203